STATISTICAL PROCEDURES IN FOOD RESEARCH

STATISTICAL PROCEDURES
IN FOOD RESEARCH

Edited by

J. R. PIGGOTT

Food Science Division, Department of Bioscience and Biotechnology,
University of Strathclyde, Glasgow, Scotland, UK

ELSEVIER APPLIED SCIENCE
LONDON and NEW YORK

ELSEVIER APPLIED SCIENCE PUBLISHERS LTD
Crown House, Linton Road, Barking, Essex IG11 8JU, England

Sole Distributor in the USA and Canada
ELSEVIER SCIENCE PUBLISHING CO., INC.
52 Vanderbilt Avenue, New York, NY 10017, USA

WITH 62 TABLES AND 113 ILLUSTRATIONS

© ELSEVIER APPLIED SCIENCE PUBLISHERS LTD 1986

British Library Cataloguing in Publication Data

Statistical procedures in food research.
1. Food industry and trade—Research—
Statistical methods
I. Piggott, J. R.
664'.0072   TP370.8

Library of Congress Cataloging-in-Publication Data

Statistical procedures in food research.

Bibliography: p.
Includes index.
1. Food—Research—Statistical methods. I. Piggott,
J. R. (John Raymond), 1950–
TX367.S73   1986   519.5'024664   86-16202

ISBN 1-85166-032-1

Phototypesetting by Interprint Limited, Malta
Printed in Great Britain by Galliard (Printers) Ltd, Great Yarmouth

PREFACE

The compilation of this book was in part prompted at a workshop on statistical methods at the 1984 Weurmann Symposium. After some confused and inconclusive discussion, it was clear that the participants in the workshop were not all familiar with the methods available. The participants wanted to learn more about them, but did not know where to start, since most of the available books were written for student or practising statisticians. A 'user's guide' to these methods was suggested as a solution, which would explain the background and provide examples of use and interpretation.

The methods described here owe much to the great statisticians, such as Pearson, Fisher, Hotelling, Bartlett and Wilks; some of the methods have seen major use in psychological and sociological research; cluster analysis has been developed as a major tool of numerical taxonomy; partial least squares regression has been considerably developed and used in chemometrics. Despite their disparate origins and development, these methods can all be used to help the food researcher to understand data—they are all tools for data analysis.

The wide availability and ease of use of computers and programs for multivariate analysis means that more researchers can use these methods, but this development is not an unmixed blessing; it means that the methods can be applied when they are not appropriate, by users who do not really understand them and uncritically accept the results.

I have asked the contributors to this book to try to explain the most common and most useful multivariate methods, after introducing the basic principles of statistical methodology and terminology. I hope the contents will be accessible to readers with little mathematical training, since the emphasis is on understanding the principles of the various methods, their applications and the interpretation of the results.

I hope this book will introduce new users to the value of multivariate analysis, and will help new and present users to gain the maximum benefits.

I am pleased to acknowledge the assistance of many colleagues, whose ideas and suggestions have made an invaluable contribution; of the authors of each chapter, who have turned my ideas into print; and of the publishers for their help. The successes of the book are theirs, the failures mine entirely.

J. R. PIGGOTT

CONTENTS

LIST OF CONTRIBUTORS

GILLIAN M. ARNOLD

University of Bristol, Department of Agricultural Sciences, Long Ashton Research Station, Bristol BS18 9AF, UK.

TIMOTHY G. BEEKER

Department of Psychiatry and Psychology, Duke University, Durham, North Carolina 27706, USA.

M. DANZART

École Nationale Supérieure des Industries Agricoles et Alimentaires, Département de Génie Industriel Alimentaire, 1 Avenue des Olympiades, 91305 Massy, France.

R. W. GUNDERSON

Department of Mathematics, Utah State University, Logan, Utah 84322, USA.

T. JACOBSEN

Bryggeriindustriens Forskningslaboratorium, Forskningsveien 1, Blindern, Oslo 3, Norway.

H. J. H. MACFIE

Food Research Institute, Langford, Bristol BS18 7DY, UK.

H. MARTENS

Norwegian Food Research Institute, Box 50, N-1432 Ås-NLH, Norway.

M. MARTENS

Norwegian Food Research Institute, Box 50, N-1432 Ås-NLH, Norway.

J. R. PIGGOTT

Food Science Division, Department of Bioscience and Biotechnology, University of Strathclyde, James P. Todd Building, 131 Albion Street, Glasgow G1 1SD, Scotland, UK.

DEREK J. PIKE

Department of Applied Statistics, University of Reading, PO Box 217, Whiteknights, Reading RG6 2AN, UK.

JOHN J. POWERS

College of Agriculture Experiment Station, University of Georgia, Athens, Georgia 30602, USA.

SUSAN S. SCHIFFMAN

Department of Psychiatry and Psychology, Duke University, Durham, North Carolina 27706, USA.

K. SHARMAN

Department of Electronic and Electrical Engineering, University of Strathclyde, 204 George Street, Glasgow G1 1XW, Scotland, UK.

L. VUATAZ

Nestlé Research Department, NESTEC Ltd, Avenue Nestlé 55, 1800 Vevey, Switzerland.

GLENN O. WARE

College of Agriculture Experiment Station, University of Georgia, Athens, Georgia 30602, USA.

ANTHONY A. WILLIAMS

University of Bristol, Department of Agricultural Sciences, Long Ashton Research Station, Bristol BS18 9AF, UK.

Chapter 1

ASPECTS OF EXPERIMENTAL DESIGN

H. J. H. MacFie

Food Research Institute, Bristol Laboratory, Langford, UK

1. INTRODUCTION

This chapter is intended to help you design better experiments. It is not a list of different designs because one can obtain these from a large number of statistical text books. Some special designs for sensory experiments are given in chapter 5 of the excellent text by Sidel and Stone (1985). The aim is to provide practical guidelines that will ensure that good design is achieved. Much of what is said relates to the design of any sort of trial. However Section 4 is devoted entirely to the specific problems encountered in designing sensory trials using panels of assessors scoring descriptive attribute profiles.

The structure of the chapter is to examine the characteristics of good design, and then some of the 'tools of the trade' developed by statisticians are discussed. The next section illustrates the problems that are likely to be faced in designing sensory trials, and provides some solutions. Finally a personal strategy for designing a good experiment is given.

2. WHAT IS GOOD DESIGN?

A good design is achieved if the answer to the following four questions, in priority order, is 'yes':

Does the experiment answer the right questions?
Is it realistic?
Is it robust?
Is it cost effective?

2.1. Does the Experiment Answer the Right Questions?

This is the cardinal principle in design and one that is very often forgotten because it is so obvious. A simple example will illustrate the point. An experimenter comes to the sensory analyst with two treatments and asks whether they are perceptually distinct. The sensory analyst takes him at his word and he carries out a triangle test, finds a difference and the following conversation takes place.

Sensory   'I am 99·9% certain that treatments A and B are perceptually distinct.'

Experimenter   'In what way are they different?'

Sensory   'You did not ask me that.'

Any team that sets out to conduct an experiment must communally and critically decide and refine the questions that need to be asked. If the questions are poorly defined, the experiment is flawed before it begins.

It is useful to classify the questions and objectives into the following categories.

2.1.1. Descriptive

Here the aim is to achieve a characterization of some treatments or samples. It is likely that this characterization will be used as a reference to compare with treatments in the experiment or previous or future characterizations. Typically one attempts to measure as many sensory attributes or physical properties as possible and then determines which vary and are therefore retained in the final profile.

A good example of an experiment with a strong descriptive objective is that of Jones *et al.* (1985). These authors wished to characterize the sensory, mechanical and chemical properties of burgers, and therefore sampled widely from the commercial market place. They studied as many sensory and physical properties as possible and then narrowed these down to a useful subset. Note that, quite correctly, no formal design structure was used in this experiment.

2.1.2. Comparative

Designs to simply compare treatments are probably the most frequently used and hence have attracted the most statistical attention. Multifactorial experiments that permit comparisons between a large number of different sources of variation are used widely in sensory testing. This topic will be discussed in more detail in Section 4 but it is useful to distinguish two types of comparative question.

(a) 'What are the differences between these treatments.'

To answer this a design that enables all treatments to be compared with each other will be required.

(b) 'Which is the best?'

The sole objective is to pick the winner. Many acceptability trials aim to answer this question. In this case there may be a large number of treatments and it will be wise to screen out the clear 'losers' using pilot trials before setting up the main experiment. 'Pick the winner' experiments are often much less complicated than those designed to elucidate the exact differences between treatments. There may be no need to use complex descriptive profiles but beware of the ancillary question:

'In what way is it better?'

2.1.3. Exploratory
Typical questions here are:

'Which of the many factors that can be varied actually influence the eating quality of a product?'
'Which of these products is not worth putting out for consumer testing.'

In this context one is usually after a quick screening procedure to filter out 'losers' before a main trial or to find out which factors do not need to be varied in the main experiment. The use of 2^n designs, in which factors are set at high and low levels and fractional replication to ignore higher order interactions, is highly recommended. For an excellent description of how to use and interpret these designs for exploratory trials, see Hunter and Hoff (1967).

Triangle tests are useful if, before embarking on large trials, confirmation is required that there *is* a difference for assessors to find and describe.

Pilot studies to estimate the residual variation are useful to determine the number of replicates required to achieve a preset precision. For example if the residual standard deviation on a set of samples is S, then a Least-Significant Difference between two means with n replicates in each group is approximately $t_\alpha(v)\sqrt{2S/n}$ at the α probability level and with v degrees of freedom in the residual. Assuming $\alpha = 0.05$ and $v > 30$ then

$$\text{LSD} = 2\sqrt{\frac{2S}{n}}$$

If the required LSD is known, the number of replicates can be calculated. This device is useful to get experimenters to exclude treatments that are not likely to be detected as different at the level of replication they can afford!

2.1.4. Confirmatory

In this type of experiment there is a structured hypothesis that needs to be tested. It may be in the form of a model of human behaviour (see Cardello *et al.*, 1985; or MacFie and Thomson, 1981 for examples) or a basic assumption about the distribution of samples. In practice these are very difficult experiments to design. Many tend to be 'supportive' of a hypothesis rather than confirmatory.

2.1.5. Relational

The general class of experiments designed to relate sensory data to physical and chemical measurements falls into this area (see for example Nute *et al.*, in press). Key rules to bear in mind are: space the samples out across the range to ensure that representative relationships can be estimated, and obtain enough samples to estimate the required models. Imposing a complex factorial design on to essentially relational designs can produce very complex regression equations.

If the relational models are to be used for predictive purposes then ideally new sets of data should be used to test performance. Alternatively the data can be split randomly into two parts and one section used to fit models and the other as a test set. This implies that the number of samples is large enough to fit models on 50% of the data.

2.1.6. Optimization

This question differs from 'pick the winner' in that it does not assume a winner is present, but assumes an optimal combination can be found.

There are two classes of optimization experiment. In the first the experimenter is not interested in the contribution of the various factors, but merely wants an optimal product. A series of tuning trials will be conducted, perhaps using Simplex optimization algorithms (see Deming and Morgan (1983) for a comprehensive literature review).

In the second type the experimenter is interested in estimating a model that will relate performance to the settings of the various factors.

Maximum performance can then be predicted. Response surface designs are the usual approach in this case (Cochran and Cox (1957); also Cornell (1981) for formulation experiments).

2.1.7. Psychological
Typical questions here are:

'What are the main sources of variation associated with individual differences in preference?'
'How do non-sensory factors influence sensory perception of response?'

The emphasis here is on the human rather than the sample. Design considerations then turn to the production of samples that are reproducible and span a sensory range. Experiments based on difference tests and multidimensional scaling (see MacFie and Thomson (1984) for a brief review and Schiffman et al. (1981) for examples) or free choice profiling (Williams and Arnold, 1985) may be suitable here.

2.1.8. Concluding Comments
The aim of classifying the questions into one or more of these broad headings is that it enables one to think more objectively about the type of design. There is always a temptation to use the design one knows how to conduct and interpret. Do not, for example, force relational or descriptive questions into the straitjacket of multi-factorial designs.

2.2. Is the Experiment Realistic?
There is absolutely no point in designing an experiment that:

1. Is over the allocated budget.
   You must either prune out some questions or go back to your sponsors and obtain more funds.
2. Will take longer than the allocated time scale.
   Sensory experiments are usually fairly simple to schedule. Our experience is that the usual error is to allow insufficient time to transfer the data to computer, analyse and interpret the results. Good experiments are then spoiled by poor presentation.
3. Cannot be analysed.
   The facilities for conducting analysis of variance by regression methods are available in most of the big statistical packages such as GENSTAT SAS, SPSS, BMDP. Hence almost any design can

be analysed but, as we shall discuss further in Section 3, the independence of factor estimation is lost if severe imbalance is present. Always write down the skeleton analysis and ensure that your current software can handle it.

2.3. Is the Experiment Robust?

Very few experiments go to plan. You should list the most likely things that could go wrong and also the *worst* things that could happen. For example in a recent experiment we were proposing to hold all our experimental material in a cold store in which temperature was not monitored at weekends. After much discussion we decided to hold the material in a commercial cold store with good temperature control facilities. In the event the unmonitored store did break down one weekend!

Build some slack into your experiment so that losses of material, low panel attendance, poor performance by some assessors and time slippage, do not cause your experiment to flounder.

2.4. Is the Experiment Cost Effective?

It may be possible to answer other questions at no extra cost. For example if one is comparing two levels of a factor A then it may be that 15 samples of each treatment are required. It is best to aim for 10 or more in this case to ensure at least 20 degrees of freedom in the residual. This would give an analysis of variance (ANOVA) table as shown below.

Source	df
Factor A	1
Residual	28
Total	29

However a 3 factorial experiment with A, B, C on 2, 2, 3 levels respectively and 3 samples in each treatment combination would give

Source	df
A	1
B	1
C	2

Interactions	
A.B	1
B.C	2
A.C	2
A.B.C	2
Residual	24

Total	35

Thus a wealth of extra information is gained for the addition of only 6 extra samples.

3. TOOLS OF THE TRADE FOR EXPERIMENTAL DESIGN

3.1. Factors versus Variables

This concept is really just notation but is essential to focus the design process.

Factors are sources of variation that can be controlled by the experimenter. Examples in sensory trials are product composition, temperature or time of processing, origin of material, brand package, etc.

Interference factors are sources of variation that are not of direct interest to the experimenter but are introduced through the natural constraints in the design. Examples are day of measurement, product batch, panel and order of assessment.

Variables are usually called response variables and are the measurements that will be made during the experiment. They may be continuous, binary or categorical.

Interference variables are quantitative sources of variation that are likely to affect the response variables. Often they are not under the direct control of the experimenter but can be monitored during the trial and the extent of their influence on the response variables can be estimated retrospectively (see Section 3.6, Covariance Analysis). Examples of interference variables are weight of sample, environmental temperature, moisture content, etc.

3.2. Randomization

This process of randomly allocating treatments to units to minimize the risk of introducing bias due to variation in associated interference variables that are not measurable is well knowm. In practice there seems rather little scope for randomization in sensory descriptive profiling. We use it sometimes for determining order of assessment in panels.

3.3. Blocking

Blocks are naturally occurring groups of experimental samples that are represented in the design by interference factors. In many sensory experiments the panel session is a block, particularly if all, or nearly all, treatments can be assessed in one session. The process of blocking is to arrange that all treatments occur in each block so that interblock differences can be removed from the analysis and do not interfere with treatment comparisons.

Sometimes the variation between blocks is used as a residual error for testing the significance of difference between levels of a factor. Consider an experiment to compare the eating quality of chickens from three different producers. An additional objective is the improvement of three experimental diets over a control diet. A known interference factor is the effect of different hatcheries. The experiment is therefore arranged so that each diet is given to units in each of four hatcheries of each producer. Assuming that the analysis is conducted on the averages across all the assessors and that two replicates were taken we arrive at the following ANOVA.

Source	df
Hatch stratum	
Producers	2
Residual	9
Total	11
Within Hatch stratum	
Diet	3
Producer diet	6
Residual	75
Total	95

The significance of difference among producers is tested against the pooled variation between hatchery means of each producer. However diet and the interaction term are tested on the within hatchery residual.

3.4. Confounding

Two factors, or effects, are said to be confounded (or aliased) in a design if it is not possible to disentangle the individual contribution of each factor in the analysis.

If an interference factor is confounded with a main factor this is poor design. In the poultry experiment of the previous section if a single diet had been applied to each hatchery then diets and hatchery effects would have been confounded.

The concept of confounding is used in two ways. We can confound interference factors because we are not interested in their effects. For example we can confound the effect of different batches of experimental material with panel session. The second use is to confound higher order interaction terms, which we expect to be small, with main effects to achieve a more parsimonious design. This is the idea behind fractional replicate designs in 2^n experiments (Cochran and Cox (1957) or any book on statistical design).

3.5. Balance

Balance in designs usually implies that all treatments appear equally often in the natural blocks. The advantage of balanced designs are two fold. First it is usually possible to eliminate the effects due to interference factors and second the estimated effects of the main factors are independent of each other. If the number of treatments exceeds the block size (i.e. if there are 8 treatments and it is only possible to taste 6 in a session) it is still worth adopting a balanced incomplete block design because the effects of the blocks can be estimated and removed from the residual (see Cochran and Cox, 1957 (p. 440) for further details; also discussion in Section 4 for practical design advice).

3.6. Covariance Analysis

This tool is used to assess the effect on the responses of interference variables that the experimenter cannot control, but can measure.

The basic concept is that the response variable is regressed on to the interference variables (covariates). If a significant correlation is attained the deviation in each observation caused by the interference variable not being at its overall mean is removed.

For example in a one-way model with one covariate an observation Y_i in treatment j would be modelled as

$$Y_i = \bar{Y} + T_j + b(X_i - \bar{X}) + e_i$$

where $\bar{Y}$ is overall mean of response, T_j is effect of jth treatment, X_i is covariate observation associated with Y_i, b is regression coefficient and e_i residual of ith observation.

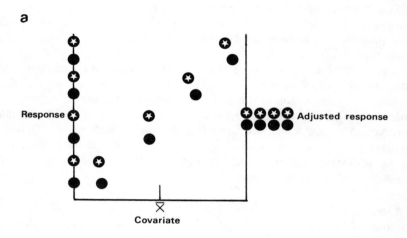

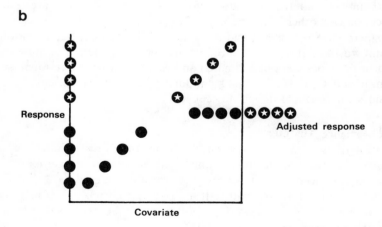

FIG. 1. Two simple examples of covariance analysis. In (a) the precision of the comparison of treatments (X, 0) is increased by adjusting for the covariate. In (b) there are treatment differences in the covariate. Adjustment removes the observed treatment difference in the response.

The adjusted value Y_{iA} would be

$$Y_{iA} = \bar{Y} + T_j + e_i$$

Two simple examples of possible outcomes of covariance analysis are shown in Fig. 1. In Fig. 1(b) the correlation between the response and the covariate across the two treatments may be genuine or it may be due to bad design. For example if the four replicates of each treatment were done on different days and the covariate was humidity, by chance all the observations might have been made on humid days. The moral is to spread the treatment combinations randomly across the range of covariation if possible.

3.7. Missing Values

Missing values are not zeroes unless the response was actually measured to be zero. If an assessor attends the panel and forgets to score an attribute it is a missing value. If he simply did not detect the attribute then it is a zero.

Designs which are not balanced should not have missing values added in to make them appear balanced to the analysis algorithm. Missing value routines are there to fill in the occasional genuine gap in the data.

3.8. Replication

Replication is the repeated sampling of particular levels of a treatment, a treatment combination, or a block. It is carried out to obtain a baseline of variation that we can use to test treatments or interactions for significance. Since replication is usually expensive it is essential to use it sparingly and in the correct place.

A simple example of the use of replication is to enable the significance of an interaction between two factors A and B, both on 3 levels to be tested. With no replication the ANOVA table is simply:

Source	df
A	2
B	2
A,B	4
Total	8

and it is only possible to test the significance of the main effects A and B against the interaction term.

With two replicates of each treatment combination there are now 27 observations and the ANOVA table is now

Source	df
A	2
B	2
A,B	4
Residual	18
Total	26

We now have 18 degrees of freedom to test the interaction and if that is of the same order as the residual we can use the residual to test the main effects.

In sensory experiments the position is usually eased by the fact that assessors provide lots of degrees of freedom for the residual. However if the experimental material is variable then replication will be necessary.

4. SPECIFIC DESIGN PROBLEMS IN SENSORY EXPERIMENTS

Let us assume that you have identified the factors and sensory attributes to be measured. The assessment is to be monadic. The problem of design of difference tests is discussed by Frijters (1984). The problem now is to allocate samples to panels, to determine the serving order, to select the number of assessors and to determine the level of replication. We shall start with easy problems and then increase the complexity of the design.

Level 1: All Treatments Can Be Assessed at One Session
In this case there are only three problems: determine the number of assessors, the number of sessions and the serving order.

The number of assessors for descriptive tests should generally exceed 8. Usually it is between 8 and 15. The more there are the less chance there is of a couple of rogue assessors distorting the means. In addition you can accommodate having to discard some assessors if their attendance is poor.

The determination of serving order is usually done systematically to ensure that, as far as is possible, serving order of each treatment occurs equally often in each session. This is easy if the number of assessors is a multiple of the number of samples. For example with 10 assessors and 5 samples one could use the following plan.

Assessor	Serving order				
A	1	2	3	4	5
B	5	4	3	2	1
C	4	5	1	3	2
D	3	1	4	2	5
E	2	4	1	5	3
F	2	3	5	1	4
G	5	2	4	1	3
H	1	3	5	4	2
I	3	1	2	5	4
J	4	5	2	3	1

If there is concern about carry over effects on certain pairs of samples, the number of times particular pairs occur together can be checked.

If there is to be more than one session then, strictly, a particular serving order should not be repeated until the complete set of permutations (given by factorial n if there are n treatments each assessed at one session) has been used up. In practice one attempts to balance as far as possible. A simple check at the end of the experiment is to calculate the average response of each treatment and overall for each serving position. If there is a significant difference then it is possible to adjust for order effects. However in a balanced experiment the effects will pass equally on to each treatment.

The number of sessions is determined by your prior beliefs about the uniformity of assessor behaviour. If all assessors have been strictly trained and are very consistent then it is *just possible* that you might be able to treat each assessor as a block and only conduct one session. The ANOVA table in an experiment with 5 treatments and 10 assessors would be:

Source	df
Assessors	9
Treatments	4
Residual	36
Total	49

The residual here is of course the Assessor Treatment interaction term and we are effectively assuming that the assessors are instruments and the residual represents random error in the 'instrumentation'.

The more likely case is that you wish to be able to examine the interaction term to see if there was any genuine disagreement and to test the discrimination of each assessor using one way F tests between and within treatments. The number of sessions will depend on the number of samples. Suppose we conduct two sessions in our previous example. The ANOVA table will now be:

Source	df
Assessors	9
Treatments	4
Assessor treatment	36
Residual	49
Total	98

This gives quite an adequate number of degrees of freedom to test the significance of the interaction term and even the contribution of each assessor to that interaction term. The degrees of freedom for the F test of each assessor are 5, 5 respectively which is a bit low. Three replicates would give 5, 10 which is better. Note that session differences have been 'lumped' into the residual.

In the third situation, the scores of the individual assessors are felt to be randomly distributed and the view is taken that the session mean is the basic data to be input to analysis of variance. In this case enough sessions must be taken to ensure adequate residual degrees of freedom. In our example six sessions are probably adequate. These would be considered as blocks in the ANOVA table

Source	df
Sessions	5
Treatments	4
Residual	20
Total	29

This level of replication is recommended when a laboratory panel should be asked to give a view on acceptability of products, taking care to observe trends caused by increasing familiarity with the material.

Level 2: Too Many Treatments to Assess in One Session
There are two situations. In the first the number of treatments is so large or take so long to assess that it is impossible for one assessor to assess all treatments. In this case a balanced incomplete blocks design (Cochran and Cox, 1957; p. 469 for index to plans) must be used to ensure that treatments occur equally often and attention must be given to balancing out serving order. Sidel and Stone (1985) give a plan for a serving rota for a five product design in which each of 40 subjects assesses 4 products once. The problem with these designs is that the number of subjects becomes fairly large. For example with each assessor tasting 5 out of 10 possible treatments, 18 blocks are required. Since one may well require 4 or 5 assessors in each block the experiment is not inconsiderable. Serving order is again balanced out across assessors within a session.

In the second case the assessors receive all the treatments but these are split into subsets at each session. Given the practical difficulties involved in presenting different subsets within a session the same set of samples is usually given to each assessor at a session. Incomplete block designs are usually rejected in favour of the straight subset strategy. The sensory analyst may be able to use prior knowledge about the relative effects of the different factors to structure the subsets. Consider the case where two factors A (2 levels) and B (5 levels) are to be studied. Five treatments can be assessed at one session. Then if the effect of differing levels of A is known to be large in proportion to variation in levels of B it will be sensible to assess all levels of B at one level of A in a session. The significance of differences in levels of A will then be compared with the pooled difference between the two sessions of each replicate.

The ANOVA table for an experiment with three complete replicates would then be:

Source	d.f.
Sessions stratum	
A	1
Residual	4
Total	5

Within session stratum

Assessors	9
B	4
Assessor A	9
Assessor B	36
A.B	4
Assessor A.B	36
Residual	196
Total	294
Grand total	295

5. DESIGNING EXPERIMENTS: STEP BY STEP

Step 1. Define your objectives as questions.
Gather together interested parties and note down all questions. Look at them and refine them. Identify ill-defined questions and clarify. Allocate priorities to your questions. Classify them into the various headings given in Section 2. A useful but unpopular strategy in research is to ask each experimenter to write a literature review that indicates clearly why the experiment is required!

Step 2. Identify the factors, interference factors and variables and response variables.
This process will begin to focus your thoughts on those aspects that you can and cannot control and measure. If you identify important aspects that cannot be controlled then consider how these can be measured or 'blocked' out of the experiment. If this cannot be achieved consider how randomization can be applied to minimize unwanted trends or biases.

Consider also the different levels of error that may be introduced by design constraints. Ask yourself about your beliefs about the assessors: are they blocks or are you going to review performance and assessor/ treatment interactions. Might you wish to conduct the analysis on panel means?

Step 3. Construct the perfect design.
Identify the ideal design or designs that will enable all the questions to be answered. Ignore at this stage any considerations of cost but make it

realistic (Section 2.2). Include any pilot studies. Write down dummy analyses to ensure that you have a clear idea of the degrees of freedom associated with significance tests. Sketch out the figures and tables that will be used in the report.

Step 4. Cut down the perfect design to take account of resource limitations.
These limitations will be either staff, instrumentation, or cost. It is usually preferable to exclude some questions and retain a good chance of answering the high priority questions rather than cutting down degrees of freedom to very low levels.

If the experiment cannot be cut down and still answer the high priority questions then get more resources! This is the advantage of constructing the perfect design first. Remember to consider whether other questions can be answered with low marginal costs.

Step 5. Criticize your experiment.
I call this process the pessimistic walkthrough. Go through each stage of the experiment *with the staff that are going to carry it out* and ask them these questions.

'What do you feel uneasy about?'
'What are the *likely* things that could go wrong?'
'What are the *worst* things that could happen?'

Plan for these eventualities and build 30% slack into your costs and time schedules. This process not only makes your experiment robust but commits your staff to making it happen.

Step 6. Write up your plans and sleep on it.
Circulate your report so that everyone has a chance to chew it over. Send it to your sponsors so that they cannot complain that they were not consulted if the results are not to their liking!

Step 7. Carry out the experiment.
If you follow each of these steps then your design should be optimal. Good luck!

REFERENCES

Cardello, A. V., Maller, O., Masor, H. B., Dubase, C. and Edelman, B. (1985). Role of consumer expectancies in the acceptance of novel foods. *J. Food Sci.*, **50**, 1707–18.

Cochran, W. G. and Cox, G. M. (1957). *Experimental Designs*, John Wiley, New York.

Cornell, J. A. (1981). *Experiments with Mixtures*, John Wiley, New York.

Deming, S. N. and Morgan, S. L. (1983). Teaching the fundamentals of experimental design. *Analytica Chimica Acta*, **150**, 183–98.

Frijters, J. E. R. (1984). Sensory difference testing and the measurement of sensory discriminability. In: *Sensory Analysis of Foods*, J. R. Piggott (Ed.), Elsevier, England, pp. 117–40.

Hunter, W. G. and Hoff, M. E. (1967). Planning experiments to increase research efficiency. *Industrial and Engineering Chemistry*, **59**, 43–8.

Jones, R. C., Dransfield, E., Robinson, J. M. and Crosland, A. R. (1985). Correlation of mechanical properties, composition and perceived texture of beefburgers. *J. Texture Studies*, **16**, 241–62.

MacFie, H. J. H. and Thomson, D. M. (1981). Perception of two-component electrocutaneous stimuli. *Perception and Psychophysics*, **5**, 473–82.

MacFie, H. J. H. and Thomson, D. M. (1984). Multidimensional scaling methods. In: *Sensory Analysis of Foods*, J. R. Piggott (Ed.), Elsevier, England, pp. 351–76.

Nute, G. R., Jones, R. C. D., Dransfield, E. and Whelehan, O. P. Sensory characteristics of ham and their relationships with composition, viscoelasticity and strength. Submitted to *J. Science Food and Agriculture*.

Schiffman, S. S., Reynolds, M. L. and Young F. W. (1981). *Introduction to Multidimensional Scaling*, Academic Press, New York.

Sidel, H. and Stone, J. L. (1985). *Sensory Evaluation Practices*, Academic Press, New York.

Williams, A. A. and Arnold, G. M. (1985). A comparison of the aromas of six coffees characterised by conventional profiling, free choice profiling and similarity scaling methods. *J. Science Food and Agriculture*, **36**, 204–14.

Chapter 2

UNIVARIATE PROCEDURES

M. Danzart

École Nationale Supérieure des Industries Agricoles et Alimentaires, Massy, France

1. INTRODUCTION

When the Food Scientist designs an experiment or organises a sampling, his aim is to use the information contained in a partial set of data to understand a phenomenon or to take a useful decision. The main problem in this respect is the variability of the responses. Indeed the same conditions do not lead to exactly similar results. Overcoming this difficulty requires the use of statistical techniques, both in a descriptive way and in an inferential way. To bring out the information we turn to the use of synthetic parameters or graphical representations, to the simplification of the distributions, to the building of models, to the performance of tests.... These processes are first performed on each of the measured characters, independently of each other. It appears that such analyses lose part of the information due to the links between the variables but nevertheless they have several qualities:

1. They rough out the problem.
2. They allow the detection of possible errors.
3. They can be used as references for the interpretation of more sophisticated analyses.
4. They are the best compromise.

Moreover, in many cases an important part of the information appears in the results of univariate analysis. This explains the success of analysis of variance and regression analysis for instance.

In the present chapter, Section 2 will give a brief description of the main summary statistics which allow maximum simplification of the data. Section 3, devoted to graphical representations, will aim at a fast

19

and better understanding of the data. Then, after briefly recalling the main distributions in Section 4, Section 5 will deal with the notions of estimation and test, which will allow us to take decisions. Section 6 will involve the classical analysis of variance. When the hypotheses required by this last technique are not satisfactory we turn to the use of non-parametric methods. Some are presented in Section 7, and Section 8 will describe the problem of possible outliers in the samples.

2. SUMMARY STATISTICS

The first results provided by any analysis are a few parameters which describe the distribution. Firstly, the field of study is given by the minimum and the maximum values. Then a central value indicates a mean position, and a parameter of dispersion specifies the credibility of this value. Sometimes, other parameters are added to allow a comparison between the actual distribution pattern and the Gaussian curve.

The parameters of position are numerous. We will consider two classes of statistics: classical parameters and robust parameters. In the first class we find the usual mean value, i.e. the *arithmetic mean* of the results

$$y. = \frac{y_1 + y_2 + \cdots + y_n}{n}$$

This also includes other means such as: geometric mean, quadratic mean, harmonic mean.... These values are useful but present the disadvantage of being too sensitive to extreme values. In particular they can give unusable information in the presence of outliers.

The second class contains statistics which avoid this weakness. They are said to be robust. The *median* is the value which divides the population into two groups of equal size, the first half with higher values, the second with lower values. To obtain this parameter we must order the measurements and pick the median value. In the case of a symmetric distribution, the arithmetic mean and the median are equal. It is clear that the median does not move much if there are outliers. Another indicator of position is the most frequent value called the *mode*. This parameter is of interest only in cases of a unimodal distribution. Some of these parameters are shown in Fig. 1 for a given pattern of distribution.

We also consider the same two classes for the dispersion parameters. The classical one is the *variance*

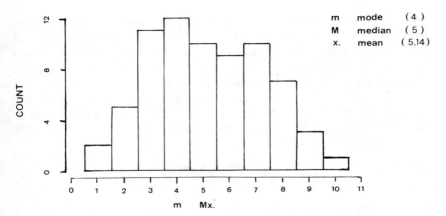

FIG. 1. Parameters of position for an example distribution.

$$\sigma^2 = \frac{1}{n-1}\sum_{i=1}^{n}(y_i - y.)^2$$

The square root of the variance, called the *standard deviation*, can also be used. This second parameter has the same units as the data and the mean. The third parameter is the *range*, the difference between the maximum and minimum values. All these statistics are sensitive to the presence of outliers.

The robust statistic generally used for dispersion is the *interquartile range*. It consists of the difference between the third quartile Q_3 and the first quartile Q_1. The first quartile is the value which separates the population into two parts, one quarter lower than Q_1 and the other greater. The third quartile separates it into two groups, three quarters lower than Q_3 and the other greater. To sum up, 25% of the results are lower than the first quartile, 25% are between the first quartile and the median, 25% between the median and the third quartile, and 25% greater than the third quartile.

Some computer programs give a *coefficient of skewness* to assess the asymmetry of the distribution. The reference value is zero. A positive value indicates a curve more extended to the right side, whereas a negative value indicates that the left side is extended. Lastly, a *coefficient of kurtosis* allows us to draw a comparison between the flattening of the distribution curve and the Gaussian curve. The value of this parameter for the Normal distribution, 3, is the reference value. A lower value indicates a more pointed curve.

It is important to keep in mind that all these statistics assume homogeneity of the population. Indeed, what would be the significance of your average temperature if you ever had your head in the oven and your feet in the freezer? This demonstrates the importance of making graphical representations to evaluate the validity of these statistics.

The univariate information is completed by the coefficients of correlation between the different variables. Each coefficient is an indicator of the relation between two characters X and Y. The most common is the linear coefficient of correlation

$$R = \frac{\sum_{i=1}^{n} (y_i - y.)(x_i - x.)}{\sqrt{\sum_{i=1}^{n} (y_i - y.)^2 \sum_{i=1}^{n} (x_i - x.)^2}}$$

This value lies in the interval $[-1, 1]$. An absolute value close to 1 indicates a strong linear dependence between the two variables. The sign specifies whether they have the same direction of variation (for a positive value) or an opposite direction of variation (for a negative value). A value close to zero indicates a linear independence between the two variables. But let us not forget that linear independence does not necessarily mean a lack of link. In the interval $[-1, 1]$ the correlation between the variables X and X^2 is null! This coefficient of correlation is widely used and one must know the precautions to take for using this tool in the right way. Firstly, the validity of its interpretation depends on the homogeneity of the population on which it was calculated. Indeed, the existence of distinct subgroups or the presence of outliers can lead to unfortunate misinterpretations. Once again, graphical representations are most useful to formulate an opinion on this homogeneity. Secondly, this coefficient expresses an observed link—but not a causal link—between the variables. Thus we must be careful in interpreting the results. For example, there is a correlation of about 0·80 between the sales of ice cream and sunglasses, but advertising the second item does not secure a sales increase for ice cream.

The link between two variables can also be shown with robust coefficients. The first one is the Kendall rank correlation coefficient τ. To calculate it we must consider the $n(n-1)/2$ pairs of points (x_i, y_i), (x_j, y_j) with $x_i < x_j$. To each pair is given a value

$$\begin{array}{ll} 1 & \text{if } y_i < y_j \\ 0 & \text{if } y_i = y_j \\ -1 & \text{if } y_i > y_j \end{array}$$

The sum S of all these values is computed and we put

$$\tau = \frac{2S}{n(n-1)}$$

τ lies in the interval $[-1, 1]$ and the same comments apply as in the previous case.

Another possibility consists in working on the ranks. Each value x_i is replaced by its ranks r_i in the set of the X results, and each y_j is replaced by its rank s_j in the Y results. If we have

$$D = (r_1 - s_1)^2 + (r_2 - s_2)^2 + \cdots + (r_n - s_n)^2$$

the Spearman rank correlation coefficient is

$$r_s = 1 - \frac{6D}{n(n^2 - 1)}$$

r_s also lies in the interval $[-1, 1]$ and the same remarks can be made.

3. GRAPHICAL REPRESENTATIONS

In order to illustrate this chapter we will consider data collected from a study on the properties of 174 clones of the cultivar Cabernet Sauvignon, in the vineyards of Bordeaux. We will consider the production of each clone as a pilot variable. The data can be extracted from Fig. 6. They all correspond to the same year and the same parcel.

3.1. Quantile Plots

A good preliminary look at a set of data is provided by quantile plots. But what is a p-quantile for a set of data? This is a value $Q(p)$ such that a proportion p of the results are lower than $Q(p)$. For instance, in the study of the production of cultivars, 95 is a 0.81-quantile because 81% of the values are smaller than 95. Each percentage is associated with a quantile. This last assertion is correct for practical use but mathematically inadequate. It is impossible with a sample of n values to exceed a precision of $1/n$ in percentage. Consequently, we will use linear interpolation between the multiples of $1/n$. In fact, the information about the quantiles needs a graphical representation for practical use. This diagram is the quantile plot. The horizontal axis represents the proportions while the vertical axis represents the quantiles of production, i.e. the ordered results (Fig. 2). This plot is easy to lay out and provides some summary statistics such as median, first and third quartile range, as shown in the figure, and a first approach to the distribution.

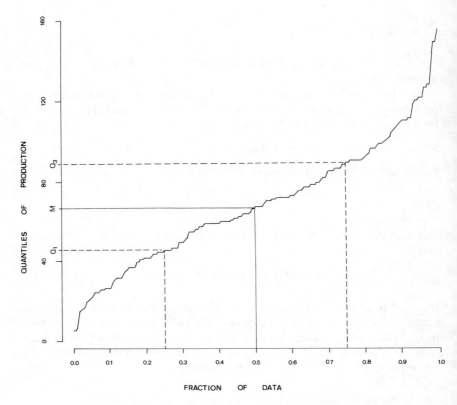

FIG. 2. Quantile plot of Cabernet Sauvignon production data.

3.2. One Dimensional Scatter Plot

Sometimes we draw up a simpler diagram where the values are plotted along a graduated axis. In case of equality we superpose two or more points. Such a scatter plot is shown for the cultivar data in Fig. 3.

Such a graphic is easily drawn and quickly obtained and gives us some information about the distribution (symmetry, range, ...) and enables us to detect outliers.

3.3. Box Plots

The previous representations contained all the information but for the purpose of further analyses, even as simple as the comparison between several groups, summary displays of the distribution are useful. A quick

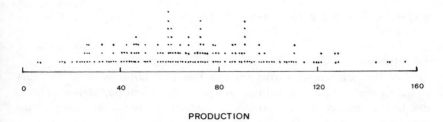

0	40	80	120	160

PRODUCTION

FIG. 3. One dimensional scatter plot of Cabernet Sauvignon production data.

method consists in the use of the Box plot (see Fig. 4). The data are represented by a rectangle whose lower bound is the first quartile ($Q_1 = Q(0\cdot25)$) and whose upper bound is the third quartile ($Q_3 = Q(0\cdot75)$). The intermediate line gives the median ($M = Q(0\cdot50)$). This box is extended by a dotted line whose lower bound is the higher of $M - 1\cdot5(Q_3 - Q_1)$ and the minimum data value; and whose upper bound is the lower of $M + 1\cdot5(Q_3 - Q_1)$ and the maximum data value. Data values lying out of this range are plotted individually and are presumed to be outliers.

This diagram gives us information about (a) a central value, the median; (b) dispersion, the interquartile range; (c) symmetry, by comparison between the lengths of the two parts of the rectangle and the dotted line; and finally points out outliers. Moreover, such diagrams are

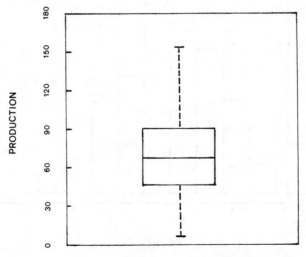

FIG. 4. Box plot of Cabernet Sauvignon production data.

useful for fast comparison between various distributions without any hypothesis.

3.4. Histograms

One of the deficiencies shown by the Box plot consists in its inability to detect the presence of distinct groups in the initial population. This is due to the absence of the distribution pattern. Therefore we always draw a histogram (see Fig. 5).

This tool is so frequently used that it is not necessary to present it more precisely. However, one must never forget that the choice of the limits between the classes greatly influences the perception of the graphic, and can induce misinterpretations. It is advisable to follow one of these two rules:

— intervals with the same length on the x-axis, and the size of class plotted on the y-axis;
— intervals with different lengths on the x-axis and a system where the surface area of each rectangle is proportional to the size of the corresponding class.

In the majority of cases, the first solution appears to be better.

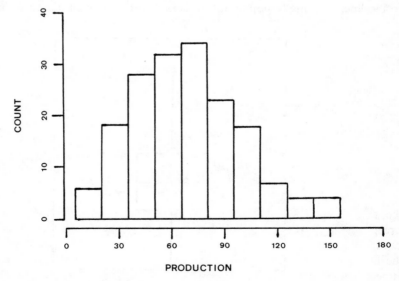

FIG. 5. Histogram of Cabernet Sauvignon production data.

3.5. Stem and Leaf Diagrams

In the presence of small populations it is also possible to draw a stem and leaf diagram. It looks like a histogram but the classes correspond to data with the same leading digits. The values with similar leading digits are plotted on the same line. The line is referenced by the leading digits, and the last digits are ordered and printed on the line. This requires a reasonable unit for the data (see Fig. 6).

We may note the diversity of such graphical representations and the ease of drawing them. As mentioned above, these graphics will be used later to confirm the results of more sophisticated analyses. For further information on this subject, refer to Chambers *et al.* (1983) or Mosteller and Tukey (1977). A short presentation is done in Martens and Russwürm Jr. (1982).

```
 0 :  67
 1 :  567
 2 :  0234556667779
 3 :  12224567778
 4 :  00112223445556666777
 5 :  00012555667789999999
 6 :  00000112233444566777789
 7 :  001122222233344577788899
 8 :  02245556668899
 9 :  00000012346667889
10 :  01246789
11 :  0001489
12 :  0117788
13 :
14 :  389
15 :  5
```

FIG. 6. Stem and leaf diagram of Cabernet Sauvignon production data.

4. ABOUT SOME DISTRIBUTIONS

The use of histograms is related to the fact that we have a better perception of the data in the presence of a visual support. This encourages the simplification of the data by fitting curves of known shapes. The first which comes to mind is the famous Gaussian curve. Its main interest lies in the frequency with which such bell-shaped distributions arise. This observation can be justified by mathematical arguments.

Gaussian curves are the graphical representations of the functions

$$x \rightarrow \frac{1}{\sqrt{2\pi\sigma^2}} \exp\left\{-\frac{(x-\mu)^2}{2\sigma^2}\right\}$$

Let us note that the mere knowledge of two parameters, μ and σ^2, is sufficient to draw the curve. Of these two parameters, the former μ represents the location value of this symmetric distribution—that is both mean and median—whereas the latter σ^2 expresses the width of the bell and corresponds to the variance. We notice the importance of the simplification, whenever it is possible; it reduces to two parameters the set of useful data. In other words, under the hypothesis of the Normality of the data, all the information is contained in the two classical parameters of mean and variance. If we go back to the example about the production of cultivars, for which the Normality of the distribution was beyond doubt (see Fig. 7), the curve $N(68\cdot76,912\cdot54)$ can be used for any decision concerning the data. In fact, a simple transformation of a $N(\mu, \sigma^2)$ variable X

$$Z = \frac{X-\mu}{\sigma}$$

leads to a standard Normal distribution. This distribution $N(0, 1)$ has

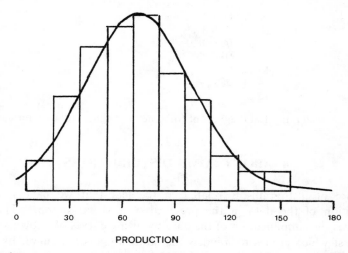

FIG. 7. Histogram of Cabernet Sauvignon production data with superimposed normal distribution.

been tabulated. For each value of ε we can have $\alpha = P(Z > \varepsilon)$, and reciprocally for each probability α we have a value ε. It allows us to compute, by difference, the probability that X lies in an interval, and this is necessary to find the probability of error for a given decision.

The lack of fit between the data and the Gaussian curve $N(\mu, \sigma^2)$ is appreciated with the help of a χ^2 test which will be presented in the next section. When the fit with the best Normal curve is bad, for example in the presence of strongly asymmetric curves, we look for a monotonic transformation of the data able to lead to a good fit. The classical changes go through log, exp, square root....

A set of distributions are derived from the Normal law. Some of them will be used in a wide range of decisions. We will quickly give a rough definition of the main ones. Some of them may appear to be contrived but they have been built out of necessity to solve statistical problems.

Chi-square Variable
If $X_1, X_2, \ldots, X_k$ are k independent variables $N(0, 1)$ then the sum of squares of these variables

$$Y = X_1^2 + X_2^2 + \cdots + X_k^2$$

is called a χ^2 (chi-square) variable with k degrees of freedom. We use the notation

$$Y \sim \chi^2(k)$$

This distribution is mainly found for the estimators of the variances.

Student Variable
If X is a variable $N(0, 1)$ and Y a χ^2 variable with k degrees of freedom, and if X and Y are independent, then the variable

$$T = \frac{X}{\sqrt{Y/k}}$$

is called a Student variable with k degrees of freedom. We use the notation

$$T \sim T(k)$$

This distribution is mainly used for the estimators of means in cases of unknown variance.

Fisher Variable

If Y and Z are two independent χ^2 variables with respectively p and q degrees of freedom then the ratio

$$F = \frac{Y/p}{Z/q}$$

is called a Fisher variable with p and q degrees of freedom. We use the notation

$$F \sim F(p, q)$$

This distribution is the most important. It allows the comparison of two variances and consequently it is used to test the validity of a model or of part of a model.

Binomial Variable

The other fundamental distribution found in the field of Food Science is the Binomial distribution. It expresses the probability of k successes from n trials, under the hypothesis that the trials are independent and the probability of success p does not depend on the trial.

$$P_{(X = k)} = C_n^k p^k (1 - p)^{n-k} \quad \text{with} \quad C_n^k = \frac{n!}{k!(n-k)!}$$

We use the notation

$$B \sim B(n, p)$$

where n is the number of trials and p the probability of success in each of the trials.

For example the number of panel members giving the correct response in a taste test is a random variable with a binomial law. This distribution is one of the basic tools for quality control and sensory analysis.

5. ESTIMATION AND TESTING

When the first phase of describing data is over, we can go on to the inferential phase. It is a matter of performing statistical analyses in order to come to the best decisions. To this end we choose a model, for example a regression model $y = \beta_0 + \beta_1 x$, and we compare this model with the experimental data. First we must find the values of the parameters, here β_0 and β_1, which lead to the best fit with the data: this is the estimation stage. Then we must take decisions about the model: is it a satisfactory model? What is the credibility of the obtained values for the parameters? This implies the acceptance of the risks linked to erroneous decisions, and is called the test phase.

5.1. Estimation

The choice of the best values for the parameters sets the problem of knowing what is a similarity between the model and the data. We must specify what criterion will be used. In most cases, the least-squares method will be favoured. It indicates that we choose values for the parameters which minimise the sum of squares of the differences between the actual results y and the values predicted by the model, $\beta_0 + \beta_1 x$. With our model

$$\sum_{i=1}^{n} (y_i - \beta_0 - \beta_1 x_i)^2 \quad \text{minimum}$$

The minimum value is called the residual sum of squares (RSS) and the values which allow us to reach that minimum are called the estimates of the parameters and are usually denoted by a circumflex (hat).

$$\text{RSS} = \sum_{i=1}^{n} (y_i - \hat{\beta}_0 - \hat{\beta}_1 x_i)^2$$

The search for the minimum is generally obtained—always for linear models—at the null point of the derivatives of the sum of squares with respect to the different parameters:

$$\frac{\partial \text{SS}}{\partial \beta_0}(\hat{\beta}_0, \hat{\beta}_1) = 0 \qquad \frac{\partial \text{SS}}{\partial \beta_1}(\hat{\beta}_0, \hat{\beta}_1) = 0$$

If the solution cannot be found by derivation, sequential methods can be used—let us remember for instance the non-linear model.

It is important to stress that the obtained values essentially depend on the sample:

$$\hat{\beta}_1 = B_1 \text{ (sample)}$$

but the function B_1 only depends on the model and on the least squares criterion. Function B_1 is called the estimator of the parameter β_1. This distinction between the estimator B_1 and the estimation β_1 is not mere subtlety on behalf of statisticians. The difference between the two notions, which allows us to extrapolate the results obtained with a given sample to a wider set, enables us to come to practical decisions. As a matter of fact, if the estimation β_1 is 2·18 and the problem is to decide whether the slope of the line is equal to 2, the numerical response is 'no'. But if we take into account the fact that 2·18 is only the image by the estimator B_1 of a given experience and that other experiences would have led to other values, then the response will depend on the variability of the phenomenon. As was mentioned before, this variability could be estimated from the data if these are representative.

5.2. Test Procedure
In order to see each step of a test procedure, let us consider an example. Suppose that you have to travel by train. How long before departure time will you leave your house? In order to take this decision you will first estimate roughly the length of the route from your house to the station. But this length is a random variable because it is influenced by many factors (walking speed, luggage weight, time spent waiting for the bus...). You know that you need a minimum of 30 min, but you are not safe from an unpleasant surprise that would considerably hold up your departure. In fact, you start considering the different probabilities of spending at least 40 min, 50 min, or 1 h. This information as a whole can be expressed under a distribution pattern of the random variable, that is the expected length of the trip (see Fig. 8).

The hatched area illustrates the probability of spending more than 1 h. The definition of the distribution is the first step. The second step is determined by the choice of risk. It is essential to remember that the value of the risk is not fixed. On the one hand, optimists will leave home 40 min before the train's departure, running a considerable risk if the

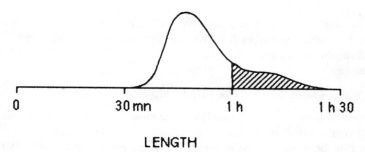

LENGTH

FIG. 8. Hypothetical distribution of travelling times to railway station.

previous distribution is correct. On the other hand, pessimists will leave home 1 h ahead and the risk taken will be much reduced. The third step consists in carrying out the experiment. The latter will either turn out to be a success—if you arrive on time—or a failure—if you miss the train. In the latter event, you will look for an explanation, decide that fate was against you, or that the risk taken was too high, or that you have misjudged the situation by using the wrong hypothesis. The first explanation is worthless to the scientist because it allows no progress. The second one is also of little consequence in so far as it is too late and your choice has been governed by reason (depending on the importance attached to taking that particular train). Besides, cutting down the risk to zero would have probably forced you to leave your house 4 h ahead for no reason. The hypothesis (or hypotheses) will therefore have to be questioned. The distribution you have chosen is probably wrong and has led you to take an unwise decision. In fact, we perform an experiment to validate or invalidate an hypothesis. It is the comparison between the results and the consequences of the hypothesis which allow you to take the decision. If the result is contradictory to what was expected under the hypothesis, then the hypothesis is rejected. Conversely, if the result is compatible with what was expected, the hypothesis is retained. The risk taken determines the threshold separating the expected values from the improbable events. This risk, α, is called the risk of the first kind. In probability terms α is the probability of rejecting the H_0 hypothesis even although it is correct

$$\alpha = P(\text{Decide } H_0 \text{ false}/H_0 \text{ true})$$

Of course there is a risk of the second kind represented by the retention of H_0 although H_0 is false.

$$\beta = P(\text{Decide } H_0 \text{ true}/H_0 \text{ false})$$

We have to emphasise that the accurate knowledge of this risk implies knowledge of the real values of the parameters. It is however possible to overcome the maximum value of the risk provided that we determine the number of experiments and the importance of the difference that needs to be pointed out. To that end, charts or data processing programs can be used. Sometimes we use the coefficient $1 - \beta$, called the power of the test. A test procedure is satisfactory if it secures simultaneously a low level α and a high power. In most practical cases, the power is not high, mainly owing to a small sample size.

To sum up, performing a test implies finding the statistic which allows us to take decisions, finding the distribution of this statistic, deciding on a risk α, and finally comparing the obtained results with those predicted under the hypothesis. In order to illustrate these steps, let us take two examples which are of great interest in the field of Food Science, namely the χ^2 test where the distribution of the estimator is a continuous law, and the triangular test where it is a discrete law.

5.3. Example 1: χ^2 Test

Let us go back to the example of the various clones of Cabernet Sauvignon. We have mentioned before that the mean of the production is 68·76 and the variance 912·5. Consequently, if we want to test the H_0 hypothesis stipulating that 'the production follows a Normal law', we first have to compute the difference between the data and the distribution $N(68·76, 912·5)$.

To do so, let us consider Fig. 7. For each of the classes, the actual size n_i is shown by the histogram and the theoretical size e_i is calculated from the corresponding Gaussian curve

$$e_i = n[P(X < a_i) - P(X < a_{i-1})] = n\pi_i$$

where the a_i are the class boundaries. We demonstrate that in this case, if k is the number of classes, the statistic

$$\chi^2 = \sum_{i=1}^{n} \frac{(n_i - e_i)^2}{e}$$

follows a χ^2 law with $k - 3$ degrees of freedom. This statistic allows us to take a decision in so far as we know that a low value corresponds to a very good fit just as a large value indicates important differences. Thus, the distribution of the studied statistic is $\chi^2(7)$ and taking a 5% risk consists in determining a threshold value (read in the χ^2 table) equal to 14.1. The value of the χ^2 statistic is then computed (Table 1). The obtained value is lower than the threshold. Therefore, we can retain the hypothesis of a Gaussian distribution.

5.4. Example 2: The Triangular Test

The principle underlying this test is as follows: in order to know if two products are perfectly distinguished by the consumer, three samples produced from the two products are presented to a judge without being named. One of the products is represented twice in the samples and the second one only once. The judge is asked to designate the sample which

TABLE 1

χ^2 TEST OF CABERNET SAUVIGNON PRODUCTION DATA

Class	1	2	3	4	5	6	7	8	9	10
n_i	6	18	28	32	34	23	18	7	4	4
π_i	0·0571	0·0808	0·1364	0·1859	0·1915	0·1591	0·1056	0·0531	0·0215	0·0090
e_i	9·93	14·06	23·73	32·35	33·32	27·68	18·37	9·24	3·76	1·58
$\dfrac{(e_i - n_i)^2}{e_i}$	1·56	1·10	0·77	0·00	0·01	0·79	0·01	0·54	0·02	3·31

$$\chi^2 = 8·11$$

appears only once in the trial. This experiment is independently replicated with other judges and then the number of correct answers is
calculated. Suppose that we get 12 correct answers out of 20. Do we have
to assume that products A and B are identical or, on the contrary, that A
and B are different? In fact among the 12 correct answers a certain
proportion may be due to pure coincidence as we know that a judge
asked to designate the unique sample will give an answer even if he does
not notice any difference between the samples. In this case, his answer
has still one chance out of three of being correct.

Let p_d be the probability of product differentiation and let p be the
probability of a correct answer. We get $p = p_d + (1 - p_d)/3$. The hypothesis
H_0 to be tested, namely 'the products are identical', is expressed by $p_d = 0$,
that is that the probability of distinguishing the products is nil, or, what
is equivalent, $p = 1/3$. The other hypothesis, namely 'the products are
different', is expressed by $p_d > 0$ or $p > 1/3$.

Let us note that the distribution of the number of correct responses is
a binomial law $B(n, p)$ where n is the number of assessors and p is the
probability of giving the correct answer. Therefore, if the hypothesis H_0
is confirmed, the law is $B(20, 1/3)$. This shows that it is possible to give
the probability for each event of k correct answers (Fig. 9). The probability of getting a minimum of 10 correct answers at random if there is
no difference between the products is equal to 9.2%

$$P(x > 10) = 0.092$$

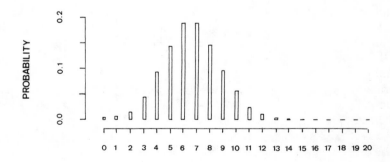

FIG. 9. Binomial distribution of frequencies of getting various numbers of correct
answers from 20 triangle tests.

Similarly, the probability of getting a minimum of 11 correct answers at random under H_0 is equal to 3·9%. These values are located one on each side of the risk of the first kind equal to 5%. Consequently, if we get a maximum of 10 correct answers, the hypothesis can be retained; on the contrary, if we get a minimum of 11 correct answers the hypothesis has to be rejected because the actual event had a probability considered as too low, and its occurrence cannot be entirely attributed to chance. In the case of our example, we are caused to reject the hypothesis of the identity of the two products. The threshold values are tabulated for various sample sizes and it goes without saying that it is not necessary to calculate them every time. This is not a potent test compared with others, such as the 2/5 test where out of five samples, one product appears twice whereas the second product appears three times. In this case, the probability of random identification of the pair is only 0·1 and the results are therefore more accurate. Moreover, it is useful to know that this test sets material problems liable to hamper its performance. For more details, consult Amerine *et al.* (1965) or Sauvageot (1982).

5.5. Confidence Interval

Sometimes, the crude response of a test procedure (yes or no) seems to be unsatisfactory. For instance when the question is not to decide if an *a priori* value is compatible with the experiment, but to know all the values of a parameter which are not conflicting with the data, another approach must be taken. That is the search for a confidence region. When only one parameter is studied the set of all possible values is an interval called the confidence interval. When two or more parameters are studied simultaneously, for a Gaussian linear model, the confidence region is an ellipse or an ellipsoid.

A set of values I_α is a confidence interval for a parameter, with confidence coefficient $1 - \alpha$, if the probability that the true value of the parameter lies in this interval I_α is $1 - \alpha$, no matter what the unknown true parameter is. The frequency interpretation is that in a long run of different situations where confidence intervals with confidence coefficient $1 - \alpha$ are used, a proportion of $1 - \alpha$ will effectively include the true value.

In order to obtain the confidence interval one must know the distribution of the estimator of the parameter. As an example, let us look at the confidence interval for the mean of a distribution. The observations are from a Normal distribution $N(\mu, \sigma^2)$ and we will call X. their arithmetic mean and Γ their estimated variance. One can see that the variable

$$T = \frac{X. - \mu}{\sqrt{\Gamma/n}}$$

has a Student distribution with $n-1$ degrees of freedom. This distribution is tabulated, and thus we can read in the table the value t such that

$$P(-t < T < +t) = 1 - \alpha$$

This formula can be written in the form

$$P(X. - t\sqrt{\Gamma/n} < \mu < X. + t\sqrt{\Gamma/n}) = 1 - \alpha$$

Consequently

$$[X. - t\sqrt{\Gamma/n}, X. + t\sqrt{\Gamma/n}]$$

is a confidence interval for parameter μ with confidence coefficient $1 - \alpha$.

The advantage of getting a large sample consists in the reduction of the width of the interval and thus better precision in the knowledge of the true value for the parameter is obtained. Nevertheless let us note that in order to double the precision the sample size must be multiplied by four!

This notion of the confidence interval is closely related to the previously presented test procedure It is equivalent to say that: the value μ_0 belongs to the confidence interval for μ with confidence coefficient $1 - \alpha$; and to decide that the hypothesis $\mu = \mu_0$ is true with a test level of α. The increase in the sample size corresponds to an improvement in the precision of the confidence region approach, and to an improvement in the power of the test approach.

5.6. One-sided or Two-sided Procedures

We must be careful; the mere statement of the hypothesis is not sufficient to obtain the correct test values or the correct confidence intervals. It is necessary to state precisely the alternative hypothesis, to decide whether a one-sided procedure or a two-sided procedure is appropriate.

For example, in a taste test, if the objective is to answer the question 'Are two products identical?' in terms of difference, we will obtain, as in the triangular test, a number of correct responses. When this number has a low value the products will be declared identical, but a high value will signify a difference between them. This is a one-sided procedure: low against high.

On the other hand, if the objective is to answer the question 'Are two products identical?' in terms of preference, we will obtain two numbers with the same importance:

n_1 the number of responses 'I prefer A'

n_2 the number of responses 'I prefer B'

If n_1 and n_2 are close, there will be no difference between the products. But if n_1 is high, the product A will be preferred (first kind of difference) and if n_1 is low the product B will be preferred (second kind of difference). This is a two-sided procedure: average against high and low.

In the case of a one-sided procedure the risk α will be taken on one side of the distribution. In the case of two-sided procedure the risk α will be split into two parts; $\alpha/2$ to the left side and $\alpha/2$ to the right side.

In terms of confidence intervals we will have one of the following kinds of interval:

$$]-\infty, a], \ [0, a] \ \text{or} \ [a, +\infty[$$

In the first case (one-sided $=>$ one limit) and an interval $[a, b]$; in the second case (two-sided $=>$ two limits).

6. ANALYSIS OF VARIANCE

The analysis of variance is a statistical technique used to decide which of several effects operating simultaneously on a process are important and what is their influence on the results. For example, we try to define the intensity of taste for different champagnes. The scores are given by a panel. It is well known that one score does not have the same significance for two different judges. The histograms for each one show that they do not have the same range of scoring. Thus we have two 'factors' influencing the results. The problem is to decide whether the real differences lie between champagnes or between judges or both. When the response is positive we must then decide which are the best and which are the worst. Most generally, the analysis of variance is suitable for the study of the effects of qualitative factors on a quantitative measurement. It implies the Normality of the distribution of the studied variable and the independence of the errors. This involves three main stages: global analysis, ranking of the effects, and study of the residuals.

6.1. One-way Analysis of Variance

The simplest model in the analysis of variance occurs when only one factor operates on the results. It is a matter of comparing k groups if the factor has k levels. The decision is not obvious because of the variability of the different measurements from the same group. It is therefore necessary to estimate this dispersion before dreaming of taking a decision. The fundamental consequence of this assertion is the absolute necessity of replications within the groups. We will call

$y_{11}, y_{12}, \ldots, y_{1n_1}$ the n_1 results of the 1st group

$y_{21}, y_{22}, \ldots, y_{2n_2}$ the n_2 results of the 2nd group

....

$y_{k1}, y_{k2}, \ldots, y_{kn_k}$ the n_k results of the kth group

Each group is characterised by its mean value $y_{i.}$, and its estimated variance $\hat{\sigma}_i^2$. This last parameter gives us information about the natural dispersion in the ith group. We assume that the different values $\hat{\sigma}_i^2$ are not significantly different, and we choose their weighted mean

$$\hat{\sigma}^2 = \frac{\displaystyle\sum_{i=1}^{n} (n_i - 1)\hat{\sigma}_i^2}{N - k} = \frac{\displaystyle\sum_{ij} (y_{ij} - y_{i.})^2}{N - k}$$

as a reference in the comparisons between the means.

In order to perform the analysis we first design a model. Each score y_{ij} is split into two parts

$$y_{ij} = \mu_i + e_{ij}$$

where μ_i represents the theoretical value of all products of the ith group and is called the model part, and e_{ij} is the difference between the mean value and a given observation, and is called the residual part. This difference is considered as a random variable as long as the sample is representative—that is collected by a representative sampling of the population. Let us note that this leads to practical consequences in the organisation of data collection. This residual variable e_{ij} is assumed to follow the classical theory of errors. This is equivalent to drawing up the hypothesis that e_{ij} is a central normal variable of variance σ^2. At least these errors are assumed to be independent. This also leads to a fundamental consequence in designing the experiment. As a matter of fact, how is it possible to draw a comparison between champagne 1 and champagne 2 if the first one is being tasted by a given person and the second one by another? The confounding of these effects will be inseparable. Finally, the model of analysis is

$$y_{ij} = \mu_i + e_{ij} \qquad e_{ij} \sim N(0, \sigma^2)$$
$$e_{ij} \text{ independently distributed}$$

We will discuss later departures from this assumption. The resolution of this model falls into two parts:

1. estimation of the parameters $\mu_1, \mu_2, \ldots, \mu_k$ and σ^2
2. testing to decide if the factor has a significant effect.

In the first part, the least-squares method is used. Through this procedure, we look for the values of the parameters μ_i which minimise the sum of the residual squares

$$SS = \sum_{ij} e_{ij}^2 = \sum_{ij} (y_{ij} - \mu_i)^2$$

which gives the best fit with the classical Euclidian distance between the data and the estimated results.

In this case of a one-factor analysis, the values obtained are the respective means of the different groups:

$$\hat{\mu}_1 = y_1., \hat{\mu}_2 = y_2., \ldots, \hat{\mu}_k = y_k., \text{ and}$$

$$\hat{\sigma}^2 = RSS/(N - k) \text{ with } RSS = \sum_{ij} (y_{ij} - y_i.)^2$$

Then, in the second part, it is a matter of deciding whether there is an effect of the factor or not. This means that we take a decision about the hypothesis H_0: '$\mu_1 = \mu_2 = \cdots = \mu_k$', called the null hypothesis. If the hypothesis is accepted, then the factor will be assumed to have no effect on the studied variable. In the opposite case, the different levels of the factor will be classified. Consider for instance the comparison between 21 types of champagne involving the criterion of taste intensity. The factor under study is the champagne which offers 21 levels. The first strategy considered can be the comparison of champagnes by pairs. But a quick calculation indicates that this procedure implies 210 comparisons (k products need $k(k-1)/2$ comparisons). If, having reached the end of this long work, no significant difference has been recorded, we will have to admit that all this work was fruitless. For this reason, it is advisable to start with a global test in order to guess if there is any chance of succeeding in these comparisons of pairs. This is the test of the null hypothesis. If the hypothesis H_0 is confirmed, the results should all be equal at a mean value common to all groups. In this case the sum of the squares will be:

$$TSS = \sum_{ij} (Y_{ij} - Y..)^2$$

where $Y..$ is the average mean. This total variance can be separated into two parts:

$$TSS = \sum_{ij} (Y_{ij} - Y_i.)^2 + \sum_i n_i(Y_i. - Y..)^2$$

The first part is the previous residual sum of squares which represents the intrapopulation variability. The second part which appears as a weighted variability of the mean values represents the part explained by the model, called the interpopulation variability. Supposing that all the means were equal, then there would be no differences among the groups and this last part would be null. Conversely, if the differences between the means are considerable when compared to the intrapopulation variance, it means that the groups are different. Therefore, it is the comparison of the two terms of the equality that enables us to make a decision. The statistic used for this purpose is as follows:

$$U = \frac{\sum_i n_i(y_i. - y..)^2/(k-1)}{\sum_{ij} (y_{ij} - y_i.)^2/(N-k)}$$

This term is a ratio of an estimation of the interpopulation variance— or mean squares of the model—and the intrapopulation variance, or residual mean squares. If the hypothesis of equality of the means is confirmed, then the U statistic follows a Fisher law with $k-1$ and $N-k$ degrees of freedom. The hypothesis will be rejected if and only if

$$U > F(k-1, N-k, \alpha)$$

The results are usually summarised in a variance analysis table (Table 2).

The F value is generally followed by an asterisk when the hypothesis is rejected at the 5% level, and by two asterisks when it is rejected at the 1% level. We must point out that the RMS value shown in this table is the estimate of σ^2 and will be useful in further analyses. In the case of the 21 types of champagnes, the results obtained are presented in Table 3.

TABLE 2
TABLE OF ONE-WAY ANALYSIS OF VARIANCE

Source of variation	SS	DF	MS	F
Factor	$\sum_i n_i(y_i. - y..)^2$	$k-1$	$SS_1/k-1$	MS_1/RMS
Residual	$\sum_{ij} (y_{ij}-y_i.)^2$	$N-k$	$RSS/N-k$	
Total	$\sum_{ij} (y_{ij}-y..)^2$	$N-1$	$TSS/N-1$	

TABLE 3
TABLE OF ANALYSIS OF VARIANCE OF 21 TYPES OF CHAMPAGNE

Source of variation	SS	DF	MS	F
Champagne	17 938	20	896·9	17·72**
Residual	62 696	1 239	50·6	
Total	80 634	1 259		

Therefore, there is a champagne effect that we must clarify in order to be in a position to designate the best types out of the whole set. Several classification methods can be considered among which two will be presented: the t-method and the S-method.

6.1.1. t-Method
We know that there are differences between the groups and the question is now to decide if two given products, namely i and j, are different or not. The mean $Y_i.$ follows a law

$$Y_i. \sim N(\mu_i, \sigma^2/n_i)$$

The same for $Y_j.$, and as they are independent we can deduce

$$\frac{(y_i. - y_j.) - (\mu_i - \mu_j)}{\sqrt{\hat{\sigma}^2(1/n_i + 1/n_j)}} \sim T(N-k)$$

as σ^2 is replaced by its estimator $\hat{\sigma}^2$. Consequently, under the hypothesis of the equality of the two means μ_i and μ_j:

$$\frac{y_i. - y_j.}{\sqrt{\hat{\sigma}^2(1/n_i + 1/n_j)}}$$

must be compared with the value given in the Student table, at $N-k$ degrees of freedom. The chosen risk must depend on the number of levels of the factor. Indeed, if there are 210 comparisons to draw, each one with the risk 5%, the global risk will be around 1. We must therefore take the risk $2\alpha/k(k-1)$ for each of the comparisons to have a global risk around α. In the presence of a high number of factor levels, the risk run for each comparison is low and allows only the differentiation of the extreme products. Such a procedure is rather conservative particularly in the case of small sample sizes.

In our example involving various types of champagnes, the experiment was balanced ($n_i = 60$ for all i). Therefore the differences between the means must be compared with the same value

$$3\cdot46\sqrt{50\cdot62(1/60 + 1/60)} = 4\cdot49$$

The ordered means of the different champagnes are shown in Table 4.

In this case we have a large number of levels of the factor, but we also have a large sample size. The extreme values, for instance champagne 21 and champagne 5, are easy to separate, but the intermediate means are all statistically equivalent, for instance champagne 7 and champagne 6 are identical although they are distant in the classification.

It is essential to remember that there is no absolute compatibility between Fisher's global test and the comparisons of the means by pairs. Indeed, the first method deals with sums of squares whereas the second one deals with absolute values. Thus, it can sometimes happen that no difference is significant, although the global nullity of the effects has been rejected. In this case it is advisable to compare different subsets using the S-method.

TABLE 4
MEAN SCORES FOR 21 CHAMPAGNES

Champagne	Mean	Champagne	Mean	Champagne	Mean
21	11·37	18	18·37	17	22·03
13	13·67	16	19·45	6	22·25
4	16·40	17	19·52	10	23·30
2	16·60	19	20·50	12	24·30
20	16·63	11	20·58	13	25·18
15	17·72	2	21·18	8	25·55
7	18·02	1	21·33	5	26·00

6.1.2. S-Method

Scheffé (1959) proposed an alternative test for studying a generalisation of the difference between means, called contrast. A contrast is a linear combination of the estimable effects with a null sum of the coefficients:

$$C = \sum_i \lambda_i \mu_i \quad \text{with} \quad \sum_i \lambda_i = 0$$

If we have $\lambda_e = 0$ whatever e except $\lambda_i = 1$ and $\lambda_j = -1$, the associated contrast is the difference between the means μ_i and μ_j. The contrasts allow comparison between two groups of products. Scheffé has shown that a contrast is significantly non-null if

$$|C| > \sqrt{(k-1)\hat{\sigma}^2 f(k-1, N-k, \alpha)(\Sigma \lambda_i^2 / n_i)}$$

where $f(k-1, N-k, \alpha)$ is the value of the Fisher statistic, at level α, used in the global test.

The advantage, with respect to the t-method, is that all the contrasts could be studied at the level α. Moreover, if the compatibility is not complete with the global F test, as in the previous case, it is always possible to find a contrast significantly non-null if the global hypothesis is rejected. On the other hand, this procedure is less powerful than the t-method, except perhaps for small sample size. In the example, the limit value for the difference between two means is 7·28, while it was 4·49 with the t-method.

6.2. Balanced Two-way Layout

When several factors act upon the result, it becomes interesting to study which one or ones have a real influence on the variation of the results. We must be able to distinguish, within the chosen model, the effects of the various factors. Consider for instance the study of 4 different types of preservation of a certain foodstuff: Roquefort cheese. The studied character is a score of general quality. Ten people will give a score for each type of preservation on 7 sessions, the total being 280 measurements. Thus the model will point out not only the effect of the type of preservation and the judge effect, but also the interaction between the two factors because *a priori*, there is no reason for all the judges to have the same appraisal of the four preservation types. Let the index i be the ith judge, the index j the jth type of preservation, and k the session index considered as the replication index. Then, the model is as follows

$$y_{ijk} = \mu_{ij} + \varepsilon_{ijk}$$

where μ_{ij} represents the effect of the studied factors and ε is the random part. The model is balanced because each judge had tasted the four products the same number of times.

The model part will be split according to the different effects mentioned above.

$$\mu_{ij} = \mu + \alpha_i + \beta_j + \theta_{ij}$$

μ is a central parameter

α_i represents the specific effect of the ith judge with respect to the average judge effect, which is null $[\Sigma\alpha_i = 0]$. It is called the main effect of the judge effect.

β_j represents the specific effect of the jth type of preservation under the same conditions $[\Sigma\beta_j = 0]$. It is called the main effect of the preservation effect.

θ_{ij} is the term of interaction between the judge i and the type of preservation j under the conditions $[\Sigma_j\theta_{ij} = 0$ for all i, and $\Sigma_i\theta_{ij} = 0$ for all $j]$.

According to this decomposition of the model part, the total sum of squares falls into four parts

$$\text{TSS} = \text{SS}_\alpha + \text{SS}_\beta + \text{SS}_\theta + \text{RSS}$$

Let us note that the first allows the appraisal of the importance of the judge effect when compared to the residual sum of squares which estimates the natural variability. The test statistic is

$$U_\alpha = \frac{\text{SS}_\alpha/I - 1}{\text{RSS}/IJ(K-1)} = \frac{JK\Sigma_i(Y_{i..} - Y_{...})^2/I - 1}{\Sigma_{ijk}(Y_{ijk} - Y_{ij.})^2/IJ(K-1)}$$

which, under the hypothesis of nullity of the judge effect, follows a Fisher law with $I-1$ and $IJ(K-1)$ degrees of freedom. This hypothesis will therefore be rejected in the case where the value of the U_α statistic computed on the sample is higher than the corresponding value given in Fisher's table. In an absolutely symmetric way, in order to test the preservation type effect, we use the U_β statistic

$$U_\beta = \frac{\text{SS}_\beta/J - 1}{\text{RSS}/IJ(K-1)} = \frac{IK\Sigma_j(Y_{.j.} - Y_{...})^2/J - 1}{\Sigma_{ijk}(Y_{ijk} - Y_{ij.})^2/IJ(K-1)}$$

which, under the hypothesis of nullity of the preservation type effect, follows a Fisher law with $J-1$ and $IJ(K-1)$ degrees of freedom. The hypothesis is rejected when the computed value of U_β is higher than the corresponding value given in Fisher's table. Finally the existence of any interaction is confirmed by the following U_θ statistic

$$U_\theta = \frac{SS_\theta/(I-1)(J-1)}{RSS/IJ(K-1)} \quad \frac{K\Sigma_{ij}(Y_{ij\cdot} - Y_{i\cdot\cdot} - Y_{\cdot j\cdot} + Y_{\cdots})^2/(I-1)(J-1)}{\Sigma_{ijk}(Y_{ijk} - Y_{ij\cdot})^2/IJ(K-1)}$$

which, under the hypothesis of nullity of interactions, follows a Fisher law with $(I-1)(J-1)$ and $IJ(K-1)$ degrees of freedom. The same procedure is used for decision.

Identically to the one-factor layout, the results are presented in a table of analysis of variance (Table 5). The results obtained from the data studied are shown in Table 6.

TABLE 5
TABLE OF TWO-WAY ANALYSIS OF VARIANCE

Source of variation	SS	DF	MS	F
Factor 1	SS_α	$I-1$	$MS_\alpha = SS_\alpha/I-1$	MS_α/RMS
Factor 2	SS_β	$J-1$	$MS_\beta = SS_\beta/J-1$	MS_β/RMS
Interaction	SS_θ	$(I-1)(J-1)$	$MS_\theta = SS_\theta/(I-1)(J-1)$	MS_θ/RMS
Residual	RSS	$IJ(K-1)$	$RMS = RSS/IJ(K-1)$	
Total	TSS	$IJK-1$	$TMS = TSS/IJK-1$	

TABLE 6
TABLE OF ANALYSIS OF VARIANCE OF 4 TYPES OF CHEESE PRESERVATION

Source of variation	SS	DF	MS	F
Judge	5 884	9	653·7	5·54**
Preservation	5 798	3	1 932·8	16·38**
Interaction	4 107	27	152·1	1·29
Residual	28 320	240	118·0	
Total	44 109	279	158·1	

Before using this table, we have to stress the importance of the order of the tests. First, we must try to find out the presence of interactions. If these are significantly non-null, it becomes difficult to consider the interpretation of the main effects. In practice, we examine the relative importance of the main effect and of the interactions. If, despite the presence of interactions, we record a great importance of the main effects, these will be studied with caution. In this case, the appropriate statistic to test the presence of a main effect of the first factor is

$$U'_\alpha = \frac{K\Sigma_{ij}(Y_{ij.} - Y_{.j.})^2/J(I-1)}{\Sigma_{ijk}(Y_{ijk} - Y_{ij.})^2/IJ(K-1)}$$

If, conversely, the interactions play a dominant part, then the separation of the effects will be very tricky. In this situation, we generally decide between two strategies: (1) Start again a one-factor analysis of variance with IJ levels of a new factor, each level being a combination of levels from the previous analysis; (2) start again one-factor analyses operating judge by judge.

The first one is suited to the cases where the best treatment, i.e. the best combination, must be determined. It would make no sense in the champagne experiment. The second one is suited to cases where the second factor, the judge effect, is a parasitic factor.

In our case, the interaction is not significant and the test statistics of the main effects will therefore be usable. Also, the nullity of interactions can be interpreted as a judge consensus on preservation types. Furthermore, we notice a strong judge effect, but this is rather common in the field of sensory analysis. Last but not least, we may consider the influence of the preservation type on the quality of Roquefort cheese.

As previously done with the one-way layout, we still have to classify the four types and distinguish those showing a real difference. The two procedures previously offered, that is the t-method and the S-method, can be applied. In our example, they both lead to the same classification

B   A   D   C

A line between two products indicates that there is no difference between them. We can therefore reject without hesitation the B type of preservation. If the C type of preservation does not imply secondary drawbacks, it can be submitted for adoption.

6.3. Other Situations

The experimental balance essential for the application of the previous model is not always reached. On the one hand, no experimenter is protected against an incident which can ruin the expected balance. Besides, if we go back to the champagne example, it appears unlikely to have 21 types of champagne tasted by each judge and to get reliable answers! Thus each judge will only taste a few samples and a partial confusion will appear between the two effects: judge and champagne. Indeed, if a judge tastes the three best champagnes and another tastes the three worst their mean values will not be comparable. This problem will therefore have to be taken into account as there is no possibility for the two effects—judge and champagne—to be analysed simultaneously. Then there will be two distinct decompositions of the total sum of squares. Each one corresponds to a specific projection. In the first one the champagne effect will be 'adjusted'. In the corresponding sum of squares, the parasitic judge effect has been eliminated and thus this first table of analysis of variance will be suited to correct comparisons between the champagnes. The value of the test statistic allows us to take the right decision. A second projection offers a table of analysis of variance adjusted for the judge effect. It can be used in the case where the judges must be compared.

As an example, let us look at the results of a given session in the experiment with the champagne. The distribution of the studied samples within the judges and the scores given are shown in Table 7.

The high scores of the sixth judge can be the consequence of his own range of scoring or alternatively of the quality of the champagnes 1, 2 and 3. Both effects are probably present in the results. As there is no replication it is impossible to estimate the interaction between the two factors. The model tries to separate the two components, judge effect and champagne effect, of the different scores. Two tables of analysis of

TABLE 7
SCORES FOR 7 CHAMPAGNES GIVEN IN ONE SESSION

Judge	Champagne 1	2	3	4	5	6	7
1		36	16				19
2	22			25	29		
3		24		19		26	
4	27			22	19		
5		29			33		26
6	29	34	35				
7	37					32	28
8		28		21		33	
9			26	16			33
10	30					25	20
11		32			37		27
12			36		19	38	
13	33	25	35				
14			29		20	31	

variance are needed to estimate correctly the importance of the different effects (Table 8 and 9).

We can see that the elements of the rows Residual and Total are identical in the two tables while the rows Judge and Champagne vary from one table to the other. In both cases the judge effect is non-significant. On the other hand the champagne effect appears to be significant in the two cases. The correct level of significance must be read in the first table, where the corresponding effect is adjusted. In this example there are not great differences between the values, because the judge effect is not significant but when the imbalance is strong and the two effects are significant the gap can be considerable.

TABLE 8

TABLE OF ANALYSIS OF VARIANCE OF CHAMPAGNE DATA FROM TABLE 7 (FIRST PROJECTION)

Source of variation	SS	DF	MS	F
Judge	522·31	13	40·18	1.55
Champagne (adjusted)	492·29	6	82·05	3·16*
Residual	571·05	22	25·96	
Total	1 585·65	41		

TABLE 9

TABLE OF ANALYSIS OF VARIANCE OF CHAMPAGNE DATA FROM TABLE 7 (SECOND PROJECTION)

Source of variation	SS	DF	MS	F
Judge (adjusted)	354·45	13	27·27	1·05
Champagne	660·14	6	110·02	4·24*
Residual	571·05	22	25·96	
Total	1 585·65	41		

The possibility of estimating correctly the different parameters in cases where the experimental design is unbalanced is very important. It allows the organisation of experiments even if the experimental constraints (time, cost, place, ...) are strong. Furthermore this possibility protects the scientist against unexpected incidents in the experiment.

6.4. Departures from Assumptions

The theory of the analysis of variance has been drawn from the mathematical model. The required assumptions are restrictive and the experimental conditions do not always secure the validity of these assumptions. Also it is important to know, in case some assumptions are not satisfactory, whether the obtained results lose or keep most of their validity. It is not the purpose of this chapter to repeat all the studies performed on the subject, but we will give some simple indications on the different departures from the assumptions. They belong to three main categories:

1. non-Normality of the distribution;
2. inequality of the variances within the different groups;
3. non-independent errors.

We have already said that in case of non-Normality of the studied variable we look for a transformation which leads to a correct fit with a Gaussian distribution. In fact, the analysis of variance is relatively robust to non-Normality, and except in pathological cases this assumption is not fundamental.

The non-equality of variances within the subgroups is more important. The imbalance in the design must not be important too. In the case where the variance is related to the mean by a function

$$\sigma^2 = f(\mu)$$

we look for a function U whose derivative is proportional to $1/\sqrt{f}$

$$U'(x) = 1/\sqrt{f(x)}$$

then the variable $Z = U(x)$ has a stabilised variance. For instance, in the study of the frequency p of a character in a population, we have

$$\sigma^2 = \frac{\mu(1-\mu)}{n}$$

then the variable $Z = \text{Arcsin}\,\sqrt{p}$ has a constant variance, roughly equal to $1/4n$.

If $\sigma^2 = \mu$, as with a Poisson law, $\sqrt{X}$ is a better variable than X. In the case of the distribution of the correlation coefficient, the variable

$$Z = \frac{1}{2} \log_e \frac{1+R}{1-R}$$

has a variance of $1/(n-3)$ and can be used for testing hypotheses.

Finally, independence of the results is the most important assumption in the linear model. The experiment must be designed and carried out to secure this assumption. If not, the results of the analysis of variance lose all their significance. For instance if in order to compare two products the first one is only tasted by judge 1 and the second one is only tasted by judge 2, there will be no possibility of separating the confounding of the judge effect and the product effect. Consequently no conclusion can be drawn from the experiment.

7. NON-PARAMETRIC METHODS

When the classical assumption of normality is not confirmed, it is still possible to call upon methods which do not require any assumption on the distribution of the studied character. These methods, which are called non-parametric methods, offer much less restrictive conditions for their application than those found in classical statistics. Moreover, the calculations are generally very simple. Nevertheless, we have to stress that such methods are only applicable if the model is not too complex and the sample size not too large. In this section, we intend to present a few of these techniques which mainly operate on ranks instead of operating on measurements.

Working on classifications and not on data offers other advantages. When the results are people's assessment of the qualities of a product, ranks eliminate the problem of scoring scales (location and dispersion) which are particular to each individual. Let us present the Mann and Whitney test for the comparison of two groups, the Kruskall and Wallis test for the comparison of k groups, and finally the Friedmann test in the presence of two factors.

7.1. Comparison of Two Groups
Suppose that we obtain the following measurement results

group 1	11	7	4	13	5	2	9	
group 2	8	12	16	14	17	20	10	6

For each measurement in group 1, we will establish the number of measurements in group 2 which are lower and then add up the obtained values. For each pair of similar values we will add 1/2. The result will be U_1. In our example:

$$U_1 = 3+1+0+4+0+0+2 = 10$$

This will also be done for each element of group 2 compared with those of group 1, to get the statistic U_2. In our case:

$$U_2 = 4 + 6 + 7 + 7 + 7 + 7 + 5 + 3 = 46$$

The sum of U_1 and U_2 is equal to the number of ordered comparisons, that is

$$U_1 + U_2 = pq$$

if there are p measurements within group 1 and q measurements within group 2. This formula can easily be verified in our example.

In order to test the hypothesis H_0: 'the two groups have the same mean', we may use the test statistic of Mann and Whitney

$$U = \min(U_1, U_2)$$

The obtained value for the sample is compared with the tabulated d value in Mann and Whitney's table. If it is lower, for a given risk α, then the samples are said to be significantly different at α level. If out of the two samples, one offers a size greater than 12, we will use the Gaussian approximation as the tabulated value

$$d = 1/2 \; (pq + 1 - \varepsilon \sqrt{pq(pq+1)/3})$$

As we may have noticed, only the respective positions of the individuals are taken into account while computing the U statistic. A simple scatter plot diagram is sufficient for fast calculations of U_1 and U_2 if one can distinguish between the individuals belonging to group 1 and those belonging to group 2.

7.2. Comparison of k Groups

When the number of groups to be compared is higher, ranks are used. In order to do so, the measurements as a whole are ordered and each one is replaced by its rank in the ordered sequence. In the case of equal scores, each one will get the mean rank. Consider for instance the cheese making industry and a study on the settling time for 4 types of milk powder, namely A, B, C and D. We get the results shown in Fig. 10.

For ranking purposes, the 52 value will be rank 1, the 56 value will be rank $(2+3)/2 = 2 \cdot 5$, etc.... For each type of powder, the ranks will be added up (Table 10).

If the four types of milk powder had the same settling time, then the mean rank of each one would be equal to the average mean rank, that is $(n+1)/2$. The Kruskall and Wallis statistic that is used is a measurement of the difference between the sum of observed ranks of one group R and

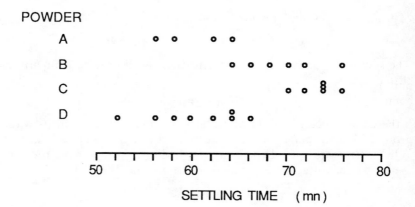

FIG. 10. Settling times of 24 samples of 4 different types of milk powder.

TABLE 10
RANKS OF MILK POWDERS FROM DATA IN FIG. 10

Powder	Ranks								Sum	Number	Mean rank
A	2·5	4·5	7·5	10·5					25	4	6·25
B	10·5	13·5	15	16·5	18·5	23·5			97·5	6	16·25
C	16·5	18·5	21	21	21	23·5			121·5	6	20·25
D	1	2·5	4·5	6	7·5	10·5	10·5	13·5	56	8	7·00

the predicted sum $n(n+1)/2$. It is equal to

$$Q = \frac{12}{n(n+1)} \left(\sum_{i=1}^{k} \frac{1}{n_i} \left(R_i - n_i \frac{(n+1)}{2} \right)^2 \right)$$

or

$$Q = \frac{12}{n(n+1)} \left(\sum_{i=1}^{k} \frac{R_i^2}{n_i} \right) - 3(n+1)$$

The random variable associated with Q follows a χ^2 law with $k-1$ degrees of freedom. Q must therefore be compared with the tabulated value of this distribution $q(k-1, \alpha)$.

If $Q > q(k-1, \alpha)$ the groups do not have the same mean

If $Q < q(k-1, \alpha)$ they do have the same mean.

In our example, the statistic Q has the value 16.86, and the tabulated value of χ^2 with 3 degrees of freedom, at the 5% level is 7.81. The powders do not have the same settling time.

As in an analysis of variance, the means have to be classified when the null hypothesis is rejected. In order to do so, the mean ranks are compared by pairs. The statistic

$$z_{ij} = (r_i - r_j)/\sigma_{ij}$$

with

$$\sigma_{ij} = \sqrt{\frac{n(n+1)}{12}\left(\frac{1}{n_i} + \frac{1}{n_j}\right)}$$

must be compared with the value given in the table of the Gaussian distribution at the level $2\alpha/k(k-1)$. In the example, the mean ranks are the following:

$$r_1 = 6{\cdot}25 \qquad r_2 = 16{\cdot}25 \qquad r_3 = 20{\cdot}25 \qquad r_4 = 7$$

In the case of the powders A and C, the value of the statistic z is $3{\cdot}07$. This value is higher than the tabulated value of a normal law at level 5/6%, $2{\cdot}635$. These two particular powders are significantly different.

7.3. Friedman Test

Consider the case of a taste test involving 5 products and organised as follows: each judge taking part in the test will simultaneously receive five samples and classify them according to his own preferences. The obtained results are as follows:

Samples	A	B	C	D	E
Judge					
1	3	2	5	4	1
2	3	2	5	4	1
3	4	1	5	3	2
4	4	1	5	2	3
R	14	6	20	13	7

Unlike the previous example, ranks are not calculated based on the results as a whole, but rather only on each judge's preferences. This requires a balanced experiment. The Friedman statistic used to decide whether the products are significantly different is as follows:

$$F = \frac{12}{nk(k+1)} \left\{ \sum_{i=1}^{k} [R_i - \tfrac{1}{2}n(k+1)]^2 \right\}$$

or

$$F = \frac{12}{nk(k+1)} \left[\sum_{i=1}^{k} R_i^2 \right] - 3n(k+1)$$

The random variable associated with F follows a χ^2 distribution with $k-1$ degrees of freedom. The decision procedure is therefore the same as the one used in the previous test. In our case

$$F = 13$$

The value of $q(4.5\%)$ is equal to 9·49. Therefore, the products are said to be significantly different at the 5% level since the actual result is higher than the tabulated value.

Means are compared using the following statistic

$$z_{ij} = (r_i - r_j)/\sigma_{ij}$$

with

$$\sigma_{ij} = \sqrt{nk(k+1)/6}$$

which is compared with tabulated values of the Gaussian distribution at level $2\alpha/k(k-1)$.

The main concepts of non-parametric statistics are presented in Hajek (1969). The possibilities of using it in the food research field are shown in Tomassone and Flanzy (1977).

8. OUTLIERS

8.1. Introduction

We have to consider the fact that this notion is a subjective concept. An observation is called a discordant observation or outlier if it appears to the scientist as standing apart from the other results. The decision that an individual is an outlier is never easy to take. When a random variable is studied, an event with a very low probability (low but not null) can occur, and then it seems abnormal, although it is not. But there is absolute need for the detection and treatment of outliers. This is mainly due to their influence on the results of the statistical procedures. This notion of weight of an individual on the parameters, or the stability of the parameters when they are calculated with and without a given result offers a possibility of pointing out problematic values. Indeed, what can be the credibility of a statistic based on only a single value? Consequently we must choose between two attitudes:

— the detection and elimination of outliers;
— the use of robust statistics, non-sensitive to the extreme values.

The second option has been partially dealt with in the paragraph concerning non-parametric methods.

When the size of the sample is small, a visual inspection is generally sufficient, but special care will be given to the extreme values. To this end, most of the diagrams previously presented are suitable. In the case of a large sample size, we introduce a model to decide whether outliers are present or not. The subjectivity of the decision is then increased by the choice of the model. Many techniques have already been proposed, such as the mixture models, i.e. models where the distribution is a mixture of two distributions (for example the mean shift model mixture of $N(\mu, \sigma^2)$ and $N(\mu + \lambda, \sigma^2)$, or the variance-inflation model mixture of $N(\mu, \sigma^2)$ and $N(\mu, a^2\sigma^2)$). Nevertheless, in this chapter we intend to present the detection of outliers in normal linear models.

8.2. Detection and Elimination of Outliers

In the linear model, one may use the studentised residuals

$$\tilde{r}_i = \frac{x_i - x.}{\hat{\sigma}}$$

Thomson (1935) has shown that

$$\frac{\sqrt{(n-2)}\,\tilde{r}_i}{\sqrt{n-1-\tilde{r}_i^2}} \sim T(n-1)$$

This formula is used to obtain the threshold values. It is advisable to note that $\tilde{r}_i$ are not independent and that the statistic allows the rejection of only one outlier, namely the outlier corresponding to the maximum value of the statistic. The uneasiness experienced at rejecting several outliers is important and due to the fact that their presence considerably increases the estimated variance if they are located on both sides of the mean, and increases both the mean and the variance when located on one side.

In order to solve this problem, we investigated the possibilities of finding procedures able to reject simultaneously several outliers, but generally the proposed models imply knowledge of the number of outliers. Finally Kitagawa (1979) used Akaike's Information Criterion (AIC). By studying a family of models where the smallest r_1 observations belonged to the inferior outlying population and the largest r_2 observations to the superior outlying population, Kitagawa was able to determine the model with the minimum AIC. The corresponding outlying populations were rejected.

8.3. Accommodation
As we have previously mentioned, the other possibility consists in the use of robust statistics. The underlying principle is to balance the measurements so as to reduce the importance of extreme values and obtain by so doing more stable estimators.

8.3.1. L-Estimators
The first idea was to use linear statistics on ranks, called L-estimators. This includes the statistics such as the median and various trimmed and Winsorised means. Tukey (1960) has shown by using a variance inflation model, that with long-tailed distributions the median is a really efficient estimator of the mean value.

8.3.2. M-Estimators
Huber (1964) proposes to change the least-squares criterion, sensitive to outliers, by the minimisation of a general criterion

$$\sum_i f(X_i - T)$$

with various functions less sensitive to discordant values. These estimators are called M-estimators. They include the arithmetic mean if $f(t) = t^2$ and the median if $f(t) = |t|$. A very efficient estimator is obtained with the function f defined by

$$f(t) = t^2/2 \qquad |t| < K$$
$$f(t) = K|t| - t^2/2 \qquad |t| \geqslant K$$

Other methods have been suggested, mainly based on the weighting of the results. The weighting can be performed using Bayesian theory or the residual values.

Lastly we must say that outliers may not necessarily be detected with the aid of univariate statistics. Multivariate analysis can point out an outlier, whereas it was not an outlier for any one of the different variables. See for example the outlier (i) in Section 4.3 of Chapter 3.

For further information we may consult De Finetti (1961), Box and Tiao (1968), Grubbs (1969), Dempster and Rosner (1971), and Beckman and Cook (1983) for a review.

REFERENCES AND BIBLIOGRAPHY

Amerine, M. A., Pangborn, R. M. and Roessler, E. B. (1965). *Principles of Sensory Evaluation of Food*, Academic Press, New York.

Beckman, R. J. and Cook, R. D. (1983). Outliers. *Technometrics*, **25**, 119–49.

Box, G. E. P. and Tiao, G. C. (1968). A Bayesian approach to some outlier problems. *Biometrika*, **55**, 119–29.

Chambers, J. M., Cleveland, W. S., Kleiner, B. and Tukey, J. W. (1983). *Graphical Methods for Data Analysis*, Duxbury, Boston.

De Finetti, B. (1961). The Bayesian approach to the rejection of outliers. In: *Proceedings of the Fourth Berkeley Symposium on Mathematical Statistics and Probability (Vol 1)*, University of California Press, pp. 199–210.

Dempster, A. P. and Rosner, B. (1971). Detection of Outliers. In: *Statistical Decision Theory and Related Topics*, Academic Press, New York, pp 161–80.

Grubbs, F. E. (1969). Procedures for detecting outlying observations in samples. *Technometrics* **11**, 1–21.

Hajek, J. (1969). *Non Parametric Statistics*, Holden-Day, San Francisco.

Huber, P. J. (1964). Robust estimation of a location parameter. *Annals of Mathematical Statistics*, **35**, 73–101.

Kitagawa, G. (1979). On the use of AIC for the detection of outliers *Technometrics*, **21**, 193–99.

Martens, H. and Russwürm Jr., H. (Eds) (1982). *Food Research and Data Analysis*, Applied Science Publishers, London.

Mosteller, F. and Tukey, J. W. (1977). *Data Analysis and Regression*, Addison-Wesley, Reading.

Piggott, J. R. (Ed.) (1984) *Sensory Analysis of Food*, Elsevier Applied Science Publishers, London.

Sauvageot, F. (1982). *L'Evaluation Sensorielle des Denrées Alimentaires*, Technique et Documentation, Paris.

Scheffé, H. (1959). *The Analysis of Variance*, Wiley, New York.

Thomson, W. R. (1935). On a criterion for the rejection of observations and the distribution of the ratio of deviation to sample standard deviation *Biometrika*, **32**, 214–19.

Tomassone, R. and Flanzy, J. (1977). Présentation synthétique de diverses méthodes d'analyse des données fournies par un jury de dégustateurs. *Ann. Techno. Agric.*, **26**(4), 373–418.

Tukey, J. W. (1960). A survey sampling from contaminated distributions. In: *Contributions to Probability and Statistics: Essays in Honor of Harold Hotelling*, Stanford University Press.

Chapter 3

A PRACTICAL APPROACH TO REGRESSION

DEREK J. PIKE

Department of Applied Statistics, University of Reading, UK

'If the doors of perception were cleansed everything would appear to man as it is—infinite.' '

WILLIAM BLAKE

1. INTRODUCTION

Regression is easy! Fifteen years ago such a statement would have required some qualification, but no longer is this the case. Simple linear regression is now no further than the nearest hand calculator. Solutions to complex multiple and nonlinear regression problems are no more remote than the nearest computer terminal. The scientist of today exists in the bewildering world of acronyms—SAS, BMDP, GLIM—able to solve problems which a short time ago could only be dreams. Why then in such an advanced numerical society does a book require a chapter about regression?

We must all recognise that the development of new techniques brings with it a correspondingly increased responsibility on all users of the techniques—scientists and statisticians alike. A technique can never be used as a substitute for thought, nor a computer terminal as a substitute for hand plotting and analysis of data. The ease of collection and analysis of large quantities of data has increased the chance of reporting invalid results because of fundamental errors of concept as well as typing and transcription errors. The scientist, who will frequently spend considerable time, effort and money in the collection of data, must recognise that at least as much time, effort and money may have to be spent in its analysis.

In this chapter simple ideas which should be well known will be treated, but briefly. Highly complex and relatively modern ideas, so often picked up and used by practising scientists, but still the subject of some debate by statisticians, will in many cases be omitted. Instead, the aims of this chapter are to heighten the consciousness of the users of regression, to illustrate techniques in the context of their problems and pitfalls, and to show how prior thought can give rise to clearer objectives and make more efficient use of available data.

In all areas of food research scientists and experimenters are interested in the relationships between quantitative response variables, y, and quantitative stimulus variables $x_1 \ldots x_k$ in the sense that y is determined by some function of the stimulus variables. Thus $y = f(\mathbf{x}; \beta)$ where β are unknown parameters which give a precise form of the function f and are estimated from data. Knowledge of a suitable functional form for f can enable a researcher to make efficient use of available resources, both practically and economically, by prediction from his fitted relationship. For example, studies might be concerned with the effect of cholesterol intake on mortality levels; the effect of time on the moisture content of stored food; the relationship between the total basic amino-acids in leaf protein concentrates and the dye binding capacity of lysine; the assessment of product acceptability as a function of varying levels of sensory variables in the product design; or the effect of enzyme concentration and incubation period on pectinesterase activity.

In practice the underlying form of the function f is unknown. Consequently the aim of research workers must be to provide response relationships which adequately describe the observed relationship and which can be used for predictive purposes. At present, and this is borne out in the recent food science and food technology literature, chosen models are largely restricted to linear models which can be fitted with any standard multiple regression package. Where nonlinear models are used, they are only used in cases where they can be turned into linear models by transformation. For example, the Michaelis–Menten equation in enzyme kinetics is transformed into the Lineweaver and Burk relationship and fitted as a linear model. It is inevitable that the choice of a suitable relationship should be influenced by statistical considerations of the method of fitting, but with modern computing facilities and recent software development this dependence should become much less important. The choice should be governed principally by the objectives of fitting a regression model.

It would be ideal if there were, in all situations where regression models are used, one and only one objective in the use of the response function. However, in regression as in experimental design, the choice is often governed by a range of conflicting objectives. These might include, in varying degrees of importance, a purely descriptive reduction of the data, a short term prediction for particular ranges of the stimulus variables, a long term prediction for the general pattern of response, and a simple interest in the 'true' underlying mechanism governing the response. With such a range of objectives, examples of which can be found in most issues of food research journals, it is perhaps not surprising that some confusion and misunderstanding exists, particularly about the choice between empirical and mechanistic models. We can present this problem diagrammatically as in Fig. 1.

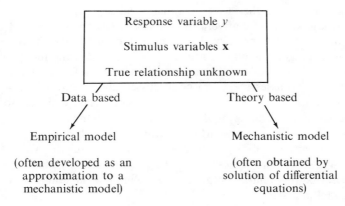

FIG. 1. Empirical and Mechanistic models.

In fact, all models are essentially empirical. The difference is that mechanistic models are obtained by consideration of the behaviour of the underlying mechanism governing the relationship. In regression the real point at issue is the extent to which it is necessary to use biologically meaningful relationships. We must be careful in our approach as Bliss (1970, p. 55) indicates. 'A mathematical model developed from an intimate understanding of the biological mechanism should be utilised whenever feasible. The agreement of a series of observations with a postulated model is a necessary but not a sufficient test of its validity. A theoretical equation, however, may acquire more constants than are needed. Thus if the proposed theoretical curve calls for six adjustable constants but describes the observations no better than an empirical curve with three constants, we would do well to re-examine our theoretical equation. Although our present concern is primarily with empirical equations, the better we understand the underlying biological process the more effectively we can select an empirical form which may be invested with biological meaning.'

The remainder of this chapter will concentrate on empirical models. The reader who wishes to investigate further the ideas of mechanistic models is referred to France and Thornley (1984), Segal (1984) and Endrenyi (1981).

2. SIMPLE LINEAR REGRESSION

It is easy to feel that the ideas of simple linear regression are so obvious and well known that relatively little space needs to be devoted to the technique. Quite the contrary. The crucial thing is to give the researcher the knowledge and the confidence to be able to study the most complex of problems successfully. All the concepts necessary for model development, fitting and assessment can be discussed and illustrated most easily using simple linear regression. Regression is concerned with relationships between stimulus variables and the response to changes in the values of these stimuli. For example Marsh *et al.* (1979) discuss the effect of varying percentages of Water Insoluble Solids, x, and the Yield Factor (percentage of tomato solids), y, in the production of Catsup.

To describe this relationship we must define a *model*, and the simplest such model is a straight line

$$y = \beta_0 + \beta_1 x + \varepsilon$$

In this model β_0 and β_1 are *unknown parameters* to be estimated and ε is a *random error* representing the level of inconsistency present in repeated evaluations of similar experimental observations. To proceed with the *estimation* of the parameters we must make *assumptions* about the nature of the random error ε. We often assume that ε has a Normal distribution with mean zero and constant variance σ^2. Thus

$$\varepsilon \sim N(0, \sigma^2)$$

We must understand what these assumptions mean and what is their importance for the fitting and evaluation of the relationship to observed data. The Normality assumption is irrelevant for the fitting of the model. It merely permits tests of significance to be performed on the results using t-tests and F-tests. It is crucial to recognise that these *are* assumptions and cannot be *proved* to be true. We can, however, rely on the fact that our results will be *robust* to mild departures from the assumptions. Assessment of the assumptions is possible after fitting the model, by using the *residuals*—the differences between the observed values and the fitted values.

2.1. Parameter Estimation and Model Assessment

To estimate the parameters β_0 and β_1 it is necessary to define a criterion by which to perform the estimation. The usual criterion is to minimise the sum of squared deviations between the observed values and the chosen model. Thus in the linear regression case with n observations we minimise

$$\sum_{i=1}^{n} \{y_i - \beta_0 - \beta_1 x_i\}^2$$

and obtain estimators

$$\hat{\beta}_0 = \bar{y} - \hat{\beta}_1 \bar{x}$$

$$\hat{\beta}_1 = \frac{\sum_{i=1}^{n}(x_i - \bar{x})(y_i - \bar{y})}{\sum_{i=1}^{n}(x_i - \bar{x})^2} = \frac{S_{xy}}{S_{xx}}$$

giving a best fitting line

$$\hat{y} = \hat{\beta}_0 + \hat{\beta}_1 x$$

The assessment of the fit of this equation and its interpretation can be carried out in a range of ways.

2.1.1. Analysis of Variance

This provides a method of partitioning the overall variation between the observations into variation which has been explained by the regression and residual or unexplained variation. Thus we can say

Total variation about the mean		Variation explained by regression		Residual variation
$S_{yy} = \sum_{i=1}^{n}(y_i - \bar{y})^2$	$=$	S_{xy}^2/S_{xx}	$+$	Residual Sum of Squares
$(n-1)$ df		1 df		$(n-2)$ df

An assessment of the significance of the regression (a test of the hypothesis that $\beta_1 = 0$) is made from the ratio of the regression mean square to the residual mean square which is an F ratio with 1 and $n-2$ degrees of freedom.

It is important that a highly significant F ratio should not seduce the experimenter into a belief that the straight line is a superb fit to the data. The F-test is simply an assessment of the extent to which the fitted line has a slope which is different from zero. If the slope of the line is near to zero the scatter of the data points about the line would need to be small in order to obtain a significant F ratio. However, a situation with a slope very different from zero can give a highly significant F ratio with a considerable scatter of points about the line. The message is simple: do not use a technique designed for one objective to try to satisfy another.

2.1.2. R^2

A summary measure of the quality of the fit is given by calculating

$$R^2 = \frac{\text{Regression Sum of Squares}}{\text{Total Sum of Squares}}$$

It is thus clear that it represents the proportion of the total sum of squares explained by the regression. Hence the larger is R^2, the better is the fit of the straight line to the data. However, again there are pitfalls. A value of R^2 equal to 0·75 is likely to be viewed with some satisfaction by experimenters. It is often more appropriate to recognise that there is still 25% of the total variation unexplained by the regression which has been performed. We must ask why this could be; and whether a more complex relationship in a single variable or inclusion of additional stimulus variables could explain much of this apparently residual variation.

2.1.3. Assessment of Individual Parameters

To a large extent (2.1.1) and (2.1.2) provide a summary assessment of the fit of the line. Frequently interest will lie in the values of particular parameters—for example the slope of the line β_1. Interpretation of such parameters is meaningless without a standard error to attach to the estimated value $\hat{\beta}_1$.

In the case of simple linear regression

$$\text{Standard error } (\hat{\beta}_1) = \sqrt{\frac{\text{Residual MS}}{S_{xx}}} = \sqrt{\frac{s^2}{S_{xx}}}$$

and we can write down a 95% confidence interval for $\hat{\beta}_1$ as

$$\hat{\beta}_1 \pm t\sqrt{\frac{s^2}{S_{xx}}}$$

where t is the 5% two-sided value of Student's t with $n-2$ degrees of freedom. The principle is exactly the same in evaluation of parameters of multiple regression equations.

2.1.4. The Fitted Line as a Predictor

Equally as important as the estimation of particular parameters is the use of the fitted line as a predictor of the likely response at values of the stimulus variable other than those used in the experiment. Once again if this prediction is to be of value it must be associated with appropriate standard errors.

If prediction is required for the *average* response at a value X_0 of the stimulus variable, the predicted response is

$$\hat{Y} = \hat{\beta}_0 + \hat{\beta}_1 X_0$$

with standard error

$$\sqrt{s^2\left[\frac{1}{n} + \frac{(X_0 - \bar{x})^2}{S_{xx}}\right]}$$

If, on the other hand, prediction is required for a specified *individual* observation at x_0, the predicted value is the same but the standard error is

$$\sqrt{s^2\left[1 + \frac{1}{n} + \frac{(X_0 - \bar{x})^2}{S_{xx}}\right]}$$

The additional s^2 here reflects the specific random error present in the individual observation for which a prediction is being made. The important point to notice is that the standard error of a predicted response depends upon the value of the stimulus variable for which prediction is required. The fitted line has been obtained from experimental data and the standard error of the predicted response is smallest at $\bar{x}$—the mean of the experimental stimulus variables. The confidence interval for the predicted value is curved and hence our prediction becomes increasingly poor as we move away from the centre of the data.

Thus prediction on the basis of a fitted regression relationship needs to be undertaken with care. This is particularly true if any attempt is made to extrapolate the results beyond the range of the data. Here there are two dangers, one practical and one statistical. The practical danger is that no evidence is available that the fitted line remains a true representation of the relationship outside the range of the observed data. Even if this assumption is reasonable the statistical problem is that the standard error which attaches to any predicted response may be so large as to render the results practically useless. Once again the message is that regression is a powerful tool to be used with care and thought.

2.2. Example

To illustrate the points made above, consider the example mentioned earlier from Marsh *et al.* (1979). They present the data in Table 1 of the Yield Factor (percentage of tomato solids in Catsup) and the Percentage of Water Insoluble Solids in the Total Solids.

TABLE 1

% Water insoluble solids, x	Yield factor y	% Water insoluble solids, x	Yield factor y
10·71	51·0	14·50	37·9
11·76	45·2	14·80	36·2
11·36	44·8	14·88	35·3
11·27	47·4	10·86	48·5
15·30	35·5	13·34	40·0
12·07	44·5	13·01	43·0
15·98	35·3	12·87	41·5
13·34	39·3	14·40	36·7
13·34	40·8	15·12	35·3
14·29	38·4	17·06	32·5
13·66	39·3	18·22	30·2
14·79	36·0	13·73	38·9

Linear regression of y on x gives a fitted relationship

$$\hat{y} = 76 \cdot 19 - 2 \cdot 65\, x \qquad \text{with } R^2 = 0 \cdot 94$$

The analysis of variance is given in Table 2 and the F-test shows that the regression coefficient β_1 is highly significantly different from zero.

TABLE 2

Source of variation	df	SS	MS	F	
Regression	1	581·27	581·27	350·4	highly sig.
Residual	22	36·50	1·66		
Total	23	617·77			

The Residual Mean Square $s^2 = 1.66$ giving a 95% confidence interval for $\hat{\beta}_1$ as

$$2.65 \pm 2.074 \sqrt{\frac{1.66}{82.98}} \quad \text{or} \quad (2.36, 2.94)$$

These results all appear to suggest the line above is an excellent fit to the data and can be used as a predictive tool. We thus look at the plot of the data and fitted line in Fig. 2. Immediately a salutory point should become clear.

The straight line regression, which appeared to be an excellent fit from the results of the automatic procedure performed above, is systematically

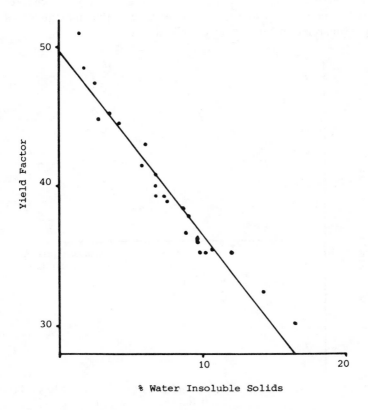

FIG. 2. Data from Marsh, Leonard and Buhlert with fitted straight line.

wrong! The true relationship is in fact curved, and this would have been obvious had these data been plotted first. This obvious observation, now clear to all readers, escapes so many experimenters that the words 'Have you plotted your data?' should be inscribed over the desk of every advisory statistician! With a single stimulus variable this is easy and is often done. With multiple regression problems this is thought to be more difficult and is thus avoided, possibly with disastrous results. The point is discussed in more detail in the context of multiple regression in Section 3. (Marsh *et al.* did not fall into this trap. They present a data plot and a fitted quadratic relationship.) We must however ask what techniques are available to help the experimenter to avoid presenting results which look excellent but which are systematically wrong. The answer lies in a study of the residuals which are the differences between the observed values and the fitted values. For this example Fig. 3 shows a plot of the residuals against the stimulus variable, x, and the inadequacy of the straight line relationship is immediately obvious.

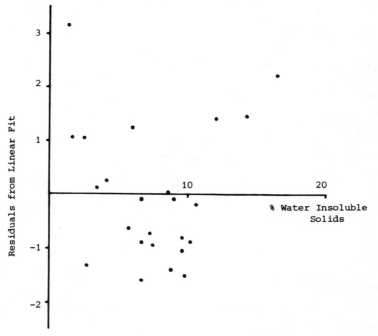

FIG. 3. Plot of residuals from straight line fitted to data from Marsh, Leonard and Buhlert.

The case for an extra term in the fitted relationship—for example, a quadratic term—seems clear; but this will not always be the case. If our intuition suggests a quadratic term might be advisable then we must expect to be able to assess the need statistically.

2.3. Quadratic Regression

To fit a quadratic relationship

$$y = \beta_0 + \beta_1 x + \beta_2 x^2$$

is a simple enough procedure by choosing β_0, β_1 and β_2 to minimise

$$\sum_{i=1}^{n} \{y_i - \beta_0 - \beta_1 x_i - \beta_2 x_i^2\}^2$$

just as for the fitting of the straight line relationship. This is done most simply by using a computer package such as MINITAB, GENSTAT, BMD-P, SAS, and many others. For the data in Table 1 we obtain a fitted line:

$$\hat{y} = 115 \cdot 1 - 8 \cdot 29 x + 0 \cdot 20 x^2 \qquad \text{with } R^2 = 0 \cdot 97$$

The Regression Sum of Squares for this quadratic is 601·04 with 2 degrees of freedom (corresponding to the fitting of β_1 and β_2). The difference between this and the value 581·27 given in Table 2 is the extra sum of squares explained by including the quadratic term and this can be used to provide an F-test of the significance of including the quadratic term in the model *in addition to* the linear term. These results are shown in Table 3 and confirm the importance of the quadratic term. A plot of the residuals (not given here) shows no apparent evidence of departures from randomness.

TABLE 3

Source of variation	df	SS	MS	F	
Extra SS for fitting quadratic term	1	19·77	19·77	24·8	highly sig.
Residual	21	16·73	0·80		

It will be clear from this example that the residuals provide information both on the size of the random error present in the data and on the extent to which a given model does not reflect the pattern of the data.

To some extent the assessment which has been used here is visual and subjective. If an alternative, more objective, evaluation were available it might be possible to advise researchers on principles to be considered in the design of their study.

2.4. Lack of Fit and Pure Error

In the study of the straight line relationship

$$y = \beta_0 + \beta_1 x + \varepsilon$$

the residual elements ε contain random variation and information on the lack of fit of the relationship. However, if a number of observations are available with the same value of x, the stimulus variable, the variation in the response values, y, can be assumed to be caused only by random variation, or *pure error*, and not by *lack of fit*. Thus, in an experiment where sets of such repeated values are available, it is possible to separate what has so far been called *residual variation* into the two components mentioned above. It is then possible to test the extent to which the lack of fit of the line is significant relative to the size of the pure error. Details of the algebra underlying the technique can be found for example in Draper and Smith (1981).

Hegedus and Zachariev (1978) present a study of the relative nutritive values (RNV) for *Tetrahymena pyriformis W* of 21 Candida yeast samples grown on n-paraffin. One investigation they present is of the relationship between Tetrahymena-RNV and protein content of the samples. In their data four pairs of samples have the same protein content and these provide 4 degrees of freedom for the assessment of pure error (sample to sample variation). Details of the fitted relationship are not given here but Table 4 contains the analysis of variance table showing the partitioning of the residual variation into Lack of Fit and Pure Error. The non-significant F ratio for Lack of Fit indicates that there is no significant and systematic departure from the straight line relationship which has been fitted.

TABLE 4

Source of variation	df	SS	MS	F
Regression	1	3598·74	3598·74	
Lack of Fit	15	906·33	60·42	0·30 not sig.
Pure Error	4	807·50	201·88	
Combined residual	19	1713·83	90·20	
Total	20	5312·57		

The implications of this result are important. Experimenters rarely think about the *design* of regression studies. Design is believed to be necessary only when factorials and randomised block experiments are being performed. With regression it is simply a question of collecting data and fitting relationships. This could not be further from the truth. The point being made here is that *some* replication of observations at the same values of the stimulus variables is to be encouraged as it provides a mechanism for objective assessment of the lack of fit of a chosen relationship. The emphasis on the word 'some' is deliberate. Replication of *every* experimental point may be wasteful of expensive resources. Replication of *no* experimental points provides no information about lack of fit. There is no single answer to the question about how much replication is necessary; but the principle should be considered and advice sought, if possible, from a statistician.

2.5. Comparison of Regressions
Frequently it will be required to extend the ideas of simple linear regression to compare the results obtained under differing conditions or for different treatments. Cloutt (1983) presents data, shown in Fig. 4, of

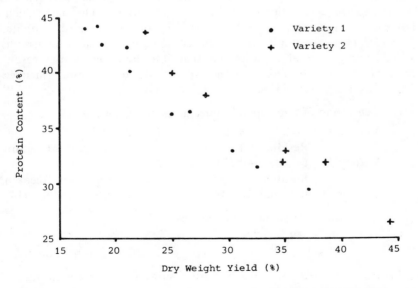

FIG. 4. Relationship between protein content and dry weight yield for two varieties of cowpea.

the relationship between protein content and dry weight yield of air classified fines fractions for two varieties of cowpea.

Straight line regressions would appear adequate to represent the data from each variety. When we compare them there are several possibilities.

(a) One straight line for both varieties,
$$y = \beta_0 + \beta_1 x$$ 2 fitted parameters

(b) Two parallel lines for the two varieties,
$$y_1 = \beta_{01} + \beta_1 x_1 \qquad y_2 = \beta_{02} + \beta_1 x_2$$ 3 fitted parameters

(c) Two lines with a common intercept,
$$y_1 = \beta_0 + \beta_{11} x_1 \qquad y_2 = \beta_0 + \beta_{12} x_2$$ 3 fitted parameters

(d) Two separate lines,
$$y_1 = \beta_{01} + \beta_{11} x_1 \qquad y_2 = \beta_{02} + \beta_{12} x_2$$ 4 fitted parameters

The best fit will always be given by (d). However, in this case if (a) is not significantly worse, it is logical to choose the simpler relationship with what is clearly a simpler and more powerful interpretation, namely that there is a single relationship with no significant difference between the varieties. Moreover, this is another situation in which a statistical comparison is possible between these competing alternatives. It is achieved in essentially the same way as was comparison between the linear and the quadratic fits of Sections 2.2 and 2.3. The basic calculations are most easily performed using any of the standard computer packages. However, it must be recognised that comparison of regressions is sufficiently general a technique that interpretation of the results requires some understanding by the experimenter of the basic principles. The ideas are illustrated here by a partial analysis of Cloutt's data.

(d) The fitting of two separate lines gives the following results:

Variety 1.	$\hat{y} = 57.73 - 0.793x$	$R^2 = 0.97$
	Residual SS $= 7.599$	8 degrees of freedom.
Variety 2.	$\hat{y} = 58.90 - 0.734x$	$R^2 = 0.97$
	Residual SS $= 6.673$	5 degrees of freedom.
Combined	Residual SS $= 14.272$	13 degrees of freedom. (B)

(a) The fitting of a single joint line gives:

$$\hat{y} = 55.68 - 0.674x \qquad R^2 = 0.92$$
Residual SS $= 40.552$ \qquad 15 degrees of freedom. (A)

The difference $(A) - (B)$ gives the extra sum of squares for fitting the two extra parameters in the separate lines. If this difference is *not significant* when compared with the mean square from fitting two lines, then one line will represent the data adequately. These results are best presented in an analysis of variance table given in Table 5.

TABLE 5

Source of variation	df	SS	MS	F	
Variation of the separate lines about the joint line	2	26·280	13·140	12·0	highly sig.
Residual	13	14·272	1·098		

The highly significant F ratio for the variation of the two separate lines about the joint line shows that a single line is not satisfactory. Inspection of the data and the fitting of two separate lines suggests that either parallel lines or lines with a common intercept might be adequate. The appropriate choice at this stage should be governed by scientific considerations of the problem being studied and not by the results from an automatic statistical routine. The evaluation of the chosen comparison is made in exactly the same way.

3. MULTIPLE LINEAR REGRESSION

Sometimes there will be more than one stimulus variable in a study, $x_1 \ldots x_k$, and we may wish to determine the way in which they affect the response variable y. For example, $x_1 \ldots x_k$ may be varying levels of ingredient in a product where the response is the product acceptability to the consumer as in Moskowitz (1981). Thus at the simplest level, if there are three stimulus variables, we could fit a multiple regression model

$$y = \beta_0 + \beta_1 x_1 + \beta_2 x_2 + \beta_3 x_3$$

(Note that we have in fact already fitted a multiple regression in Section 2 when we looked at a quadratic relationship. The term in x^2 is treated exactly as if it were a separate variable x_2 in a multiple regression.)

More complex models are possible including quadratic terms such as x_1^2 and cross product terms like $x_1 x_2$ (analogous to a two factor interaction in analysis of variance). Indeed such complex multiple regression models can easily be fitted using packages available for almost any type of computer, however small. Unfortunately the prevalence of such packages has encouraged unthinking analysis of data; and the production of models which do not reflect the pattern of variation present in the data, or which contain unnecessarily many parameters. Study of a data set prior to analysis and the use of simple graphical techniques can easily avoid such problems and can isolate appropriate models before the computer is used at all. Generally simple hand plotting is all that is needed, but the advent of SAS/GRAPH has provided a new dimension for the scientist who wishes to display data pictorially.

3.1. Data Plotting and Model Selection

The most effective way to illustrate these ideas is by an example. The one chosen here is from Moskowitz (1981) in a study which investigates the effects of spice level, total solids and thickener in a three-component sauce on the overall acceptability level judged by a group of 45 panellists. The relative levels of the three components and the average response of the panellists is given in Table 6. Thus in this case

y = mean overall acceptability level

x_1 = spice level

x_2 = total solids

x_3 = thickener level.

TABLE 6

Spice level (x_1)	Total solids (x_2)	Thickener level (x_3)	Overall acceptability (y)
1·75	1·75	1·75	15
1·75	1·75	0·25	29
1·75	0·25	1·75	40
1·75	0·25	0·25	30
0·25	1·75	1·75	20
0·25	1·75	0·25	18
0·25	0·25	1·75	29
0·25	0·25	0·25	14
1·75	1·00	1·00	67
0·25	1·00	1·00	30
1·00	1·75	1·00	54
1·00	0·25	1·00	48
1·00	1·00	1·75	76
1·00	1·00	0·25	54
1·00	1·00	1·00	49

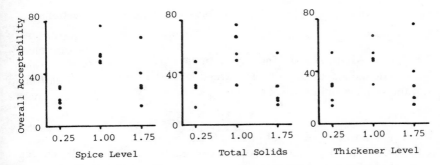

FIG. 5. Relationship between overall acceptability and level of individual components in a three-component sauce.

An indication of graphical summarisation of these data is given in Fig. 5, where it can be seen that the response to all three factors shows evidence of curvature—evidence which is stronger for spice level and for total solids than it is for thickener. The wide variation in the plotted points suggests either that there is considerable inconsistency in the response of panellists, or that more than one variable is required to describe the response pattern, or both.

In Fig. 6 we see a hand contour plot of spice level against total solids where the variation previously observed is largely resolved. Similar patterns are observed in the other two possible such contour plots and suggests the need for a model containing linear and quadratic terms in all three variables. The need for cross-product terms is not quite so

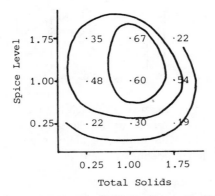

FIG. 6. Contour plot of overall acceptability against spice level and total solids from a three-component sauce.

evident at this stage. These data will be studied further in Sections 3.2 and 3.5.

3.2. Fitting Methods and Model Assessment

We can define a general multiple regression model with n observations, k variables and p unknown parameters as:

$$\mathbf{y} = \mathbf{X}\boldsymbol{\beta} + \boldsymbol{\varepsilon}$$

where $\mathbf{y}$ is an $n \times 1$ vector of observations;

$\mathbf{X}$ is an $n \times p$ matrix of known form. It is based on the chosen experimental design and the model to be fitted and is made up from the k variables under study.

$\boldsymbol{\beta}$ is a $p \times 1$ vector of parameters.

$\boldsymbol{\varepsilon}$ is an $n \times 1$ vector of residual elements.

The simplest way to understand this vector notation is to see it in the context of simple linear regression with, for example, five observations $(x_1, y_1), \ldots, (x_5, y_5)$. Thus for the ith observation

$$y_i = \beta_0 + \beta_1 x_i + \varepsilon_i$$

where there are two parameters β_0 and β_1 and a residual element ε_i for that observation. The full set of observations can be written as in Table 7 with the vector notation equivalent beside it.

TABLE 7

$y_i = \beta_0 + \beta_1 x_i + \varepsilon_i$	$\mathbf{y}$	$=$	$\mathbf{X}$	$\boldsymbol{\beta}$	$+$	$\boldsymbol{\varepsilon}$
$y_1 = \beta_0 + \beta_1 x_1 + \varepsilon_1$	$\begin{bmatrix} y_1 \\ y_2 \\ y_3 \\ y_4 \\ y_5 \end{bmatrix}$	$=$	$\begin{bmatrix} 1 & x_1 \\ 1 & x_2 \\ 1 & x_3 \\ 1 & x_4 \\ 1 & x_5 \end{bmatrix}$	$\begin{bmatrix} \beta_0 \\ \beta_1 \end{bmatrix}$	$+$	$\begin{bmatrix} \varepsilon_1 \\ \varepsilon_2 \\ \varepsilon_3 \\ \varepsilon_4 \\ \varepsilon_5 \end{bmatrix}$
$y_2 = \beta_0 + \beta_1 x_2 + \varepsilon_2$						
$y_3 = \beta_0 + \beta_1 x_3 + \varepsilon_3$						
$y_4 = \beta_0 + \beta_1 x_4 + \varepsilon_4$						
$y_5 = \beta_0 + \beta_1 x_5 + \varepsilon_5$						

The theory underlying the fitting of such a model is standard and the reader should refer, for example, to the excellent and detailed exposition in Draper and Smith (1981). In this chapter general results will be summarised and a few guidelines presented.

3.2.1. The Principle of Least Squares

For the model $\mathbf{y} = \mathbf{X}\boldsymbol{\beta} + \boldsymbol{\varepsilon}$, the assumption is usually made that $E(\boldsymbol{\varepsilon}) = \mathbf{0}$ and $V(\boldsymbol{\varepsilon}) = \mathbf{I}\sigma^2$ so that the elements of $\boldsymbol{\varepsilon}$ are uncorrelated. Note that the belief, sometimes expressed, that the columns of **X** should also be uncorrelated is totally mythological. To recognise this it is only necessary to understand that a quadratic is a multiple regression model with correlated 'independent variables'!

The parameters of β are estimated by minimising $\Sigma_{i=1}^{n} \varepsilon_i^2$, the sum of squared residuals. A summary measure of the quality of the fitted model can be obtained by using the R^2 statistic, the square of the *multiple correlation coefficient*. Thus if a model with p parameters is fitted, then

$$R^2 = 1 - \frac{\text{Residual Sum of Squares}}{\text{Total Sum of Squares}}$$

3.2.2. The 'Extra Sum of Squares' Principle

In any multiple regression study it is important to be able to assess whether particular terms should or should not be included in the model. If, in addition to the assumptions made above, we can assume that the residuals ε are Normally distributed, then it is possible using the extra sum of squares principle to perform an F-test for the inclusion of individual terms in the model. Note that scanning the t-values in a computer output, based on the full model, and omitting the non-significant terms may give quite the wrong result *unless* all the stimulus variables are *totally* uncorrelated. This point will be expanded in Section 4.

The extra sum of squares is that portion which is added to the regression sum of squares (and hence removed from the residual sum of squares) when an extra term is included in the model in addition to those already present. This extra sum of squares is then compared with the Residual Mean Square using an F-test. A significant F-value indicates that the term in question should be included in the model.

As an example, consider the data already given in Table 6. If we had already fitted a model

$$y = \beta_0 + \beta_1 x_1 + \beta_{11} x_1^2 + \beta_2 x_2$$

and wanted to ask whether a term in x_2^2 (Total Solids^2) was important as well, we could proceed as follows:

1. Fit the model $y = \beta_0 + \beta_1 x_1 + \beta_{11} x_1^2 + \beta_2 x_2$ giving a residual sum of squares

$$RSS_4 = 2157 \cdot 90 \qquad \text{with 11 degrees of freedom.}$$

2. Fit the model $y = \beta_0 + \beta_1 x_1 + \beta_{11} x_1^2 + \beta_2 x_2 + \beta_{22} x_2^2$ giving a residual sum of squares

$$\text{RSS}_5 = 1300 \cdot 40 \qquad \text{with 10 degrees of freedom.}$$

3. Extra Sum of Squares for fitting x_2^2 is $\text{RSS}_4 - \text{RSS}_5 = 857 \cdot 50$ with 1 degree of freedom.

4. Significance test for x_2^2 is

$$F = \frac{\text{RSS}_4 - \text{RSS}_5}{\text{RSS}_5 / 10} = 6 \cdot 59 \qquad\qquad \sim F_{1,10}$$

The conclusion is that the term in x_2^2 is important in addition to those terms already included.

This extra sum of squares principle forms the basis for all the automatic variable selection procedures in multiple regression packages.

3.3. Variable Selection Procedures

Multiple regression is an art, not a science. Of course rules exist to assist the scientist, but evaluation of an adequate representation of a response as a function of many possible stimulus variables is a minefield for the unwary. The challenge is to effect a compromise between including enough terms in the model to obtain greater accuracy of prediction, and keeping the final model as simple as possible. Any scientist embarking on a computer study of a multiple regression problem should try to acquire a basic understanding of the methods being employed. This has two purposes: one is to enable short cuts to be taken where possible and the second is to enable the scientist to understand *apparent* inconsistencies in the results which are obtained from different methods. Excellent reviews of the techniques can be found in Draper and Smith (1981) and Hocking (1976).

3.3.1. All Possible Regressions

Where there are more than a few variables this technique is unnecessarily expensive both in time and effort. It consists of performing regressions on all possible subsets of stimulus variables and extracting from the results the best subset of terms by use of a particular criterion. The three main criteria, which are closely related to each other, are:

(a) *The value of R^2*. The higher R^2 becomes the better is the regression. *However*, introduction of a new variable *never decreases R^2*, and no test is available on R^2 to determine what constitutes a significant increase.

(b) *The residual mean square, s^2.* As more variables are included in order of importance the value of s^2 will generally reduce and then increase. For each variable in turn the significance of the reduction in s^2 can be judged by an F-test as outlined in Section 3.2.

The drawback to each of these methods is that, unless the variables included in two competing models are such that one is a subset of the other, no direct comparison is possible. Thus we cannot say that a model including x_1 and x_2 is better or worse than one including x_1, x_3 and x_4.

(c) *The C_p statistic* (Mallows (1973), for example). This method is appealing on three counts. First, it uses the full model with all terms as a base of reference. Second, it makes an adjustment for the number of terms included in the model. Third, it provides a graphical means of presenting the results and choosing an appropriate model. A possible drawback is still the lack of a significance test to compare different subsets. Mallows defines

$$C_p = \frac{\text{RSS}_p}{\hat{\sigma}^2} + 2p - n$$

where RSS_p = Residual SS when only p terms are included in the model

$\hat{\sigma}^2$ = Residual MS from the full model

n = number of observations.

If there is no bias in the chosen model then Mallows shows that the value of C_p should on average be equal to p. The technique is thus to plot C_p against p and to choose the simplest possible model with C_p near to but preferably less than p.

For example, in a study of an artificial set of data with five variables, if the C_p plot were given as in Fig. 7 the conclusion would be to use all variables except variable 1, or possibly all except variables 1 and 5.

3.3.2. Forward Selection and Stepwise Procedures

This technique selects at each stage the term which by its inclusion in the model produces the greatest reduction in the Residual Sum of Squares. Put in a different way, this selected term will have the greatest F-value calculated using the extra sum of squares principle. The way in which this term is assessed for inclusion in the model differs slightly according to the computer package being used. For example, the F-value might be checked to ensure that it is greater than some pre-selected value or percentage point of the appropriate F-distribution. This is effectively the

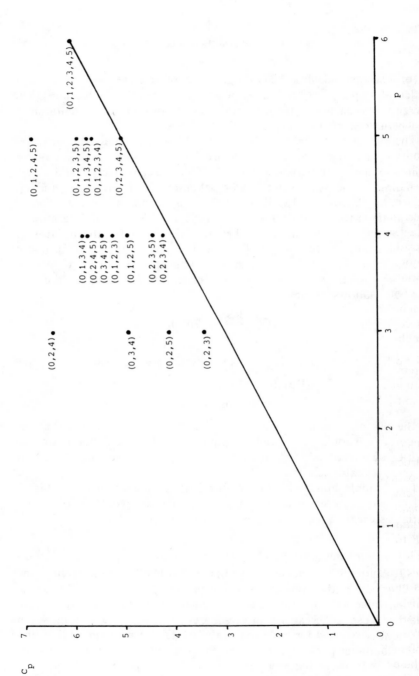

FIG. 7. Example of a C_p plot.

case with GENSTAT, SAS, SPSS, and BMD-P where this value is referred to as 'F to include'. Early releases of GENSTAT included the extra term if it resulted in a reduction in the value of the residual mean square. This is equivalent to using an 'F to include' of 1 and meant that a forward selection procedure in GENSTAT would automatically offer more terms for *possible* inclusion in the model than the other packages. The careful choice of words in the preceding sentence is quite deliberate. It is a mistake for any scientist to accept without question the results given by any computer package. Default options for the inclusion of extra terms (and the exclusion in a stepwise procedure) differ between packages. Their thoughtless and automatic use can easily lead to anomalous results. A good general guideline is to set the inclusion level to give more terms than are needed, and the exclusion level to give fewer. Appropriate values are likely to differ for different problems.

This simple procedure has the disadvantage that once a term is included it cannot subsequently be discarded. This may frequently be necessary where the stimulus variables are correlated with one another. Inclusion of subsequent variables may render redundant a variable previously thought to be important. This can be overcome by use of a stepwise procedure where at each stage the current set of model terms is studied to see whether it contains any redundant terms which can be omitted. This is achieved by

3.3.3. Backward Elimination

This procedure, when employed on its own and not as part of a stepwise procedure, starts from the full model. At each stage the term selected for possible elimination is the one which, by removal, results in the smallest increase in the Residual Sum of Squares. Thus it is the term with the *smallest F*-ratio calculated on the extra sum of squares principle. This again is compared to ensure that it is less than a preselected F-value, the 'F to remove'. If this is so then the term is removed from the model set. This simple procedure alone can be costly on computer time for problems with a large number of terms for possible inclusion in the model. It is more efficient as part of a stepwise procedure.

3.3.4. Interpretation of the Fitted Model

We have discussed briefly the assessment of the fit of a model by the use of such statistics as R^2, or an F-test, or the residual mean square, but these can be misleading. For example, an R^2 value of 0·7 may seem to be satisfactory until it is appreciated that the regression model has still failed to explain 30% of the overall variation in the observations. Is this all due to random error or is there anything systematically wrong with the fitted model? All the available information is contained in the residuals.

$$\hat{\varepsilon} = \text{observed value} - \text{fitted value}$$

The scientist engaged on a regression study would be better served, but considerably more aggravated, if all regression packages could refuse to print out any standard results until satisfied that the scientist had studied and deemed acceptable a range of plots of the residuals. This is perhaps a dream, but it is a route all responsible scientists should try to follow. The simplest procedure is to plot the residuals $\hat{\varepsilon}$ against the fitted values and against each stimulus variable in turn. If the model is adequate we expect the residuals on average to take the value zero and to have a variance which is not dependent either on the size of the fitted value or on the value of the input variable being considered.

A more extensive discussion of the investigation of residuals can be found in Draper and Smith (1981).

3.3.5. Example
We return to the data of Moskowitz (1981) given in Table 6 and summarised graphically in Figs. 5 and 6. These suggested that there was a curved response to all three stimulus variables and that there was no clear indication of interaction between them. The analysis has been performed using

  (i) variable selection techniques;
  (ii) an all possible regression technique, followed by a C_p plot.

(i) Forward selection and backward elimination using SAS led to identical results summarised below.

Fitted relationship
$$\hat{y} = -9.47 + 80.44x_1 - 35.56x_1^2 + 58.89x_2 - 31.11x_2^2 \quad (R^2 = 0.75)$$
(Std errors)   (24.70)   (12.12)   (24.70)   (12.12)

Analysis of variance

Source of variation	df	SS	MS	F
Regression	4	3 840.0	960.0	7.4
Residual	10	1 300.4	130.0	
Total	14	5 140.4		

Three points are clear. First the variable x_3 (thickener) is excluded entirely from the model, and second no interaction terms are included either. Indeed, when all the terms *are* included in the model the R^2 value is 0·83, but the residual mean square is also much larger at 175·5. It should therefore be clear that R^2 alone is insufficient as a criterion for model choice. Removal of terms will appear to be foolish because of the reduction in R^2, but in fact the reduction in the value of the residual mean square more than outweighs the apparent loss. The final point however is that the fitted relationship is still not a very good predictor of the overall acceptability of the product and it is necessary to investigate whether there are any anomalies in the fit as shown by the residuals. A plot of the residuals against the fitted value is shown in Fig. 8 and against the individual stimulus variables in Fig. 9.

In studying these pictures, especially with only 15 observations in total, it is essential not to try to read into them more than is immediately obvious, or patterns which do not make scientific sense. The only clear point to note is that the point circled on these plots—a large negative residual—is *consistently* separate from observations with similar stimulus variables. It corresponds to the point with a high level of all three variables and suggests that there may be a threshold level for the combination of variables beyond which the acceptability drops dramatically. Further investigation may lead to modifications to the *form* of the model to accommodate such occurrences.

(ii) The study of all possible regressions and the C_p plot given in Fig. 10 has been based on the three linear and three quadratic terms only, taking account of the previous results. In addition a quadratic term is only included in the model when the linear term is already present. The results of the C_p plot confirm those of the variable selection procedure, but show that a possible alternative model could include a linear term in x_3. There is some evidence for this in the residual plot of Fig. 9(c), evidence which would be much stronger but for the presence of the circled residual.

In summary, the results presented here do not give a complete analysis of the results. They show automatic procedures together with an interpretation of the results which form a starting point for further discussion and evaluation which could lead to an improved modelling and understanding of the underlying mechanism of the problem. A final note is that here the forward selection and backward elimination procedures led to the same results. This will not always happen, especially if there are correlations between the stimulus variables. Moskowitz has

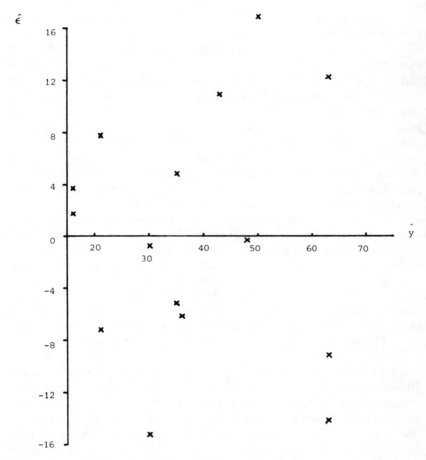

FIG. 8. Residuals plotted against the fitted values for the data of Moskowitz.

avoided these problems by the use of a carefully chosen experimental design.

4. PROBLEMS AND PITFALLS OF MULTIPLE REGRESSION

The main dangers in the use of multiple regression techniques are those which occur because an automatic routine is being employed, on a computer, with large data sets, and with no real understanding of the

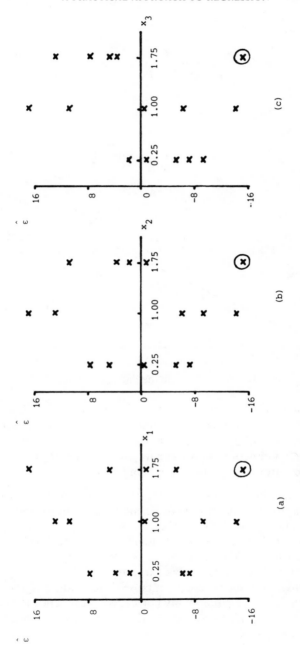

FIG. 9. Residuals plotted against individual stimulus variables for the data of Moskowitz.

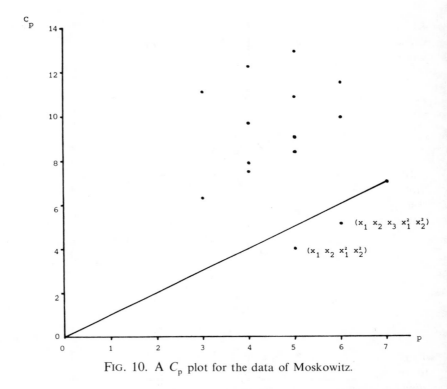

FIG. 10. A C_p plot for the data of Moskowitz.

underlying structure of the data. Multiple regression techniques can sometimes be as misleading as on other occasions they can be informative. The art of multiple regression lies in the scientist using his expert knowledge in conjunction with the computer to unravel the mystery of his data. The automatic routines are being used:

(a) to decide which terms in the model have coefficients significantly different from zero. Thus a coefficient can only be judged relative to its standard error because the *values* of the coefficients are scale-dependent. A parameter estimate near to zero can have a small or a large effect on the predicted response depending upon the order of magnitude of the stimulus variable;

(b) to estimate the model coefficients when the values of the stimulus variables may be quite highly correlated. In practice this situation can give misleading results if automatic variable selection procedures are applied thoughtlessly.

4.1. The Effect of Correlated Stimulus Variables

Consider the artificial data set given in Table 8 where a response variable y is being described by two stimulus variables x_1 and x_2.

TABLE 8

y	480	600	620	650	650	650	680	740	810	920
x_1	43	28	31	34	30	26	35	27	34	33
x_2	223	163	164	188	172	149	205	188	210	225

In this case data plotting does not reveal a clear pattern either by plotting y against x_1 and x_2 separately or by a contour plot of the response to both variables. On the other hand the regression fits are interesting.

Regression on x_1 alone   *Regression on x_2 alone*

$$\hat{y} = 889 - 6\cdot25\,x_1 \qquad \hat{y} = 387 + 1\cdot55\,x_2$$
$$t \text{ value, 8 df} = -0\cdot79 \qquad t \text{ value, 8 df} = 1\cdot03$$

Regression on x_1 and x_2

$$\hat{y} = 547\cdot1 - 31\cdot15 \quad x_1 + 6\cdot00\,x_2$$
$$t \text{ values, 7 df,} - 4\cdot80 \qquad 4\cdot95$$

Thus in this case forward selection or stepwise regression could well fail to *include* either variable while backward elimination would fail to *eliminate* either variable. The clue to the apparent paradox lies in the correlation matrix given in Table 9.

TABLE 9

ρ	y	x_1	x_2
y	1	$-0\cdot27$	$0\cdot34$
x_1		1	$0\cdot77$
x_2			1

Whilst neither variable alone is highly correlated with the response variable, y, they are highly correlated with one another. In combination they are able to explain a reasonable proportion of the variation in y. Bliss (1970) gives an example of the reverse situation where two variables are each effective predictors of y when considered separately, but taken together, neither *appears* important. This is an example where forward selection and backward elimination would lead to identical results, namely that only the better of the two single variables is required.

4.2. Interpretation of Marginal Effects

A fundamental reason for doing regression must be to enable the scientist to predict the outcome from future, but similar, experiments performed using different levels of the stimulus variables. In addition it would be valuable if marginal effects of individual variables can be assessed. That is, if a regression relationship is obtained as

$$y = \beta_0 + \beta_1 x_1 + \beta_2 x_2$$

then we should like to be able to say that a marginal change of one unit in x_1 would cause a corresponding change of β_1 units in y. Unfortunately if x_1 and x_2 are correlated, a marginal change of one unit in x_1 is also likely to cause a change in x_2 and this too will have an effect on the value of y. This would be true in the example given by Ostrowski-Meissner (1981) where an equation is presented relating protein extraction efficiency (Y) from herbage as a function of crude protein levels (Z) and the herbage dry matter concentration (X). An assessment of the effect on Y of a change in X cannot ignore the fact that this change will give rise to a corresponding change in Z.

This is probably best expressed by the splendid example from Mohammed *et al.* (1982) who are studying the relationship between sensory crispness of apples (y) and three stimulus variables:

equivalent sound level (x_1)
work done during fracture (x_2)
fracture rate (x_3)

They give a wide range of regression equations, many of which fit equally well. Amongst them are the following three, all of which appear to provide a good fit to the data.

$\log y = \quad 1 \cdot 20 \qquad\qquad\qquad +0 \cdot 12 \, x_3$	$R^2 = 0 \cdot 91$
$\log y = -11 \cdot 67 + 7 \cdot 96 \, \log x_1$	$R^2 = 0 \cdot 89$
$\log y = \quad 2 \cdot 06 - 0 \cdot 15 \, \log x_1 + 1 \cdot 52 \, \log x_2 - 0 \cdot 02 \, x_3$	$R^2 = 0 \cdot 97$

The marginal effects of the fracture rates are therefore that in the first case an increased fracture rate increases the sensory hardness, in the second it has no effect and in the third it reduces it! Once again, high levels of correlation between x_1, x_2 and x_3 are preventing sensible decisions being taken about marginal effects.

An obvious but not always practical solution is to ensure that in multiple regression studies the levels of the stimulus variables **x** are chosen so that their intercorrelations are low. If it is possible to *design* such an experiment then automatic fitting procedures are less liable to give anomalous results and the estimates of the fitted parameters can be interpreted directly. The experimental design work in response surface methodology—see the reviews by Mead and Pike (1975), Steinberg and Hunter (1984)—provides techniques by which this can be achieved.

4.3. Outlying Observations

Outlying observations can basically be of two types, and both can have a misleading effect on the fitted multiple regression model. They are:

(i) a data point which appears to be anomalous giving a response inconsistent with the remaining data points;

(ii) a data point with a stimulus level far removed from the stimulus levels of the remaining data points. This observation may or may not have a response level consistent with the relationship governing the remaining observations. But in any case this single observation will have an undue effect on the fitted relationship.

These are illustrated in Fig. 11 by data from Cloutt (1983) of the relationship between protein content and dry weight yield for air classified fines fractions of cowpea. The anomalous observations of types (i) and (ii) have been artificially added.

Fitting straight line models to the three data sets we obtain:

Original data	$\hat{y} = 57{\cdot}73 - 0{\cdot}79x$	$R^2 = 0{\cdot}97$
Data + outlier (i)	$\hat{y} = 53{\cdot}66 - 0{\cdot}67x$	$R^2 = 0{\cdot}59$
Data + outlier (ii)	$\hat{y} = 54{\cdot}19 - 0{\cdot}66x$	$R^2 = 0{\cdot}94$

Some simple regression packages, for example MINITAB, will give an indication of residuals which are either unacceptably large (case (i)) or observations which have an unacceptably strong influence on the fitted relationship (case (ii)). In either situation neither the existence of the outlier nor its nature will be clear from the statistical output of many packages. The relevant information lies in the residuals and every effort should be made to plot these. In the case of a multiple regression with many stimulus variables there is an increasing tendency just to plot the residuals $\hat{\varepsilon}$ against the fitted values $\hat{y}$. This can very often fail to indicate errors in the model because of outliers of case (ii). Anomalous outliers of case (i) will usually show up clearly whichever way the residuals are plotted. However, an anomalous observation with a *stimulus* variable a

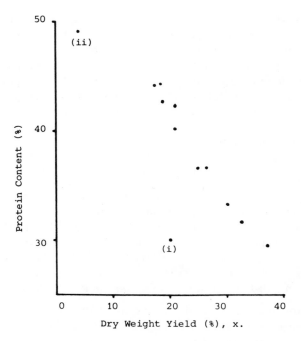

FIG. 11. Plot showing two types of outlier.

long way from the other variables is quite likely to have a small residual
as the relationship will be forced to fit the point quite well. This will,
however, induce a patterned relationship with the residuals across the
range of the stimulus variable concerned. Thus it is important to plot the
residuals against the stimulus variables as well as against the fitted value.
Figure 12 shows the three residual plots for the data of Fig. 11 and the
typical residual patterns for the two types of outlier are clearly visible.

4.4. Multiple Regression as a Tool in Calibration
Instrument calibration no longer seems to be the problem for the food
researcher which once it was. The time when balances had to be zeroed
and ranges of scales checked and adjusted to eliminate bias has been
replaced by the digital read-out, self zeroing world of electronics.
Complex instruments, such as spectrophotometers, are now supplied
with an attached microcomputer, to present results quickly and efficiently in a form which is easily assimilated by the research worker.

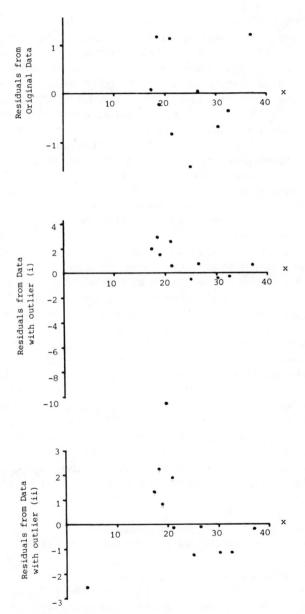

FIG. 12. Residual plots indicating the effects of the two types of outlier.

This does not, of course, mean that calibration has become redundant. More precisely it has become the responsibility of the manufacturer to ensure that the modern 'black box' approach does not mislead the researcher nor produce results which are incorrect. In consequence, any instrument, so marketed, will only be as good as the staff who determine the calibration technique and those who program the microcomputer. Researchers should expect clear and detailed information on the form of the calibration procedure and the extent of any errors inherent in the results because of the calibration. Again, scepticism may not pay direct dividends, but unquestioning acceptance of automatic calibration devices could lead to disaster. These worries are echoed by Kowalski (1983).

An example of the use of multiple regression in automatic calibration occurs in the assessment of protein content of cereals by infra-red reflectance spectrophotometers (Lakin, 1978) using techniques pioneered by Norris and Hart (1965). Typically calibration is performed by assessing a number of standard samples using about six different wavelengths. The chosen calibration equation would, for example, be chosen as that equation which best fits the data using four of the six wavelengths. This equation would be calculated by the microcomputer and stored for use in analysing subsequent samples of unknown constitution. If this equation is to be accepted as an adequate predictive tool for all samples two requirements are essential. First, the choice of wavelengths should provide a satisfactory range of validity for the calibration equation and, second, the resultant equation should fit the data from the standard samples very well. It is not, for example, true that a very good fit over a narrow range of wavelengths is necessarily better than an adequate fit over a wide range of wavelengths. Near infra-red reflectance spectroscopy is a widely used technique in food research as can be seen by the bibliography of Osborne (1983). Important evaluations of this technique and the calibrations used in practice can be found in papers by Norris, Arneth, and Jensen and Martens in the book edited by Martens and Russwurm (1983).

5. NONLINEAR REGRESSION MODELS

At the outset it is necessary to define 'nonlinear' and to make clear the difference between linear and nonlinear models. A linear model is a relationship between stimulus and response which is linear in the unknown parameters. Thus both the straight line $y = \beta_0 + \beta_1 x$ and the quadratic $y = \beta_0 + \beta_1 x + \beta_2 x^2$ are linear models. (Some authors confusingly refer to the latter as a nonlinear model.) By contrast a nonlinear model is one in which the parameters are not naturally separated in this way. Examples of nonlinear models are:

(i) the exponential growth relationship $y = \beta_0 e^{\beta_1 x}$
(ii) the Michaelis–Menten equation of enzyme kinetics $v = Vs/K + s$.

The major advantage of nonlinear models is that frequently they will represent the biological phenomena being studied better than polynomial models. Specific disadvantages of the polynomial family are that it does not include an asymptotic relationship and that the quadratic form is symmetrical about the optimum. The major disadvantage of nonlinear models has always been that they are harder to fit than linear models. As a consequence researchers have either avoided the problem by using other models, or they have resorted to the use of transformations to turn them into linear models. The first approach is incorrect and the second may be highly inefficient. With modern computing facilities and software, there should now be little difficulty in approaching the problem directly and solving it. This section provides a discussion and criticism of current approaches and attempts to suggest how such problems might be solved in the future.

5.1. Transformation to Linearity

Under certain conditions it is possible to utilise a nonlinear model which can be transformed to linearity and fitted using standard linear regression techniques. For example, the exponential growth relationship

$$y = \beta_0 e^{\beta_1 x}$$

can be transformed to

$$\log_e y = \log_e \beta_0 + \beta_1 x$$

and a plot of $\log_e y$ against x yields a straight line. This seems too good to be true—and so it is! The apparent beauty of the mathematics and the simplicity of fitting the relationship obscures the need to consider the nature of the assumptions needed to perform the fitting. In fact, the full model is

$$\log_e y = \log_e \beta_0 + \beta_1 x + \epsilon$$

where the residual elements ϵ are additive elements assumed to have zero mean and a constant variance σ^2. The transformation means that these residual errors must have been multiplicative in the original model. Almost without exception these residual errors are forgotten in the search for a transformation to linearity. The research worker and the statistician should always ask:

(i) is there any good reason for transforming?
(ii) does a chosen transformation give a spread of residual errors compatible with the required assumptions? If not, then biased estimates of the parameters could result.

A serious example of this type of problem is the almost universal tendency to fit the Michaelis–Menten equation of enzyme kinetics

$$v = \frac{Vs}{K+s}$$

by the Lineweaver and Burk double reciprocal transformation

$$\frac{1}{v} = \left(\frac{1}{V}\right) + \left(\frac{K}{V}\right)\frac{1}{s}$$

where v is the reaction velocity and s is the substrate concentration. The parameters V and K are respectively the maximum velocity of the reaction and the half-saturation constant. The use of this technique, and other related linearising transformations, has been shown to be unreliable by Dowd and Riggs (1965). A more general discussion can be found in Currie (1982). The important point to make is that this need no longer be a problem for food researchers. Nonlinear models of this and more complex types can be fitted *directly* by the use of such packages as GLIM, SAS and MLP. The scientist is now able, and should be encouraged, to demand more than ever before from the statistician. It has always been possible to develop suitable models for particular types of problem. It is now possible to fit such models and to estimate their parameters directly and efficiently.

5.2. Nonlinear Models for Enzyme Kinetics

The aim of this section is briefly to outline two types of nonlinear model which are suitable for use in enzyme kinetics and which can be fitted very simply, for example, by the NLIN procedure in SAS.

5.2.1. Inverse Polynomials

These were first introduced by Nelder (1966) and as a general family of functions can be seen to have an important role in this area.

(a) The inverse linear $y = x/(\beta_0 + \beta_1 x)$ is exactly the Michaelis–Menten equation discussed earlier with $\beta_0 = K/V$, $\beta_1 = 1/V$.

(b) The inverse quadratic $y = x/(\beta_0 + \beta_1 x + \beta_2 x^2)$ is a function with a simple nonsymmetric optimum. This can arise in two ways. Either in the case where the velocity of the enzyme reaction is inhibited by the substrate, or where the enzyme activity is stimulated by the presence of a metal ion (Reed, 1975).

(c) Multifactor inverse polynomials $y = \Pi_{i=1}^{k} x_i / P(\mathbf{x})$ where $P(.)$ is a polynomial in $x_1 \ldots x_k$. In the example of Zetalaki–Horvath (1981) pectinesterase activity was related to enzyme concentration for a range of different incubation periods. This example would lend itself very well to the fitting of a two variable inverse polynomial with enzyme concentration and incubation period as the stimulus variables.

5.2.2. Logistic Functions

Nelder (1961) introduced the very flexible, four parameter logistic function

$$y = \frac{\beta_0}{[1 + e^{-(\beta_1 + \beta_2 t)/\theta}]^\theta}$$

where β_0, β_1, β_2 and θ are the parameters. The inclusion of the extra parameter θ permits the function to behave in a nonsymmetric way about its point of inflexion. Nour El-Dien *et al.* (1981) present data on yeast growth with time for different concentrations of whey lactose. Any situation like this in growth studies where an initial phase of exponential growth is followed by an inhibition due to limiting nutrient will be well represented by a form of logistic function.

The aim of this section has been to provide indications of the potential now available to food researchers for the development and fitting of nonlinear functions to data. A wider indication of the types of nonlinear function which are available can be found in the book by Ratkowsky (1983).

6. POSTCRIPT ON EXPERIMENTAL DESIGN

The main objective of this chapter has been to provide guidelines to the experimenter for the considered and careful use of multiple regression

98 DEREK J. PIKE

techniques in practice. The techniques are powerful and today they are easier than ever to use and misuse. An awareness of the pitfalls of unthinking analysis is crucial in the interpretation of computer output. However, it is vital to introduce one final idea, which really requires a book to itself. Why in most regression books does experimental design never get mentioned?

There are several reasons, some very sound. However, the root cause is a failure by research workers to recognise the need to design a regression study, and a failure by statisticians to inform experimenters of the potential benefits, in terms which are easily understood. Much of the pioneering work of Box and his co-workers in the 1950s has not been used as fully as it should and it has to a large extent been obscured by the subsequent developments in more mathematical statistics to which it has led. (See the discussion in Mead and Pike (1975) for example.) The choice of an experimental design for a regression study involves answering three questions.

(i)   How should the stimulus levels be chosen? How many different levels? What should the levels be?
(ii)   How many replicate observations should be taken?
(iii) Is it necessary to consider blocking the experiment? For example, this might be the case if only a small number of experiments were possible in any one day and differences were likely between days.

To illustrate the importance of the first question it is necessary only to consider the choice of stimulus levels to fit a straight line. A number of experimenters asked how they would choose stimulus levels for a set of twelve observations invariably produce a range of suggestions. A typical selection is given below.

1. Twelve observations equally spaced over the range of experimentation.
2. Four equally spaced points each replicated three times.
3. Three equally spaced points each replicated four times.
4. Two points at the ends of the range of experimentation each replicated six times.

If the objective is to estimate the slope of the straight line, *and the line really is straight*, the fourth suggestion will minimise the variance of the estimated slope. The efficiencies of the other designs expressed as the inverse of the ratio of the variances relative to the best design are respectively 39%, 56% and 64%.

The importance of design should now be clear. It is sufficient here to say in conclusion that any design chosen to fit a response curve or surface must depend upon the function to be fitted, the expected number of parameters to achieve an appropriate representation of the data, and the objectives of the researcher performing the experiment. With these ideas in his mind, the researcher should be in a position to improve the efficiency of his work by careful design of his experiment and thoughtful analysis of his results.

REFERENCES

Bliss, C. I. (1970). *Statistics in Biology*, Vol. II, McGraw-Hill, New York.

Cloutt, P. (1983). A study of component fractionation of legume flours by air classification. Unpublished Ph.D. thesis, University of Reading.

Currie, D. (1982). Estimating Michaelis–Menten parameters: Bias, variance and experimental design. *Biometrics*, **38**, 907–19.

Dowd, J. E. and Riggs, D. S. (1965). A comparison of estimates of Michaelis–Menten kinetic constants from various linear transformations. *J. Biol. Chem.*, **240**, 863–9.

Draper, N. R. and Smith, H. (1981). *Applied Regression Analysis*, 2nd edn, John Wiley, New York.

Endrenyi, L. (Ed.) (1981). *Kinetic Data Analysis: Design and Analysis of Enzyme and Pharmacokinetic Experiments*, Plenum Press, New York.

France, J. and Thornley, J. H. M. (1984). *Mathematical Models in Agriculture*, Butterworths, London.

Hegedus, M. and Zachariev, Gy. (1978). Assessment of quality of single-cell proteins with *Tetrahymena Pyriformis W*. *Acta Alimentaria*, **7**, 141–54.

Hocking, R. R. (1976). The analysis and selection of variables in linear regression. *Biometrics*, **32**, 1–51.

Kowalski, B. R. (1983). Intelligent instruments of the future. In: *Food Research and Data Analysis*, H. Martens and H. Russwurm, Jr. (Eds), Applied Science Publishers, London.

Lakin, A. L. (1978). Determination of nitrogen and estimation of protein in foods. In: *Developments in Food Analysis Techniques, I*, R. D. King (Ed.), Applied Science Publishers, London.

Mallows, C. L. (1973). Some comments on C_p. *Technometrics*, **15**, 661–75.

Marsh, G. L., Leonard, S. J. and Buhlert, J. E. (1979). Yield and quality of Catsup produced to a standard solids and consistency level. II. Influence of handling practices, break temperature and cultivar. *J. Food Processing and Preservation*, **3**, 195–212.

Martens, H. and Russwurm, H. (Eds) (1983). *Food Research and Data Analysis*, Applied Science Publishers, London.

Mead, R. and Pike, D. J. (1975). A review of response surface methodology from a biometric viewpoint. *Biometrics*, **31**, 803–51.

Mohammed, A. A. A., Jowitt, R. and Brennan, J. G. (1982). Sensory and instrumental measurement of food crispness. II—in a high moisture food. *J. Food Engineering*, **1**, 123–47.

Moskowitz, H. R. (1981). Enhanced efficiency of product development and engineering via consumer feedback. *Acta Alimentaria*, **10**, 113–28.

Nelder, J. A. (1961). The fitting of a generalisation of the logistic curve. *Biometrics*, **17**, 89–110.

Nelder, J. A. (1966). Inverse polynomials, a useful group of multi-factor response functions. *Biometrics*, **22**, 128–41.

Norris, K. H. and Hart, J. R. (1965). Direct spectrophotometric determination of moisture content of grain and seeds. *Proc. 1963 Int. Symposium on Humidity and Moisture, Principles and Methods of Measuring Moisture in Liquids and Solids*, **4**, 19–25. New York, Reinholt.

Nour El-Dien, A., Halasz, A. and Lengyel, Z. (1981). Attempts to utilize whey for the production of yeast protein. Part I—Effect of whey concentration of ammonium sulphate and of phosphate. *Acta Alimentaria*, **10**, 11–25.

Osborne, B. G. (1983). *A Bibliography of Applications of Near Infrared Reflectance Spectroscopy to Food Analysis*, Flour Milling and Baking Research Association, Chorleywood, Rickmansworth, Hertfordshire.

Ostrowski-Meissner, H. T. (1981). Optimization of protein extraction from pasture herbage, quantitative and qualitative considerations. *J. Food Processing and Preservation*, **5**, 7–22.

Ratkowsky, D. A. (1983). *Nonlinear Regression Modelling: A Unified Practical Approach*, Marcel Dekker, New York.

Reed, G. (Ed.) (1975). *Enzymes in Food Processing*, 2nd edn. Academic Press, New York.

Segal, L. A. (1984). *Modelling Dynamic Phenomena in Molecular and Cellular Biology*, Cambridge University Press, Cambridge.

Steinberg, D. M. and Hunter, W. G. (1984). Experimental design: review and comment (with discussion). *Technometrics*, **26**, 71–130.

Zetalaki-Horvath, K. (1981). Factors affecting pectinesterase activity. *Acta Alimentaria*, **10**, 371–8.

Chapter 4

RESPONSE SURFACE METHODS

L. VUATAZ

Nestlé Research Department, NESTEC Ltd, Vevey, Switzerland

1. INTRODUCTION

In Food Science and Technology, modelling by means of functional models expressing physical, chemical or thermodynamical laws is generally restricted to well defined unit operations which involve heat transfer, mass transfer, growth of a biomass or concentration changes of chemical entities.

Very often, however, the processes to be studied are too complex in nature to be modelled in this way. Complexity may be inherent in the process itself, in the sense that the process involves conditions for which no adequate model exists. Complexity may also arise from the fact that the technologist wishes to study the dependence of a model parameter on several technological variables. An example of these two situations is as follows.

In well defined conditions of temperature, pH, concentration and so on, the losses of a chemical entity in a solution may be modelled by a function of time obtained by integration of a differential equation. The order of the reaction is generally estimated from the data. As an example, a second order reaction is expressed by

$$y^{-1} = y_o^{-1} + kt$$

or

$$l\% = 100 - 100(1 + y_o kt)^{-1}$$

where $l\% = (y_o - y)y_o^{-1}\,\%$ is the relative loss in % and y_o is the starting concentration of the chemical under study. The above expressions are functional models and the measurements of concentration at various times may be used to estimate k.

If the technologist is interested in the dependence of k on technological variables, the experiment which consists of measuring y for increasing values of t can be repeated in different conditions involving different pH values, temperatures, concentrations and so on. Obviously, there is no overall functional model for this type of investigation.

The technologist may also be interested in modelling the losses in viscous or solid food products where the kinetics valid for solution may no longer apply. Moreover, he may also wish to investigate, in this type of food, the dependence of the losses on technological variables like pH, viscosity, moisture, temperature, percentages of definite ingredients and so on. Obviously, time becomes a technological variable in this context where, once again, no overall functional model is available.

In each situation the experimenter has the possibility of resorting to response surface methods (RSM). It is interesting to note that relatively few papers, in the area of food science and technology, are devoted to applications of RSM. This is certainly due to the fact that most food technologists do not know about the existence of these methods. Among the few scientists who read Chapter 8A in Cochran and Cox (1957), many must have abandoned the idea on realizing that a RSM design with 4, 5 or 6 technological variables may involve 30–50 trials. Many scientists prefer to follow their own 'feeling'. They are convinced they will obtain a good insight into the problem after performing few trials. Experience shows, however, that technologists adopting this strategy usually end up running more trials than required by RSM designs, and even at this point, are still far from understanding the process.

While drafting the present article the author became acquainted with the monograph by Gacula and Singh (1984) in which Chapter 7, which comprises 60 pages, is entitled 'Response Surface Designs and Analysis'.

Since the present article was intended to be much shorter, ample reference will be made to Gacula and Singh, especially when dealing with the various RSM designs. The reader will find, in that article, very well documented numerical examples showing how to perform the calculations in relation to different experimental situations encountered in RSM. The present article may be considered as complementary. Other useful articles devoted to RSM are Chapter 8A in Cochran and Cox (1957), and the review by Mead and Pike (1975). The reader will find, in these articles, references to the many papers by Box, Wilson and Hunter who were pioneers in this field.

The first part of the present article shows how to obtain a reliable polynomial model. In the second part, this model is used to investigate the response surface, that is, to localize the optimum within the region of interest and to study the shape of the response surface around the optimum.

2. HOW TO OBTAIN A QUADRATIC POLYNOMIAL MODEL

2.1. Notation and Definitions

Vectors will be denoted by bold low case characters and matrices by bold upper case characters. Vectors will be column vectors, and row vectors will be noted as transposed vectors.

As an example, a vector $\mathbf{y}$ of n responses will be of size $(n \times 1)$ and its transpose will be $\mathbf{y}'$ of size $(1 \times n)$. Similarly, if $\mathbf{X}$ is a matrix of size $(n \times p)$, its transpose will be $\mathbf{X}'$, of size $(p \times n)$.

In Food Science and Technology, the objective of a process is to transform a food product. The operating conditions of the process are defined by the *technological variables* (called experimental factors in Gacula and Singh), which will be denoted by x_j, $j = 1, \ldots, p$. The transformed product is characterized by a variable of interest, and the aim is to optimize this variable, called, the *response* and noted as 'y'.

In this article, we shall consider only scalar responses.

An *experiment* will consist of a set of n trials. Its objective is to obtain information about the unknown function

$$y = f(\mathbf{x}; \mathbf{\beta}) \tag{1}$$

where $\mathbf{x}$ is the $(p \times 1)$ vector of the technological variables and $\mathbf{\beta}$ is the $(g \times 1)$ vector of the model parameters.

Figure 1 shows some responses to a process which is determined by two technological variables, x_1 and x_2. The plane spanned by x_1 and x_2 is the *technological plane*. Each point of this plane defines a possible trial. The values of x_1 and x_2 at which trials are performed are the *levels* of the technological variables. In Fig. 1, x_{11} and x_{21} are the levels of x_1 and x_2, respectively, of the first trial which has produced the response y_1. The set of the levels of the technological variables is the design of the experiment. Still in relation to Fig. 1, these levels can be put into the form of a matrix of size (7×2), called *the design matrix* $\mathbf{D}$,

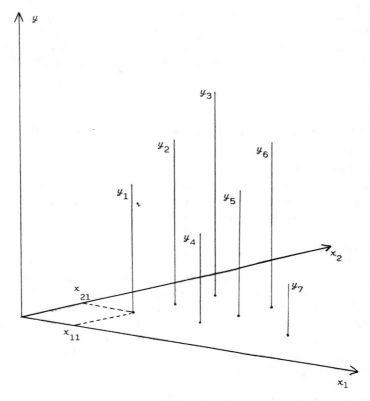

FIG. 1. Responses at 7 points of the technological space.

$$\mathbf{D} = \begin{bmatrix} x_{11} & x_{12} \\ x_{21} & x_{22} \\ \vdots & \vdots \\ x_{71} & x_{72} \end{bmatrix} \qquad (2)$$

The region of the technological space which has been explored by the design is the *region of interest*.

The three-dimensional surface which provides the best fit to the points y_i, $i = 1, \ldots, 7$, in Fig. 1, is the *response surface*. Examples of response surfaces are given in Gacula and Singh, Figs 7.3 and 7.4.

In Food Science and Technology the experimenter usually begins with a natural product whose exact composition may depend on its origin and conditions of growth. It will be assumed, in this article, that all the trials of an experiment involve samples of the same batch of raw material. In this way, the responses to the process operating conditions will be due to the process itself, and not to variations in the raw material. Studying how the characteristics of the raw material influence the response for constant operating conditions is another type of problem, because these characteristics are not under experimenter control, in contrast to the technological variables which are set to definite levels.

2.2. Justification of the Quadratic Polynomial Model

Any function (1) can be approximated by a second degree polynomial (3) in a restricted region of the technological space,

$$y = \beta_o + \sum_{j=1}^{p} \beta_j x_j + \sum_{j=1}^{p} \beta_{jj} x_j^2 + \sum_{j<k=2}^{p} \beta_{jk} x_j x_k \tag{3}$$

For $p=2$, the second order Taylor expansion of (1) around the point (x_{o1}, x_{o2}) is

$$f(x_1, x_2; \boldsymbol{\beta}) = f(x_{o1}, x_{o2}) + (x_1 - x_{o1}) \left(\frac{\partial f}{\partial x_1} \right)_o +$$

$$(x_2 - x_{o2}) \left(\frac{\partial f}{\partial x_2} \right)_o + \tfrac{1}{2}(x_1 - x_{o1})^2 \left(\frac{\partial^2 f}{\partial x_1^2} \right)_o +$$

$$\tfrac{1}{2}(x_2 - x_{o2})^2 \left(\frac{\partial^2 f}{\partial x_2^2} \right)_o + \tfrac{1}{2}(x_1 - x_{o1})(x_2 - x_{o2}) \left(\frac{\partial^2 f}{\partial x_1 \partial x_2} \right)_o$$

The subscript 'o' means that the values of the derivatives are taken at the point (x_{o1}, x_{o2}). If we set $x_{o1} = x_{o2} = 0$, which is always possible through a scale translation, we obtain

$$y = \beta_o + \beta_1 x_1 + \beta_2 x_2 + \beta_{11} x_1^2 + \beta_{22} x_2^2 + \beta_{12} x_1 x_2 \tag{4}$$

where

$$\beta_o = f(0, 0), \quad \beta_j = \left(\frac{\partial f}{\partial x_j} \right)_o, \quad j = 1, 2,$$

$$\beta_{jj} = \frac{1}{2} \left(\frac{\partial^2 f}{\partial x_j^2} \right)_o \quad \text{and} \quad \beta_{12} = \frac{1}{2} \left(\frac{\partial^2 f}{\partial x_1 \partial x_2} \right)_o$$

A necessary, but not a sufficient, requirement for the success of RSM applications, is that the region of interest should not be larger than the region where (3) is a good approximation to (1).

Now, an RSM experiment, like any experiment, does not take place in a deterministic context. In particular, the observed value of the ith response $(i = 1, \ldots, n)$ unavoidably involves a random component (an unobservable disturbance) which expresses the departure of the observed value from the unknown true value of the ith response. As a result of this, (4) must be written as

$$E(y_i) = \beta_0 + \cdots + \beta_{12} x_{i1} x_{i2} \tag{5}$$

where $E(y_i)$ is the expected value of the ith response, or

$$y_i = \beta_0 + \beta_1 x_{i1} + \beta_2 x_{i2} + \beta_{11} x_{i1}^2 + \beta_{22} x_{i2}^2 + \beta_{12} x_{i1} x_{i2} + \varepsilon_i \tag{6}$$

Both errors of response measurement and model inadequacy contribute to the random component ε_i. One of the objectives of a good experimental design will be to discriminate between these two causes of departure from the unknown true value.

2.3. Estimation of the Model Parameters

If, in (6), x_{i1}^2, x_{i2}^2 and $x_{i1} x_{i2}$ are replaced by x_{i3}, x_{i4} and x_{i5}, respectively, (6) can be written as

$$y_i = \beta_0 + \sum_{j=1}^{5} \beta_j x_{ij} + \varepsilon_i \tag{7}$$

Moreover, setting $x_0 = 1$ turns (7) into

$$y_i = \sum_{j=0}^{5} \beta_j x_{ij} + \varepsilon_i \tag{8}$$

(7) and (8) are multiple regression equations.

Accordingly, the estimation procedures used in multiple regression can be applied to RSM. In this article, we shall restrict our attention to the classical least squares estimators.

When the numbers of trials and technological variables are n and p, respectively, the design matrix (2) of size (7×2) takes the size $(n \times p)$ and an element of this matrix is $x_{ij}, i = 1, \ldots, n; j = 1, \ldots, p$. As already mentioned, the ith row of a design matrix consists of the levels assigned to the p technological variables in the ith trial. The design matrix is extended to form the matrix $\mathbf{X}$. The extension is achieved by putting a column of 1's on the left, and columns which account for second order terms on the right. The ith row of a matrix $\mathbf{X}$ is

$$\mathbf{x}'_i = [1, x_{i1}, \ldots, x_{ip}, x_{i1}^2, \ldots, x_{ip}^2, x_{i1} x_{i2}, \ldots, x_{i, p-1} x_{ip}]$$

The numerical values of the second order terms are obtained from the numerical values of the first order terms, that is, from levels in the matrix $\mathbf{D}$.

The least squares procedure of estimation assumes that the ε_i are random variables independently and identically distributed, with

$$E(\varepsilon_i) = 0, \qquad\qquad V(\varepsilon_i) = \sigma^2 \text{ and}$$
$$\mathrm{Cov}(\varepsilon_i, \varepsilon_{i'}) = 0, \ i \neq i', \tag{9}$$

where V and Cov mean 'variance' and 'covariance', respectively.

In matrix notation, the quadratic model is written as

$$\mathbf{y} = \mathbf{X}\boldsymbol{\beta} + \boldsymbol{\varepsilon} \tag{10}$$

where $\mathbf{X}$ is the extended design matrix of size $(n \times g)$, $\boldsymbol{\beta}$ is a $(g \times 1)$ vector, $\mathbf{y}$ and $\boldsymbol{\varepsilon}$ are both $(n \times 1)$ vectors. When (9) is fulfilled, the least squares estimate of $\boldsymbol{\beta}$ is

$$\mathbf{b} = (\mathbf{X}' \mathbf{X})^{-1} \mathbf{X}' \mathbf{y} \tag{11}$$

Referring to (6), the components of the vector $\mathbf{b}$ are

$$\mathbf{b}' = [b_o \, b_1 \, b_2 \, b_{11} \, b_{22} \, b_{12}]$$

These estimates are unbiased, that is,

$$E(\mathbf{b}) = \boldsymbol{\beta} \tag{12}$$

If, in addition to (9), the ε_i are normally distributed, then $\mathbf{b}$ follows a multivariate normal distribution with mean $\boldsymbol{\beta}$ and variance–covariance matrix

$$V(\mathbf{b}) = \sigma^2 (\mathbf{X}' \mathbf{X})^{-1} \tag{13}$$

If we refer once more to (6), (13) shows that the variances of $b_o, b_1, b_2, b_{11}, b_{22}$ and b_{12} are the diagonal terms of the matrix $\sigma^2 (\mathbf{X}' \mathbf{X})^{-1}$, and that the other terms express the covariances between any pair of these estimates.

As in the multiple regression theory, σ^2 is estimated by the residual mean square

$$s^2 = (n-q)^{-1} \sum_{i=1}^{n} (y_i - \hat{y}_i)^2 \tag{14}$$

where q is the number of estimated parameters and $\hat{y}_i$ is the ith calculated response value

$$\hat{y}_i = \mathbf{x}_i' \mathbf{b}$$

As a result of this, (13) is estimated by

$$\hat{\mathbf{V}}(\mathbf{b}) = s^2 (\mathbf{X}'\mathbf{X})^{-1} \tag{15}$$

Furthermore, the variance of a value $\hat{y}_o$ calculated from the model at the point $\mathbf{x}_o$ is

$$V(\hat{y}_o) = \sigma^2 \mathbf{x}_o' (\mathbf{X}'\mathbf{X})^{-1} \mathbf{x}_o$$

which is estimated by

$$\hat{V}(\hat{y}_o) = s^2 \mathbf{x}_o' (\mathbf{X}'\mathbf{X})^{-1} \mathbf{x}_o \tag{16}$$

The expressions (15) and (16) show the dependence of $\hat{\mathbf{V}}(\mathbf{b})$ and $\hat{V}(\hat{y}_o)$ on $\mathbf{X}$, that is, on $\mathbf{D}$ since $\mathbf{X}$ is just an extension of $\mathbf{D}$. This dependence is the very reason why appropriate experimental designs must be used in RSM (as in any experimental domain). In particular, a good design will produce reliable estimates of $\boldsymbol{\beta}$, that is, small values of the diagonal terms of (15).

The concept of estimate reliability, as expressed by the variance of the estimates, must be well understood. It can be illustrated as follows, using the simple regression

$$y_i = \alpha + \beta x_i + \varepsilon_i$$

for the sake of simplicity.

If the experimenter had the possibility of repeating his experiment of n trials a large number of times, say N times, he would obtain N values b_k ($k = 1, \ldots, N$) from which an estimate of $V(b)$ could be calculated as

$$V_N(b) = (N-1)^{-1} \sum_{k=1}^{N} (b_k - \bar{b})^2$$

where

$$\bar{b} = N^{-1} \sum_{k=1}^{N} b_k$$

Obviously, $V_N(b)$ should be numerically close to $\hat{V}(b)$ if the N repetitions have been carried out in exactly the same conditions. In the simple regression, we have

$$\hat{V}(b) = s^2 \left[\sum_{i=1}^{n} (x_i - \bar{x})^2 \right]^{-1}$$

Note that, in the above conceptual experiment, the term $\Sigma_{i=1}^{n}(x_i - \bar{x})^2$ is constant, and s^2 is averaged over the N repetitions.

Now, in practice, a *single* experiment will generally be performed, yielding a single value of b. It is thus highly desirable that this estimate be not too far from the unknown parameter value, especially when the regression is to be used to make predictions. As an example, the probability that b will be within $\pm 5\%$ of the value $\beta = 10$, say, i.e.

Prob $\{10 - 0.5 \leqslant b \leqslant 10 + 0.5\}$ is equal to

0·886 when $V(b) = 0.1$
0·683 when $V(b) = 0.25$
0·383 when $V(b) = 1$

2.4. Experimental Designs

All the technical problems concerning the experimental designs in RSM have been reviewed extensively in Gacula and Singh, including the methods of performing the required calculations. The objective of this section is thus restricted to comment on some points which might be of concern to the experimenter. The points (b), (c), (d), (h), (i) and (j) are requirements to the success of the RMS application.

(a) First of all, the reason for coding the levels of the technological variables is to have homogeneous scales on the axes which span the technological space, that is, to generate a spherical symmetry which makes the subsequent study of the RS much easier.

(b) All pertinent technological variables should be identified. The inclusion of a non-pertinent variable unnecessarily inflates the experiment. On the other hand, ignoring a pertinent variable may result in a significant lack-of-fit unless, by chance, the level of the ignored variable is constant over the whole experiment.

(c) The choice of the actual levels assigned to the technological variables is of utmost importance. As already mentioned, an ideal situation would be that the region of interest be not larger than that part of the technological space where the quadratic model is a valid representation of the unknown model. On the other hand, the actual range of the levels ($x_{max} - x_{min}$ in actual units) should be large enough to permit a good discrimination between the responses. In other words, the range of the levels should be large enough to detect curvatures of the response surface when they exist. A further point to keep in mind is that the responses obtained at some design points may be bad responses from the point of view of quality. These responses are nevertheless necessary to define the shape of the response surface.

(d) The most popular designs in RSM are the so-called central composite rotatable designs (CCRD) (Cochran and Cox (1957) and Gacula and Singh). They consist of three sets of experimental points. The first set is a traditional factorial design with 2^p points, whose coded levels are ± 1 for each of the p variables. These 2^p points are the vertices of a p-dimensional cube centred at the origin of the coded system of reference. The distance of these points from the origin is $p^{1/2}$. The second set is a star of $2p$ points on the axes of the system of reference, at a distance $2^{p/4}$ from the origin. The third set consists of points at the origin. Their objective is to provide an estimate of the variance of the experimental error and their number is chosen so as to make the design rotatable. Table 1 gives the CCRD for $p=4$.

Table 2 shows the distances of the points from the origin in the first and second sets, respectively, for $p=3$, 4 and 5.

In these CCRDs, the region of interest will be a p-dimensional sphere of radius slightly larger than $\text{Max}[p^{1/2}, 2^{p/4}]$. How much

TABLE 1

1st Order Part				2nd Order Part (axial points)			
x_1	x_2	x_3	x_4	x_1	x_2	x_3	x_4
-1	-1	-1	-1	-2	0	0	0
-1	-1	-1	1	2	0	0	0
-1	-1	1	-1	0	-2	0	0
-1	-1	1	1	0	2	0	0
-1	1	-1	-1	0	0	-2	0
-1	1	-1	1	0	0	2	0
-1	1	1	-1	0	0	0	-2
-1	1	1	1	0	0	0	2
1	-1	-1	-1				
1	-1	-1	1	Central part:			
1	-1	1	-1	7 points			
1	-1	1	1				
1	1	-1	-1	0	0	0	0
1	1	-1	1				
1	1	1	-1				
1	1	1	1				

TABLE 2

DISTANCES OF THE CCRD POINTS FROM THE ORIGIN

p	1st set $p^{1/2}$	2nd set $2^{p/4}$
3	1·732	1·682
4	2	2
5	2·236	2·378

larger? Owing to the definition of the region of interest given in (c), a precise and general rule cannot be formulated. If the levels of the technological variables have been chosen adequately, the radius of the region of interest might be larger than Max $[p^{1/2}, 2^{p/4}]$ by 10–20%.

From a practical point of view, the points in the second set must be considered as extreme points, even when $p = 3$ or 4, because they involve a technological variable with an extreme value. Accordingly, it would be wise to check the feasibility of the trials at these points, before starting the experiment.

(e) The concepts of independence and interaction should be clear in the experimenter's mind.

Two variables x_j and $x_k (j < k = 2, \ldots, p)$ are said to interact when the effect of one of them depends on the level of the other: they are physically dependent. In a quadratic polynomial model, the coefficient b_{jk} measures the amplitude of this interaction, which can be tested for significance. Now, in any CCRD, the columns associated with the terms x_j, x_k and $x_j x_k$ in the **X** matrix are orthogonal to one another: their scalar products are zero. This means that the contributions of the interacting variables x_j and x_k to the regression sum of squares, as well as the contribution of their interaction, are estimated independently of one another. On the other hand, it may happen that x_j and x_k in the **X** matrix are not orthogonal, see (h) below, in spite of the fact that they are physically independent. When it is so, the contributions of these two physically independent variables are not estimated independently of each other. The two estimates have a non-null covariance: Cov $(b_j, b_k) \neq 0$. In these conditions, the test for statistical significance is conditioned.

(f) The programs for multiple regression in the statistical packages can be used to obtain the required least squares solution in the context of the RSM. Most of these programs perform a column centring of the matrix $\mathbf{X}$, including the first column of 1s which disappears with this technique. In general, the coefficient b_0 appears under the name of intercept. It is calculated as $b_0 = \bar{y} - \Sigma_{j=1}^{p} b_{jj} \bar{x}_j^2$ in the designs where $\bar{x}_j = 0$.

(g) Regarding the order in which the trials are performed, the experimenter may be tempted to resort to randomization to comply with the basic theoretical requirements of the statistical tests. If a random sequence of the trials does not raise any operating trouble, it might be used. As a rule, however, it is probably best to follow an order which minimizes the troubles which might be sources of error. Furthermore, the control points from which the variance of the experimental error is estimated should be scattered throughout the experiment. In this way, the presence of any trend should be detected. Obviously, the randomization is within the blocks when a design is arranged in blocks as in Gacula and Singh, p. 258.

(h) Sometimes, the experimenter discovers that, in one or more trials, the actual levels of one or more technological variables were out of control, that is, were not those assigned in the $\mathbf{X}$ matrix. In this situation, it is best to calculate the coded values corresponding to the incorrect x_{ij} values, and to use them for the least squares estimation. Obviously, this results in a loss of orthogonality between some columns in the $\mathbf{X}$ matrix and introduces non-null covariances between some estimates. This is, however, much less harmful than using incorrect x_{ij} values to preserve the orthogonality.

(i) It may also happen that, without the knowledge of the experimenter, some levels of some technological variables did not agree to the values assigned in the $\mathbf{X}$ matrix. This is the situation known in the literature as the 'errors-in-variables' regression. Extensive computer simulations of experiments in RSM have been carried out by one of the author's collaborators (Dr H. Rahim), to investigate the effect of this type of error on the statistical properties of the estimates and of the values predicted by the model. As expected, this type of error induced biases of the estimates and an inflation of their variance, which was sometimes dramatic. An unexpected result, however, was the rejection of the model validity, tested by comparing the lack-of-fit mean square with the experimental error mean square, which occurred with a probability *much higher* than the nominal value. Accordingly, the unexpected rejection of the model validity should prompt the experimenter to check the levels of technological variables.

(j) When the process to be investigated by the RSM involves a transient state, the experimenter must wait until the steady state is reached to take the sample from which the response is measured.

(k) It may be useful, at the end of this chapter, to make explicit the simple transformation which relates the two scales.

If the variable to be coded is the temperature (noted T), the extreme levels corresponding to the axial points are T_{max} and T_{min} to which correspond x_{max} and x_{min} on the coded scale. If we set $\Delta T = T_{max} - T_{min}$, $\Delta x = x_{max} - x_{min}$ and $\bar{T} = (T_{max} + T_{min})/2$, the relations are

$$x = (T - \bar{T})\frac{\Delta x}{\Delta T} \tag{17a}$$

and

$$T = \bar{T} + x\frac{\Delta T}{\Delta x} \tag{17b}$$

Example: In a CCRD with $p = 3$, the coded levels are $-1.682, -1, 0, 1$, 1.682. If the two extreme temperatures are 30 and 70°C, we have $\bar{T} = 50$ and $\Delta T = 40$. Moreover, $\Delta x = 3.364$. Accordingly, the actual temperature at the coded levels -1 and 1 are 38·1 and 61·9°C, respectively.

3. HOW TO EXPLOIT A RESPONSE SURFACE

In the previous chapter, we have seen how to obtain a quadratic polynomial model

$$y = b_o + \sum_{j=1}^{p} b_j x_j + \sum_{j=1}^{p} b_{jj} x_j^2 + \sum_{j<k=2}^{p} b_{jk} x_j x_k \tag{18}$$

which was a reliable mathematical representation of the process, within the region of interest. The quantities unknown to the experimenter were the regression coefficients, the estimates of which were obtained in a single experiment.

In this chapter, the situation changes completely. The estimated regression coefficients are known and may be considered as fixed. The quantities unknown to the experimenter are the levels of the technological variables which optimize the response. More generally, the problem will be to study what happens to the response, when moving within the region of interest. Obviously, all the information obtained in this study of the response surface will be conditional on the values of the coefficients.

In this context, the quadratic polynomial model is the algebraic representation of a $(p+1)$-dimensional quadric surface which extends from $-\infty$ to $+\infty$ along each of the technological axes. Obviously, only that part of the surface whose projection on the technological space is the region of interest will be the actual response surface.

The first step, in this study, is to localize the stationary point, that is, the point of the response surface where the response is optimum. This is achieved by solving the p linear equations

$$\frac{\partial y}{\partial x_j} = 0, \qquad j = 1, \ldots, p \tag{19}$$

where y is given in (18).

In matrix notation, the p equations (19) become

$$\mathbf{M}\mathbf{x}_p = \mathbf{k} \tag{20}$$

where $\mathbf{x}_p$ is the $(p \times 1)$ vector of the technological variables. The solution of (20) is

$$\mathbf{x}_{sp} = \mathbf{M}^{-1}\mathbf{k}$$

where $\mathbf{x}_{sp}$ is the vector of the coordinates of the stationary point, $\mathbf{M}$ is the $(p \times p)$ symmetrical matrix

$$\begin{bmatrix} 2b_{11} & b_{12} & \cdots & b_{1p} \\ & 2b_{22} & \cdots & b_{2p} \\ & & \ddots & \vdots \\ & & & 2b_{pp} \end{bmatrix}$$

and $\mathbf{k}$ is the $(p \times 1)$ vector

$$\mathbf{k}' = [-b_1 - b_2 \cdots -b_p]$$

In order to know whether the stationary point is a maximum, a minimum or a minimax, (18) is put into its so-called canonical form

$$y = y_s + \sum_{j=1}^{p} \lambda_j z_j^2 \qquad (21)$$

where y_s is the response at the stationary point. Equation (18) becomes Eqn. (21), when referred to the natural axes of the quadric of which it is the algebraic representation. This transformation is obtained first by shifting the origin of the technological system of reference to the stationary point, and second, by rotating this system to make it coincide with the natural axes of the quadric. The z_j are the so-called canonical variables. They are functions of the technological variables. These functions are expressed, in matrix notation, as

$$\mathbf{z} = \mathbf{A}'(\mathbf{x}_p - \mathbf{x}_{sp})$$

where $\mathbf{x}_p - \mathbf{x}_{sp}$ corresponds to the shift, and $\mathbf{A}$ to the rotation. The columns of $\mathbf{A}$ (or the rows of $\mathbf{A}'$) are the eigenvectors of $\frac{1}{2}\mathbf{M}$. The elements of the jth eigenvector are the direction cosines of the jth canonical axis, with respect to the shifted original system of reference. The eigenvectors are defined by

$$\tfrac{1}{2}\mathbf{A}'\mathbf{M}\mathbf{A} = \mathbf{\Lambda}$$

where $\mathbf{\Lambda}$ is a $(p \times p)$ diagonal matrix, the elements of which are the coefficients λ_j of (21), i.e. the eigenvalues of $\frac{1}{2}\mathbf{M}$.

If, in a process, the interactions between the technological variables are weak, the coefficients $b_{jk}(j \neq k)$ in (18) will be numerically small with respect to the other coefficients, $\frac{1}{2}\mathbf{M}$ will be close to the diagonal matrix $\mathbf{\Lambda}$, (that is, b_{jj} is numerically close to $\lambda_j(j = 1, \ldots, p)$ and the shifted original axes will almost coincide with the canonical axes. In these conditions, $\mathbf{A}$ is close to an identity matrix.

Equation (21) shows that the stationary point is a minimum when $\lambda_j > 0, j = 1, \ldots, p$, and a maximum when $\lambda_j < 0$. Otherwise, the stationary point is a minimax, that is, a minimum for certain variables and a maximum for others.

Furthermore the response surface is a $(p+1)$-dimensional ellipsoid when all the λ_j have the same sign, and a $(p+1)$-dimensional hyperboloid otherwise. The size of λ_j shows how rapidly the response changes along the jth canonical axis.

Two situations must be considered, depending on the position of the stationary point with respect to the region of interest.

First situation. The stationary point is inside the region of interest. It must be emphasized that the case where the stationary point is a maximum (minimum) when a minimum (maximum) was searched for, is to be treated by the methodology developed for the second situation (see below), where the expected optimum is on the boundary of the region of interest.

When the nature of the stationary point meets the experimenter's expectation, the problem is theoretically solved. All that remains to be done is to plot two-dimensional contour lines for constant values of the response. Figure 2 shows such a plot for $p=2$, where the stationary point is a maximum. The two technological variables, in this plot, are temperature and concentration. The design points are represented, together with the coded system of reference, x_1 and x_2. The canonical axes are z_1 and z_2. When $p>2$, $p(p-1)/2$ two-dimensional plots may be obtained by giving definite values to all the variables, except the two of interest. How to solve this problem algebraically is indicated in Gacula and Singh.

Contour lines like those in Fig. 2 may be obtained from the variables either in coded or in original form. When they are coded, the coefficients

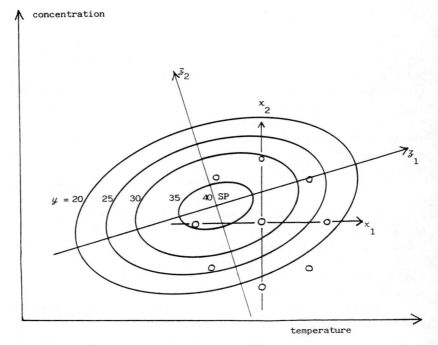

FIG. 2. The stationary point (SP) is a maximum inside the region of interest.

are the least squares estimates of (18). In the other case, new values of the coefficients must be calculated by replacing x_j in (18) by (17a), that is,

$$x_j = (v_j - \bar{v}_j) r_j$$

where v_j denote the jth variable on the original scale and $r_j = \Delta v_j / \Delta x_j$.
   For $p = 2$, the new model is

$$y = b'_o + b'_1 v_1 + b'_2 v_2 + b'_{11} v_1^2 + b'_{22} v_2^2 + b'_{12} v_1 v_2$$

where

$$b'_o = b_o - b_1 \bar{v}_1 r_1 - b_2 \bar{v}_2 r_2 + b_{11} \bar{v}_1^2 r_1^2 + b_{22} \bar{v}_2^2 r_2^2 + b_{12} \bar{v}_1 \bar{v}_2 r_1 r_2$$
$$b'_1 = b_1 r_1 - 2 b_{11} \bar{v}_1 r_1^2 - b_{12} \bar{v}_2 r_1 r_2$$
$$b'_2 = b_2 r_2 - 2 b_{22} \bar{v}_2 r_2^2 - b_{12} \bar{v}_1 r_1 r_2$$
$$b'_{11} = b_{11} r_1^2, \ b'_{22} = b_{22} r_2^2 \quad \text{and} \quad b'_{12} = b_{12} r_1 r_2$$

Second situation. The stationary point is outside the region of interest. Figure 3 shows, for $p = 2$, a stationary point which is a minimax outside this region.

   The problem, here, is to find the optimum (maximum or minimum of the response) which is necessarily *on the boundary* of the region of interest. If this region is defined as the p-dimensional sphere $\mathbf{x}'_p \mathbf{x}_p = r^2$ (or $\Sigma_{j=1}^{p} x_j^2 = r^2$ in scalar notation), the problem is to find the value of $\mathbf{x}_p$ which optimizes the response on the boundary of the region of interest, that is, with the constraint

$$\mathbf{x}'_p \mathbf{x}_p = r^2$$

This is a classical optimization problem which is solved through the Lagrange's function, Bass (1956),

$$F = y - \mu(\mathbf{x}'_p \mathbf{x}_p - r^2)$$

where μ is the Lagrange's multiplier. The solution to the problem consists of solving the $(p+1)$ equations

$$\frac{\partial F}{\partial x_j} = 0 \qquad j = 1, \ldots, p$$

$$\frac{\partial F}{\partial \mu} = 0$$

In matrix notation we have

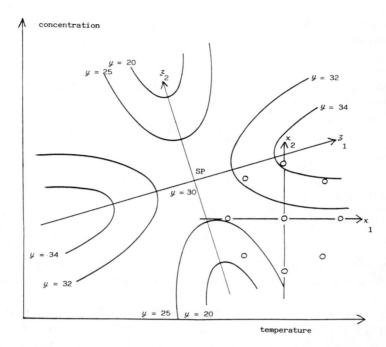

FIG. 3. The stationary point (SP) is a minimax outside the region of interest.

$$\mathbf{x}_p = (\mathbf{M} - 2\mu \mathbf{I}_p)\mathbf{k} \tag{22a}$$

$$\mathbf{x}'_p \mathbf{x}_p = r^2 \tag{22b}$$

where $\mathbf{I}_p$ is the $(p \times p)$ identity matrix.

Due to the non-linear constraint (22b), the direct solution of the system (22) is best replaced by an *indirect search* carried out by expressing the x_j as functions of μ, that is, as the ratios of two determinants, as shown in (23) for $j=1$ and $p=3$,

$$x_1 = \frac{\begin{vmatrix} -b_1 & b_{12} & b_{13} \\ -b_2 & 2(b_{22}-\mu) & b_{23} \\ -b_3 & b_{23} & 2(b_{33}-\mu) \end{vmatrix}}{\begin{vmatrix} 2(b_{11}-\mu) & b_{12} & b_{13} \\ b_{12} & 2(b_{22}-\mu) & b_{23} \\ b_{13} & b_{23} & 2(b_{33}-\mu) \end{vmatrix}} \tag{23}$$

Moving μ from $-\infty$ to $+\infty$ induces a *trajectory* within the p-dimensional technological space. In other words, each numerical value of μ induces numerical values of $x_j (j=1,\ldots,p)$ through expressions of which (23) is just a three-dimensional example. In other words there is a one-to-one correspondence (mapping) between the value of μ on the real line and the points which constitute the trajectory within the technological space. The distance of each point from the origin is calculated as $(\Sigma_{j=1}^p x_j^2)^{1/2}$, and when this distance is equal to r, the point is on the boundary of the region of interest.

The trajectory starts and ends at the origin because $\mu = \pm \infty$ implies that $x_j = 0$.

Furthermore, the trajectory passes through the stationary point when $\mu = 0$ and enjoys discontinuities when μ assumes the values λ_j.

One of the author's collaborators (Dr R. Munoz-Box) has shown (unpublished work) that the value of μ which corresponds to the constrained maximum (on the boundary of the region of interest) is larger than the largest λ_j, and that the value of μ which corresponds to the constrained minimum is smaller than the smallest λ_j. Accordingly, the region between the two extreme λ_j where the trajectory has a very complex shape due to p discontinuities does not need to be investigated.

The program devoted to RSM written by Dr R. Munoz-Box (available on request) includes an output for this indirect search with the following structure:

μ	x_1	x_2	$\ldots\ldots\ldots\ldots\ldots$	x_p	$d=(\Sigma_{j=1}^p x_j^2)^{1/2}$	y
μ_1	x_{11}	x_{21}	$\ldots\ldots\ldots\ldots\ldots$	x_{p1}	d_1	y_1
μ_2	x_{12}	x_{22}	$\ldots\ldots\ldots\ldots\ldots$	x_{p2}	d_2	y_2
.	.	.		.	.	.
.	.	.		.	.	.
.	.	.		.	.	.

In summary, μ_1 must be slightly larger than the largest eigenvalue, and the increments $\Delta\mu$ must be positive, if the response is to be maximized. μ_1 must be slightly smaller than the smallest eigenvalue, and the increments $\Delta\mu$ must be negative, if the response is to be minimized.

If the radius of the region of interest has been defined exactly, finer searches with smaller increments are performed until $d=r$ is obtained. In most cases, however, the uncertainty regarding the exact position of the boundary of the region of interest makes this refinement useless. The relevant information is the values of the response in the domain where this boundary is likely to be.

Experience has shown that, in Food Science and Technology, many response surface studies involve a stationary point which is a minimax outside the region of interest. Accordingly, the above methodology is very useful.

As in the first situation, all that remains to be done is to plot two-dimensional contour lines which show the behaviour of the response within the region of interest, and more particularly in the vicinity of the optimum.

4. MISCELLANEOUS TOPICS RELATED TO RESPONSE SUR-FACE METHODOLOGY

4.1. Experiments with Mixtures

It may happen, in Food Science and Technology, that the technological variables are the proportions of the constituents of a mixture. The problem is to find the optimal composition, with respect to a response of interest.

The proportions of the constituents add up to unity. As a first result of this constraint, the technological space generated by p constituents is a $(p-1)$-dimensional simplex, i.e. an equilateral triangle for three variables, a regular tetrahedron for four variables, etc., the vertices of which correspond to the pure constituents.

As a second result of this constraint, the quadratic polynomial which represents the response surface does not have the form of (3). The reader interested in this method is referred to Cornell (1981).

4.2. Evolutionary Operation (EVOP)

A review of the subject has been presented by Hunter and Kittrel (1966). The fundamental paper on the subject, however, goes back to Box (1957) where that author writes that 'a process should be run so as to generate product plus information on how to improve the product'.

From a practical point of view, EVOP involves slight systematic variations in the operating conditions, which are large enough to induce, in the long run, detectable response differences, but not large enough to generate off-specification products. EVOP is thus a variant of RSM which may be used in a plant without interrupting the process.

4.3. Sequential Procedures

At first sight, sequential procedures are certainly more appealing to the experimenter in Food Science and Technology, than monolithic designs which may comprise up to more than 50 trials (when, for example, 6 technological variables are involved, see Cochran and Cox (1957)). This feeling is based on the belief that sequential procedures can be interrupted at any time without impairing the information already gathered by that time. Moreover, some experimenters certainly know that, when two groups are compared, sequential procedures lead to decisions with fewer trials, on the average, than required by the designs where the sample size has been fixed in advance.

The possibility of using sequential procedures in RSM will therefore be briefly discussed. See the paper by Mead and Pike (1975) for further references.

First of all, a sequential procedure implies that the response is available within a relatively short time. There are many situations, however, where this requirement is not fulfilled in Food Science and Technology. A good example is the biological value of a protein, the assessment of which needs about one month. On the other side, the response may be the result of a sensory evaluation. In this case, the experimenter very often prefers to wait until all the products are available for testing, and an incomplete block design will generally be used for the sensory assessment (Cochran and Cox, 1957). Moreover, a response of considerable interest is the keeping quality. For practical reasons, the experimenter may prefer also here to wait until all the products are available to start the storage study.

The most popular sequential technique to reach the optimum (or a point near the optimum) of a process, within the region of interest, is the simplex procedure, see, for example, Baasel (1965), and Nakai *et al.* (1984). This technique, however, does not produce a response surface. If necessary, the experimenter can perform some trials around the optimum to get an idea of the shape of the response surface in this part of the technological space. The simplex procedure can also be used to localize the optimum very roughly (still within the region of interest or on its boundary) when no *a priori* information is available. Then, a central composite rotatable design can be carried out with the maximum of security, to provide all the information which has been described in the previous chapters.

4.4. Path of Steepest Ascent

When no *a priori* knowledge is available regarding the shape of the response surface and the possible location of the stationary point with respect to the region of interest, it is recommended to start with a first order design in a 'corner' of the technological space. From this first restricted experiment a direction, called the path of steepest ascent, is obtained, see, for example, Motycka *et al.* (1984) and Cochran and Cox (1957). A point is chosen on this path of steepest ascent, which becomes the origin of a new first order design, and produces a new path of steepest ascent. The process is repeated until the region where an optimum takes place is localized. A central composite rotatable design can be performed in this region. This procedure may be considered as a semi-sequential technique.

ACKNOWLEDGEMENTS

The author is greatly indebted to three colleagues, P. Leathwood, R. Munoz-Box and H. Rahim, for their helpful comments on an earlier version of this chapter.

REFERENCES

Baasel, W. D. (1965) Exploring response surfaces to establish optimum conditions. *Chem. Eng.*, **72**, 147–152.

Bass, J. (1956). *Cours de Mathématiques*, Masson et Cie, Paris.

Box, G. E. P. (1957). Evolutionary operation: a method for increasing industrial productivity. *Appl. Statist.*, **6**, 81–101.

Cochran, W. G. and Cox, G. M. (1957). *Experimental Designs*, John Wiley, London.

Cornell, J. A. (1981). *Experiments with Mixtures, Designs, Models, and the Analysis of Mixture Data*, John Wiley, New York.

Gacula, M. C., Jr. and Singh, J. (1984). Response surface designs and analysis. In: *Statistical Methods in Food and Consumer Research*, Food Science and Technology, A Series of Monographs, Academic Press, New York, pp. 214–72.

Hunter, W. G. and Kittrell, J. R. (1966). EVOP, a review. *Technometrics*, **8**, 389–96.

Mead, R. and Pike, D. J. (1975). A review of response surface methodology from a biometric viewpoint. *Biometrics*, **31**, 803–51.

Motycka, R. R., Devor, R. E. and Bechtel, P. J. (1984). Response surface methodology approach to the optimization of boneless ham yield. *J. Food Sci.*, **49**, 1386–9.

Nakai, S., Koide, K. and Eugster, K. (1984). A new mapping supersimplex optimization for food product and process development. *J. Food Sci.*, **49**, 1143–8, continued on p. 1170.

Chapter 5

DISCRIMINANT ANALYSIS

JOHN J. POWERS and GLENN O. WARE

College of Agriculture Experiment Station, University of Georgia, Athens, Georgia, USA

1. INTRODUCTION

In sensory and chemical analysis, measurements are frequently made concurrently on several variables of two or more treatment groups for the primary purpose of determining whether the groups can be distinguished from each other. Illustrations of application might be the differentiation of decaffeinated and caffeine-containing coffee upon sensory grounds or, upon either sensory or chemical grounds, various brands of low-calorie and of regular cola beverages or a particular herb grown in different major producing areas. A statistical procedure for identifying the variables useful for such differentiation is discriminant analysis (DA), first introduced by Fisher in 1936. The essential purpose of DA is classification of an item into one of the several mutually exclusive groups on the basis of its measured response variables. It is thus of especial value to *predict* the class to which unknown samples belong.

Throughout much of its life, DA has been more a tool in the offing than a practical, everyday one. The reason is obvious. DA, as is true for other multivariate analysis (MVA) procedures, involves lengthy and at times complex mathematical computation. Until high speed computers and 'user friendly' computer packages made the process simpler, routine applications of DA were just not practical. The number of papers dealing with its application have flowered in recent years whereas they were sparse prior to the late 1960s.

1.1. Goals
The purposes of this chapter are to (1) describe the main features of the

different methods of DA, (2) illustrate, with examples, use of each procedure, (3) point out the problems associated with DA in general and each of the DA methods, (4) advise of precautions which need to be taken to minimize such problems, including those related to the use of various computer packages, and (5) forewarn the prospective user of pitfalls to be avoided either in carrying on the analysis or in interpreting the results.

2. OVERVIEW OF DISCRIMINANT ANALYSIS

2.1. The Linear Discriminant Function

Fisher introduced the linear discriminant function in 1936. His basic concept was that, through a transformation of the measured variables to a new scale, a linear combination of the variables could be found such that the mean distance between classes would be maximized.

This form of DA is closely related to the method of regression analysis. Whereas regression analysis uses a weighted combination of continuous quantitative variables for predicting an item's response on a continuous quantitative scale, DA uses a weighted combination of the quantitative variables to predict the discrete class to which an item belongs.

The general form of the discriminant function is given by

$$L = b_1 x_1 + b_2 x_2 + \cdots + b_p x_p$$

where L is a weighted linear composite score. These measurements have thus been reduced to a single composite score, L. When the X_i's have a multivariate normal distribution, L then has a univariate normal distribution. It is assumed that the variance–covariance (VC) matrices of the p measurements are homogeneous for all classes.

The objective in employing linear discriminant analysis (LDA) is to find the set of bs (i.e. weights) which will result in the group differences being as dramatic as possible. This maximizes the ratio of the between-group variability to the within-group variability of L.

Success in being able to discriminate between the groups depends upon the ratio of the between-group variability to the within-group variability. To illustrate the concept, let us consider a very simple example involving two-group discrimination as a function of a single variable. Figure 1 shows three different situations of two groups of observations, A and B, measured on the variable, X_1. For two treatment groups of equal size with equal within-group variances, the cut-off scores

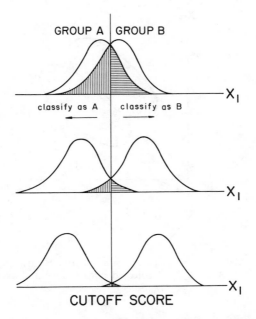

GROUP A | GROUP B

classify as A   classify as B

X_1

X_1

CUTOFF SCORE X_1

FIG. 1. The probabilities of misclassification decrease as the distance between the group means increases in relation to the within-group variability. Horizontal hatching: members of group A misclassified as members of group B; vertical hatching: members of group B misclassified as members of group A.

are located midway between the two groups. As the distances between the means becomes greater in relation to the within-group variability, the greater is the probability of success in being able to discriminate between the two groups, i.e. fewer misclassifications result.

Now consider Fig. 2 showing two groups of observations, A and B, measured on two variables X_1 and X_2. A look at the projection onto the X_1 axis of the plotted points corresponding to the two groups shows considerable overlap. Projection of the plotted points onto the X_2 axis likewise results in considerable overlapping. However, upon observing the scatter points of the two groups, we can discern two rather distinct groups corresponding to groups A and B which can be separated by a straight line. If X_1 and X_2 are projected onto an axis perpendicular to this line, then one can see how the two measurements can be combined into a single composite measurement on a rotated axis for the purpose of distinguishing between the two groups.

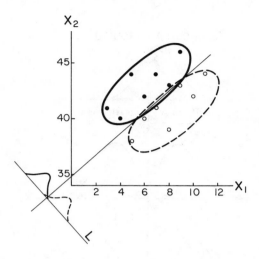

FIG. 2. Observed data points for two groups, A and B, measured on response variables, X_1 and X_2, projected onto the rotated axis, L.

When only two groups are considered, a single linear discriminant function can serve to discriminate between the groups. When three or more treatment groups exist, one axis does not necessarily exhaust the discrimination potential. The first discriminant function derived is the one that maximally separates group differences. A second function is then derived which is orthogonal to the first and separates the groups further based on the remaining information not contained in the first function. This process continues until all possible functions are derived. The total number of all functions is one less than the number of groups or equal to the number of response variables to be used whichever is smaller. Usually in most applications the number of variables will exceed the number of groups, and thus, there is at most $G-1$ discriminant axes where G denotes the total number of groups. The term 'at most' is used since in many instances only one or two different functions are required for reliably discriminating between each of the several groups.

2.2. Criteria–Evaluation–Classification

Once the discriminant functions have been determined, questions arise from the analysis as to: (1) whether or not the discriminant functions succeed in discriminating between the groups, (2) which variables are most important in discriminating between the groups, and (3) how to use the discriminant functions to classify items into the various groups.

There are a number of indices used as a measure of the criterion of discrimination. It is not our intention to define these indices in terms of their statistical properties, but rather to let the reader know they provide a basis for evaluating the statistical significance of discriminant functions.

Wilks' lambda (or U statistic) is a general statistic used as a measure for testing the differences among group centroids, i.e. group means for the rotated axes. All groups are assumed to have homogeneous VC matrices. The smaller the value for the U statistic, the more significant are the centroid differences. Rao's V is a generalized distance measure, and attains its largest value when there is maximal separation between groups. Mahalanobis' D^2 is based on the squared distances between group centroids and also attains its largest values when maximal separation is achieved. Rao's V and Mahalanobis' D^2 are used primarily in stepwise discriminant analysis (SDA).

The determination of the importance of variables in DA is analogous to determining the importance of variables in multiple regression analysis. In regression analysis, the absolute magnitude of the standardized regression coefficients can be used as a measure of variable importance. Likewise in DA, the absolute magnitude of the standardized discriminant coefficients is one indicator of the importance of the variables used for discrimination. Another indicator of variable importance is the absolute magnitude of the correlation between the composite linear score and each of the variables. The variable having the largest absolute correlation with the composite score is the one which contributes the most to discrimination.

Questions about how the discriminant functions are used to classify items relate to procedures for establishing boundaries between the groups. Since the composite scores have a univariate distribution, cut-off scores can be computed for the discriminant function. The cut-off scores represent boundaries between the various classes to which items are to be assigned, and therefore, the task is to determine the cut-off scores that result in the fewest number of errors in classification. Determining cut-off scores for two-group discrimination is fairly straightforward but becomes much more complicated for multiple-group discrimination since there can be more than one discriminant function involved.

A rather general classification procedure is to measure the squared Euclidean distance of each item to the mean of each treatment group. One then may assign the item to the group for which the squared

Euclidean distance is smallest. Mahalanobis (1936) proposed a generalization to the squared Euclidean distance approach, now known as Mahalanobis' D^2 procedure which adjusts the squared distance by utilizing the inverse of the pooled within-groups VC matrix. Green (1978) points out in his text that the relationship of Mahalanobis' D^2 to Fisher's discriminant function is that both procedures produce exactly the same classification assignments. However, classification using Mahalanobis' D^2 is much simpler than using the sequential classification procedure with a set of discriminant equations.

Some authors as well as computer programs utilize Mahalanobis' concept to develop a set of classification equations, one for each group, using the inverse of the pooled matrix. The classification functions are derived in such a fashion that an item is classified into the group for which it has the highest score.

It should be pointed out that Fisher's linear discriminant function, Mahalanobis' D^2 procedure as well as the latter classification functions assume that the xs are multivariate normally distributed with homogeneous matrices. However, by utilizing the individual VC matrices separately for each group with Mahalanobis' D^2 or the classification equation discussed above, the assumption that the VC matrices are homogeneous is no longer required.

2.2.1. Illustrative Example

We will now consider an example of two-group discriminant analysis to illustrate the features introduced in the preceding sections. For purposes of discussion, let's suppose that two products, A and B, have been measured on two separate response variables, X_1 and X_2 as previously shown in Fig. 2. As pointed out earlier, two rather distinct groups of points corresponding to the two products are clearly distinguishable and therefore a linear composite function of these two variables for purposes of discriminating between the two products should be attainable.

The linear discriminant analysis for this hypothetical example is presented in Table 1. Although the set of bs in the linear discriminant function, $L = b_1 X_1 + b_2 X_2$, are chosen to maximize the differences between groups relative to the differences within group, they are not unique. For example the bs can be scaled up or down by multiplying by any arbitrary constant producing the same maximum difference between groups. Assuming X_1 and X_2 are univariate normally distributed, the bs associated with the standardized discriminant function, $L = 1 \cdot 55176\ X_1 + 1 \cdot 56190\ X_2$, produce a normally distributed variable having an overall

TABLE 1

ILLUSTRATION OF VARIOUS COMPUTATIONAL COMPONENTS FOR LINEAR DISCRIMINANT ANALYSIS

Variable	Pooled covariance matrix X_1	Pooled covariance matrix X_2	Standardized discriminant function coefficients	Unstandardized discriminant coefficients	Multiple correlations between composite scores and discriminating variables	Classification functions coefficients Group A	Classification functions coefficients Group B
X_1	4·6667	3·5000	-1·55176	-0·7183263	-0·31204	-17·44402	-15·31274
X_2	3·5000	4·16667	1·56190	0·7651737	0·33023	24·97297	22·70270
Constant	—		—	-27·10901	—	-485·2800	-404·8476

Wilks' lambda; 0·28030; $X^2 = 13·99$; Significance level = 0·0009

Group A

Observed data X_1	Observed data X_2	Discriminant scores L_A	Mahalanobis' D^2 D_A	Mahalanobis' D^2 D_B	Classification scores C_A	Classification scores C_B
3	42	2·8733	2·94	19·99	511·25	502·73
4	40	0·6246	2·32	6·02	443·86	442·01
5	44	2·9670	2·20	19·81	526·31	517·51
6	42	0·7183	0·65	4·91	458·92	456·79
7	44	1·5303	0·25	9·34	491·42	486·88
8	43	0·0468	2·32	2·59	449·01	448·87
9	46	1·6240	2·29	11·93	506·48	501·66

	X_1	X_2	L_A
Means	6	43	1·4835
Std Dev.	2·16025	1·91485	1·1211

Group B

Observed data X_1	Observed data X_2	Discriminant scores L_B	Mahalanobis' D^2 D_A	Mahalanobis' D^2 D_B	Classification scores C_A	Classification scores C_B
5	38	-1·6240	11·93	2·29	376·47	381·29
6	40	-0·8120	5·84	1·01	408·98	411·38
7	41	-0·7652	5·12	0·57	416·50	418·77
8	39	-3·0138	20·48	2·59	349·11	358·06
9	43	-0·6175	5·21	1·23	431·56	433·55
10	42	-2·1550	13·81	1·02	389·14	395·54
11	44	-1·3430	10·26	2·29	421·64	425·63

	X_1	X_2	L_B
Means	8	41	-1·4835
Std Dev.	2·16025	2·16025	0·8620

mean of zero and unit variance within each group. Since there are only two groups, the discriminant function can be used to classify observations; accordingly an observation would be classified into group A if its discriminant score is greater than zero and into the group B if its score is less than zero.

The standardized discriminant scores are difficult to use in practice when classifying new observations because the measurement values for the new samples are 'raw' values. The discriminant function can be formulated on the basis of the original measurements of X_1 and X_2 similar to regression analysis which will include a constant term to adjust for the means. The unstandardized discriminant function, $L = -27{\cdot}1091 - 0{\cdot}7183263\,X_1 + 0{\cdot}7651737\,X_2$, can be used with the original scale of measurements for classification purposes. The discriminant scores produced by the unstandardized function are presented in the columns designated L_A and L_B. The means for groups A and B are $1{\cdot}4835$ and $-1{\cdot}4835$, respectively, providing an overall mean of zero with a pooled within-group variance equal to 1. Wilks lambda (or U statistic) indicates that the two centroids are significantly different with $X^2 = 13{\cdot}99$ ($p \leqslant 0{\cdot}0009$).

If we assume that the probability of occurrence of the two groups, A and B, is equal and that misclassification costs are equal, the cut-off score is the average of the two group means $(-1{\cdot}4835 + 1{\cdot}4835)/2 = 0$. The basis for classification would then be to assign an observation to group A if the discriminant score is greater than zero, and into group B if the discriminant score is less than zero. Based on the discriminant scores, all 14 observations are correctly classified. The process of using the discriminant functions for classification purposes when there exists more than two groups is not very practical.

When there are more than two groups, we generally prefer to use the Mahalanobis distance method. The generalized squared distance function weighted by the inverse of the VC matrix,

$$D_j^2 = (\mathbf{x} - \bar{\mathbf{x}}_j)'\,\mathrm{Cov}^{-1}(x - \bar{x}_j)$$

is computed for each observation where x denotes an observation to be classified, $\mathbf{x}_j$ is the vector of mean response for group j, and Cov^{-1} is the inverse of the VC matrix. Columns designated D_A and D_B are the computed squared distances of each observation from the means of Groups A and B. An observation is then classified into the group for which D_A or D_B is minimum. As can be seen, all 14 observations are correctly classified into their respective Groups A and B.

When the expected sizes of all population groups are equal, classification functions can also be derived as a function of the inverse of the pooled VC matrix and the column vector of the group means. The coefficient vector and constant term for the equations for group j are computed as:

$$\text{Coefficient vector} = \text{Cov}^{-1}\,\bar{x}_j,$$
$$\text{Constant term} = -\tfrac{1}{2}\bar{x}'_j\,\text{Cov}^{-1}\,\bar{x}_j$$

The classification functions for Group A and B are given as follows:

$$\text{Group A} \quad C_A = -485{\cdot}2800 - 17{\cdot}44402\,X_1 + 24{\cdot}97297\,X_2$$
$$\text{Group B} \quad C_B = -404{\cdot}8476 - 15{\cdot}31274\,X_1 + 22{\cdot}70270\,X_2$$

Classification scores are generated for both C_A and C_B for all observations as shown in the columns designated as C_A and C_B. An observation is classified into the group for which the classification score is larger. The classification scores result in all seven observations of each group being correctly classified. For unequal population sizes the classification functions can be modified to reflect the *a priori* inequalities by adding a term to the classification function that adjust for group size (Tabachnick and Fidell, 1983).

As in regression analysis, the absolute magnitude of the standardized coefficients can be used as a measure of importance for the discriminating variables. The absolute standardized coefficients for X_1 and X_2 are, respectively, $1{\cdot}55176$ and $1{\cdot}56190$. Correlations between the discriminant composite scores and the variables X_1 and X_2 can also indicate the relative importance of the discriminating power of each variable. The correlation of the composite scores with X_1 is $-0{\cdot}31204$ while that with X_2 is $0{\cdot}33023$. X_2 shows a slightly better discriminating power than X_1 although as we observed earlier, neither X_1 or X_2 singularly is sufficient for discriminating between the groups.

For the illustrative example, the VC matrices were shown to be homogeneous. However, if the VC matrices for the treatment groups are not equal, then the statistical procedures for discriminant analysis are modified appropriately. The interested reader should refer to texts such as those of Green (1978), and Tabachnick and Fidell (1983), and to the documentation of the various computerized statistical packages.

2.3. Nearest Neighbor Discrimination

A rather general nonparametric classification method which is commonly referred to as nearest-neighbor (NN) discriminant analysis classifies observations into groups based on the squared distance of the observations to the k nearest neighbors. Given an observation to classify, NN discriminant analysis looks at the k observations closest to it.

There are two approaches, Euclidean distance and Mahalanobis' D^2 distance, which are commonly utilized in NN discriminant analysis. The observation is placed in the group containing the highest proportion of the k nearest neighbors. If the treatment groups are of equal size and k is specified as the class size, then the NN discriminant procedure gives essentially the same classification results as LDA.

2.4. Canonical Discriminant Analysis
There is a third form of DA known as canonical discrimination analysis (CDA) which is a variant of canonical-variate analysis (CVA). CDA provides estimates of the distances between classes and the probabilities of the distances being greater. Furthermore, the geometric location of the means for the classes may be plotted to permit visualization of how close or far apart the classes are. If the positions of individual samples are plotted instead of the means, the amount of intermingling of samples may likewise be visualized.

2.5. Stepwise Discriminant Analysis
A basic problem in DA is deciding which of the response variables to include in the analysis. One approach to screening the variables is to consider all possible combinations of response variables. Based on some specified criterion, the 'best' equation is selected. 'Best' in this sense means that no other combination of variables provides better discrimination. However, this approach requires a considerable amount of computational time especially when there are a large number of response variables.

SDA is a method for seeking out subsets of variables most useful to discriminate between the treatment groups. It is very similar to the method of stepwise regression analysis (SRA), and several approaches are available for selecting a subset of variables to provide a good discrimination model. Most of the techniques available are based primarily on either a forward-selection or backward-elimination process.

The forward-selection approach begins with no variables in the model. At each step, the variable is entered that contributes most to the discriminating power measured by some method of criterion selection. Some forward-selection procedures provide the option for also deleting a variable after each step if its contribution to the discriminating functions falls below a specified significance level.

The backward-elimination approach begins with all variables in the model. At each step the variable that contributes the least to the discriminatory power as measured by some criterion is removed from the equation. The process continues until all remaining variables meet the criterion to stay in the equation.

The user of SDA needs to keep in mind some reservations with respect to the process. One imperfection is that many significance tests are performed; consequently some of the apparently significant relations observed represent random covariation, 'significance' by chance alone. Also, the combination of variables selected may not be the 'best' for that number in the equation. For example, in the forward-selection approach, the second variable is selected for its contribution after the first. Therefore, if a five-variable equation is selected, then the fifth variable was the one that made the most contribution to the four-variable combination selected in the previous step. The five-variable equation may not consist of the combination of five variables which provides the 'best' discrimination.

Despite these limitations, the stepwise approaches are especially useful in exploratory research where one needs to screen a large set of response variables in order to find a smaller subset that will provide good discriminating power.

2.6. Discriminant Analysis Computer Programs

Several computerized statistical software systems provide the researcher with a variety of DA programs. Three systems, widely used, are the Statistical Analysis System (SAS) (1985), the Biomedical Computer Programs (BMDP) (1979), and the Statistical Package for the Social Sciences (SPSS) (1975). SAS and SPSS provide separate programs for doing multiple-group linear discrimination and SDA. The 1979 version of the BMDP package provides only a SDA program. Prior versions provided SDA and MDA programs. Although the reader should obviously consult each of the three manuals for specific details as to the various options available, it is also important however to discuss here some of the similarities and differences of the programs.

The DISCRIM program of the SAS package prints out discriminant function coefficients, but it does so only if the pooled covariance matrix is used to calculate the squared generalized distance. A test of homogeneity is applied to the VC matrices for each group. If the test is significant, i.e. heterogeneity exists among the VC matrices, then the generalized distance between groups is calculated using the individual VC matrices for each group and in that case a linear discriminant function is not calculated. Instead a quadratic function is produced. Inasmuch as pooled sensory scores are almost invariably somewhat heterogeneous, the linear discriminant function coefficients are hardly ever available as a part of the regular statistics printed out for such data. If one utilizes the CDA program, however, one can secure both the standardized canonical coefficients and the raw canonical coefficients. From the latter, calculations can be made as to which class an individual specimen probably belongs. If the individual VC matrices are heterogeneous, there is bias in that a specimen is more likely to be assigned to a class with wide dispersion than to one more homogeneous.

The SPSS program provides greater freedom to the investigator. The classification functions for each class are printed. As explained above, the specimen is assigned to the class, the classification functions of which yield the highest weighted mean. There are as many sets of classification coefficients as classes.

All three systems have a SDA program. The BMDP program provides for either forward selection or backward elimination based on the multivariate F value specified by the user. SAS also provides for either the forward or backward process. SAS requires that the user specify a significance level or a partial R^2 value for variables either to enter or to stay in the equation. The SAS package suggests that a moderate significance level of 0·10–0·25 be used. Wilks' lambda, the likelihood ratio criterion, is used as the measure at each step for determining which variable contributes the most or least to the discriminating power depending on which option is selected.

The SPSS program provides for an even wider selection of means of carrying on or making decisions at each step than do the SAS and BMDP programs. The SPSS program permits the selection of variables to be based on Wilks' lambda as does the SAS program. The criterion is the overall multivariate F ratio for the test of differences among the group centroids. The variable which maximizes the F ratio also minimizes Wilks' lambda, a measure of group discrimination. This test takes into consideration the differences between all the centroids and the homogeneity within the groups. A second criterion which may be used is maximization of the Euclidean distance between the two closest groups. A third criterion is the maximin F value which maximizes the smallest F ratio between pairs of groups. The F ratio is the test of the Mahalanobis

D^2 value, i.e. the Euclidean distance, but the second and the third criteria do not necessarily yield the same results when the groups are of unequal size. A fourth criterion is the minresid procedure which is a measure of 1·0 minus the square of the multiple correlation between the set of discriminating variables being considered and a dummy variable. Basically the thing being estimated is the residual variation. The fifth criterion is Rao's V, a generalized distance measure. The variable selected is the one which contributes the largest increase in V when added to the previous variables. This amounts to the greatest overall separation of the groups.

Aside from the algorithms involved, the investigator naturally is interested in the amount of information provided by the different programs. The SAS program summarizes, for example, only the statistics attached to each variable selected. Classification functions are not given. The BMDP and SPSS programs list out the classification functions which avoids having to run the entire stepwise process over if one wants to add merely one more case. The fact that the classification functions are not printed out as a part of the SAS program is not a serious disadvantage, for the primary function of the stepwise process is to select variables. The actual yielding of a classification matrix is useful but classification can be achieved in other ways, e.g. by use of LDA. Moreover, even after the set of classification variables is first determined by SDA, the investigator may want to edit the list further. When that is done, the classification functions need to be re-calculated because the weight each variable has assigned to it depends in part on the other variables making up the combination of variables.

One difference between the packages is that the criterion for entry and deletion is specified as an F value for the BMDP program whereas, as stated above, the SAS program requires a significance level or partial R^2 value to be specified. For the BMDP program, the first F to enter is the same as the univariate F for the variable with the highest F value. The F to enter is computed thereafter from a one-way analysis of covariance where the covariates are the previously entered variables. In essence, at each stage for the forward-step procedure the variable is entered that contributes most to the discriminatory power of the model as measured by Wilks' lambda, the likelihood ratio criterion. The SAS package cautions that when many significance tests are performed each at some given level, let's say, 5%, the overall probability of rejecting at least one true null hypothesis is much larger than 5%; accordingly, if the investigator wants to guard against including any variables that do not contribute appreciably to the discriminatory power of the model, he or she should specify a very small probability level. If however, one wants to choose the model providing the best discriminatory power, one needs only to guard against choosing more parameters than can be reliably estimated with the given sample size. Vuataz (1981) re-affirms the points above. He ran simulation tests. He recommends that the F-to-enter and the F-to-delete should not be set too high. He states further that the probability of identical products being declared different increases as the number of descriptors necessary to their complete description increases.

3. ILLUSTRATED APPLICATIONS

So far the methods of DA and available computer programs have been described in general terms to sketch out their background. Further description can be presented more effectively if various facets of DA are coordinated with actual illustration of applications and interpretation of results.

3.1. SDA

A typical application of SDA is that utilized by Godwin *et al.* (1977) to determine whether untrained judges were capable of differentiating among the quality attributes of six lots of blue cheese. A dairy techno-logist wished to learn whether (1) cheese experts, (2) the trained assessors of a typical dairy-products judging team and (3) consumers would agree in their evaluation of the quality of the blue cheese. He had expert cheese buyers from six companies each select a specimen which they considered to represent blue cheese of high quality. Each expert in turn graded the cheese selected by himself and the five others. The trained assessors of the dairy judging team likewise graded the six products. Using profile analysis, 25 consumers scaled the intensities of 28 attributes of the cheese. The responses of nine of the panelists were deleted because the panelists were not discriminating for enough of the 28 attributes (Powers, 1979, 1984a,b). Table 2 lists the 28 descriptive terms employed and the F value for each term based on the pooled response of the 16 panelists retained. The individual F values may be obtained from the P7M program since the 1979 version of BMDP prints out an univariate analysis for each variable.

Table 3 lists the order in which the various terms of Table 2 were selected to yield an effective combination of classifying terms. Based on

TABLE 2
F VALUES OBTAINED UPON EXAMINING 6 LOTS OF BLUE CHEESE, THE CHEESE HAVING BEEN SCALED FOR 28 ATTRIBUTES BY 16 ASSESSORS, TRIALS REPLICATED 3 TIMES

Term	F value	Term	F value
Veining, extent of	56·84	Acceptability	3·43
Moldiness, amount of	45·18	Solvent-like	2·95
Whiteness of curd	34·07	Saltiness	2·65
Pastiness	27·19	Acidulousness	2·48
Yellowness of curd	24·67	Unpleasant aftertaste	2·42
Dryness	18·99	Ammonia-like	2·24
Appearance of curd	17·16	Astringency	2·17
Crumbliness	15·37	Bitterness	2·16
General appearance	12·56	Sweetness	2·00
Oiliness	7·24	Pleasant aftertaste	1·75
Graininess	6·96	Body	1·20
Blueness of curd	5·26	Balance of flavor	1·06
Pepperiness	5·26	Mustiness	0·84
Flavor	4·38	Soapiness	0·68

experience, the F value to enter or delete a variable was set at 2·0. One thing the reader may observe is that some terms having low F values were selected in preference to others having higher F values. Note that graininess and pepperiness, having F values of 6·96 and 5·26, respectively,

TABLE 3
ORDER OF ENTRY OF CLASSIFYING TERMS AND ASSOCIATED STATISTICS, BMDP PROGRAM p7M, 281 DF, F VALUE TO ENTER OR DELETE A TERM = 2·0.

Step	Term entered	F value	Multivariate F	U statistic	df
1	Veining	56·84	56·83	0·4972	5/280
2	White	33·36	44·33	0·3116	5/279
3	Pasty	28·00	39·44	0·2075	5/278
4	Mold, amount of	17·73	34·45	0·1573	5/277
5	Yellow	13·09	30·58	0·1272	5/276
6	Crumbly	6·12	26·51	0·1145	5/275
7	Flavor	5·34	23·55	0·1044	5/274
8	Oily	4·28	21·21	0·0968	5/273
9	Astringent	4·27	19·42	0·0898	5/272
10	Appearance	2·50	17·74	0·0859	5/271
11	Bitter	2·37	16·36	0·0823	5/270
12	Solvent	2·63	15·26	0·0785	5/269
13	Curd	2·53	14·33	0·0749	5/268
14	Balance	2·16	13·49	0·0720	5/267

were not selected, but solvent and balance, having F values of 2·95 and 1·06, were. The purpose of DA is to seek out the combination of tests which provides the greatest amount of information in aid of classification. If one test is highly correlated with another or·moderately correlated with several and these other tests have already been included in the step process, the correlated terms would not be providing new information useful for discrimination but only information partially redundant with that already available. A variable which by itself is not a great discriminator but which is not well correlated with any other variable already in use is more likely to add to the discrimination power than one which is correlated. Examination of the correlation matrix revealed that graininess was correlated with such terms as pastiness and crumbly. Pepperiness was related to several of the other terms. It thus was not selected. If an attribute such as saltiness or pepperiness is common to all the products, then it is a good descriptor but it may not be a good discriminator. Palmer (1974) has pointed out that this distinction should always be kept in mind. Piggott and Jardine (1979) contend that Wu et al. (1977) were in error in dropping apt descriptors though they were ineffective as discriminators. Powers (1984b) commented upon the desirability of making a case by case decision. Some of the other kinds of statistics listed in Table 3 are obvious whereas a comment perhaps needs to be made about others. The fourth column of Table 3 lists the multivariate F values. They decline as new, but less effective, components are added to the classifying function. When F was set at 4·0, the program ran through the ninth step. That fact may be seen from Table 3. Column 5 lists the U statistic. It corresponds to Wilks' lambda criterion, and in a crude sense it can be looked upon as an error term. The smaller the value becomes, the closer is the classification coming to perfection. The degrees of freedom (df) have of course their usual meaning. At the first step, there were 5 df for the six products and 281 df as a remainder once the 1 general df and the 5 df for products had been removed. The reason there were 287 df total instead of 288 is that there was one set of evaluations missing (6 products × 3 replications × 16 assessors = 288).

Table 4 depicts the classification matrix based on the 14 tests listed in Table 3. The 'jackknifed' designation indicates that the case being classified was not utilized in calculating the weighting values for the 14-term classification functions used to assign cases to classes. When all the cases, including the one being assigned to a class, were included, the success was 76·3%, only marginally higher than the jackknifed clas-

TABLE 4

JACKKNIFED CLASSIFICATION MATRIX, 6 LOTS OF CHEESE, 287 CASES CLASSIFIED

Cheese lot	Percent correct	Number of cases classified into lot						
		A	B	C	D	E	F	Total
A	81·3	39	1	2	1	1	4	48
B	72·9	1	35	4	2	4	2	48
C	64·6	3	5	31	4	3	2	48
D	70·8	1	4	9	34	0	0	48
E	77·1	1	4	1	0	37	5	48
F	53·2	7	5	3	1	6	25	47
Total	70·0	52	54	50	42	51	38	287

sification. The reason a case being classified should not be included in establishing the classification function is that it biases the function since it is a contributor to its own determination.

Before proceeding, a 'case' needs to be defined. In the instant trial, a case is one set of scores assigned by one assessor. There are thus 287 cases (Table 4). One of the features of the BMDP package is that the assignment of cases is printed out with a notation as to the true class and the class to which the case was assigned.

3.1.1. SDA Computer Packages
To illustrate differences between computer packages, most of the summary table from the forward-selection procedure of the SAS program (1982) is set forth in Table 5. Table 6 shows the SAS summary table for backward elimination applied to the same data set. There is another option, designated 'stepwise', which permits a variable once selected to be deleted if its contribution to discrimination becomes nonsignificant.

In several respects, the SAS summary table gives considerably more information to guide the investigator than does the BMDP summary table.

3.2. Standardization
Before leaving SDA, one phase of the process should be mentioned. Standardization is not necessary to calculate a linear discriminant function (Fisher, 1936; Goulden, 1952). Most computer programs standardize the variables, but that is done to make possible or simplify certain

TABLE 5

SUMMARY TABLE, SAS PROGRAM STEPDISC, FORWARD SELECTION, 287 CASES OF BLUE CHEESE, EVALUATED, PROBABILITY TO ENTER OR DELETE SET AT 0·15

Step	Variable entered	Number in	Partial R^2	F statistic	Prob. > F	Wilks' lambda	Prob. > lambda	Average squared canonical correlation	Prob. > asscc
1	Veining	1	0·50	56·84	0·000	0·497	0·000	0·101	0·000
2	White	2	0·37	33·36	0·000	0·312	0·000	0·175	0·000
3	Pasty	3	0·33	27·00	0·000	0·207	0·000	0·226	0·000
4	Mold	4	0·24	17·73	0·000	0·157	0·000	0·265	0·000
5	Yellow	5	0·19	13·09	0·000	0·127	0·000	0·292	0·000
6	Crumbly	6	0·10	6·12	0·000	0·114	0·000	0·306	0·000
7	Flavor	7	0·09	5·34	0·000	0·104	0·000	0·318	0·000
8	Oily	8	0·07	4·28	0·001	0·097	0·000	0·326	0·000
9	Astringent	9	0·07	4·27	0·001	0·090	0·000	0·334	0·000
10	Appearance	10	0·04	2·50	0·031	0·086	0·000	0·341	0·000
11	Bitter	11	0·04	2·37	0·040	0·082	0·000	0·348	0·000
12	Solvent	12	0·05	2·63	0·024	0·078	0·000	0·354	0·000
13	Curd	13	0·05	2·53	0·029	0·749	0·000	0·359	0·000
14	Balance	14	0·04	2·16	0·582	0·072	0·000	0·363	0·000
15	Salty	15	0·04	1·99	0·080	0·069	0·000	0·369	0·000
16	Sweet	16	0·03	1·86	0·102	0·067	0·000	0·373	0·000

TABLE 6

BACKWARD ELIMINATION OF CLASSIFYING VARIABLES, SAS PROGRAM STEPDISC, 287 CASES OF BLUE CHEESE, PROBABILITY TO ENTER OR DELETE VARIABLE SET AT 0·15

Step	Variable deleted	Number in	Partial R^2	F statistic	Prob. > F	Wilks' lambda	Prob. > lambda	Average squared canonical correlation	Prob. > asscc
0		28						0·402	0·000
1	Soapy	27	0·01	0·34	0·889	0·053	0·000	0·401	0·000
2	Blue	26	0·01	0·67	0·649	0·053	0·000	0·399	0·000
3	Body	25	0·02	0·72	0·611	0·054	0·000	0·397	0·000
4	Astringent	24	0·02	0·84	0·052	0·055	0·000	0·395	0·000
5	Unplaft	23	0·02	0·86	0·508	0·056	0·000	0·393	0·000
6	Grainy	22	0·02	0·92	0·467	0·057	0·000	0·391	0·000
7	Dry	21	0·02	1·19	0·314	0·058	0·000	0·389	0·000
8	Musty	20	0·03	1·33	0·250	0·059	0·000	0·387	0·000
9	Appearance	19	0·02	1·22	0·298	0·060	0·000	0·384	0·000
10	Plesaft	18	0·02	1·32	0·256	0·062	0·000	0·380	0·000

other calculations. In standardization the means are set to zero and the raw measurement values are scaled in terms of the standard deviation.

3.3. LDA

An application of SDA was illustrated first because SDA logically should precede LDA when the data set is at all voluminous. If SDA is not applied to remove some of the chaff, then all the variables will be included in the classification functions even though many of the variables are really useless as classifying agents. If SDA does not precede LDA, generally at least two LDA calculations are needed. First, all the data are analyzed. From the print-out of the correlation coefficients of each variable with the discriminant functions, one may observe where the last major decrease in the coefficients occurs. Investigators often then decide subjectively to eliminate variables below the last major drop on the ground they contribute little to the discriminant function. That method is basically the scree process (Cattell, 1966). A more objective procedure is to carry on SDA first, delete variables possessing little classifying power, then apply LDA. When that is done, one secures directly a LDA function not encumbered with terms detracting from effectiveness. The advantage LDA has as compared with SDA is that it is more practical if one wants to predict the class to which an unknown specimen should be assigned (see Section 2.3).

Tables 7 and 8 illustrate the process of using the classification coefficients to calculate the weighted means which in turn are used to assign unknown specimens to a class. The original data were GLC peak areas for a product of a food company with four branch plants in North America. There was no question about the acceptability of the product. It was well within quality-assurance bounds. Indeed, sensory differences could be detected only with sensitive and carefully applied difference tests. The company wished to learn whether chemical analysis could be used to corroborate decisions made on the basis of sensory analysis.

Application of SDA with the multivariate F to enter or delete a variable set at 2·0 and 1·8, respectively, yielded a combination of seven GLC peaks which allowed product discrimination to be attained. Classification coefficients and constants for the seven variables are listed in the upper part of Table 7. The U-statistic for the seven steps indicated that probably four peaks would suffice to effect product resolution; accordingly a second SDA was made with the number of variables restricted to four. The resulting coefficients and constants are listed in the lower part of Table 7. From the classifying coefficients (Table 7) for the

TABLE 7

COMPARISON OF CLASSIFYING COEFFICIENTS AND CONSTANTS FOR THE ASSIGNMENT OF SAMPLES TO A CLASS

Variable class	Seven-term classifying functions			
	1	2	3	4
GC-38	292·61	1 393·16	− 76·24	− 44·61
GC-32	94·05	− 179·15	957·98	1 459·31
GC-21	5·51	− 85·35	106·77	− 16·48
GC-1	24·01	27·14	71·48	81·66
GC-30	1 155·68	3 983·25	− 2 789·00	− 839·89
GC-13	248·58	1 065·58	− 382·86	555·55
GC-20	166·27	− 428·33	222·04	− 738·76
Constant	− 427·00	− 1 117·17	− 1 164·82	− 1 273·08

	Four-term classifying functions			
	1	2	3	4
GC-38	78·61	855·63	171·37	− 18·24
GC-32	279·05	64·19	447·17	539·38
GC-21	31·10	35·78	52·27	33·79
GC-1	28·82	32·97	50·85	44·06
Constant	− 327·93	− 643·06	− 912·58	− 735·42

four-term functions and the measurement values listed in Table 8, an illustration is first given of the calculation of a weighted mean. The classification coefficients were based on four replicate determinations. The bottom portion of Table 8 shows the procedure used to assign unknown specimens to a class. In this instance, the specimens designated Products 1 and 4 actually were individual samples analyzed as replicates five or six. Two replicate sets of determinations were held back to learn whether the weighted means based on four replicate determinations would indeed predict the class to which a product truly belonged. Both samples were assigned to their true classes when the four-term functions were used, but Product 4 was not assigned to class 4 when the seven-term functions were used. The fact that the functions with several terms were not more efficient than the functions with a lesser number of terms should be noted. The reader should note too that one cannot take a subset and use the same weighting values as the members of the subset had in the larger set. The coefficients have to be re-calculated. The ratios among the coefficients are unique to the particular set of variables.

TABLE 8

ILLUSTRATION OF ASSIGNMENT OF A SPECIMEN TO A CLASS VIA
LDA MEASUREMENT VALUES FOR SPECIMEN, AS PEAK
AREA/TOTAL GLC AREA

Measurement	Value	Measurement	Value
GC-38	0·300	GC-30	0·439
GC-32	0·925	GC-13	0·035
GC-21	8·975	GC-20	0·586
GC-1	0·225		

Calculation of weighted mean for class 1, four-term function (see Table 8)

$$Z = 78·61(0·300) + 279·05(0·925) + 31·10(8·975) + 28·82(0·225) - 327·93$$
$$Z = 23·58 + 258·12 + 279·12 + 6·48 - 327·93 = 239·37$$

	Weighted means calculated			
		Weighted means		
Real identity	Class 1	Class 2	Class 3	Class 4
Product 1, 4-terms	239·37	1.56	33·02	71·21
Product 1, 7-terms	1 985·76	− 14 280·06	716·21	− 7 712·55
Product 4, 4-terms	799·2	206·31	934·79	1 122·49
Product 4, 7-terms	2 448·55	− 356·24	− 1 171·12	− 7 152·03

3.4. Canonical Discriminant Analysis

SDA or LDA tells the analyst the class to which an individual specimen probably belongs, but the results are nominal. For the former at least, the investigator does not know how far apart the classes are. Canonical analysis overcomes that deficiency. Figure 3 shows relations among the six cheese samples when their plotting positions were calculated based on canonical variables 1 and 2. Options available in the P7M program of the BMDP package permit calculation of the mean coordinates for the samples and a plot such as Fig. 3. The user of the program may likewise specify that the plotting position of each case be depicted. CDA may furthermore be used to provide a quantitative measure of the distance between classes. Table 9 lists in the portion of the table above the diagonal the interclass distances between the six blue cheese products. In the portion below the diagonal are listed the probabilities of the dis-

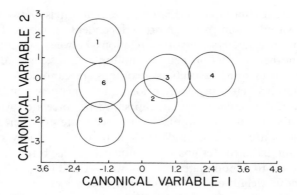

FIG. 3. Geometric representation of the six blue-cheese products based on canonical discriminant analysis.

TABLE 9

MAHALANOBIS DISTANCE[a] BETWEEN BLUE-CHEESE PRODUCTS AND PROBABILITY OF THE DISTANCE BEING GREATER

| Product | Product | | | | | |
	1	2	3	4	5	6
1		3·72	3·66	4·48	3·93	2·66
2	0·00		2·69	2·72	2·50	2·65
3	0·00	0·00		2·56	3·49	2·98
4	0·00	0·00	0·00		4·49	4·06
5	0·00	0·00	0·00	0·00		2·41
6	0·00	0·00	0·00	0·00	0·00	

[a]Values above the diagonal are the Mahalanobis distance; values below the diagonal are the probability levels. Probability shown only to the second decimal place; in actuality, all probabilities were < 0·000000.

tances being greater. As is obvious, there is less than 1×10^{-6} probability that the classes are not significantly different.

CDA is a variant of canonical analysis. Inasmuch as canonical correlation is described in Chapter 9, distinctions between canonical-variate and canonical-correlation analysis need not be discussed other than to re-affirm that canonical analysis involves the establishment of relations between *sets* of variables. Simple correlation between two single variables is a special case of canonical analysis as is either multiple correlation or regression. As to multiple regression, the relation is between a single dependent variable and two or more independent variables. The general case of canonical analysis involves relations between sets of variables. There is another distinction between multiple regression and canonical analysis which in some respects is fortuitous. In canonical analysis one does not have to make any assumption as to dependency/independency. When chemical differences merely happen to be correlated with the sensory ones, the assumption would be inappropriate, for then the chemical differences are no more independent than the sensory ones. Since one does not have to designate a canonical set as being dependent— or in fact have to denominate it in any way—there is less of a tendency to place undue weight on the import of one set as compared with others.

Sensory data can in fact be either dependent or independent. Sensory acceptability or the grade of a product depends upon one's response to the individual sensory properties. In that case, the individual attributes— though sensory—are truly independent variables. The chemical composition or various physical properties of a material such as color, viscosity or elasticity may determine one's sensory response to individual attributes. In that case, the sensory attributes are dependent. If there is mere correlation and not a true cause-and-effect relation, neither set, as already stated, should preemptively be considered to be the independent one. Though the sets need not be verbally described sometimes particular variables are forced to be in a designated set. The investigator may wish to match chemical measurements versus a set of sensory responses (see Section 5.2) or attitudinal versus behavioral responses to food.

In CVA, the objective is to find a linear combination of set X and of Y measurements such that the correlation is maximized. A further objective then is to find a second set of correlations which likewise is at a maximum, but is zero correlated with the first set. The number of linear correlations cannot exceed the number of variables in the X or Y set, whichever is smaller. Thorndike (1978) cautions that the sample size should be at least 10 times greater than the number of variables and that for small sets of variables an additional 50 cases should be included.

Figure 3 was obtained upon applying the P7M program of the BMDP package and Table 9 by applying the CANDISC program of the SAS (1982) package. The CANDISC program could have been used to print out a plot of the 287 cases, the means of the six products, or both. Had the 287 cases been plotted, moderately severe intrusion of the plotting points for one product into the confidence zones of other products would have been evident. Overlapping of the frequency distribution curves for individual samples (cases) though the products means are significantly different was illustrated earlier (Fig. 1). Only two of the confidence limits (Chatfield and Collins, 1980) for the means of the blue cheese overlapped (Fig. 3). For the typical sensory application, the frequency distribution curves almost always overlap some. Three obvious reasons suggest themselves. Firstly, products being examined are normally already well within a rather restricted range of acceptability (Powers, 1979, 1981a). Secondly, the error of measurement for sensory evaluation is likely to be greater than for most chemical or physical measurements. It is virtually impossible for an assessor—even a highly trained one—to reproduce his (her) responses from day to day with the same constancy as can be attained upon using typical, well-established chemical/physical methods. Thirdly, product–assessor interaction adds still further to dispersion. For the three reasons given, it would have been the exception had none of the 48 cases for one product intruded into the confidence zones of any of the other five products.

3.5. Nearest-neighbor Procedure

The fourth method of DA to be illustrated by example is the NN procedure. Instead of using the responses of the 16 assessors of blue cheese as has been done so far, a subgroup of nine of the 16 assessors will be employed. The subgroup of nine was selected from the 16 assessors by cluster analysis (discussed in Chapter 10) so as to lessen product–assessor interaction. That was done for two reasons. One was to document that assessors often follow different pathways in judging the specific and hedonic qualities of products; yet the conclusions drawn from their responses lead to the same conclusion, e.g. the products or classes are different (or not different). Discussion of that subject will be reserved until we come to 'ramifications' (Section 4). The second reason was to permit a comparison of SDA and NN with confounding caused by product–assessor interaction reduced somewhat.

The upper part of Table 10 shows the jackknifed classification resulting when the assessments of the panelists comprising the cluster of 9 were analyzed by SDA. The lower part of the table displays the results when the NN procedure was applied to the same data set. While the results differ somewhat, they agree in general. Product 6 was misclassified the most often by the SDA procedure. The process for assigning cases to a class was explained earlier for that procedure. By the NN procedure, products 3 and 6 tied for frequency of misclassification. The NN procedure does not require that the classes have multivariate normal distributions. Assignment to a class can either be according to the Mahalanobis distance between X_1 and X_2 based on the total-sample VC

TABLE 10

COMPARISON OF PERCENTAGE EFFICIENCY IN THE CLASSIFICATION OF 162 CASES
OF CHEESE PRODUCTS BY SDA AND NN PROCEDURES, 9 MEMBER CLUSTER

Product	Percentage correct	SDA jackknifed classification Cases classified into groups						Total
		1	2	3	4	5	6	
1	66·7	18	0	2	0	1	6	27
2	77·8	1	21	3	1	0	1	27
3	59·3	2	4	16	3	1	1	27
4	63·0	0	1	9	17	0	0	27
5	63·0	2	3	2	0	17	3	27
6	37·0	6	4	2	0	5	10	27
Total averages	61·1	29	33	34	21	24	21	162

NN CLASSIFICATION SUMMARY, DISTANCE FUNCTION: $D^2(X,Y)=(X-Y)'\text{COV}^{-1}(X-Y)$

Product	Number of cases (top row) and percentage classified into product (bottom row)						Total
	1	2	3	4	5	6	
1	15	4	3	1	1	3	27
	55·6	14·8	11·1	3·7	3·7	11·1	100·0
2	1	14	6	1	1	4	27
	3·7	51·9	22·2	3·7	3·7	14·8	100·0
3	2	7	8	4	2	4	27
	7·4	25·9	29·6	14·8	7·4	14·8	100·0
4	5	3	4	13	0	2	27
	18·5	11·1	14·8	48·2	0·0	7·4	100·0
5	2	4	1	0	12	8	27
	7·4	14·8	3·7	0·0	44·4	29·6	100·0
6	3	5	6	2	3	8	75
	11·1	18·5	22·7	7·4	11·1	29·6	100·0
Total	28	37	28	21	19	29	162
percentage	17·3	22·8	17·3	13·0	11·7	17·9	100·0

matrix:

$$D^2(X_1, X_2) = (X_1 - X_2)'\text{COV}^{-1}(X_1 - X_2)$$

or optionally the Euclidean distance,

$$D^2(X_1 X_2) = (X_1 - X_2)'(X_1 - X_2)$$

Using the NN rule, the k smallest distances are saved. Of these k distances, let n_i represent the number of distances that correspond to group i. The posterior probability of membership in group i is:

$$P_i = \frac{m_i \text{prior}_i}{\Sigma m_j \text{prior}_j}$$

The observation, in other words, is placed in the class containing the highest proportion of the k nearest neighbors, or, optionally, the proportion of NN items according to a prior probability level set for the classes. Unless there is a tie for largest or unless the maximum probability is less than the threshold specified, X_2 is classified into a group designated as 'other'.

4. RAMIFICATIONS

So far the basis for classification has not been defined other than to say that the classes should be discrete. There ought to be strong, advance and independent evidence that discrete classes exist. A sensory problem was chosen to illustrate different facets of DA, classification being one, for sensory data invariably provoke more problems and more complex ones than occur in the analysis of the typical chemical or physical data set.

4.1. Classification

By definition one of the rudimentary elements of DA is that there be classes. The classification in Table 4 was made on the assumption that there were six classes, but that might not have been so. Two of the buyers might have purchased cheese from the same source. That occurrence is unlikely, but possible. Even if the cheese were bought from different sources, two of the lots might have been so close together in their characteristics as not to constitute distinct classes. There is always an element of doubt when there is not advance, strong, external evidence of there being some certain number of classes. From a pragmatic point of view however, if DA permits the samples to be assigned to the assumed classes, then for all practical purposes classes exist. If classification is poor, however, the investigator may be in doubt. He or she does not know whether the tests were inappropriate to detect class differences or the number of assumed classes was in error. The analysis of Godwin *et al.* (1977) and the various analyses illustrated here demonstrate that the six means were significantly different. They could represent a continuum, but the canonical plotting positions of Fig. 3 lend little weight to that assumption. There being as good a reason to assume that the products form classes as to believing they are a continuum, there is no reason to reject DA as being an inappropriate method of analysis.

We can presume that Fisher (1936) knew, based on taxonomic criteria, that three classes of irises existed and that his 150 specimens belonged to some one of the three classes. In sensory analysis, that same certainty often does not prevail. If such things as brand labels or formulations are used as the basis for classification, they may be misleading. Producers often market the very same product under two or more different labels. We have encountered a situation where the five lots furnished to us for statistical analysis were represented as being five different formulations or process variations (Powers, 1984a), but such variations do not necessarily result in distinct sensory classes. Unlike the blue-cheese trial where MVA ultimately indicated that the six lots of cheese most probably represented six sensory classes, as definitive an answer could not be given for the five re-formulation or process-variable products. Not every process or formulation variation leads to a sensory difference. In fact, when ingredient substitution is being considered, the firm involved generally hopes that the substitution will not lead to a sensory change.

In our early studies we used blend ratios to form the classes because at that time we felt the only class we could be fairly sure of was the mathematical ratio produced by blending two different foods in known ratios. Powers and Keith (1968) assumed they had four classes because the two kinds of coffee (Arabica and Robusta) used were types well recognized by the trade as being distinctly different; the other two specimens were a 40:60 and a 60:40 blend of the two distinct kinds of coffee. Young *et al.* (1970) blended Coca-Cola® and Pepsi-Cola® in known ratios; Milutinović *et al.* (1970) did likewise with tomato-juice. The latter group blended canned juice and a juice made from reconstituted tomato powder, again on the presumption that the canned and the reconstituted juices were so different that distinct classes would be formed if the two products were combined in different blend ratios. Application of the triangular test (Bengtsson, 1943) subsequently demonstrated the two cola beverages and the two tomato-juice starting materials were in fact sensorially different.

Though not as acceptable as knowing in advance that classes truly exist, chemical differences have evidentiary value. For the coffee, the cola beverages and the tomato juice trials, GLC examination supported the supposition that the blend ratios were producing different products. The illustrations to follow further document the evidentiary role chemical analysis may play as well as point out applications of physical-chemical analyses. Powers *et al.* (1977) and Godwin *et al.* (1978), using sensory results, attempted to classify four brands of canned green beans, three of frozen beans and one of fresh beans. Eight distinct classes did not result. (Upon classifying the cases as canned or frozen beans, the percentage success was 96%.) When GLC measurements were used as the classifying agent, the 32 specimens available were all assigned based upon only 4 GLC peaks to the appropriate one of the eight classes. There was thus evidence that the eight lots of beans represented eight classes, but that could not be demonstrated sensorially.

Lin (1983) applied DA to the sensory properties and GLC measurements made on four lots of soy sauce. One product was a hydrolyzed soy sauce and three were fermented products. There was thus fair assurance that at least two classes existed, chemically- and fermentatively-produced soy sauce. Among the three fermented products, one was a fancy-grade product, the second was a regular-grade product, both produced in Japan, and the third was a regular-grade product produced in the USA —all by the same company. A basic question was: were the two regular products alike? Lin had two panels, one composed of Orientals, the other of Occidentals. Both panels detected differences in the three lots of fermented soy sauce, but the differences were not great enough to truly claim the products formed three distinct classes. There was no doubt that the hydrolyzed soy sauce was distinctly different from the other three. Just as was true when Godwin *et al.* (1978) applied GLC analysis, Lin was able to classify 18 specimens of the three fermented soy sauces into the appropriate 'class' based on 8 GLC peaks. It could be argued that the three fermented products represent a continuum and that DA was not appropriate. From a practical point of view, if one succeeds in 'classifying' 100% of the specimens into certain groups, the groups are sufficiently discrete to be considered as being classes. From the same point of view, if the classes are close together, they may be looked upon as being a continuum. That was true for some of the blend ratios for the cola beverages and tomato-juice referred to above. If SRA instead of LDA be applied to the data set, the conclusions drawn may be almost identical. At times, there are advantages to using multiple regression instead of LDA to predict relations between the measurement values and a single entity such as flavor desirability. One should not get too wrapped up in theoretical considerations. Provided prudent assumptions are made, either DA or regression analysis may apply depending upon how discrete the classes actually are.

The illustrations above were given in detail for two reasons. If the existence of classes is based on dubious grounds such as brand or formulation differences, use of a supplemental form of analysis is often desirable to learn whether the second method will confirm the first. Powers (1984a) suggested that PCA should be applied to try to verify whether there are as many groups as assumed classes. Piggott and Jardine (1979) followed that procedure when they were evaluating nine brands of Scotch whisky and one of Irish whiskey. From their results it is obvious that there were not 10 distinct sensory classes.

4.2. Analytical Considerations

In presenting tables to illustrate the bare analyses themselves, some considerations were temporarily by-passed though they are important in carrying on analysis or in interpreting the results. Even though the P7M program of the BMDP package prints out an univariate analysis of the data set as well as the SDA phases, the investigator should give consideration to carrying on univariate analysis first. Occasionally univariate analysis will reveal that MVA is unnecessary. To illustrate, when Godwin (1984) applied ANOVA to his data, he observed that any one of several of the high-performance-liquid-chromatographic peaks measured in examining five grades of tea of the same type permitted separation of each of the five grades from the other four. Usually the investigator is not so fortunate, but even if not, initial univariate examination often minimizes computer costs in spite of the investigator needing to go on to MVA.

Univariate analysis to examine for outliers is desirable, for they influence the validity of DA results drastically. A third reason, but one which is less important today than it once was, is that some programs have a limitation as to the number of variables permitted. Today most of the major packages do not have a limitation, but some programs for microcomputers do. If so, the investigator may decide to reduce the number of variables being considered by deleting those having nonsignificant univariate F values. There is risk to that. A variable nonsignificant by itself may contribute to significance when coupled with another variable (see Sections 2.2.1 and 4.2.1). However deleting a variable on the basis of its having a nonsignificant univariate F value may be a less risky procedure than trying to examine all the variables on a batch-wise basis. Powers et al. (1977) and Godwin et al. (1978) chose the first course of action in their study of green beans. They had measurement values for 85 objective tests and evaluations for 31 sensory attributes. Since the 1975 version of BMDP could accommodate only 80 variables, they decided to eliminate nonsignificant variables so as to get below the limitation. The alternative of splitting the variables into batches so that all might be examined multivariately has a flaw too. In sub-grouping data, there is risk of a term being effective when used in combination with another test but of that fact failing to be detected because one of the terms is initially in one batch and the other in a second batch. Inclusion of several of the same terms in different batches lessens the likelihood of that untoward event occurring. Eventually, of course, the terms reduced in number have to be examined while all are in the same set.

4.2.1. Colinearity

The mere fact that ANOVA shows that a test is effective does not necessarily mean that it will be used as a discriminator. Among the tests retained because they are effective as discriminators of product differences, some may still not be useful—see Section 3.1—because they are correlated with other tests. If effective tests are substantially correlated, SDA will usually reject all but one for the reasons explained in Section 3.1. SDA is thus initially a winnowing process to eliminate chaff or colinear tests; then it is a ferreting process to seek out the combination of tests which is the most effective for the classification of samples. As mentioned above, occasionally tests, nonsignificant according to ANOVA, are included in the DA combination of tests. Not evident from Table 8 is the fact that GLC peak No. 13 by itself was non-effective as a discriminator. Its univariate F value was 1.10. It was selected as one member of the classifying function because in combination with the others it did aid significantly in discrimination. Even though two illustrations have been given of tests nonsignificant by themselves being included in the discriminating set, that occurrence is rare.

4.2.2. Deletion of Variable Already Selected

None of the illustrations given so far illustrate the fact that sometimes a variable already selected may later be deleted from the most effective combination. Table 11 illustrates that occurrence. The data came from the study of Powers et al. (1977) and Godwin et al. (1978). Note that sweet was the 11th variable selected. At the 15th step however it was deleted. Three other variables had come into the step process in the meantime. Those terms in combination with the terms selected earlier

TABLE 11

SDA ARRAY OF SENSORY AND OBJECTIVE TESTS POOLED

SDA step	Variable entered	Variable removed	F value	U statistic	F to enter or remove	Approximate F-statistic	df
1	GC34		66·46	0·0491	66·46	66·46	7/23
2	GC33		39·53	0·0045	32·35	45·57	7/22
3	GC1		25·04	0·0004	30·07	42·17	7/21
4	Color-2		19·48	0·0001	15·55	36·50	7/20
5	GC21		16·09	0·0000	13·12	33·82	7/19
6	GC39		15·47	0·0000	14·09	33·96	7/18
7	GC26		6·94	0·0000	11·57	34·32	7/17
8	LC7		33·07	0·0000	8·29	34·03	7/16
9	CR8		29·36	0·0000	7·98	34·58	7/15
10	GC32		16·37	0·0000	6·19	34·73	7/14
11	Sweet		5·53	0·0000	5·46	35·04	7/13
12	GC35		8·75	0·0000	4·88	35·47	7/12
13	FPER		4·32	0·0000	4·26	35·87	7/11
14	GC18		16·27	0·0000	4·64	37·14	7/10
15		Sweet	5·53	0·0000	3·95	36·57	7/11
16		GC32	16·37	0·0000	3·60	36·90	7/12
17	Slimy		3·97	0·0000	5·45	38·41	7/11

contributed more to the coefficient of determination than did sweetness. Inasmuch as $F = 4 \cdot 0$ had been set as the criterion to accept or delete a variable, sweetness was deleted as was GC32. The reader should note that when these two terms were removed as classifiers, two df were temporarily regained.

4.3. Percentage Success
When the jackknifed classification was given (Table 4) for the blue cheese trial, the reader—especially one used to dealing with objective measurements—might have thought that success of only 70% is low. As already noted, Godwin *et al.* (1978) using GLC data were 100% successful in classifying samples of green beans after only the fourth step. In contrast, our experience (Powers and Quinlan, 1974; Powers, 1979, 1981a, 1982a, 1984a) is that success in classification based on sensory evaluation alone rarely exceeds 90% and more commonly the success level is approximately 80% (Brown and Clapperton, 1978; Levitt, 1974; Hwang-Choi, 1982).

The sensory profiling system used was essentially that of Stone *et al.* (1974) except a practice was followed which Sidel and Stone (1976) do not recommend. They specify that trained assessors should be used for profile analysis. Our experience is that consumers, provided they are properly instructed as to what is expected of them, are considerably more consistent and discriminating in their evaluations than many people give them credit for. The experience of Wu *et al.* (1977) attests to that. In evaluating white and red wines, their untrained panelists (consumers) were quite consistent and adept at evaluating most of the 33 attributes specified. In the blue cheese study 16 out of the 25 panelists were efficient—though untrained—at scaling the intensities of the specific attributes. Piggott and Canaway's (1981) experience with untrained panelists was likewise gratifying.

4.4. Cluster Analysis
That the 16 panelists who appraised the blue cheese did not all respond in unison should not be unexpected inasmuch as they were consumers. Even trained assessors do not always scale products as one. They too cause product–assessor interaction (Powers, 1984b). Sometimes such interactive effects need to be minimized before DA procedures can be fully effective.

Table 12 shows how the 16 panelists clustered out when Ward's minimum variance hierarchical cluster analysis (SAS, 1982) was applied

TABLE 12

CLUSTER ANALYSIS APPLIED TO 16 ASSESSORS WHO WERE EFFECTIVE FOR MOST ATTRIBUTES UPON EVALUATING THE BLUE CHEESE PRODUCTS

Number of Clusters	Assessors															
	2	3	10	11	12	13	15	16	17	18	19	20	21	22	24	25
1	X	X	X	X	X	X	X	X	X	X	X	X	X	X	X	X
2	X	X	X	X	X	X	X	X	X	X	X	X	X	X	X	X
3	X	X	X	X	X	X	X	X	X	X	X	X	X	X	X	.
4	X	X	X	X	X	X	X	X	X	X	X	X	X	X	.	.
5	X	X	X	X	X	X	X	X	X	X	X	X	X	.	.	.
6	X	X	X	X	X	X	X	X	X	X	X	X	.	.	.	.
7	X	X	X	X	X	X	X	X	X	X	X	.	.	.	.	.
8	X	X	X	X	X	X	X	X	X	X	.	.	.	.	.	.
9	X	X	X	X	X	X	X	X	X	.	.	.	.	.	.	.
10	X	X	X	X	X	X	X	X	.	.	.	.	.	.	.	.
11	X	X	X	X	X	X	X	.	.	.	.	.	.	.	.	.
12	X	X	X	X	X	X	.	.	.	.	.	.	.	.	.	.
13	X	X	X	X	X	.	.	.	.	.	.	.	.	.	.	.
14	X	X	X	X	.	.	.	.	.	.	.	.	.	.	.	.
15	X	X	X	.	.	.	.	.	.	.	.	.	.	.	.	.
16	X	X	.	.	.	.	.	.	.	.	.	.	.	.	.	.

to the scale values assigned by the 16 respondents. Clustering was based on the 14 terms listed in Table 3. Panelists 2 and 3 will not be considered further. When SDA was applied to the responses of the panelists comprising each of the other two clusters, note that it revealed that the members of the two different clusters were not making their discriminations of product differences upon the basis of the same terms nor the same order of terms (Table 13).

Hwang-Choi (1982) raised her average percentage success in classifying three cheese products when her 10 panelists were sub-divided into three clusters more homogeneous than the panel as a whole. That did not happen here. Forming the two major clusters of 5 and 9 consumers resulted in success scarcely greater than for the panel as a whole (Table 4). Unlike Hwang-Choi who started out with trained assessors and thus individuals who were more concordant in their responses since screening/elimination had already taken place, the blue-cheese panelists were not initially screened other than to represent different demographic considerations. The first few clustering steps were inadequate to reduce panelist heterogeneity markedly. Note that panelist 25 does not fit too well in the cluster of 9 and that there is also a major break between panelists 18 and 19. Powers (1984a) has pointed out that, for trained assessors, if the cluster is not compact, the remedy is further training. Training is out of the question for consumers. One has to accept them as they come. The first two stages of clustering, which were really incipient clustering only, did not result in a major reduction of panelist heterogeneity. Even one stage of clustering did reveal, however, that the consumers were not all responding alike though prior ANOVA had shown all were efficient at discerning differences in the attributes of the panelist heterogeneity markedly. Note that panelist 25 does not fit too did so via different pathways is not uncommon. Piggott (1984) commented that Wilkin et al. (1983) had to have different weighting values for different panels of trained assessors evaluating the organoleptic qualities of distillers' spirits. Even as trained assessors, we humans are still individuals and we act as such.

4.5. Number of Terms

Table 7 demonstrated that sometimes the greater the number of terms the less reliable is the classification process. That re-affirms the point made by Vuataz (1981), i.e. that as the number of descriptors increases the probability of products being misclassified may likewise increase. In effect, as one includes more and more descriptors, but they are also of

TABLE 13
COMPARISON OF ORDER AND TERMS USED IN SDA WHEN PANEL OF 16 ASSESSORS SUBGROUPED INTO TWO CLUSTERS OF 5- AND 9-MEMBERS TO YIELD GREATER HOMOGENEITY

Terms[a] and order of entry	Five-member cluster		Terms[b] and order of entry	Nine-member cluster	
	F to enter or remove	U statistic		F to enter or remove	U statistic
Veining	25·5	0·397	Mold, amount of	29·9	0·51
White	15·0	0·209	Pasty	24·4	0·29
Oily	7·1	0·146	White	16·06	0·19
Mold, amount of	6·3	0·105	Veining	9·21	0·14
Acidity	4·3	0·083	Yellow	3·88	0·13
Pasty	4·1	0·066	Flavor	3·23	0·12
Yellow	2·3	0·057	Curd	3·16	0·10
Flavor	2·5	0·049	Solvent	2·09	0·10
Balance	2·2	0·043			

[a] Approximate F value at 9th step = 7·78.
[b] Approximate F value at 8th step = 11·5.

progressively lower discriminating power, they begin in some instances to damp product discrimination rather than to enhance it. The investigator may want to make two or three calculations, cutting off the step process at different levels, to learn whether essentially as good classification can be secured with a few classifiers as with several or utilize the SDA option (BMDP, 1979) of printing a jackknifed classification after each step. If five will do the job, there is not only no need to use 15, the risk of being in error may actually increase.

4.6. MANOVA

Sometimes multivariate analysis of variance (MANOVA) is used in conjunction with DA for the analysis of data. MANOVA will not be discussed in detail, for to do so would require a whole chapter unto itself. Its utilization to supplement or to complement DA needs however to be mentioned.

DA and MANOVA, in many respects, are opposite branches arising from the same node of the tree of MVA. They are oriented differently, but like branches of the same tree, they are otherwise alike. The basic principles are the same. Considerations affecting validity are generally the same. Several of the calculation steps and significance tests are founded upon the same premises. In objective however, the two procedures are oriented differently. MANOVA involves joint examination of the measurement values to learn whether treatments have effected significant differences in a product. DA assumes that the designated classes are different.

Before carrying on DA, MANOVA is sometimes applied to the data set to learn whether the measurement values result in a significant difference between classes. Inasmuch as there is an assumption that the classes are different, application of MANOVA in effect is a test to determine whether the variables as a whole distinguish one class from another. If significance is obtained, one has learned little more than would have been learned by using SDA without any editing of the data. MANOVA does have however uses for other purposes related to DA. It is often used to test descriptors or assessors for effectiveness.

Piggott and Jardine (1979) applied MANOVA in their study of whisky flavor. They treated the whiskies as the sample groups and the descriptors as the variables. If there is large dispersion within samples, this indicates that the assessors are not agreeing in their use of the terms. If there is large dispersion between samples, thus the samples are detectably different, then there is agreement in the use of the terms and overall they are effective as product discriminators. We (Powers, 1982a,b,c, 1984a,b; Powers *et al.*, 1984, 1985) have likewise used MANOVA to examine the performance of assessors, chiefly each assessor separately instead of the assessors pooled. The publications cited above point out the value and the limitations of MANOVA as a means of evaluating the performance of assessors.

The chief value of MANOVA is to determine whether treatments applied to a product cause significant differences. It thus should be brought into play at a second stage of research. DA tells the investigator whether certain variables combined are correlated with classes. The relations may be purely correlative or they may be causal as to product differences. If one wants to learn whether they cause product differences, then it is time to turn to experiments where the variables are purposely changed in concentration or force. If the treatments are shown to cause the product to be significantly different, there is then some evidence that causal relations exist.

4.6.1. Degrees of Freedom
Sometimes the investigator cannot utilize MANOVA in lieu of DA to determine whether the products (classes) are different. The chemical data used to explain calculation of a weighted mean (Tables 7 and 8) will be used to illustrate that point. While not necessary to determine whether the products differed (SDA having already shown that), MANOVA was applied to the data set with the intent to illustrate its use. The writer (JJP) of this section instructed his technician to make a MANOVA examination of the chemical data. She asked how many of the GLC peaks were to be used. There were 38. Without thinking, the writer said 'Use all of them'. A singular matrix resulted because the design of the experiment did not provide sufficient df. There were only 16 df (4 products, 4 replications). The SDA had gone to completion successfully as far as the seven effective peaks were concerned because only one df is removed as each step is included. The multivariate F value had dropped below the F value specified before the number of df had been exhausted. When variables were deleted to bring the number of variables below 12, MANOVA likewise indicated the existence of differences between products. Lack of df is generally not a problem when sensory data are being analyzed because the responses of each assessor contribute as many df to each replication as there are assessors. When panelist results are pooled, lack of df may then prevent certain kinds of analyses or restrict the

extent to which the analysis can be made. A comparison of the results we obtained when DA was applied to the 287 cases of blue cheese and the 'near-miss' of Godwin et al. (1977) illustrates that point. Godwin et al. (1977) analyzed the blue-cheese data with the panelists' responses pooled. In doing so, they then had only 18 df (6 products × 3 replications). By the twelfth step they were 100% successful in assigning each of the 18 samples to the class to which it belonged. Had 13 steps been required, the analysis would have aborted for lack of df. Powers (1979, 1982c, 1984a) and Powers et al. (1985) have pointed out that for all forms of MVA one has to have an ample number of df either through replication, number of products or factor levels; otherwise the investigator may find that he or she cannot perform certain kinds of analyses for lack of df.

Though some failures were encountered in classifying the 287 samples of blue cheese into their own real classes (Table 4), CVA for class means, the analysis of Godwin et al. (1977) and MANOVA—all demonstrated that there were significant differences between classes. In terms of practical usefulness though, efficiency in the classification of each individual specimen should be the basis of judgement as to whether adequate classification is being attained. The thing the user is generally interested in is whether or not individual samples are likely to be assigned to the appropriate class.

4.7. Verification

In illustrating SDA itself, consideration was not given to the introduction of new samples to verify that the set of classifying tests is indeed effective. Persson and von Sydow (1972) pointed out that tests should be conducted anew with different samples, preferably procured months apart and for sensory analysis that the members of the panels should be different. Powers et al. (1977) and Godwin et al. (1978) carried on their trials a year apart (1975 and 1976) with entirely different brands of green beans and with panels almost 100% different in composition. If entirely new experiments cannot be utilized, then part of the data should be held back to learn whether the discriminant function or set of classifying variables arising from part of the data will hold true when applied to the portion withheld. Powers and Quinlan (1973) verified the discrimination function they calculated by having an entirely different person analyze a second set of samples, with the identity of the samples coded, to learn whether the discriminant function 'worked'. They succeeded in classifying correctly 19 out of 20 unknown samples.

4.8. Applying SDA to Training of Assessors

Traditional applications of SDA were employed as illustrations above. A use which may be made of SDA is to pinpoint causes of product–assessor interaction. Two-way ANOVA will show whether interaction exists and cluster analysis may be used to sub-divide assessors into groups more homogeneous in their responses, but at the training stage one wants to overcome heterogeneity, not merely segregate it, so as to 'save' would-be assessors rather than having to eliminate them because they in effect are outliers. One of the jobs the sensory technologist attempts to do is to train his or her assessors so that they act as one in the magnitude and direction of their responses. The ideal of having no product–assessor interaction can seldom be met, but it can be minimized through training. SDA may be used to give guidance to the sensory technologist as to where the greatest effort needs to be expended in training. Normally one wants to have tests which enable products to be assigned to the class to which they belong. In the case of assessors, we would like not to be able to assign them to the class to which they belong, themselves as individuals. If SDA is applied to the responses of assessors and they can be separated into discrete classes, that, of course, is one expression of product–assessor interaction. The important thing however is that SDA gives the technologist an array of sensory tests most effective in permitting classification to be attained, thus the chief cause of interaction. The technologist thereby knows which attributes need to be worked upon the most so as to lessen product–assessor interaction. Godwin (1984) used that procedure quite effectively as a guide to train his 10 assessors. Table 14 shows the summary list of terms used to 'classify' his assessors. Godwin had used an F value of 2·0 to enter the step process and 1·5 to remove a variable. Before applying SDA, he had utilized PCA to learn whether his panel of 10 constituted one homogeneous group or more logically should be partitioned into sub-groups. Powers (1984a,b) and Powers et al. (1985) have pointed out that the PCA results may be used to permit each assessor to visualize where he or she stands in relation to the other members of the panel. Two-dimensional graphs sometimes suffice; if not, a three-dimensional model may be constructed with movable and adjustable posts to enable an assessor to see for himself or herself whether (1) he or she is truly an outlier, (2) is mildly aberrant as compared with the majority or (3) constitutes a part of the core of the panel. With the increasing use of microcomputers, instead of using physical models, three-dimensional graphs can now be displayed or printed (Grotch, 1983). Provided one has the appropriate software to rotate the three-

TABLE 14

APPLICATION OF SDA TO TERMS USED BY 10 TRAINEES, EVALUATING FIVE TYPES OF TEA, TO LEARN WHICH TERMS WERE MOST EFFECTIVE TO CLASSIFY THE TRAINEES (AND THUS ARE THE CHIEF CAUSES OF PRODUCT–ASSESSOR INTERACTION), 190 CASES

Step No.	Variable entered	F value	F to enter or remove	U statistic	Approximate	df
1	Malty	34·32	34·32	0·368 2	34·32	9/180
2	Floral	21·41	11·95	0·230 0	21·59	9/179
3	Resinous	21·40	11·57	0·175 1	18·06	9/178
4	Pungent	12·95	10·89	0·093 4	16·31	9/177
5	Sweet	14·38	7·60	0·067 2	14·55	9/176
6	Brisk	9·00	6·50	0·050 4	13·23	9/175
7	Metallic	8·89	6·26	0·038 1	12·31	9/174
8	Bitter	5·22	4·13	0·031 3	11·29	9/173
9	Aroma	5·82	3·63	0·026 3	10·45	9/172
10	Grassy	15·65	3·24	0·022 5	9·75	9/171
11	Color	3·13	2·36	0·020 0	9·07	9/170
12	[a]Flavor	1·914	(0·967)			
13	[a]Body	5·406	(0·205)			
14	[a]Harsh	4·289	(1·489)			

[a]Terms not used, failed to meet specified F value of 2·0.

dimensional figure so as to change the angles of viewing, each assessor may see for himself or herself as training progresses how compatible he or she is becoming with the rest of the assessors. Figures 4, 5 and 6 illustrate the value of display.† The points in the three cubes are the plotting positions of Fisher's three species of iris (Grotch, 1984). Note that tilting and rotation of the cubes permits class distinctions to be readily visualized. The same sort of process can be used to permit each assessor to visualize his (her) agreement with other members of the panel.

Because three of the four variables examined by Fisher accounted for most of the variance between species, three-dimensional depiction sufficed to illustrate relations among the species. The question may be asked: is graphical representation of any value when a greater number of variables is necessary to resolve product differences? Dr Stanley L. Grotch of the Lawrence Livermore National Laboratory of the

† Figures 4, 5 and 6 are taken from Grotch (1984) with permission of the publisher, D. Reidel Publishing Co., Dordrecht, The Netherlands, and the Lawrence Livermore National Laboratory, University of California. The work was performed under the auspices of the US Department of Energy.

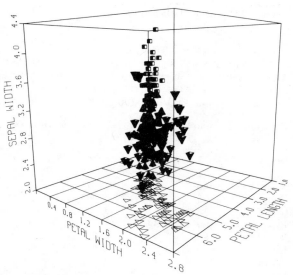

FIG. 4. Fisher's iris data seen using 'best' three dimensions, the three species being depicted as cubes, pyramids and inverted triangles (Reproduced by permission of D. Reidel Publishing Company, Lawrence Livermore National Laboratory and the US Department of Energy).

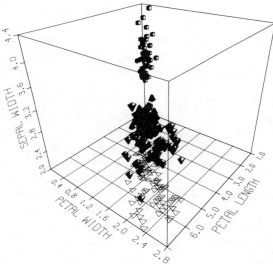

FIG. 5. Tipping of Fig. 4 vertically so as to improve the separation of the species symbolized by the cubes (Reproduced by permission of D. Reidel Publishing Company, Lawrence Livermore National Laboratory and the US Department of Energy).

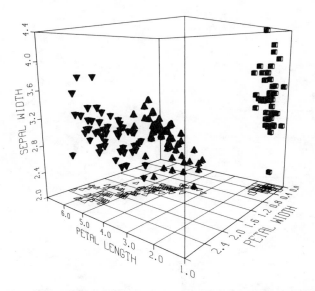

FIG. 6. Rotation of Fig. 4 through 90° permits the classes depicted by the pyramids and inverted triangles to be separated from each other (Reproduced by permission of D. Reidel Publishing Company, Lawrence Livermore National Laboratory and the US Department of Energy).

University of California kindly agreed to apply his program to data sets less exemplary than that of Fisher. One of these involved the analysis, both sensorially and chemically, of three kinds of onions (Dodo, 1985). Two were ordinary yellow and red globe onions. The third was a species, Grano-Granex, known for its mild and sweet taste, especially when grown in the soil surrounding Vidalia, Georgia (USA). Although seven GLC peaks were necessary to fully resolve sample differences, the first three dimensions gave evidence of product differences (Figs. 7 and 8).

If one wishes to examine more than three variables, then reduction of dimensionality is necessary for graphical representation. Though only seven peaks were necessary to differentiate among the three species, several of the other 45 GLC peaks were also significant as to product differences. Dr Grotch reduced the 45 peaks to three principal components. Figure 9 shows that Vidalia onions are clearly different from the other two kinds. The viewer can visualize for himself (herself) that through rotation and tilting of the cube a line of demarcation between the yellow and red onions could likewise be made evident.

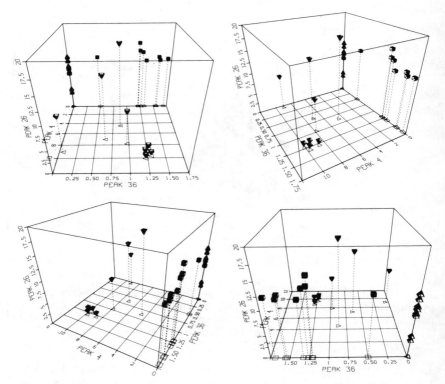

FIG. 7. Effect of rotating the axis so as to facilitate visualization of class differences. Cubes stand for the yellow onions; pyramids, for the red onions; and the inverted triangles, for the Vidalia onions.

Graphic depiction of product differences is particularly important in quality assurance. Production managers and general managers of higher authority often do not wish to take the time to examine typical DA output. They are more likely to institute necessary action if facts are simply or visually presented. Since the advent of microcomputers and with the proper program, graphic representation of product differences has become quite feasible.

4.9. Sharpening Up the Focus
In choosing a strict sensory problem to illustrate different DA methods and one where each case could not be successfully classified, the reader

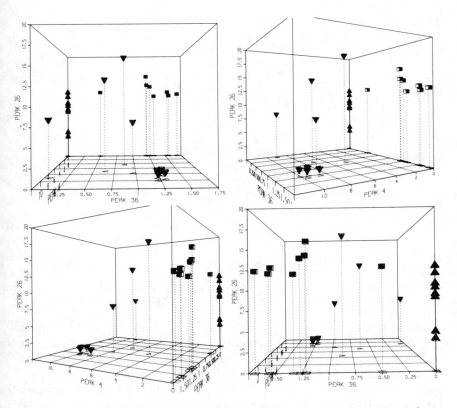

FIG. 8. Influence of tilting of the representation so as to bring out product differences more clearly.

might be left with the impression that DA is not particularly useful in practical application. Doubts of the reader need to be allayed. From the Godwin *et al.* (1977), the Lin (1983) and Dodo (1985) results cited, the reader should note that unequivocal results can often be obtained when objective data are the basis for classification. Additional citations to successful applications will be given in Section 5. The fact that product differences often are more readily demonstrable from objective measurements than from sensory ones generates a problem if the objective procedure is to be used in quality control. The confidence limits for the objective measurements may have to be set at an entirely different probability level than usual if QC ranges for sensory and objective

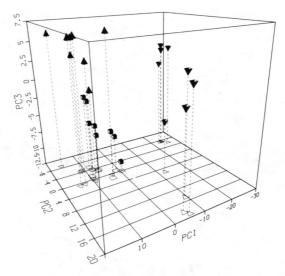

FIG. 9. Geometric representation of three types of onions based upon 45 GLC peaks having been reduced to three principal components.

determinations are to coincide. Intrusion of some of the plotting points of one product into the confidence limits of other products is not always a bad sign. Products might in fact be so close in their characteristics that clear resolution of product differences would be possible to establish only with an excessive amount of testing, and, as pointed out by Powers (1984a), further attempts to resolve such differences might not be justifiable economically. If, on the other hand, overlapping of plotting points is caused by product–assessor interaction, often there are ways to reduce or to segregate that form of error. When product–assessor interaction is caused by mere use of different portions of the scale, standardization of the scoring values will reduce that error somewhat. If the assessors are using the descriptive terms in different ways, application of PCA (Piggott and Jardine, 1979) or cluster analysis (Powers, 1979, 1981a,b, 1982c, 1984a,b) is often quite effective.

5. INDUSTRIAL AND QA APPLICATIONS

While a few of the examples above dealt with industrial problems, further illustrations should perhaps be given to document the value of DA in an industrial context.

Among major uses of LDA is the examination of raw products and finished goods to learn whether they comply with quality assurance (QA) specifications. As to raw goods, products may be out of bounds because of adulteration, false representation of some sort, improper storage or anyone of a dozen other reasons. If adulteration or mistreatment is gross, it generally may be detected with simple tests. Today however adulteration is often quite sophisticated especially when it is highly lucrative. Those who cheapen the food by adulteration are quite likely to tamper with several of the components in an effort to confound those trying to establish that adulteration has occurred. Even if adulteration is not involved, the same situation may prevail. Products, as pointed out earlier, usually do not deviate from normal because of one component only being rather aberrant but because several are, though all do so only in minor ways. The QA department thus has to decide whether individually or cumulatively the deviations are sufficient to constitute departure from an acceptable or specified sensory zone.

5.1. Adulteration

Cabezudo *et al.* (1981) applied LDA to the GLC profiles of 36 genuine Spanish vinegar samples, 16 genuine vinegar samples not having undergone complete acetification and 26 samples considered to be fraudulent for failure to comply with the Spanish regulations. Three discriminant functions consisting of 12 terms were generated; then 98 additional samples were prepared in the laboratory to simulate different industrial practices (or malpractices). With only one exception, the authors were able to classify correctly 57 genuine vinegar samples and 31 samples incompletely acetified. As to fraudulent samples (secured from the market or simulated in the laboratory) 12 out of 88 cases failed to be detected. When adulteration amounted to less than 20% by volume, some fraudulent samples were correctly classified as such whereas others were not. The authors concluded that 86% of adulterated samples could be detected from GLC and DA analysis. Inasmuch as C^{14} analysis can also be used, the percentage of fraudulent samples detectable would be somewhat higher than 86%. When classification is erratic, a procedure which often works is to transform the measurement values in some manner (Powers and Quinlan, 1973) or to calculate new sets of discriminant functions (Powers and Quinlan, 1974; Powers *et al.*, 1978). Using the main discriminant function, Powers and Quinlan (1974) could resolve differences among three bourbon whiskies but resolution of differences between two others was intractable. When a new discriminant function was calculated over the narrow range of ambiguity, the two brands initially non-resolvable became tractable to separation.

5.2. Quality Specifications

Sometimes adulteration is not at issue, merely whether raw products produced in different growing regions (Gillette, 1984a) or of different varieties (Stenroos and Siebert, 1984) can be identified as to the country of origin or the variety and whether they are sensorially different. Gillette reported that a herb grown in five countries could be separated by DA applied to GLC profiles. The sensory panel could not resolve differences between the herb grown in two countries, but it could as to the others. The GLC profiles and DA permitted all five products to be differentiated. Gillette (1984b) reports that the company involved has carried on 100 + determinations since the initial discriminant functions were calculated and that joint use of sensory and chemical analysis is proving of value in the evaluation of products for purchase. Figures 10 and 11 illustrate the same sort of situation. They were derived from raw data provided by McCormick and Company, Inc. A herb grown in eight different areas was compared sensorially and chemically. When the P7M program of the BMDP package (1979) was applied to the sensory attributes evaluated, products 2, 3 and 5 could be differentiated from

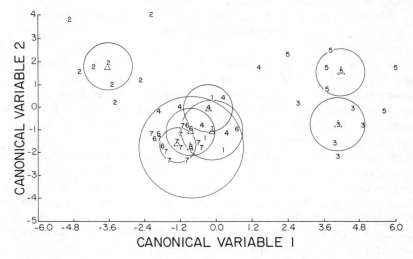

FIG. 10. Canonical discriminant analysis applied to sensory evaluation of a herb grown in eight different major producing areas.

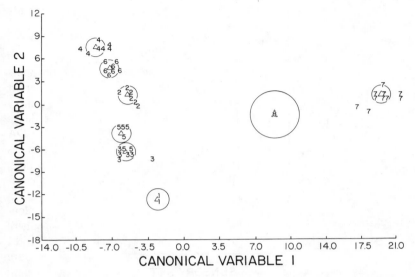

FIG. 11. Canonical discriminant analysis applied to various chemical measurements made on the same herb samples as shown in Fig. 10.

each other and from the other five products, but, as is obvious, five of the products could not be distinguished from each other. When the chemical data were analyzed differences among the eight products could be resolved. If the sensory results alone are considered, then products 1, 4, 6, 7 and 8 appear to be almost equal inasmuch as there is not a statistical difference among any of them. No doubt there are subtle sensory differences, however, too minute or variable for even a trained sensory panel to consistently detect. The chemical data lend some support to that supposition, for they indicate that the products did in fact differ from each other. Canonical correlation is beyond the scope of this chapter (see Chapter 9), but its application is appropriate here to throw additional light on the two sets of data. While there appears to be little correlation between the sensory and chemical relations of the spice from each of the growing locations, there is in fact some underlying correlation as Fig. 12 makes evident. The first canonical variate for the sensory set of determinations is on the abscissa; the set of GLC determinations is on the ordinate. There is a clearcut relation between the sets of sensory and chemical determinations. That fact cannot be noted from Figs. 10 and 11. Their patterns bear little resemblance to each other. Powers (1981a,b)

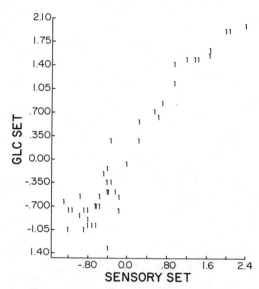

FIG. 12. Canonical correlation analysis applied to a set of the four most discriminatory sensory attributes and to a set of 15 chemical measurements.

has commented upon the difference between deriving chemical patterns—as a consequence of analysis leading to separation and quantitation of the compounds—as distinguished from human judgement where some of the sensory signals are apparently integrated rather than all of them being responded to separately.

Stenroos and Siebert (1984) applied various pattern recognition (ARTHUR and SIMCA) and other MVA methods (SDA, NN, Bayesian classification) to the essential oil profiles of 148 hop samples grown in North America and Europe. The SIMCA-Jacobi, SIMCA principal component, SDA, NN, and Bayesian classification methods were 100, 96, 80, 77 and 32% successful in classifying the samples. Stenroos and Siebert reported that the original 177 GLC peaks could be reduced to as few as 12–13 peaks which still retained the necessary discriminating information, that some of the smaller peaks had the greatest discriminating power and, as Powers and Keith (1968) pointed out much earlier, such information can guide priorities for further peak identification.

Moret *et al.* (1984) likewise reported comparisons of MDA and NN. They studied the aroma components of Venetian white wines. MDA resulted in 94·9% correct classification whereas the NN procedure was 71·8% successful. Powers (1979, 1981a,b, 1982b,c,d, 1984a,b) has cited many other publications dealing with the application of DA to various food products. Others, e.g. Coomans *et al.* (1979), have done so as to chemical applications.

5.3. Sensory or Objective Standards

If chemical or physical determinations could replace sensory evaluation, there often would be manifest advantages in terms of time and expense, but objective tests are unlikely to supplant sensory ones. In fact in some industries just the opposite has taken place. The on-line sensory evaluation described by Wilkin *et al.* (1983) illustrates the latter situation. William Grant & Sons, Ltd rejected chemical evaluation as the sole QA means to decide whether its distillers' spirits were in compliance with specifications. Though one or more chemical differences may be great enough to be statistically significant, chemical differences are not necessarily highly correlated with sensory differences. Sensory differences may occur without there being any plausible chemical reason. To determine compliance with sensory specifications, organoleptic evaluation offered a direct route provided a means could be found to weight the importance of different sensory notes in determining organoleptic acceptability. Initially, the company characterized acceptable and nonacceptable distillers' spirits for several attributes. LDA was then applied to determine weighting factors which should be assigned to each sensory attribute (Piggott and Canaway, 1981). Once that had been done, almost immediate decisions could be made as to compliance with the quality standard from calculation of the product of the weighted means and the assessors' scale values pooled.

An examination of products upon a multicriteria basis is more difficult to initiate simply because the training of assessors is more complex and time-consuming (Powers, 1984b). One has to be careful too—as has already been pointed out—to distinguish between provincialism and generality. When different panels are used, weighting factors may be needed for each panel until the panels have been brought into close conformity through training and discussion of results *inter alios* and with the sensory leader. Piggott (1984) commented that the classifying functions calculated for Wilkin *et al.* (1983) have been modified some as experience has been accumulated. Part of the need for modification was to refine the weighting factors to make them more general; the major need was to compensate for changes in the composition of the panels.

Because of all the interplay possible among variables, probability levels are difficult to establish for the decision made. As data are accumulated however, the factors which are real and general should arise out of the sea of possibilities. At that stage, since the quality of a food depends upon relations among a multiplicity of attributes, multivariate evaluation becomes several-fold more useful than single, simple tests. The need for proper initial design of experiments, a sound data base and the use of appropriate statistical methods to bring into focus these relations is obvious. They are imperatives not to be ignored.

6. SUMMARY

DA is being used increasingly in research and for various industrial purposes. The widespread availability of computers and associated software have made practical the benefits of DA. One of the objectives of this chapter was to point out considerations the user should keep in mind as DA is applied. MANOVA received scant treatment, but there were reasons for that. Textbooks on MVA generally describe MANOVA more exhaustively than they do DA; thus the need for extensive description is less. Furthermore, if one were to describe all the variations of MANOVA, depending on how rigorously one wants to examine various relations, a whole chapter unto itself would be required. Perhaps more pertinent is the fact that nonstatisticians generally are less intimidated from utilizing MANOVA than DA simply because MANOVA seems to be but an extension of ANOVA, and most of today's food scientists are well grounded in the elements of univariate analysis.

MANOVA is often of value in the examination of data before the application of DA so as to make judgements about the effectiveness of descriptors or of assessors. For these and other applications it rarely is an end in itself. Just as ANOVA tells only part of the story if significance is obtained, the same is true for MANOVA. Other tests need to be applied to flesh out the skeletal findings. To illustrate, all ANOVA tells the investigator is that significance does or does not exist. If it does, the user still does not know whether only one treatment differs from all others or significant differences among treatments are more general. Mean separation tests need to be applied to learn the particulars as to where treatments differ significantly. MANOVA is useful for a global survey of relations, but one has to resort to other tests to examine such relationships more closely. In some respects the same is true as to DA methods. Only rarely will a single DA examination of data suffice. The initial conclusions have to be refined through repeated editing and examination of the data set.

Finally, as was stressed with respect to provincialism and generality, the first use of DA is but the beginning of application. Just as a delta at the mouth of a river builds up by accretion, so too are the first few DA trials merely the first deposits of the many more needed. For the full merits of DA to be attained, sufficient experience and accumulation of data needs to be acquired to provide—not footing still shifting—but solid ground for the support of decisions made.

ACKNOWLEDGEMENTS

Support for preparation of this chapter was provided in part from tax funds allocated by the Georgia General Assembly to the Georgia Agricultural Experiment Stations of the University of Georgia. Appreciation is expressed to Mrs Kathleen Shinholser for her considerable skill and flexibility in carrying out the various kinds of statistical analyses, to Ms Cathy C. Burch for her skill and patience in making many word-processing changes and to Ms Marianne Gillette, McCormick and Co., Inc., Hunt Valley, Maryland for providing the herb data used.

REFERENCES

Bengtsson, K. (1943). Provsmakning som analysmetod statistisk behandling av resultaten. *Svenska Bryggareforeningens manadsblad*, **58**(3), 102–11, 149–57.
BMDP Biomedical Computer Programs (1979). P-series, University of California Press, Berkeley, California USA, 876 pp.
Brown, D. G. W. and Clapperton, J. F. (1978). Discriminant analysis of sensory and instrumental data on beer. *J. Inst. Brew.*, **84**, 318–23.
Cabezudo, M. D., Herraiz, M., Llaguno, C. and Martin, P. (1981). Some advances in alcoholic beverages and vinegar flavour research. In: *The Quality of Foods and Beverages*, G. Charalambous and G. Inglett (Eds), Academic Press, New York, pp. 225–40.
Cattel, R. B. (1965). The scree test for the number of factors. *Multivariate Behavior Research*, **1**, 245–76.
Chatfield, C. and Collins, A. (1980). *Introduction to Multivariate Analysis*, Chapman and Hall, London, p. 158.
Coomans, D., Massart, D. L. and Kaufman, L. (1979). Optimization by statistical

linear discriminant analysis in analytical chemistry. *Analytica Chimica Acta*, **119**, 97–122.

Dodo, Hortense (1985). Sensory and chemical analysis applied to three species of onion. Master of Science thesis, University of Georgia, Athens, Georgia GA, USA, 49 pp.

Fisher, R. A. (1936). The use of multiple measurements in taxonomic problems. *Ann. Eugen.*, **VII**, 179–88.

Gillette, M. (1984a). Applications of descriptive analysis. *J. Food Protection*, **47**, 403–9.

Gillette, M. (1984b). Personal communication.

Godwin, D. R. (1984). Relationships between sensory response and chemical composition of tea. Ph.D. dissertation, University of Georgia, Athens, GA, USA, 201 pp.

Godwin, D. R., Bargmann, R. E. and Powers, J. J. (1978). Use of cluster analysis to evaluate sensory-objective relations of processed green beans. *J. Food Sci.*, **43**, 1229–34.

Godwin, D. R., Washam, C. J. and Powers, J. J. (1977). Selection of blue cheese quality descriptors. *J. Dairy Sci.*, **60** (Suppl. 1), 42.

Goulden, C. H. (1952). *Methods of Statistical Analysis*, 2nd edn. John Wiley, New York, pp. 378–93.

Green, P. E. (1978). *Analyzing Multivariate Data*. The Dryden Press, Hinsdale, Illinois, USA.

Grotch, S. L. (1983). Three-dimensional and stereoscopic graphics for scientific data display and analysis. *IEEE Computer Graphics and Applications*, **3**(8), 31–43.

Grotch, S. L. (1984). Three-dimensional graphics for scientific data display and analysis. In: *Chemometrics. Mathematics and Statistics in Chemistry*, B. R. Kowalski (Ed.), D. Reidel, Dordretch, Holland.

Hwang-Choi, I. K. (1982). A case study of the use of standard methods to analyze multivariate sensory data. Ph.D. dissertation, University of Georgia, Athens, GA, USA, 162 pp.

Levitt, D. J. (1974). The use of sensory and instrumental assessment of organoleptic characteristics via multivariate statistical methods. *J. Texture Studies*, **5**, 183–200.

Lin, A. C. (1983). Chemical and sensory analysis of soy sauce. Ph.D. dissertation, University of Georgia, Athens, GA, USA, 113 pp.

Mahalanobis, P. C. (1936). On the generalized distance in statistics. *Proceedings, Natl. Institute of Science, Calcutta*, Vol. 12, 49–55.

Milutinovic, L., Bargmann, R. E., Chang, K. Y., Chastain, M. and Powers, J. J. (1970). Comparison of flavor and volatiles of tomato products and of peanuts. *J. Food Sci.*, **35**, 224–8.

Moret, I., Scarponi, G. and Cescon, P. (1984). Aroma components as discriminating parameters in the chemometric classification of Venetian white wines. *J. Sci. Food Agric.*, **35**, 1004–11.

Palmer, D. H. (1974). Multivariate analysis of flavour terms used by experts and non-experts for describing tea. *J. Sci. Food Agric.*, **25**, 153–64.

Persson, T. and von Sydow, E. (1972). A quality comparison of frozen and refrigerated cooked sliced beef. 2. Relationships between gas chromatographic data and flavor scores. *J. Food Sci.*, **37**, 234–9.

Piggott, J. R. (1984). Personal communication.

Piggott, J. R. and Canaway, P. R. (1981). Finding the words for it—methods and uses of descriptive sensory analysis. In: *Flavour '81*, P. Schreier (Ed.), Walter de Gruyter and Co., Berlin, pp. 33–46.

Piggott, J. R. and Jardine, S. P. (1979). Descriptive sensory analysis of whisky flavour. *J. Inst. Brew.*, **85**, 82–5.

Powers, J. J. (1979). Correlation of sensory evaluation data with objective test data. In: *Sensory Evaluation Methods for the Practicing Food Technologist*, IFT Short Course, 1979–1981, Institute of Food Technologists, Chicago, Illinois, USA, pp. 9–1 to 9–34.

Powers, J. J. (1981a). Perception and analysis: a perspective view of attempts to find causal relations between sensory and objective data sets. In: *Flavour '81*, P. Schreier (Ed.), Walter de Gruyter, Berlin, pp. 103–31.

Powers, J. J. (1981b). Multivariate procedures in sensory research: scope and limitations. *Master Brewers Association of the Americas Tech. Quarterly*, **18**(1), 11–21.

Powers, J. J. (1982a). Materials and training exercises for workshop on sensory analysis. South African Association for Food Science and Technology, Johannesburg, 52 pp.

Powers, J. J. (1982b). Sensory-instrumental correlations, review and appraisal. 2 Teil. *Lebensmittel Technol.*, **15**(1), 6–11.

Powers, J. J. (1982c). Sensory-instrumental correlations, review and appraisal. Further considerations in analysis. Part III. *Lebensmittel Technol.*, **15**(2), 2–6.

Powers, J. J. (1982d). Techniques of analysis of flavours. Integration of sensory and instrumental methods. In: *Food Flavours. Part A. Introduction*, I. D. Morton and A. J. MacLeod (Eds), Elsevier, Amsterdam, pp. 121–68.

Powers, J. J. (1984a). Using general statistical programs to evaluate sensory data. *Food Technol.*, **38**(6), 74–84.

Powers, J. J. (1984b). Current practices and application of descriptive methods. In: *Sensory Analysis of Foods*, J. R. Piggott (Ed.), Elsevier Applied Science Publishers, London, pp. 179–242.

Powers, J. J. and Keith, E. S. (1968). Stepwise discriminant analysis of gas chromatographic data as an aid in classifying the flavor quality of foods. *J. Food Sci.*, **33**, 207–13.

Powers, J. J. and Quinlan, M. C. (1973). Subjective-objective evaluation of model odor systems. *Lebensm-Wiss. u. Technol.*, **6**(6), 209–14.

Powers, J. J. and Quinlan, M. C. (1974). Refining of methods for subjective-objective evaluation of flavor. *J. Agric. Food Chem.*, **22**, 744–9.

Powers, J. J., Cenciarelli, S. and Shinholser, K. (1984). El uso de programas estadísticos generales en la evaluacíon des los resultados sensoriales. *Revista de Agroquimica y Tecnologia de Alimentos*, **24**(4), 469–84.

Powers, J. J., Godwin, D. R. and Bargmann, R. E. (1977). Relations between sensory and objective measurements for quality evaluation of green beans. In: *Flavor Quality: Objective Measurement*, R. A. Scanlan (Ed.), ACS Symposium Series No. 51, American Chemical Society, Washington, D.C. USA, pp. 51–70.

Powers, J. J., Shinholser, K. and Godwin, D. R. (1985). Evaluating assessors' performance and panel homogeneity using univariate and multivariate statistical analysis. In: *Progress in Flavour Research* 1984, *Proceedings of the*

4th Weurman Flavour Research Symposium, J. Adda (Ed.), Elsevier, Amsterdam, pp. 193–210.

Powers, J. J., Smit, C. J. B. and Godwin, D. R. (1978). Relations among sensory and objective attributes of canned Rabbiteye (Vaccinium ashei Reade) blueberries. II. Cluster and discriminant analysis examination. Lebensm-Wiss. u. Technol., 11, 275–8.

SAS (1982). User's Guide to Statistical Analysis Systems, SAS Institute, Cary, North Carolina, USA, 584 pp.

SAS (1985). User's Guide: Statistics Version 5, SAS Institute, Cary, North Carolina, USA, 956 pp.

Sidel, J. L. and Stone, H. (1976). Experimental design and analysis of sensory tests. Food Technol., 31, 32–8.

SPSS—Statistical Package for the Social Sciences. (1975). McGraw-Hill, New York, 661 pp.

Stenroos, L. E. and Siebert, K. J. (1984). Application of pattern-recognition techniques to the essential oil of hops. Am. Soc. Brew. Chem. J., 42(2), 54–61.

Stone, H., Sidel, J., Oliver, S., Woolsey, A. and Singleton, R. C. (1974). Sensory evaluation by quantitative descriptive analysis. Food Technol., 28, 24–34.

Tabachnick, B. G. and Fidell, L. S. (1983). Using Multivariate Statistics, Harper and Row, New York.

Thorndike, R. M. (1978). Correlation Procedures for Research, Gardner Press, Inc., New York, p. 184.

Vuataz, L. (1981). Information about products and individuals in multicriteria description of food products. In: Criteria of Food Acceptance, J. Solms and R. L. Hall, (Eds), Forster Verlag AG, Zurich, Switzerland, pp. 429–46.

Wilkin, G. D., Webber, M. A. and Lafferty, E. A. (1983). Appraisal of industrial continuous still products. In: Flavour of Distilled Beverages: Origin and Development, J. R. Piggott (Ed.), Ellis Horwood Limited, Chichester, England, pp. 154–65.

Wu, L. S., Bargmann, R. E. and Powers, J. J. (1977). Factor analysis applied to wine descriptors. J. Food Sci., 42, 944–52.

Young, L. L., Bargmann, R. E. and Powers, J. J. (1970). Correlation between gas-chromatographic patterns and flavor evaluation of chemical mixtures and of cola beverages. J. Food Sci., 35, 219–23.

Chapter 6

METHODS TO AID INTERPRETATION OF MULTIDIMENSIONAL DATA

J. R. PIGGOTT

Food Science Division,
Department of Bioscience and Biotechnology,
University of Strathclyde, Glasgow, UK

and

K. SHARMAN

Department of Electronic and Electrical Engineering,
University of Strathclyde,
Glasgow, UK

1. INTRODUCTION

This chapter is concerned with a group of procedures whose main use is to aid interpretation of complex multivariate data. They are *descriptive* procedures, in that they model or describe data in a way which can be more easily understood by the researcher; whereas *inferential* procedures allow conclusions to be drawn from a data set, such as that one set of samples is significantly different, in the statistical sense, from another set. Perhaps the most commonly used of all multivariate procedures is principal components analysis (PCA), while principal coordinates analysis (PCO) and factorial correspondence analysis (FCA) can be used for broadly similar purposes, but have received less exposure in food science and technology.

A group of techniques generally known as factor analysis (FA) has been developed for the modelling of complex data. Many ways of carrying out factor analysis have been proposed, and PCA is one of the best known. Norusis (1985) briefly described some of the more common methods, and there are many books for the interested reader (e.g. Rummell, 1970; Mulaik, 1972; Cattell, 1973; Harman, 1976).

The main difference between PCA and other forms of FA is that PCA is simply a mathematical transformation of the raw data, whereas the others require an input from the analyst in the form of an initial hypothesis, and might make assumptions about the distribution of the data (Gower, 1983). The FA model assumes that the observed variables are manifestations of a number of unobservable factors; firstly a set of general factors, which affect all variables, and secondly a set of specific factors which affect one variable each, whereas the PCA model simply transforms the original variables. Examples of factor analysis of food science data can be found (e.g. Harper and Baron, 1951; Baker, 1954; Harper, 1956; Baker *et al.*, 1961), but the method is little used and will not be discussed further. One problem which does arise, though, is in the terminology used to describe these techniques, especially in North American literature, where factor analysis is used to describe the particular method of principal components analysis. A careful reading of reports can be required to determine exactly which procedure has been used.

1.1. The Data Matrix

The data matrix upon which these techniques operate is usually a rectangular matrix of observations on variables arranged in the following manner:

$$\mathbf{X} = \begin{bmatrix} x_{11} & x_{12} \cdots x_{1P} \\ x_{21} & \\ \vdots & \\ x_{N1} & x_{NP} \end{bmatrix} \Bigg\} N \tag{1}$$

$$\underbrace{}_{P}$$

where x_{ij} denotes the ith observation or sample of the jth variable. In most practical cases in food science, the observations are samples of food or beverage, chosen to cover (as far as is known) the product space or technological space. The samples may be drawn from what is already available, or may be created by changing technological variables. Various terms have been used to describe these observations—subjects, objects, samples, cases, or observational taxonomic units (OTU). *Objects* is the term which will be used hereafter.

There are in total N observations of P variables available for data analysis. The individual elements of the data matrix, x_{ij}, are commonly called the *scores* of each object for each variable. It is important to note that these scores may be summary statistics of a much larger set of observations. For example, a multi-sample experiment may well produce a set of T observations for each object i on each variable j. This leads to a three-way data matrix of samples on objects on variables. A two-way, objects versus variables, data matrix can be constructed by calculating the mean value of each score,

$$x_{ij} = \frac{1}{T} \sum_{k=1}^{T} x_{ijk} \qquad (2)$$

where x_{ijk} is the kth sample, or experimental outcome, describing object i in terms of the variable j.

The above data matrix, which is the starting point for most statistical analysis techniques, can be used to give a simple geometric interpretation of the raw experimental data. The *columns* of the data matrix, $\mathbf{X}$, can be thought of as vectors in an N-dimensional hyperspace, with each column defining the location of a *variable point* in this space. Thus by examining the relationships between the various columns of $\mathbf{X}$, it is possible to investigate the relationships between the variables in the experiment. Alternatively, the *rows* of the data matrix may be viewed as defining a set of N points in a P-dimensional hyperspace. These points represent each *object* using the variables as coordinates. The relationships between the various objects are then analysed by comparing the rows of the data matrix.

The *variables* are usually either sensory variables (attributes or descriptions) or physico-chemical variables such as gas chromatographic peak areas or other chemical measures. The variables can be measured on any of the scales in the common classification, i.e. binary or dichotomous scales, nominal or qualitative scales, ordinal scales, interval scales and ratio scales. The last two can be collectively called quantitative scales. The importance of this is that the methods described here can be applied to some, but not all, these kinds of data.

In many cases, the units of measurement are straightforward and can be entered directly into the data analysis, but it is sometimes not so simple, and a transformation of the data might be required. In mass spectroscopy, for example, 2 molecules which are extremely similar, but in one of which a hydrogen atom has been replaced by deuterium, will give completely different mass spectra if the m/z numbers are used as variables. The autocorrelations of the mass spectra have suitable properties for multivariate analysis (Wold *et al.*, 1984), though after such a transformation interpretation might be less easy because the autocorrelations have no obvious meaning.

Some means of dealing with missing data is also required. The simplest method is to omit the rows or columns containing missing data, but this inevitably causes some loss of information. The analyst must decide whether this loss is acceptable, because any means of estimating missing values carries the risk of distorting the analysis. Where a large proportion of data in a row or column is missing (more than, say, one third), it is probably safer to omit the row or column. However, where only a few cells of the data matrix are empty, the missing values can be estimated, by for example the mean of the variable. Alternatively, the covariance or correlation matrix can be calculated for each pair of variables from all the data available for that pair, though this runs the risk of creating an inconsistent matrix (Norusis, 1985).

It was mentioned above that the data matrix, $\mathbf{X}$, can be considered either as describing the variables in terms of the objects, or as describing each object in terms of the variables. This leads to two main classes of analytical techniques called R- and Q-techniques. R-techniques are primarily concerned with relationships amongst the variables of the experiment, and examine the interplay between the various columns of the data matrix. A starting point for most R-techniques is a summary of the raw data in terms of a correlation or covariance matrix of the sampled variables. For a data matrix of N objects on P variables, the covariance matrix, $\mathbf{C}$, is a $P \times P$ symmetric matrix whose element at row i, column j, is the sample covariance of variable i with variable j, averaged over all the objects. That is

$$c_{ij} = \frac{1}{N} \sum_{k=1}^{N} (x_{ki} - \bar{x}_i)(x_{kj} - \bar{x}_j) \tag{3}$$

where $\bar{x}_k$ is the mean of the observations on the kth variable,

$$\bar{x}_k = \frac{1}{N} \sum_{i=1}^{N} x_{ik} \tag{4}$$

If the variables have been assigned arbitrary multiplicative scales, it is often convenient to summarise the data in terms of the sample correlation matrix, $\mathbf{R}$. This procedure amounts to replacing the original data by a new set, which has been prescaled to have unit variance, and recalculating the covariance matrix. The element of the correlation matrix at row i, column j represents the true sample correlation between variables i and j, and is computed as

$$r_{ij} = \frac{c_{ij}}{\sqrt{(c_{ii}c_{jj})}} \tag{5}$$

The diagonal elements, $\{r_{ii}, i = 1, \ldots, P\}$, of the correlation matrix are always unity. Due to the normalisation of the data in the formation of the correlation matrix, $\mathbf{R}$, it has less degrees of freedom than the covariance matrix $\mathbf{C}$. Use of the $\mathbf{R}$ matrix is thus sometimes preferable, and can improve the quality of the results, especially when the available number of samples or objects is small.

The alternative viewpoint of the data considers relationships amongst the objects, and employs coefficients of association between the *rows* of the data matrix. Analytical techniques for this class of problem normally start with a matrix of distances between the object points in P-dimensional space. This matrix, called the $\mathbf{Q}$ matrix, is a symmetric $N \times N$ matrix, whose element at row i, column j, is the Euclidean squared 'distance' between the objects i and j, with coordinates in P-space given by the observations on each of the P variables,

$$q_{ij} = \sum_{k=1}^{P} (x_{ik} - x_{jk})^2 \tag{6}$$

The technique of principal components analysis is an R-technique, and is primarily used to explain the original data in terms of a new, reduced set of variables. Principal coordinates analysis is dual to PCA and is a Q-technique, whereas factorial correspondence analysis uses both representations of the data and is referred to as a QR-technique.

2. PRINCIPAL COMPONENTS ANALYSIS

2.1. Introduction

PCA is an invaluable procedure, and can be applied to almost any multivariate data set as an exploratory technique to great advantage. Further descriptions can be found in Cooley and Lohnes (1971), Harris (1975), Chatfield and Collins (1980) and Lefebvre (1983). Stungis (1976) presented a brief glossary of some of the terms encountered in multivariate analysis and reviewed some of the methods, and Tomassone and

Flanzy (1977) reviewed the application of some multivariate methods to sensory data.

There are two main functions of PCA; firstly, in indicating relationships among groups of variables in a data set, and secondly in showing relationships between objects. The data matrix can be visualised as describing a multi-dimensional space, with one dimension for each variable, and each sample can be represented as a point in the space. In simple cases where there are only a few variables, the structure of the sample space can be understood by simple inspection, or two-dimensional plots, of the data. This can be done even when there are many objects. Relationships between variables can then be investigated by simple correlation or regression analysis. However, when there are many variables such visualisation of the sample space becomes more difficult, if not impossible. It is in these cases where PCA can make a contribution.

The effect of PCA is to reduce the dimensionality of the sample space. If 25 variables have been measured, the raw data matrix represents a 25-dimensional space, and a full display of the space requires a number of dimensions equal to the lesser of the number of variables and one less than the number of objects. PCA proceeds by searching for *linear combinations of variables* which account for the maximum possible proportion of variance in the original data. If two or more variables are strongly correlated, then the majority of the variance (or information) in the data can be explained by drawing a new axis through the centre of the group of observations, so that the sum of squared residual distances is a minimum. The remaining (small) proportion of variance in the data can then be explained by constructing a second new axis, orthogonal to the first. It is easy to see from this simple case that PCA can only simplify a data set if the original variables are correlated. If they are not, then it is not possible to draw any new axis which can explain more of the variance in the data than the original variables. This is the case where the objects form a circular group in the two dimensions. However, when the objects form an elliptical group, a principal component can be constructed which explains a large proportion of variance.

As a simple example, consider the case of an experiment resulting in N observations on two variables. The raw data matrix is of size N rows by 2 columns, with elements denoted by $\{x_{ij}\}$. The data matrix can also be represented by the two $N \times 1$ column vectors $\mathbf{x}_1$ and $\mathbf{x}_2$, defining the locations of the two variable points in the object space. Principal components analysis of these data proceeds by obtaining the coordinates of two new variables y_1 and y_2, from a linear combination of the original column vectors x_1 and x_2,

$$y_1 = a_{11}x_1 + a_{12}x_2$$
$$y_2 = a_{21}x_1 + a_{22}x_2 \tag{7}$$

The constants of this transformation (a_{11}, a_{12}, a_{21} and a_{22}) are chosen by PCA in such a way that the transformed columns are orthogonal,

$$y_1'y_2 = 0 \tag{8}$$

(y' is the transpose of y), and are further constrained so that the first principal component explains as much of the variance in the original data as possible. The principal component transformation defined by (7) amounts to a scaling and rotation of the variable axes in the object space. In this special case of only two variables, the transform constants can be calculated by hand to yield

$$y_1 = \frac{1}{\sqrt{2}}(x_1 + x_2)$$

$$\tag{9}$$

$$y_2 = \frac{1}{\sqrt{2}}(x_1 - x_2)$$

If the original observations were standardised before the transformation then the variances of each principal component are found to be

$$\mathrm{var}(y_1) = y_1'y_1 = (1 + r_{12})$$
$$\mathrm{var}(y_2) = y_2'y_2 = (1 - r_{12}) \tag{10}$$

where r_{12} is the sample correlation coefficient between the two variables. Note that this result clearly shows the effect of the correlation of the variables on the variance explained by each component. If the two original variables are perfectly correlated, $r_{12} = 1$, and all of the data variance is contained in the first transformed variable described by the vector y_1. On the other hand, if the two original variables are totally independent, $r_{12} = 0$, the variance of each principal component becomes identical, and nothing is achieved by the PCA transformation.

The foregoing can be readily extended to three or more dimensions. In three dimensions, the first principal component corresponds to the longest axis of the ellipsoid of objects, the second to the next longest axis, at right angles to the first, and the third and final to the remaining axis, at right angles to the first two. From these two cases, it is clear that for a

PCA to provide a complete explanation of a set of data, as many components are necessary as there were dimensions in the original object space. However, the power of the method lies in its ability to select dimensions which explain more variance than a single variable. Thus a set of, say, 25 variables may be reduced to five components, with the loss of only a quarter of the variance in the original data. The actual reduction in dimensionality achieved depends on the structure of the original data, and the taste of the analyst in selecting maximum explanation or maximum simplicity. The two- and three-dimensional examples discussed above can be easily extended to examples in spaces of greater dimensionality. In this case, the components correspond to ever-decreasing axes of the hyper-ellipsoid of objects. If the objects plot as a hyper-sphere in the n-dimensional space, PCA cannot help as in the two-dimensional case of a circular cloud of points.

In the general case, an experiment will produce an $N \times P$ data matrix of N observations on P variables, and P principal components are required to completely describe the original data. It can be shown that the calculation of the principal component transformation is intimately linked with the eigenvectors and eigenvalues of the sample **R** matrix of variable correlations. The eigenvectors, $\mathbf{u}_i$, and eigenvalues, λ_i, are solutions of the well-known matrix eigen-equation

$$\mathbf{R}\mathbf{u}_i = \lambda_i \mathbf{u}_i \qquad (i = 1, \ldots, P) \tag{11}$$

If **R** is a standard covariance or correlation matrix, then it is known that all of the eigenvalues have magnitude greater than or equal to zero, and can be arranged in descending order

$$\lambda_1 \geqslant \lambda_2 \geqslant \cdots \geqslant \lambda_P \tag{12}$$

The corresponding set of eigenvectors can be normalised to form an orthonormal set of P basis vectors,

$$\mathbf{u}_i' \mathbf{u}_j = \begin{cases} 0 & i \neq j \\ 1 & i = j \end{cases} \tag{13}$$

The elements of these normalised eigenvectors are then used as the coefficients of the principal component transformation. The ith principal component is expressed as a linear combination of the original variables, weighted by the elements of the ith eigenvector, and can be written in the form

$$\mathbf{y}_i = \mathbf{X}\mathbf{u}_i \tag{14}$$

If the data matrix $\mathbf{X}$ has been standardised (i.e. the columns have zero mean and unit variance) then the variance of this component is

$$\text{var}(\mathbf{y}_i) = \mathbf{u}_i' \mathbf{X}' \mathbf{X} \mathbf{u}_i \qquad (15)$$

$$= \mathbf{u}_i' \mathbf{R} \mathbf{u}_i \qquad (16)$$

$$= \lambda_i \qquad (17)$$

Thus the variance of each component is given by an eigenvalue of the variable correlation matrix. Consequently, the component $\mathbf{y}_1$, corresponding to the largest eigenvalue of $\mathbf{R}$ will explain most of the given data if the remaining eigenvalues are much smaller. On the other hand, if the distributions of the original variables are such that the eigenvalues are all approximately equal in magnitude, each principal component will contribute a similar amount to the variance or information in the data and no variable reduction will be possible. If the principal component vectors $\{\mathbf{y}_i\}$ are expressed in an $N \times P$ matrix, $\mathbf{Y}$,

$$\mathbf{Y} = [\mathbf{y}_1, \ldots, \mathbf{y}_P] \qquad (18)$$

then the complete principal component transformation is compactly described by the equation,

$$\mathbf{Y} = \mathbf{X} \mathbf{U} \qquad (19)$$

where $\mathbf{U}$ is a $P \times P$ matrix whose columns are the normalised eigenvectors of the $\mathbf{R}$ matrix. The elements of the transformed data matrix $\mathbf{Y}$ are effectively the scores of each object in terms of the new variables. Note also that the principal component transformation can easily be inverted to express the original data in terms of the principal components as

$$\mathbf{X} = \mathbf{Y} \mathbf{U}' \qquad (20)$$

In the case where the covariance matrix has been the starting point for analysis, the interpretation of the PCA is rather different because the size of the variation in the original units of measurement affects the variance explained by given components, and thus the order and construction of the components. This application of PCA has been discussed by Vuataz (1977), and some striking examples of the effects of different scalings of the data were given by Zhou et al. (1983). They showed the importance of using the appropriate scaling for a particular problem.

Other scalings are possible, such as normalising each row (or column) of the data matrix to a constant sum. Such normalising can produce misleading results, if for example one variable's values are very much

larger than the others (Wold *et al.*, 1984). In such a case, a change in the
large value causes changes in all the others, and therefore produces
negative correlations. Where the values are of suitable sizes, however,
this transformation can reduce the effect of different scale ranges being
used, e.g. sensory analysis judges using different parts of a scale. A side
effect of this is that the rank of the matrix is reduced by the effect of
closure (Zhou *et al.*, 1983), because the rows or columns are constrained
to add up to the normalising constant.

The main outputs from a PCA are concerned with the relationships
amongst the variables and objects. The transformed data matrix, **Y**,
presented above (18), describes the scores of each original object for each
transformed variable. This matrix shows the relationships between the
objects and the principal component variables. The relationships of the
original variables to the transformed variables can be viewed by calculating the *component loadings* and *communalities* for each variable. The
loadings are the correlations between the original and PCA transformed
variables, with the loadings of the ith variable on the jth component
being calculated from the formula (for a standard data matrix)

$$l_{ij} = \frac{1}{\lambda_j^{1/2}} \sum_{k=1}^{N} x_{ki} y_{kj} \tag{21}$$

This effectively conveys the extent to which the jth principal component
depends on the ith original variable. This loading achieves a maximum
value of one (or minus one) when the principal component and original
variable are completely correlated.

The communality of a particular variable shows how much of the data
variance, due to that variable, is explained by a set of K principal
components. It is computed as the sum of the squared loadings of the
variable on each of the components. For the ith variable, the communality with the first K principal components is

$$h_i = \sum_{j=1}^{k} l_{ij}^2 \tag{22}$$

A communality close to unity for a given value of K indicates that the
variable is approximately explained by the first K principal components.
It is also sometimes useful to compute the communalities over a subset of
a given set of principal components to determine which components are
strongly associated with which variables, though this can be a computationally tedious task if the number of variables and/or components
is large.

Loadings can be plotted on components as vectors in the reduced dimensional component space. The maximum loading is 1, since this corresponds to complete correlation and therefore to all variance explained. If all (or most) variance in a variable is explained by one component, the variable can have only small or zero loadings on other components. If two components provide a satisfactory representation of the data, the complete model can be portrayed as a two-dimensional plot. This can be visualised as a two-dimensional projection of the original multi-dimensional space, being the particular two-dimensional projection which explains the maximum possible proportion of variance in the data. The variables having large loadings on one or both components (i.e. long vectors) are well explained by the two-dimensional model; variables having small loadings are not well explained, and can be visualised as vectors pointing out of the plane of the projection.

The objects can be plotted as points in the two-dimensional space, similarly as if projected from the original multi-dimensional space. The components are by definition orthogonal and therefore uncorrelated, so the observations will form a roughly circular cloud.

If a three-dimensional PCA is required, the three-dimensional space resulting can be viewed in a similar way, as a three-dimensional projection of the original multi-dimensional space. It can be portrayed as a three-dimensional model, as a perspective drawing of the space, or as a set of two-dimensional projections which is the simplest way. Various methods of displaying such spaces have been used (Grotch, 1984), and Tufte (1983) gave some guidance for displaying complex data, and presented some examples of very clear graphics carrying a lot of information. PCAs having more than three dimensions can be portrayed as a series of two-dimensional plots. This can be either as exclusive pairs, or as consecutive pairs, or as every possible pair, though the last option becomes impractical with a large number of components. The number of plots required is $n(n-1)/2$, so for six components, 15 plots would be necessary. One solution has been to use the 'spider's web' type of plot favoured by flavour profile analysis, the spokes or axes of the plot being components. The scores for an object can then be plotted as a closed curve around the web (Aishima, 1979; Hashimoto and Eshima, 1980).

2.2. Number of Components

A number of criteria have been suggested for choosing the number of components for the solution:

  1. *The eigenvalue equals 1·0* has been suggested as the cut-off point.

This is based on the idea that a component having an eigenvalue of 1·0 is explaining only the average proportion of variance in the data. This is because the sum of the eigenvalues of a full-rank matrix (i.e. a correlation matrix calculated from data where no variables are perfectly correlated and where there are more observations than variables) equals the number of eigenvalues which equals the number of rows and columns. Therefore the average eigenvalue is 1·0, and so eigenvalues greater than 1·0 correspond to a disproportionately large proportion of variance.

2. *The scree test* is based on a plot of eigenvalues versus component extracted. It tends to fall quickly at first, and then levels out and falls more slowly, as residual or random variance is explained by subsequent components. The cut-off should be at the point where the curve levels out.

3. *The proportion of variance* explained can be useful, if the analyst has some previous idea of the acceptable proportion of variance, or proportion of error in the data. The total variance in the data is given by the sum of the **R** matrix eigenvalues, and from the above the variance of the ith principal component is just the eigenvalue, λ_i. It is thus a simple matter to compute the proportional variance explained by the ith component by examining the **R** matrix eigenvalues. The total proportion of variance accounted for by the first K components is found to be

$$P_K = \frac{\lambda_1 + \lambda_2 + \cdots + \lambda_K}{\lambda_1 + \lambda_2 + \cdots + \lambda_P}$$

$$= \frac{\lambda_1 + \cdots + \lambda_K}{P} \quad \text{(for a correlation matrix)}$$

(23)

In the special case that this quantity is close to one then it is probable that only K underlying variables are necessary to describe the observations. If two or more of the original variables are completely dependent, the rank of the data matrix will be reduced, and one or more of the eigenvalues will become zero. In this case, all of the data variance can be explained by $K < P$ components.

4. *The meaningfulness criterion* suggests that components are ignored when they become impossible to interpret.

5. *The communalities* (sums of squared loadings) for each variable can be helpful, in that one or more low communalities after a particular number of components shows that a significant proportion of variance of those variables remains to be explained.

6. The *Bartlett significance test* was proposed by Bartlett (1950) to test the significance of the remaining $P - K$ roots of a correlation matrix. The statistic calculated is

$$\chi^2 = - \{n - \tfrac{1}{6}(2P + 5) - \tfrac{2}{3}K\} \log_e R_{P-K} \qquad (24)$$

where $n = N - 1$, which follows an approximate χ^2 distribution with $1/2(P - K + 2)(P - K - 1)$ degrees of freedom (Bartlett, 1951). R_{P-K} is given by

$$R_{P-K} = |R| \Big/ \left\{ \lambda_1 \lambda_2 \cdots \lambda_K \left[\frac{P - \lambda_1 - \lambda_2 - \cdots - \lambda_K}{P - K} \right]^{P-K} \right\} \qquad (25)$$

Since R is a correlation matrix, the sum of all the eigenvalues equals P, and their product equals the determinant, $|R|$. Thus

$$R_{P-K} = \left(\frac{G}{A} \right)^{P-K} \qquad (26)$$

so

$$\chi^2 = \left(N - \frac{2P + 11}{6} - \frac{2K}{3} \right) (P - K) \log_e \left(\frac{A}{G} \right) \qquad (27)$$

where N is the number of objects or observations in the data matrix, K is the number of principal components to be retained ($< P$), A is the arithmetic mean of the eigenvalues corresponding to the components which are rejected, and G is the geometric mean of these eigenvalues,

$$A = \frac{1}{(P - K)} \sum_{i = K + 1}^{P} \lambda_i \qquad (28)$$

$$G = \left[\prod_{i = K + 1}^{P} \lambda_i \right]^{1/(P-K)} \qquad (29)$$

This expression is appropriate if the largest eigenvalues have already been eliminated; if a complete set of χ^2 approximations is calculated, Bartlett proposed an alternative multiplying factor, $(n - P + 1/2)$, corresponding to $K = P - 2$. By comparing the test statistic with the χ^2 percentiles from tables, it is possible to estimate whether the data can be represented by a reduced number of variables. K is normally chosen to result in the most likely χ^2 value.

For example, suppose in an experiment involving 30 objects and 4 variables, the correlation matrix eigenvalues were found to be

$$\lambda_1 = 2 \cdot 00, \quad \lambda_2 = 1 \cdot 80, \quad \lambda_3 = 0 \cdot 12, \quad \lambda_4 = 0 \cdot 08$$

and Bartlett's test is to be used to decide the number of components to retain. Using $P = 4$ and $N = 30$ in Eqn. (27) gives the following values for the Bartlett statistic for different values of K:

K	Bartlett statistic	Degrees of freedom	90% point of χ^2 distribution
0	90·3	9	14·68
1	74·4	5	9·24
2	1·0	2	4·61

Starting with $K = 0$, the computed Bartlett statistic is compared with the appropriate χ^2 distribution from tables, using the degrees of freedom given above. In this example, two components would be chosen, since 1·0 is less than 4·61, the 90th percentile for the χ^2 distribution with two degrees of freedom. The value for $K = 1$ is too large to be associated with the χ^2 distribution for five degrees of freedom. For comparison, the table below shows the proportion of variance explained by retaining the leading K components (as computed using Eqn. (23)).

K	Proportion of variance explained
1	0·50
2	0·95
3	0·98
4	1·00

This clearly shows that the first two components alone account for the majority (95%) of the variation in the data matrix.

Malinowski and Howery (1980) described a number of further tests which can be used when the analyst has some estimate of experimental error, all intended to partition the eigenvalues into primary (those associated with real variation) and secondary (those associated with error) sets. This is achieved by comparison of the eigenvalues with various estimates of error, to decide which eigenvalues are significantly different from zero and therefore belong to the primary set. They concluded that none of the criteria is completely satisfactory, and that in practical cases most or all of the tests are likely to be useful and should be employed in deciding how many components to take.

2.3. Sample Size and Repeatability

Principal components analysis as a mathematical procedure makes no assumptions about the distributions of the variables used (Gower, 1966). However, no estimate of population principal components can be made unless distributions are specified. Dudzinski *et al.* (1975) used a Monte Carlo method to study the effect of various sample sizes, and concluded that normality did not seem to be of prime importance for repeatability, which depended more on the ratios of consecutive eigenvalues. The larger the ratio, the smaller sample size was required for adequate repeatability. This ratio will be large where the population sampled has a strong structure, i.e. where the cloud of objects in space has a long major axis. The corresponding point is that, where the eigenvalues are small, i.e. the cloud is more nearly spherical and the extraction of principal components has limited value and a low proportion of variance will be explained, repeatability is likely to be poor. They also recommended the use of the correlation matrix, rather than the dispersion (variance–covariance) matrix for the sake of improved repeatability. With a fixed sample size, inspection of the eigenvalues (or proportion of variance explained) or their ratios for successive components can assist in deciding how many components to take. The method of 'boot-strapping' (Diaconis and Efron, 1983) or cross-validation (Wold *et al.*, 1984) can also be used to guard against taking components which are too dependent on the actual objects used. In cross-validation, the analysis is repeated several times with different subsets of objects omitted, and the scores of the omitted objects are estimated from the model. The number of components chosen is that which gives the minimum residual sum of squares for the omitted objects. The power of the model to explain the data and reduce the residuals of the objects present clearly increases as the number of parameters in the model (that is components) increases, but the validity of the model and the extent to which it can be generalised decrease.

2.4. Factor Rotation

Component or factor rotation has been practised since the early days of factor analysis and PCA, as an aid to interpretation of results. In graphical rotation, the analyst simply rotated the factors or components by eye until he found what he thought was the best fit; in analytical rotation, the components are rotated to a predetermined mathematical criterion. Graphical rotation has fallen out of use over recent years, as faster computers have become available and better criteria have been proposed.

The ultimate aim of factor rotation is to obtain a more meaningful description of the data in terms of a set of factors, and if possible to find a simple factor structure (Thurstone, 1947). In terms of the original factors or principal components, $\mathbf{Y}$, which have been standardised to have unit column variance, the data matrix $\mathbf{X}$ can be represented by

$$\mathbf{X} = \mathbf{Y}\mathbf{L}' \qquad (30)$$

where $\mathbf{L}$ is the $(P \times K)$ matrix of loadings of the P variables on the K factors. The process of factor rotation introduces a new set of factors, $\mathbf{F}$, obtained by rotating the original factors, $\mathbf{Y}$, using a $K \times K$ rotation matrix, $\mathbf{G}$,

$$\mathbf{F} = \mathbf{Y}\mathbf{G} \qquad (31)$$

In terms of these rotated factors, the original data are now described by

$$\mathbf{X} = \mathbf{F}\mathbf{L}_R' \qquad (32)$$

where $\mathbf{L}_R$ is the $(P \times K)$ matrix of loadings of the variables on each of the rotated factors. From a geometrical viewpoint, the columns of the rotated factor matrix $\mathbf{F}$ are a set of unit axes in a K-dimensional coordinate system for describing each object. The rotation may be orthogonal, in which case the rotated factors are uncorrelated and the coordinate axes are orthogonal, or oblique, where correlation between the factors is allowed. The oblique rotation is inherently more flexible and realistic by not assuming that the underlying factors affecting the data are unrelated, but is usually more computationally tedious to apply. One advantage of using an orthogonal rotation however is that it is relatively easy to evaluate the loadings on the rotated factors. In this case the rotated factor loadings are given by

$$\mathbf{L}_R = \mathbf{L}\mathbf{G} \qquad (33)$$

In food science, orthogonal rotation has been most commonly used, and the methods most used are probably Varimax and Quartimax (Kaiser, 1959; Cooley and Lohnes, 1971). A small disadvantage of rotation is that the components must be rotated after the preferred number of components has been chosen. The first four of, for example, six rotated components might bear little relationship to the first four components, selected and then rotated. Rotation is trivial if a two-component solution is chosen, because the analyst can perform the rotation equally well by turning the page; however, when more components are used, the rotation can best be carried out by calculation and new components plotted.

In both methods, the rotation is carried out to maximise the variance of the squared loadings. In Quartimax rotation, the variance is maximised within variables, while the Varimax method, on the other hand, maximises variance within factors. The effect is that Quartimax tries to simplify *variables* by producing one or more large loadings and the rest as near to zero as possible. The Varimax method simplifies *factors*, so that for each factor there are a few high loadings and the remainder near zero.

Both Quartimax and Varimax rotations use internal criteria to find the rotated solution. It is also possible to rotate components to some external criterion, for example to see if the object configuration produced is similar to that produced by a different analysis. This is the procedure that Procrustes rotation uses, as discussed in Chapter 7. Alternatively, the principal component loadings can be rotated to see if some external effect, a hypothesised factor, is present in the data. This can be achieved either by regression of the hypothesis factor on the loadings vectors (Malinowski and Howery, 1980), or by extraction of the hypothesis factor from the correlation matrix (Cooley and Lohnes, 1971).

2.5. Examples
Two examples will be considered, to introduce the application of PCA to data sets resulting from chemical analysis and from sensory analysis. The major difference between these two kinds of data is that chemical data is likely to be virtually free of error, whereas sensory data is likely to contain a large proportion of error. This difference affects the interpretation of results.

2.5.1. Chemical Data
The first example is applied to data of Lehtonen (1983a,b). He analysed a set of distilled beverages for volatile and non-volatile phenols, and published the entire data set. A discriminant analysis was carried out, but no further multivariate analysis was published. The measured phenols

TABLE 1

VOLATILE AND NON-VOLATILE PHENOLS MEASURED IN DISTILLED BEVERAGES
(Adapted from Lehtonen, 1983a,b)

Number		Concentration ($mg\ litre^{-1}$)	
		Mean	Standard deviation ($n = 68$)
1	Phenol	0·062 1	0·062 8
2	o-Cresol	0·032 6	0·045 4
3	m-Cresol	0·016 8	0·016 1
4	p-Cresol	0·026 3	0·035 7
5	Guaiacol	0·083 4	0·171 7
6	p-Ethylphenol	0·154 0	0·398 7
7	p-Ethylguaiacol	0·187 1	0·327 0
8	Eugenol	0·141 6	0·258 6
9	p-(n-Propyl)guaiacol	0·043 4	0·166 2
10	Gallic acid	2·773 1	2.583 2
11	Vanillic acid	0·336 5	0·356 3
12	Syringic acid	0·606 0	0·681 1
13	Vanillin	0·870 1	0·923 5
14	Syringaldehyde	1·723 1	1·774 4
15	Ferulic acid	0·004 4	0·012 6

and summary statistics are shown in Table 1. Calculation of the correlation matrix was straightforward, followed by extraction of eigenvalues and eigenvectors.

At this point, a decision must be made about the number of components to be used in the solution. In the present example, the appropriate statistics are shown in Table 2. The Bartlett statistic showed a large number of significant components, and application of other tests suggested that about four components should be accepted (scree test, eigenvalue). However, examination of the communalities showed that variation in vanillin and ferulic acid was not well accounted for; the fifth component significantly increased the communality for ferulic acid, and the sixth component for vanillin. Inspection of the original data showed that only one sample had a high value for ferulic acid, and that one sample had a high value for vanillin. These two final components were necessary to accommodate two unusual samples. An exploratory data analysis, such as simple plotting of distributions (Tukey, 1977; Hoaglin et al., 1983), by hand or using a program such as MINITAB, can be useful to identify outliers before any multivariate analysis is carried out.

In the present case, six components were chosen, acknowledging that the last two were of little general interest, and probably would not

TABLE 2

EIGENVALUES OF THE CORRELATION MATRIX OF PHENOL CONCENTRATIONS, PROPORTIONS OF VARIANCE AND BARTLETT'S χ^2

Number	Eigenvalue	Proportion of variance explained	Cumulative proportion of variance	χ^2	Degrees of freedom
1	6·032 0	0·402 1	0·402 1	1 710	119
2	3·829 6	0·255 3	0·657 4	1 423	104
3	2·434 0	0·162 3	0·819 7	1 139	90
4	0·851 7	0·056 8	0·876 5	835	77
5	0·755 0	0·050 3	0·926 8	716	65
6	0·579 3	0·038 6	0·965 4	547	54
7	0·220 7	0·014 7	0·980 1	304	44
8	0·088 7	0·005 9	0·986 1	179	35
9	0·067 5	0·004 5	0·990 6	139	27
10	0·054 2	0·003 6	0·994 2	104	20
11	0·035 2	0·002 3	0·996 5	67	14
12	0·022 5	0·001 5	0·998 0	41	9
13	0·016 2	0·001 1	0·999 1	25	5
14	0·009 5	0·000 6	0·999 7	10	2
15	0·003 9	0·000 3	1·000 0	0	0

appear in a slightly different sample set. This led to a six-dimensional space, the components accounting for progressively smaller proportions of variance in the data. Interpretation of the resulting components must be the next stage of the analysis. This can best be done by inspecting variable loadings and sample scores, shown in Figs. 1 and 2. The components can be viewed as representing uncorrelated sources of variation in the original data, i.e. the variation in the original data was a result of six underlying factors, whose independent variation caused the observed data. In many practical cases, some variables will be highly correlated with only one component, their values being affected by only one underlying factor; other variables will have high correlations with more than one component, their values being affected by more than one underlying factor.

Thus examination of Fig. 1 showed that a group of variables was heavily loaded on component 1, and o-cresol and m-cresol had smaller loadings. Similarly, a group of variables had large negative loadings on the second component, and gallic acid, vanillin and ferulic acid had smaller loadings. For both components, there was only one group of variables, all positively correlated with each other; there were no negative

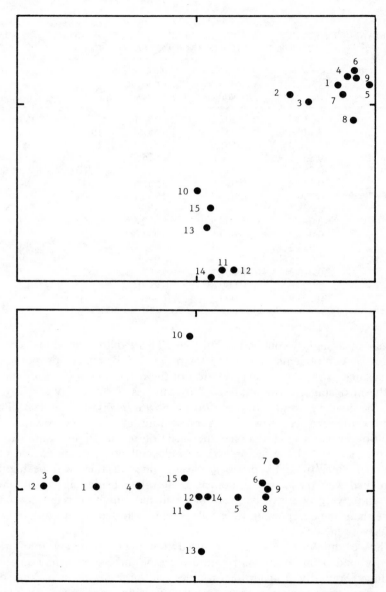

FIG. 1. Loadings of 15 volatile and non-volatile phenols on the first and second (top) and third and fourth (bottom) principal components, from data of Lehtonen (1983a,b). The phenols are identified in Table 1.

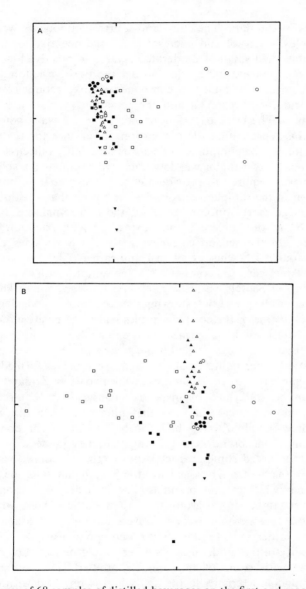

FIG. 2. Scores of 68 samples of distilled beverages on the first and second (A) and third and fourth (B) principal components, from data of Lehtonen (1983a,b). □ Scotch whisky; ▼ U.S. whiskey; ■ Other whisky; △ Cognac; ▲ Brandy; ○ Dark rum; ● White rum.

correlations in the data. The third and fourth components were rather more complex. o-Cresol and m-cresol had large negative loadings, and other variables had small or moderate negative or positive loadings. On the fourth component, gallic acid had a large positive loading, and all others were small. The final two components took account of variation in ferulic acid (positive on 5) and the remaining variation in vanillin (positive on 6). The largest loading on component 6 was about 0·6, the square of this representing the proportion of variance for that variable accounted for by the component. This was low, but as discussed above, the communality of vanillin was low after five components, so the sixth component was required to provide a complete explanation of the data.

Inspection of the sample scores in Fig. 2 showed that a group of dark rums had large scores on component 1, the two remaining dark rums obviously being very different and having much in common with the white rums. On the second component, three US whiskies had large scores, the fourth US whiskey again being rather different—less characteristically 'American'. On component 3, the samples with extreme scores were a group of Scotch whiskies and again the dark rums. The Scotch whiskies were well spread out, showing that they varied considerably. On component 4, some of the cognac samples had large positive scores, and the Indian whisky a large negative score. The US whiskies, with moderate negative scores, clearly had some similarity. Detailed examination showed some further points; that the Japanese whiskies formed a group with some similarity to the Scotch; that the two New Zealand whiskies were so similar, confirmed by inspection of the data, that they might have been the same material; and that nine rums were likewise very similar. Three Scotch whiskies had sizeable scores on component 4, in the direction of the brandies, suggesting that they possessed a 'Scotch' character, but shared some characteristics of the brandies. It is notable that some of the Scotch whiskies had little Scotch character, being in the area of other whiskies and brandies. The fifth and sixth components showed a very tight central group with a few outliers; a US whiskey on component 5, the Indian whisky positive on component 6 and another US whiskey rather outside the group on component 6.

The stability of the model described here could be tested by repeating the analysis with some of the samples omitted. Two samples were apparently uncharacteristic, so the analysis was repeated without them. Comparison with the previous analysis showed slight differences, but no clear simplification. Sample scores are shown in Fig. 3. Components 1, 2 and 3, though reversed, were similar to those in the original analysis. The

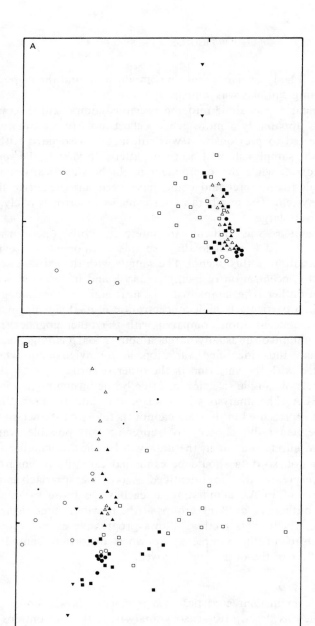

FIG. 3. Scores of samples of distilled beverages on the first and second (A) and third and fourth (B) principal components, after elimination of two samples, from data of Lehtonen (1983a,b). Symbols are as in Fig. 2.

brandies still had positive scores on component 4, and the disposition of the remaining samples was similar.

Component 5 was similar to the previous component 6, confirming that it was apparently a more general effect, not simply caused by the outlier referred to previously. It was still largely associated with ferulic acid, and the samples showed no clear pattern. In view of the very small amounts found, while this component might be statistically sensible, it was difficult to interpret and could have been an artefact of the data recording system. The numbers were so small that error is likely to have been relatively large.

Component 6 was difficult to interpret. Only one variable, p-ethylguaiacol, had a small loading, so this component was explaining residual variation in this phenol. The sample with the extreme score had the highest concentration of p-ethylguaiacol, and in this case was identified as an outlier. The sample with the next highest score, a cognac, did not contain a particularly high concentration of p-ethylguaiacol, but had the highest concentration compared with the other cognacs, i.e. both samples contained unusually large amounts of p-ethylguaiacol. The analysis had thus identified variation in p-ethylguaiacol which was uncorrelated with the variation in the other phenols.

The effects of sample selection must be borne in mind when interpreting any PCA. The analysis will describe the data set presented to it. Effects not represented in the data cannot therefore be shown, so samples should be carefully chosen to represent all possible variations. Conversely, effects present in the data will be shown, whether they are general or not, so data should be examined carefully to ensure that if outliers are present they are identified. A possible approach is to carry out a series of PCAs, eliminating at each stage those samples which appear as outliers or outlying groups at the previous stage (MacFie and Gutteridge, 1982). This method allows progressive examination of the 'fine structure' of the sample space when distortion caused by the leverage effect of the outliers is removed.

2.5.2. Sensory Data

One of the main characteristics of a sensory data set, collected by a method such as descriptive sensory analysis, is that it contains a large proportion of errors, or noise. The problem for the analyst is therefore two-fold: firstly, separation of useful information from error; and secondly, the display of the information in a form in which it can be interpreted. This second problem is the same as that in the example above. The first problem can also be partly overcome by PCA. As described above, PCA seeks to explain the maximum proportion of variance in the data by assembling correlated variables into linear combinations. Thus the proportion of variance in a variable which is correlated with other variables is explained in a principal components model, while the uncorrelated variation is not explained until a later component. Thus, if there are many more variables than sources of variation, the variables will form correlated groups. The error, on the other hand, as long as it is random and uncorrelated, will be left out, and only explained by the PCA in later components. Maxwell (1977) warned against over-reliance on this effect, but in practice it seems to effect a valuable selection of the data. Some correlation inevitably appears by chance, but as a general rule, if there are only one or two large loadings on a component, the analyst should inspect the results carefully and decide whether these components are showing useful information or merely random error. This should not be taken as a recommendation to use many more variables than are necessary. This not only increases the probability of correlations appearing by chance, but if variables are redundant, in that they are measuring an effect already measured by other variables, they contribute only to the error and not to the information collected. The statistics cannot give a certain answer, though the tests above are a useful guide; the analyst must interpret the results in the light of any other information available.

Sixteen samples of fruit drinks were profiled by a panel of assessors using a vocabulary of 27 descriptive terms (Table 3) to give a data matrix of 16 objects by 27 variables, which was subjected to PCA. A large proportion of error could be expected in the data, so the principal components model was not expected to explain all or nearly all the variance. Eigenvalues and percentage variance explained are shown in Table 4. A plot of eigenvalue against component is shown in Fig. 4. Applying the same criteria as before, the number of components necessary to describe the data was chosen.

The eigenvalues of the correlation matrix (Table 4), and corresponding proportions of variance extracted, suggested that two or three components would be satisfactory, but many communalities were still low. Four components provided a more satisfactory solution, but three communalities were still low. If five components were taken, one communality was low, but this term, *spicy*, did not appear to be very important from examination of the profiles. Component 5 accounted for the residue of variance in *sulphury* and *sulphitic* (which had high scores

TABLE 3

TERMS USED FOR DESCRIPTIVE SENSORY ANALYSIS OF ORANGE DRINKS

Abbreviation	Term	Score	
		Mean	Standard deviation ($n=16$)
Fra	Fragrant	1·049	0·509
Swe	Sweaty, rancid	0·394	0·282
Nut	Nutty, coconut	0·216	0·180
Bur	Burnt, phenolic	0·152	0·161
Gra	Grassy	0·293	0·136
Sos	Sour, acid smell	0·569	0·257
Sic	Sickly	0·587	0·365
Mou	Mouldy, musty	0·187	0·149
Pun	Pungent, acrid	0·285	0·186
Oil	Oily, fatty	0·354	0·141
Sol	Solvent	0·078	0·065
DMS	Sulphury (DMS)	0·208	0·177
Sws	Sweet smell	1·422	0·719
Spi	Spicy	0·182	0·136
Min	Minty	0·071	0·065
SO_2	Sulphitic, SO_2	0·676	0·515
Fes	Fruity (estery)	0·588	0·411
Fot	Fruity (other)	1·081	0·707
For	Fruity (orange)	1·560	0·815
Fle	Fruity (lemon)	0·380	0·301
Soa	Soapy	0·222	0·107
Van	Vanilla	0·236	0·288
Flo	Floral	0·397	0·280
Smo	Smooth	0·350	0·194
Swt	Sweet taste	1·883	0·590
Sot	Sour taste	0·934	0·365
Bit	Bitter taste	0·491	0·340

for sample number 8, sample number 10 and sample number 12) not related to other variables. *Sulphury* and *sulphitic* were already loosely related to component 3. On component 5, sample number 8 had an extreme score, while sample number 10 and sample number 12 were among the central group. Four components were therefore accepted as providing the best representation of the data.

Examination of the plots of variable loadings on components (Fig. 5) showed a very unclear picture, with many variables having moderate loadings. This was a case where a rotation might make interpretation of the components easier. The results of applying two rotations to the first

TABLE 4
EIGENVALUES OF THE CORRELATION MATRIX OF DESCRIPTIVE TERMS AND PROPORTIONS OF VARIANCE

Number	Eigenvalue	Proportion of variance	Cumulative proportion of variance
1	12·437 6	0·460 7	0·460 7
2	5·564 7	0·206 1	0·666 8
3	0·541 0	0·094 1	0·760 9
4	1·744 8	0·064 6	0·825 5
5	1·098 2	0·040 7	0·866 2
6	0·878 8	0·032 5	0·898 7
7	0·698 9	0·025 9	0·924 6
8	0·514 1	0·019 0	0·943 6
9	0·432 8	0·016 0	0·959 7
10	0·372 5	0·013 8	0·973 5
11	0·284 3	0·015 3	0·984 0
12	0·231 2	0·008 6	0·992 6
13	0·111 5	0·004 1	0·996 7
14	0·061 1	0·002 3	0·998 9
15	0·028 6	0·001 1	1·000 0

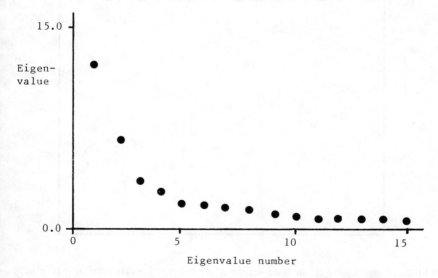

FIG. 4. Eigenvalues of correlation matrix of terms used for descriptive sensory analysis of orange drinks.

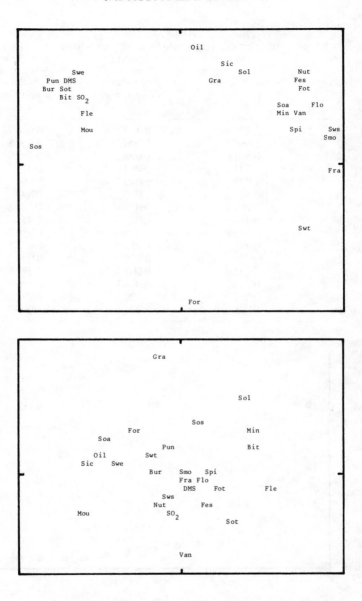

FIG. 5. Loadings of terms used for descriptive sensory analysis of orange drinks on the first and second (top) and third and fourth (bottom) principal components. Abbreviations are shown in Table 3.

four components are shown in Figs. 6 and 7. Neither rotation was clearly 'better' or more easily interpreted. On components 1 and 2, Quartimax produced tighter groups of high loadings, but Varimax reduced the small loadings more. On components 3 and 4, the reverse appeared to be the case. Both were more readily interpreted than the unrotated loadings. In general, Varimax seems to be the preferred rotation where a rotation is used, despite the general similarity of these results.

Having selected the preferred number of components and rotation, interpretation proceeded as before. Sample scores on four Varimax components are plotted in Fig. 8.

A further use of PCA is in the investigation of hedonic data. Hedonic data were collected from 13 assessors, who examined the orange drink samples and provided a matrix of samples by assessors. This was processed in exactly the same way, treating the assessors as variables and the samples as objects, to give a matrix of loadings of assessors on components. Two components were selected, to provide a much simplified model of the assessors' behaviour. Sample scores were next superimposed, to provide a representation of the samples likely to be preferred by individuals or groups of assessors. Note that in interpretation of this much reduced-rank model, the length of the assessor's vector showed how well the two-dimensional representation had explained the data. Assessors with short vectors were not well accounted for, and were a clear indication that the model was incomplete. However, the quality of the data must be considered also. It is very easy to 'overanalyse' and construct elaborate models founded on chance and error.

To aid interpretation of such analyses, measured variables can also be plotted as vectors on such a plot. To do this, it is only necessary to calculate the correlations between the variables and the component scores, and plot such correlations. This is shown in Fig. 9. The variables could be sensory data, as in this case, or physico-chemical or other measures.

Interpretation of these results was straightforward. The loadings plot of assessors on components represented correlations between assessors, i.e. those plotted close together were likely to share likes and dislikes, though the actual scale values used might vary. The similarity was greatest when the assessors' loadings were large on the components used—assessors with low loadings on these components were not well accommodated by the model. In this case, the proportion of variance accounted for was 63%, and all assessors were relatively well accommodated. The lowest communality on 2 components was 0·45.

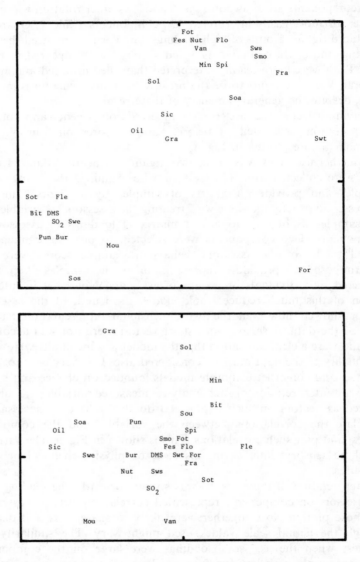

FIG. 6. Loadings of terms used for descriptive sensory analysis of orange drinks on four components rotated by the Quartimax method. Abbreviations are shown in Table 3.

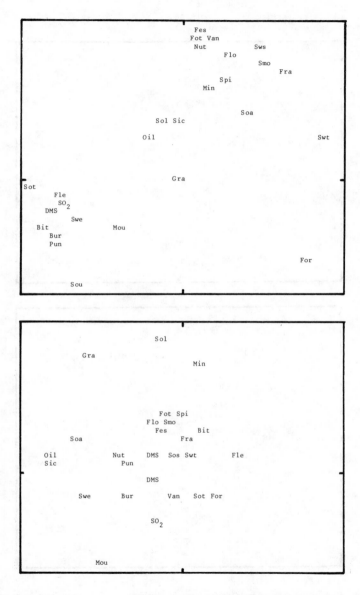

FIG. 7. Loadings of terms used for descriptive sensory analysis of orange drinks on four components rotated by the Varimax method. Abbreviations are shown in Table 3.

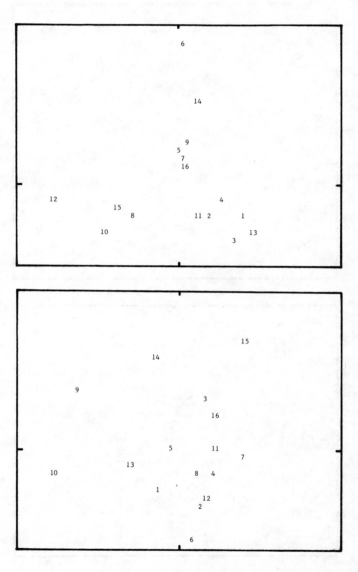

FIG. 8. Scores of 16 samples of orange drinks on four principal components rotated by the Varimax method.

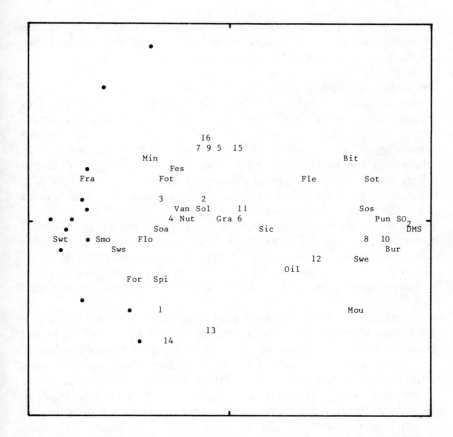

FIG. 9. Loadings of assessors (filled circles) on two principal components, calculated from hedonic data on orange drinks, plotted with sample scores and correlations between scores and descriptive terms. The samples are identified by numbers as in Fig. 8, and the abbreviations for descriptive terms are shown in Table 3.

Component 1 was unipolar, showing that there was a measure of agreement among the assessors, whereas the variations among assessors were described by component 2. The plot of sample scores showed that three samples were disliked by all, five samples were liked by assessors 1 and 7, and three samples were liked by assessors 6, 10 and 11.

The plot of descriptive terms shows the terms associated with the disliked samples, and with the samples liked by the various groups of assessors. This provides one route towards the problem of relating physico-chemical or sensory data to hedonic or acceptability data. Other methods are discussed in Chapters 8 and 9.

2.6. Other Applications

There are many examples of PCA in the bibliography of Martens and Harries (1983), where the purpose and interpretation of the analysis were similar to the examples above, but it has some other less common applications. It can be used to separate a number of underlying 'effects', where they can be measured only indirectly as the sum of the several effects present. Kowalski (1983) gives as an example the use of PCA to separate co-eluting materials in gas chromatography. Infra-red spectra are taken repeatedly during elution of the peaks, and a PCA carried out using the wavelengths as variables and the successive scans as objects. If there are two components in the peak, then two principal components will be necessary to explain the variation in the spectra. This is an example of the resolution of complex curves into the components of the mixtures which gave rise to them (Shurvell and Dunham, 1978; Sharaf and Kowalski, 1981).

A similar example of the use of PCA of spectral data was reported by Cowe and McNicol (1985). Near-infra-red spectra for sets of wheat and barley samples were collected, and reflectance measurements taken at 681 wavelengths. The usual method of calibration of such instruments is multiple regression, but this is unsatisfactory where such a large number of variables (wavelengths) is used. In this case, PCA allowed the majority of the variation in the spectra to be described by six principal components, and virtually all the variation by 10 components. The component scores were then used as predictor variables for multiple regression. The components were by definition uncorrelated, so selection of the components to use in the multiple regression was a simple matter. It was only necessary to choose those components having the highest correlations with the variable to be predicted, until an acceptable value of R^2 was reached. An unusual output display was used in this report, the coefficients of each component being plotted against the wavelength. This was used as an alternative to a loadings plot for identifying the variables which were important in a component. It is only possible where the variables form a continuum such as wavelength, since it is clearly nonsensical to use for example unrelated chemical measures as the scale for such a plot.

Hill and Goodchild (1981) presented a PCA of some unusual data;

wheat yields for the shires of the Western Australia wheat belt over a period of 47 consecutive years. The analysis was carried out by treating the shires as variables and the years as objects. The shires could thus be separated into groups which tended to vary together, and the variation interpreted by reference to external data, such as meteorological or socioeconomic data. They considered that this method of analysis was the only one which permitted a meaningful picture of the variation in yield to be assembled.

Ratkowsky and Martin (1974) applied PCA to the residuals matrix after removing the treatment effect in an experiment on apples. The pooled SSCP matrix was converted to a correlation matrix for extraction of components. They emphasised the importance of using such an 'unstructured' matrix. This is similar to the problem in factor analysis of heterogeneous sample sets (Cattell, 1965; Gower, 1966), where analysis of the whole data set provides factors which do not well describe the complete data set or the sub-sets. The action recommended in that case was to analyse the sub-groups separately, and then to analyse the whole data set in the form of its sub-group means. This problem is analogous to a simple regression or correlation where a line is constructed between two groups of points (Chapter 3). The line might not adequately describe the relationship between the variables either between or within the two groups.

Martens (1979) used principal components analysis (and maximum likelihood factor analysis) to examine the amino acid spectra of millet grain grown under different conditions. The raw data were in the form of a rectangular matrix of amino acids (variables) versus millet samples (objects), and the problem was to determine the number and amounts of proteins (or co-varying protein groups) contributing to the overall variation in amino acid composition. The raw variables were weighted to allow for variation in the analytical uncertainty of the determinations, so that greater importance was attached to the more precise determinations. MacFie and Gutteridge (1982) used a similar weighting method. Martens and Bach Knudsen (1980) used similar procedures to examine the amino acid spectra of barley proteins. Vallis et al. (1983) described the use of PCA to estimate amounts of constituents in mass spectra of mixtures after Pyrolysis-MS. The mass spectra were normalised so that the intensity of the most abundant ion was 100, or so that the sum of intensities was 100, in order to allow for the effect of different sample sizes. Elliott et al. (1971) used PCA to reduce the number of GC peaks measured over a series of hop oils before carrying out discriminant analysis. Newell (1981) described the use of PCA to estimate the 'effective precision' of analytical methods, i.e. precision plus bias, when no reference method known to be correct was available. The main interest in this case was the unexplained variance in the PCA, since this could not have been due to the systematic effect of the actual composition of the samples.

3. PRINCIPAL COORDINATE ANALYSIS

PCO is a type of metric multi-dimensional scaling procedure, and attempts to provide a description of the objects in the data using a reduced set of $K(<P)$ underlying factors. The starting point for this class of techniques is an $N \times N$ matrix of distances, $\mathbf{Q}$, between each object in the data, as discussed above in Eqn. (6). Each row of this distance matrix can be viewed as describing the coordinates of each object in a space of N dimensions. The purpose of PCO is to reduce the dimensionality of this space, while attempting to keep the distance matrix of the objects in this new space as close as possible to the original object distance matrix. MacFie and Thomson (1984) gave as an example the construction of a map showing the relative positions of a number of UK towns from a matrix of distances between them. This is accomplished using the eigenvectors and eigenvalues of the distance matrix $\mathbf{Q}$, as follows.

Employing the singular value decomposition it is possible to represent the original data matrix in the form

$$\mathbf{X} = \sum_{i=1}^{\min(N,P)} \lambda_i^{1/2} \mathbf{v}_i \mathbf{u}_i' \qquad (34)$$

where the $(N \times 1)$ column vectors, $\{\mathbf{v}_i\}$, are the eigenvectors of the 'distance' matrix $\mathbf{Q} = \mathbf{XX}'$, the vectors $\{\mathbf{u}_i\}$ are the $(P \times 1)$ eigenvectors of the correlation matrix $\mathbf{R} = \mathbf{X}'\mathbf{X}$, and the scalars $\{\lambda_i\}$ are the non-zero eigenvalues, which are identical for both the $\mathbf{Q}$ and $\mathbf{R}$ matrices. Note that the distance matrix $\mathbf{Q}$ employed here is a function of the Euclidean distance between two objects, defined in eqn. (6). Further discussion of the relationship between the eigenvectors $\{\mathbf{u}_i\}$ and $\{\mathbf{v}_i\}$ can be found below. The PCO simplification is obtained by approximating the relationship (34) using only the largest eigenvalues. That is, an *estimate* of the original data is given by

$$\hat{\mathbf{X}} = \sum_{i=1}^{K} \lambda_i^{1/2} \mathbf{v}_i \mathbf{u}_i' \qquad (35)$$

where $K < \min(N, P)$. This can be interpreted as describing each object in a K-dimensional sub-space of reduced factors. The new factors are the rows, $\mathbf{u}_i'$, which form a set of unit axes in the P-dimensional variable space. The principal coordinates of the objects are the weights applied to these axes, and are found to be

$$c_{ij} = \lambda_i^{1/2} v_{ij}, \quad \begin{aligned} j &= 1 \cdots K \\ i &= 1 \cdots N \end{aligned} \tag{36}$$

where c_{ij} is the jth coordinate of the ith object in the reduced space. These coordinates can subsequently be plotted to yield a new interpretation of the original data.

In common with PCA, PCO has certain optimal data reduction properties. For example, it can be shown that the resulting distance matrix of objects in the reduced space is closest to the original matrix (in the least squares sense) when the PCO factorisation is used. Furthermore, the variance of the objects in K-space, using the first K principal coordinates, is greater than any other choice of K coordinates.

Gower (1966) commented that the method of PCO was computationally more convenient than PCA because less calculation was involved. This is especially so in the case where there are more variables than objects, because a smaller matrix is processed (a distance matrix of objects, rather than a correlation matrix of variables). This is unlikely to be important where sufficient computer power is available, but for large data sets on small computers it could be an attraction. The disadvantage, of course, compared with PCA is that the relationships between the variables and the coordinate axes are not explicitly provided as they are by the coefficients or loadings in PCA.

However, the $\mathbf{R}$ and $\mathbf{Q}$ matrix eigenvectors required by PCA and PCO respectively are related through the singular value decomposition of the data matrix, introduced above. This leads to the possibility of reducing the computational workload in special cases of PCA, when there are fewer objects than variables.

The singular value decomposition of the standardised data matrix $\mathbf{X}(N \times P)$ is given by

$$\mathbf{X} = \mathbf{V}\mathbf{D}^{1/2}\mathbf{U}' \tag{37}$$

where $\mathbf{V}$ $(N \times K)$ is a matrix whose columns are the K leading eigenvectors of $\mathbf{Q} = \mathbf{X}\mathbf{X}'$, and $\mathbf{U}$ is a $P \times K$ matrix whose columns are the eigenvectors of $\mathbf{R} = \mathbf{X}'\mathbf{X}$. The matrix $\mathbf{D}$ is a diagonal matrix of corresponding non-zero eigenvalues; these are the same for both the $\mathbf{Q}$ and

R matrices. K is the minimum dimension of the data matrix, i.e. K is the smaller of N and P. Since the eigenvector matrices **V** and **U** are orthonormal, it can be shown that

$$\mathbf{V} = \mathbf{XUD}^{-1/2} \tag{38}$$

and

$$\mathbf{U} = \mathbf{X'VD}^{-1/2} \tag{39}$$

These two results show that it is possible to obtain the **Q** matrix eigenvectors from the **R** matrix eigenvalues and eigenvectors, and vice versa. The bulk of the computational workload in PCA and PCO is involved with the calculation of the eigenvalues and eigenvectors of the **R** or **Q** matrix, and this increases exponentially with the size of the matrix being decomposed. This computation can be minimised by employing the above results. For example, if a PCA is being performed on data with $N < P$, it would make sense, if P is large, to compute the eigenvalues and eigenvectors of $\mathbf{Q} = \mathbf{XX'}$ (a $N \times N$ matrix), instead of those of $\mathbf{R} = \mathbf{X'X}$ (a $P \times P$ matrix), and then use the relationship above (39) to obtain the desired **R** matrix eigenvectors. This was the method used by Cowe and McNicol (1985).

It is also possible to use (38) and (39) to analyse the data using PCA and PCO simultaneously, while only employing a single matrix eigenstructure calculation.

PCO is also useful where a mixture of variables is used. Gibbs *et al.* (1978) reported cluster analysis and PCO of *Staphylococcus aureus* strains, characterised by a mixture of dichotomous, qualitative and quantitative measures, using Gower's (1971) similarity measure. A PCA would have been possible on the dichotomous (binary) and quantitative data, but it is difficult to include qualitative (nominal) data in a PCA. It can be done by regarding each value of the nominal variable as a separate binary variable, but the result is rather unsatisfactory.

Wrigley *et al.* (1981) used PCO to examine electrophoregrams of cereal proteins in an attempt to classify 80 cereal genotypes. The distance matrix used was a Euclidean distance based on estimated intensity of 34 bands on a four-point scale. They commented that the result was disappointing, two axes accounting for only 38% of variance. They appear to have missed the implication of this, which is that their data were too complex to be adequately represented in two dimensions; further axes were necessary. A PCA was not carried out, though it might in these circumstances have been useful.

Bryant and Cowan (1979) reported a PCO of 235 strains of *Saccharomyces cerevisiae*, characterised by five brewing properties. The brewing properties were assessed on a three point scale from 1 to 5. With so few variables and so many objects, it is astonishing that a PCA was not carried out. However, the structure of the data was such that the PCO provided a useful separation of the effects present into two factors.

Laing and Willcox (1983) reported a PCO of a set of mixtures of hexenal and decenal, on Euclidean distances calculated from odour quality profile data. The analysis provided a very clear picture of the mixtures in two dimensions. This was taken as evidence that there was no significant interaction between the compounds, though the proportion of variance explained by two dimensions was not stated, and the third was apparently rejected because it could not be interpreted.

Campbell and Williams (1976) used PCO as Gower suggested as a computationally more convenient alternative to PCA, on three data sets on bananas. The three sets of principal coordinates were compared using canonical correlation, and the correlation coefficients then calculated over all objects between the original attributes (variables) and the scores on the canonical axes. This procedure provided a means of interpreting the canonical axes, similar to the calculation of correlations between variables and principal component scores, as was described above for the orange drink hedonic data.

Clark and Menary (1981) used PCO as a method of cluster analysis, having calculated a similarity matrix using the Canberra metric (Lance and Williams, 1967). They also commented that use of the Euclidean distance as a measure of similarity in place of the Canberra metric did not result in any important changes in coordinates or interpretation.

4. FACTORIAL CORRESPONDENCE ANALYSIS

FCA was originally developed and popularised by Benzecri and co-workers (e.g. Benzecri, 1969, 1982) for the analysis of contingency tables, where the cells contain frequencies of occurrences. Division by the grand sum of the table then provides estimates of probabilities in each cell. Since a contingency table is essentially a two-way classification of a set of observations, neither rows nor columns of the matrix need be regarded as distinctly 'variables' or 'objects'. Benzecri (1982) used the term 'element' for both rows and columns of the matrix. In order to plot both sets of elements on one plot, a fully symmetrical treatment of the data table is attractive. This is achieved by calculating a χ^2 distance as the similarity measure for both rows and columns, providing two square matrices of similarity measures. The analysis then yields two sets of coordinates which can be plotted on the same axes to display relationships between the elements.

The use of FCA of tables of measured variables followed, as the attraction of plotting variables and objects on the same axes was obvious. This can be achieved by the use of the 'profile distance' as the similarity measure between rows and columns. The suitability of FCA for a particular data set then depends on whether the profile distance is an appropriate similarity measure for both variables and objects. Zhou et al. (1983) pointed out that since the rows and columns of a data table are not inherently symmetrical, a symmetrical treatment of rows and columns will not necessarily produce a better solution.

The starting point for FCA is a matrix of frequency or measurement data resulting from the experimental observations. The first step in the analysis is to apply a symmetrical scaling to these data in order to achieve a measure of similarity between the rows (objects) and columns (variables) of the data matrix. In the case of frequency measurements, the scaled data matrix, $\mathbf{W}$, is obtained from the original data matrix, $\mathbf{X}$, by normalising each element, x_{ij}, by the square roots of the row and sum totals of $\mathbf{X}$,

$$w_{ij} = \frac{x_{ij}}{(\Sigma_k x_{ik} \cdot \Sigma_k x_{kj})^{1/2}} \tag{40}$$

This particular data normalisation has the important property that the *Euclidean* distances between the points whose coordinates are the rows of $\mathbf{W}$ are in fact the χ^2 profile distances between the original experimental objects. Similarly, the Euclidean distances between the points whose coordinates are the columns of $\mathbf{W}$ are the profile distances between the original experimental variables. The definition of the profile distance between elements i and j is given by

$$d_{ij}^2 = \sum_k \frac{x_{++}}{x_{+k}} \left(\frac{x_{ik}}{x_{i+}} - \frac{x_{jk}}{x_{j+}} \right)^2 \tag{41}$$

where

$$x_{+k} = \sum_i x_{ik}$$ = sum of kth column, where i and j are rows, or kth row where i and j are columns

$$x_{i+} = \sum_k x_{ik} \quad = \text{sum of } i\text{th row (or column)} \tag{42}$$

$$x_{j+} = \sum_k x_{jk} \quad = \text{sum of } j\text{th row (or column)}$$

$$x_{++} = \sum_{ik}\sum x_{ik} = \text{grand sum of matrix}$$

This profile distance measures the 'similarity' between a pair of objects by calculating a weighted average of the squared differences between the variable coordinates of each object, where each variable coordinate is normalised by the average measurement on the object. The term x_{++}/x_{+k} appearing in the above formula scales the component of the distance measure due to the kth variable by the average score of the kth variable. In this way a symmetrical object/variable scaling is applied to the data.

The second step in FCA is to apply both principal components and principal coordinates analyses to the scaled data matrix **W**. Since PCA and PCO provide factor analysis in terms of a Euclidean distance measure, this yields a factor analysis of the data in terms of the χ^2 profile distance measure defined above. PCA of the **W** matrix will provide a description of the variables in terms of a set of factors, while PCO will yield a description of the objects in terms of a set of underlying factors. Since the scaling involved in computing **W** is symmetrical with respect to the objects and variables, and since the eigenvalues of PCA and PCO are identical, it is possible to plot both the objects and variables in terms of the same set of factors. Thus a simultaneous Q and R factor analysis is applied to the experimental data. It is shown above that it is possible to extract the Q and R factors of **W** simultaneously by using the singular value decomposition. A further point of interest is that, due to the particular scaling employed in FCA, factor analysis will always produce a largest eigenvalue of unity. This eigenvalue and the associated factor are ignored in the analysis.

4.1. Survey Data Example

Pepper and Milson (1984) carried out a questionnaire survey of six sectors of the food service industry to investigate the use of fast foods in Scotland. They presented their data as a series of tables of response rates to the questions. After conversion from their relative response rates to actual frequencies, this study provided a data matrix of 30 rows (questions) by 6 columns (kinds of establishment). The entries in each cell of

TABLE 5

FOOD SERVICE INDUSTRY SECTORS AND SUMMARY STATISTICS OF FACTORIAL
CORRESPONDENCE ANALYSIS
(Pepper and Milson, 1984)

Abbr.	Sector	Weight	Relative contribution of factor				Sum over four factors
			1	2	3	4	
Empl	Employees' food services	223	0·119	0·306	0·005	0·473	0·903
Hotl	Hotels and restaurants	335	0·528	0·319	0·035	0·098	0·980
Educ	Educational establishments	383	0·062	0·000	0·922	0·001	0·985
Hosp	Hospitals	571	0·174	0·720	0·095	0·010	1·000
Scol	School meals	457	0·939	0·001	0·003	0·056	1·000
Cafe	Cafes, etc.	108	0·000	0·425	0·212	0·040	0·678

the matrix were the numbers of establishments which served various kinds of foods or thought various factors of preparation and presentation were important. The responding establishments and questions are shown in Tables 5 and 6.

The data matrix was analysed by FCA. The first decision which the analyst must make is again how many factors should be used for the solution. The eigenvalues and percentage explained of the association matrix (Table 7) are again the most useful guides, but in this case there was no clear cut-off point corresponding to the scree test, where the rate of decrease of the eigenvalues changed suddenly. The plot of eigenvalue against factor number was nearly straight, and two factors explained 68% of variance. For more detailed consideration, the two-way output of the analysis must be examined.

Among the summary statistics for the data matrix, the weights of each element (row and column totals) provide a warning—elements with very low weights must obviously be interpreted with caution since a small number of observations is likely to make them unreliable. In this case, only 7 cafes out of a possible 50 returned forms.

The most useful output from the analysis is the proportion of each element explained by each factor and the accumulated totals over a series of factors, and the coordinates of each element on the factors. The first factor explained 41% of the data, but the proportion of each element explained varied greatly. The second factor explained an additional 28%, and accommodated the elements rather better. However, the accumulated contributions of factors to elements were still very low for 'use of baked potatoes', 'importance of preparation skill' and frequencies of use of dehydrated foods and canned foods. This showed that changes in frequencies in these were not related to the other elements. The third factor explained 'use of baked potatoes' satisfactorily, but the accumulated explanation for 'use of canned foods' was still rather low. This was not explained until the fourth factor. Thus, two factors explained much of the data, but some elements were not well accommodated.

In the case of the columns of the matrix, hotels and schools were well explained by the first factor, and hospitals by the second. Educational establishments were explained by the third factor, and the residue in employees' food services by the fourth.

Detailed examination of the factors has shown that, in some cases, the representation provided by two factors was not very good; however, for the sake of simplicity and reliability two factors were considered to provide an adequate model. The elements plotted on the first two factors are shown in Fig. 10. It was immediately apparent that use of Indian, Chinese and Italian foods and frozen desserts, use of cooked/chilled foods and importance of pleasant surroundings were outliers, the only close relationship being between use of Indian and Chinese foods. Inspection of the data table showed that they did indeed have similar use profiles across the responding establishments.

Detailed inspection of Fig. 10 showed a general trend from commercial establishments (on the lower left) to institutions (on the upper right), though school meals services have recently begun to operate in a more commercial manner. It is interesting that, despite this tendency, the school meals services responded very differently from the hotels, restaurants and cafes. The commercial establishments were characterised by the use of cooked/chilled foods, soups and sandwiches and frozen desserts, and by regarding time taken in preparation as important. The institutions, on the other hand, were characterised by regarding as important cost, skill level and equipment required, ease of storage and ease of opening, and by their use of chicken and pies, burgers and pizza. The cost and resources pressure on the institutions was clearly evident. The central cluster was of loosely related or poorly explained elements, not clearly associated with either extreme of the identified trend.

The direction orthogonal to the commercial-institutional trend, i.e. from the lower right to the upper left, was less easy to interpret. The upper left quadrant could be characterised as less 'traditional', using oriental foods and (expensive) frozen foods. The lower right quadrant,

TABLE 6
QUESTIONS ASKED AND SUMMARY STATISTICS OF FACTORIAL CORRESPONDENCE ANALYSIS
(Pepper and Milson, 1984)

Abbr.	Question	Weight	Relative contribution of factor				Sum over four factors
			1	2	3	4	
Types of fast foods served:							
Fish	Fish and chips	40	0·353	0·431	0·037	0·004	0·825
Chic	Chicken or pies and chips	32	0·624	0·109	0·044	0·174	0·950
Indi	Indian foods	10	0·102	0·362	0·491	0·025	0·979
Chin	Chinese foods	6	0·071	0·800	0·011	0·118	1·000
Ital	Italian foods	11	0·477	0·157	0·350	0·014	0·999
Burg	Burgers and hot dogs	32	0·737	0·066	0·000	0·019	0·822
Soup	Soup, sandwiches and rolls	36	0·079	0·322	0·406	0·130	0·937
Pota	Potato bakes	19	0·054	0·005	0·712	0·054	0·825
Froz	Frozen sweets and desserts	11	0·529	0·054	0·176	0·189	0·947
Pizz	Pizzas	28	0·056	0·301	0·553	0·071	0·981
Regarded as very or extremely important:							
Cost	Cost	56	0·072	0·650	0·013	0·255	0·989
	Technical skills required	28	0·023	0·6??	0·000	0·074	0·740

		%					
	Customer preferences						
	(row partially cut off)	37	0·558	0·554	0·162	0·392	0·967
Time	Time taken to produce a product	34	0·000	0·518	0·399	0·009	0·925
Stor	Ease of storage	22	0·794	0·000	0·145	0·003	0·942
Open	Ease of opening packaging	10	0·279	0·346	0·005	0·033	0·663
	Used at least 2/3 times per week:						
Prep	Pre-prepared foods	44	0·053	0·107	0·332	0·507	0·998
Frig	Refrigerated foods	58	0·538	0·248	0·213	0·000	0·999
Froz	Frozen foods	59	0·985	0·001	0·004	0·005	0·995
Dehy	Dehydrated foods	30	0·040	0·003	0·223	0·312	0·578
Cans	Canned and bottled foods	60	0·021	0·022	0·012	0·936	0·992
Chil	Cooked/chilled foods	28	0·196	0·655	0·006	0·128	0·985
Raw	Basic raw ingredients	67	0·350	0·015	0·001	0·633	0·999
	Regarded as important:						
Fast	Fast service	29	0·220	0·228	0·277	0·133	0·858
Attr	Attractively served food	40	0·421	0·012	0·525	0·043	1·000
Plea	Pleasant surroundings	20	0·944	0·022	0·015	0·012	0·993
Chee	Cheerful service	26	0·928	0·016	0·031	0·020	0·995
Valu	Value for money	43	0·212	0·128	0·647	0·001	0·988
Clea	Cleanliness	31	0·455	0·002	0·226	0·017	0·700

TABLE 7
EIGENVALUES AND PROPORTIONS OF VARIANCE OF ASSOCIATION MATRIX OF
ELEMENTS IN TABLES 5 AND 6

Number	Eigenvalue	Proportion of variance	Cumulative proportion of variance
2	0·0263	0·4064	0·4064
3	0·0179	0·2768	0·6832
4	0·0119	0·1834	0·8667
5	0·0056	0·0871	0·9538
6	0·0030	0·0462	1·0000

First eigenvalue = 1·000 000 60.

and especially the schools, was associated with the provision of pleasant and cheerful surroundings, presumably in the absence of the scope to do much with the food. The first two factors can therefore be broadly interpreted as contrasting commercial with institutional establishments, and attention to food with attention to surroundings. As discussed previously, further factors can be extracted from the data, but do not appear to be very useful. Some of the row and column totals were very low, which restricts the use of the data and the scope for interpretation.

4.2. Other Applications

There are very few examples of FCA in the food science literature, reflecting the relatively recent development of the method and its rather specialised applications. Tomassone and Flanzy (1977) described the use of FCA of tables of rank data, where a number of assessors rank a set of products for a specified characteristic. Many characteristics can be accommodated, in principal, simply by putting many such tables side-by-side. Dumont (1984) used FCA to examine consumer acceptability of beef samples, Richard and Coursin (1979) for orange juice processing and Sauvant et al. (1973) in an investigation of goats' milk. Danzart (1983) presented a FCA of quality scores for chickens, as a means of displaying and understanding the interaction between assessors and chickens.

5. COMPUTER PROGRAMS

SPSS (SPSS, 1983; Norusis, 1983, 1985) and its derivative SCSS (Nie et al., 1980) include a routine, FACTOR, which will extract and rotate factors by a variety of methods, including principal components analysis.

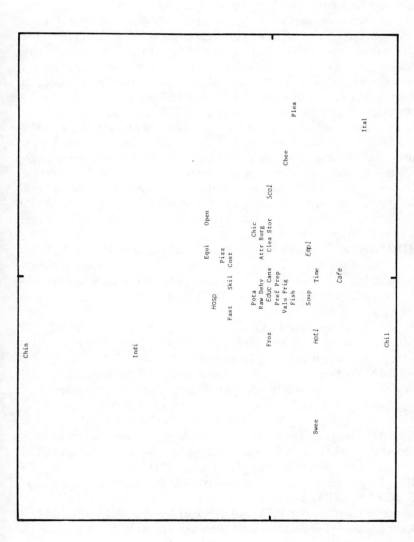

FIG. 10. Coordinates of food service establishments and survey questions plotted on the first two factors, from correspondence analysis of data from Pepper and Milson (1984). Abbreviations are shown in Tables 5 and 6.

The output available includes the correlation matrix, eigenvalues, communalities, loadings and rotated loadings, residuals of the correlation matrix and factor scores. Using the facilities for mathematical manipulation and transformation of data, it should also be possible to carry out correspondence analysis and principal coordinate analysis. The MANOVA routine can also be used to carry out PCA of a covariance or correlation matrix of residuals. This can be useful in searching for the sources of variation in the residual term of a MANOVA model, as referred to above and discussed by Vuataz (1977).

SAS (Helwig and Council, 1979) and BMDP (Dixon et al., 1981) are generally similar to SPSS in the way in which they handle data and in the facilities available. Both include routines for factor analytic procedures, and allow a variety of extraction methods and rotations. There are slight differences in the output from these packages. Using the facilities for data manipulation and the MATRIX procedure of SAS, other analyses can also be carried out. GENSTAT (Alvey et al., 1982) also provides a routine for PCA, and is the only widely available package which explicitly provides a PCO.

MINITAB, while primarily an interactive package for EDA, tabulation, regression, ANOVA, etc., has some facilities for data manipulation, and includes a routine for extraction of eigenvalues and eigenvectors. Thus, it can be used for PCA, PCO, and FCA, using its facility to execute a stored procedure.

Meyer (1974) announced CONSTEL, a program to carry out PCO of quantitative, 'multi-category' and binary data, using Gower's (1971) similarity measure. Benzecri (1982) published BENTAB2, a listing of a FORTRAN program for correspondence analysis. This program should be straightforward to modify for most medium and large computers, and it is possible that it could be modified to run on a desktop machine at least for small data sets. Cooley and Lohnes (1971) published listings of FORTRAN programs for many multivariate procedures including PCA and rotation, and these have been successfully adapted to run on CP/M microcomputers. Blackith and Reyment (1971) provided listings of FORTRAN programs for similar multivariate procedures, and included PCO. For ACT, IBM and similar desktop computers there should be no problems in carrying out PCA and PCO, at least.

Other packages for desktop computers are available, but are generally speaking very much slower, less versatile and less powerful than those running on mainframe and minicomputers. The National Computing Centre (NCC Microsystems Centre, 11 New Fetter Lane, London EC4

1PU. Tel: 01-353 4875) maintains a directory of software packages available for microcomputers, and prospective users are advised to enquire since new programs are regularly released.

REFERENCES

Aishima, T. (1979). Examination and discrimination of soy sauce by computer analysis of volatile profiles. *Agric. Biol. Chem.*, **43**, 1711–18.

Alvey, N., Galwey, N. and Lane, P. (1982). *An Introduction to GENSTAT*, Academic Press, London.

Baker, G. A. (1954). Organoleptic ratings and analytical data for wines analysed into orthogonal factors. *Food Res.*, **19**, 575–80.

Baker, G. A., Amerine, M. A. and Pangborn, R. M. (1961). Factor analysis applied to paired preferences among four grape juices. *J. Food Sci.*, **26**, 644–7.

Bartlett, M. S. (1950). Tests of significance in factor analysis. *Brit. J. Psychol. (Stat. Section)*, **3**, 77–85.

Bartlett, M. S. (1951). A further note on tests of significance in factor analysis. *Brit. J. Psychol. (Stat. Section)*, **4**, 1–2.

Benzecri, J.-P. (1969). Statistical analysis as a tool to make patterns emerge from data. In: *Methodologies of Pattern Recognition*, S. Watanabe (Ed.), Academic Press, New York.

Benzecri, J.-P. (1982). *L'Analyse des Données Vol. II: L'Analyse des Correspondances*, Dunod, Paris.

Blackith, R. E. and Reyment, R. A. (1971). *Multivariate Morphometrics*, Academic Press, London.

Bryant, T. N. and Cowan, W. D. (1979). Classification of brewing yeasts by principal co-ordinates analysis of their brewing properties. *J. Inst. Brew.*, **85**, 89–91.

Campbell, S. J. and Williams, W. T. (1976). Factors associated with maturity bronzing of banana fruit. *Aust. J. Exp. Agric. Anim. Husb.*, **16**, 428–32.

Cattell, R. B. (1965). Factor analysis: an introduction to essentials. *Biometrics*, **21**, 405–35.

Cattell, R. B. (1973). *Factor Analysis*, Greenwood Press, Westport, Conn.

Chatfield, C. and Collins, A. J. (1980). *Introduction to Multivariate Analysis*, Chapman and Hall, London.

Clark, R. J. and Menary, R. C. (1981). Variations in composition of peppermint oil in relation to production areas. *Economic Botany*, **35**, 59–69.

Cooley, W. W. and Lohnes, P. R. (1971). *Multivariate Data Analysis*, John Wiley, New York.

Cowe, I. A. and McNicol, J. W. (1985). The use of principal components in the analysis of near-infrared spectra. *Appl. Spectrosc.*, **39**, 257–66.

Danzart, M. (1983). Evaluation of the performance of panel judges. In: *Food Research and Data Analysis*, H. Martens and H. Russwurm (Eds), Applied Science, London.

Diaconis, P. and Efron, B. (1983). Computer-intensive methods in statistics. *Scientific American*, **248**(5), 96–108.

Dixon, W. J., Brown, M. B., Engelman, L., Frane, J. W., Hill, M. A., Jennrich, R. I. and Toporek, J. D. (1981). *BMDP Statistical Software*, University of California Press, Berkeley.

Dudzinski, M. L., Norris, J. M., Chmura, J. T. and Edwards, C. B. H. (1975). Repeatability of principal components in samples: normal and non-normal data sets compared. *Multivariate Behavioral Research*, **10**, 109–17.

Dumont, B. L. (1984). Importance relative des caractères sensoriels (tendreté, saveur, jutosité) sur l'acceptabilité de la viande de boeuf par les consommateurs. *Sci. Aliments*, **4**, H.S. III, 27–31.

Elliott, S. C., Hartmann, N. A. and Hawkes, S. J. (1971). Analysis of blends of mixtures using multivariate statistics. *Anal. Chem.*, **43**, 1938–9.

Gibbs, P. A., Patterson, J. T. and Harvey, J. (1978). Biochemical characteristics and enterotoxigenicity of *Staphylococcus aureus* strains isolated from poultry. *J. Appl. Bacteriol.*, **44**, 57–74.

Gower, J. C. (1966). Some distance properties of latent root and vector methods used in multivariate analysis. *Biometrika*, **53**, 325–38.

Gower, J. C. (1971). A general coefficient of similarity and some of its properties. *Biometrics*, **27**, 857–74.

Gower, J. C. (1983). Data analysis: multivariate or univariate and other difficulties. In: *Food Research and Data Analysis*, H. Martens and H. Russwurm (Eds), Applied Science, London.

Grotch, S. L. (1984). Three-dimensional graphics for scientific data display and analysis. In: *Chemometrics: Mathematics and Statistics in Chemistry*, B. R. Kowalski (Ed.), Reidel, Dordrecht.

Harman, H. H. (1976). *Modern Factor Analysis*, Chicago University Press, Chicago, Ill.

Harper, R. (1956). Factor analysis as a technique for examining complex data on foodstuffs. *Applied Statistics*, **5**, 32–48.

Harper, R. and Baron, M. (1951). The application of factor analysis to tests on cheese. *Brit. J. Appl. Phys.*, **2**, 35–41.

Harris, R. (1975). *A Primer of Multivariate Statistics*, Academic Press, New York.

Hashimoto, N. and Eshima, T. (1980). Multivariate analysis of the sensory pattern of beer flavour. Report Res. Lab. Kirin Brewery Co. Ltd, No. 23, 19–31.

Helwig, J. T. and Council, K. A. (Eds) (1979). *SAS User's Guide*, SAS Institute, Box 8000, Cary, N. Carolina.

Hill, J. and Goodchild, N. A. (1981). Analysing environments for plant breeding purposes as exemplified by multivariate analyses of long term wheat yields. *Theor. Appl. Genet.*, **59**, 317–25.

Hoaglin, D. C., Mosteller, F. and Tukey, J. W. (Eds) (1983). *Understanding Robust and Exploratory Data Analysis*, John Wiley, New York.

Kaiser, H. F. (1959). Computer program for Varimax rotation in factor analysis. *Educ. Psychol. Measurement*, **19**, 413–20.

Kowalski, B. R. (1983). Intelligent instruments of the future. In: *Food Research and Data Analysis*, H. Martens and H. Russwurm (Eds), Applied Science, London.

Laing, D. G. and Willcox, M. E. (1983). Perception of components in binary odour mixtures. *Chem. Sens.*, **7**, 249–64.

Lance, C. N. and Williams, W. T. (1967). Mixed data classifying programs: 1. Agglomerative systems. *Austr. Computer J.*, **1**, 15–20.

Lefebvre, J. (1983). *Introduction aux Analyses Statistiques Multidimensionelles*, Masson, Paris.

Lehtonen, M. (1983a). Gas-liquid chromatographic determination of volatile phenols in matured distilled alcoholic beverages. *J. Assoc. Off. Anal. Chem.*, **66**, 62–70.

Lehtonen, M. (1983b). High-performance liquid chromatographic determination of non-volatile phenolic compounds in matured distilled alcoholic beverages. *J. Assoc. Off. Anal. Chem.*, **66**, 71–8.

MacFie, H. J. H. and Gutteridge, C. S. (1982). Comparative studies on some methods for handling quantitative data generated by analytical pyrolysis. *J. Anal. Appl. Pyrolysis*, **4**, 175–204.

MacFie, H. J. H. and Thomson, D. M. H. (1984). Multidimensional scaling methods. In: *Sensory Analysis of Foods*, J. R. Piggott (Ed.), Elsevier Applied Science, London.

Malinowski, E. R. and Howery, D. G. (1980). *Factor Analysis in Chemistry*, John Wiley, New York.

Martens, H. (1979). Factor analysis of chemical mixtures. *Anal. Chim. Acta*, **112**, 423–42.

Martens, H. and Bach Knudsen, K. E. (1980). Fractionating barley proteins by computer factor analysis. *Cereal Chem.*, **57**, 97–105.

Martens, H., Wold, S. and Martens, M. (1983). A layman's guide to multivariate data analysis. In: *Food Research and Data Analysis*, H. Martens and H. Russwurm (Eds), Applied Science, London.

Martens, M. and Harries, J. M. (1983). A bibliography of multivariate statistical methods in food science and technology. In: *Food Research and Data Analysis*, H. Martens and H. Russwurm (Eds), Applied Science, London.

Maxwell, A. E. (1977). *Multivariate Analysis in Behavioural Research*, Chapman and Hall, London.

Meyer, J. A. (1974). CONSTEL: A FORTRAN program for factor and cluster analysis of mixed data. *Behav. Res. Methods Instrum.*, **6**, 506.

Mulaik, S. A. (1972). *The Foundations of Factor Analysis*, McGraw-Hill, New York.

Newell, G. J. (1981). A new procedure for comparing methods in food science. *J. Food Sci.*, **46**, 978–9.

Nie, N. H., Hull, C. H., Franklin, M. N., Jenkins, J. G., Sours, K. J., Norusis, M. J. and Beadle, V. (1980). *SCSS: A User's Guide to the SCSS Conversational System*, McGraw-Hill, New York.

Norusis, M. J. (1983). *SPSS-X Introductory Statistics Guide*, McGraw-Hill, New York.

Norusis, M. J. (1985). *SPSS-X Advanced Statistics Guide*, McGraw-Hill, New York.

Pepper, A. W. and Milson, A. (1984). The use and acceptability of convenience and fast-foods in the food service industry in Scotland. *Int. J. Hospitality Management*, **3**(2), 63–9.

Ratkowsky, D. A. and Martin, D. (1974). The use of multivariate analysis in identifying relationships among disorder and mineral element content in apples. *Austr. J. Agric. Res.*, **25**, 783–90.

Richard, J. P. and Coursin, D. (1979). Utilisation de quelques méthodes informatiques à l'expertise des jus de fruits. *Ind. Alim. Agric.*, **96**, 433–40.

Rummel, R. J. (1970). *Applied Factor Analysis*, Northwestern University Press, Evanston, Ill.

Sauvant, D., Fehr, P.-M., Rodolphe, F., Tomassone, R. and Delage, J. (1973). Etude des interrelations entre les critères de production et de composition lipidique du lait de chèvre par deux méthodes d'analyse factorielle. *Ann. Biol. anim. Biochim. Biophys.*, **13**, 107–29.

Sharaf, M. A. and Kowalski, B. R. (1981). Extraction of individual mass spectra from gas chromatography–mass spectrometry data of unseparated mixtures. *Anal. Chem.*, **53**, 518–22.

Shurvell, H. F. and Dunham, A. (1978). The application of factor analysis and Raman band contour resolution techniques to the study of aqueous Zn(II) chloride solutions. *Can. J. Spectrosc.*, **23**, 160–5.

SPSS (1983). *SPSSX User's Guide*, McGraw-Hill, New York.

Stungis, G. E. (1976). Overview of applied multivariate analysis. ASTM Special Technical Publication 594, ASTM, Philadelphia, Penn.

Thurstone, L. L. (1947). *Multiple-factor Analysis*, University of Chicago Press, Chicago, Ill.

Tomassone, R. and Flanzy, C. (1977). Présentation synthétique de diverse méthodes d'analyse de données fournies par un jury de dégustateurs. *Ann. Technol. Agric.*, **26**, 373–418.

Tufte, E. R. (1983). *The Visual Display of Quantitative Information*, Graphics Press, Cheshire, Conn.

Tukey, J. W. (1977). *Exploratory Data Analysis*, Addison-Wesley, Reading, Mass.

Vallis, L., MacFie, H. J. H. and Gutteridge, C. S. (1983). Differentiation of simple biochemical mixtures by pyrolysis–mass spectrometry: some geometrical considerations. *J. Anal. Appl. Pyrolysis*, **5**, 333–48.

Vuataz, L. (1977). Some points of methodology in multidimensional data analysis as applied to sensory evaluation. In: Nestlé Research News 1976/77, C. Boella (Ed.), Nestlé Products Technical Assistance, Lausanne.

Wold, S., Albano, C., Dunn, W. J., Edlund, U., Esbensen, K., Geladi, P., Hellberg, S., Johansson, E., Lindberg, W. and Sjöström, M. (1984). Multivariate data analysis in chemistry. In: *Chemometrics: Mathematics and Statistics in Chemistry*, B. R. Kowalski (Ed.), Reidel, Dordrecht.

Wrigley, C. W., Robinson, P. J. and Williams, W. T. (1981). Association between electrophoretic patterns of gliadin proteins and quality characteristics of wheat cultivars. *J. Sci. Food Agric.*, **32**, 433–42.

Zhou, D., Chang, T. and Davis, J. C. (1983). Dual extraction of R-mode and Q-mode factor solutions. *Math. Geol.*, **15**, 581–606.

Chapter 7

THE USE OF GENERALISED PROCRUSTES TECHNIQUES IN SENSORY ANALYSIS

GILLIAN M. ARNOLD AND ANTHONY A. WILLIAMS

University of Bristol, Department of Agricultural Sciences, Long Ashton Research Station, Bristol, UK

1. INTRODUCTION

In sensory profiling suppose an assessor scores N samples for V attributes or descriptive terms. The results can be displayed in an $N \times V$ matrix where each row refers to a particular sample and each column refers to a particular attribute. These data may be considered as representing a configuration of N points in V dimensions. Procrustes Analysis originated as a method for matching two such configurations arising when two assessors scored the same set of samples (Hurley and Cattell, 1962). The analysis involved the mathematical operations of transformation to a common origin, rotation/reflection of axes and possibly an isotropic scale change, by which one configuration was made to approach the other as nearly as possible. This closeness was measured by the Procrustes Statistic which is the sum of the squared distances between the two assessments of each sample in the adjusted configurations.

Early work with this technique restricted attention to only two configurations (Schonemann, 1966; Schonemann and Carroll, 1970; Gower, 1971; Sibson, 1978, 1979). However, in practice in sensory profile work many more than two assessors, say M, are likely to be involved and each will produce a configuration. Two basic extensions of Procrustes Analysis as described above exist. In the first, all possible pairs of configurations are compared, whereas in the second, the configurations are compared simultaneously as a group.

In the pairwise approach the profile information is summarised in an $M \times M$ matrix, whose ijth element is the Procrustes Statistic between the configurations i and j. Relationships amongst the configurations (i.e. the assessors) are determined by a multidimensional scaling of this matrix, each assessor being represented by a point (Krzanowksi, 1971; Gower, 1976). In this approach however, the information about the samples is not recovered and no consensus configuration is obtained (Banfield and Harries, 1975; Harries and MacFie, 1976).

In the second method, known as generalised Procrustes analysis, the configurations are iteratively matched in a Procrustes sense to a common consensus configuration. This consensus configuration is the mean of the transformed configurations, and replaces the panel mean of the untransformed configurations. Using the transformed configurations a dissimilarity matrix for assessors can be obtained and used as a replacement for the $M \times M$ matrix of a pairwise Procrustes analysis with almost identical results (Langron, 1981). Thus the generalised Procrustes method gives the vital sample information in its consensus configuration as well as the assessor information which is the only output of the pairwise approach. As a consequence it provides a far more useful method of analysis for examining sensory data than the pairwise approach.

2. GENERALISED PROCRUSTES ANALYSIS AND PROFILE DATA

2.1. Sources of Variation

Profiling has moved a long way since it was first conceived by the A. D. Little Corporation in the 1950s (Caul, 1957). As commonly practised now, a large number of samples of a product are presented to a panel of trained/selected assessors who, by discussion and the use of standards, devise a precisely defined list of terms which describe the various sensory attributes of the product, in particular those varying over the samples of interest. These terms are then incorporated into a score sheet for use in subsequent assessments of the product. A measure of the amount or intensity of each attribute in a sample can thus be recorded.

Because of this training and discussion within the panel it is usual to assume that all assessors are scoring the attributes in a similar manner, but no training can eliminate all variation in usage. Some sources of variation are:

(i)   Assessors vary in the overall level of the scores they give.
(ii) Assessors use different terms or combinations of terms to describe the same stimulus.

(iii) Assessors vary in their range of scoring.
(iv) In extreme cases, assessors perceive different stimuli in the same product.
(v) Assessors show variation in their use of terms and scales between sessions.

2.2. Relationship between Sources of Variation and Generalised Procrustes Analysis

The various stages in a generalised Procrustes analysis can adjust for some of the above types of variation, and will thus produce a consensus configuration which has more meaning with respect to the samples than the untransformed mean configuration. To illustrate this we will take a set of simulated data representing the scoring of 4 samples (1, 2, 3, 4) by 5 assessors (A, B, C, D, E) on two attributes say bitterness and astringency. This is an oversimplification of real profiling situations, but it will serve to pinpoint more clearly the effects of the different stages of the analysis.

Figures 1–4 show graphically the results of each stage of the analysis, with consecutive columns of Table 1 giving the equivalent Procrustes Statistic for each assessor after that stage. In Fig. 1 the original two-dimensional configurations for each assessor are shown, with a point for each sample in each configuration specified by the scores for each attribute. There are no clear patterns of sample differences apparent from this graph. The first stage of a generalised Procrustes analysis is that of translating each configuration to be centred about a common origin (Fig. 2), which makes adjustment for scoring at different levels of the scale by different assessors (source (i)). This is analogous to the removal of an assessor 'main effect' in a univariate analysis of variance. As a

TABLE 1

PROCRUSTES STATISTICS BEFORE AND AFTER EACH STAGE OF THE ANALYSIS TOGETHER WITH INDIVIDUAL SCALING FACTORS

Assessor	Original	Translation	Rotation/ reflection	Scaling	Scaling factor
A	7·214	5·331	1·354	0·808	0·915
B	18·648	16·885	1·237	0·911	0·953
C	28·454	5·158	0·959	0·277	0·903
D	3·822	2·458	2·331	0·379	1·834
E	8·056	4·787	4·862	4·637	0·888
Total	66·194	34·619	10·743	7·012	

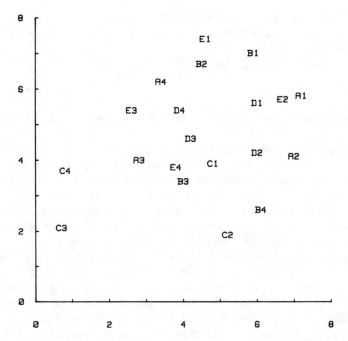

FIG. 1. Untransformed configurations of simulated data set: Astringency versus Bitterness. Assessors A, B, C, D, E. Samples 1, 2, 3, 4.

consequence assessor C has been brought more into agreement with the other assessors, as is clearly shown by the relatively large reduction in the equivalent Procrustes statistic.

The next stage is to match these centred configurations as well as possible by rotation and reflection of axes, still maintaining the intersample distances for each assessor (Fig. 3). This allows for differing interpretation of terms by different assessors (source (ii)); in this example the Procrustes statistic associated with assessor B is greatly reduced, indicating a different interpretation of the terms bitterness and astringency compared to the other assessors.

The final stage (in practice carried out simultaneously with the previous stage) allows for an isotropic scale change to each configuration, adjusting therefore for differences in range of scaling for different assessors (source (iii)). The final configurations thus obtained (Fig. 4) can be seen to have brought much greater agreement between configura-

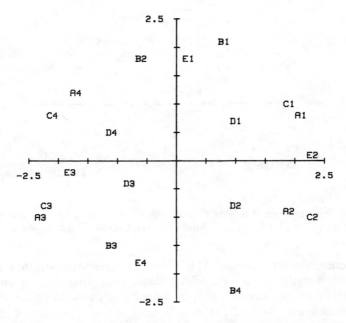

FIG. 2. Centred configurations (after translation): Astringency versus Bitterness.

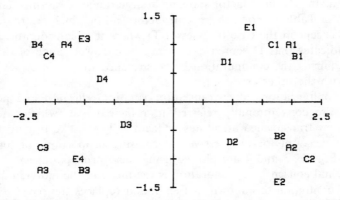

FIG. 3. Centred configurations after rotation/reflection referred to principal axes:
Principal Axis 2 versus Principal Axis 1.

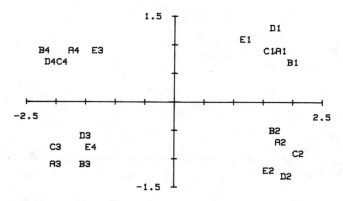

FIG. 4. Final configurations after translation, rotation/reflection and scaling referred to principal axes: Principal Axis 2 versus Principal Axis 1.

tions, especially for assessors A, B, C and D. Assessor E still has a large Procrustes statistic after this final stage, indicating that, even after adjustment for sources of variation (i)–(iii), this assessor perceives the samples differently from the other assessors. In fact Figs. 3 and 4 seem to infer that, for assessor E, samples 3 and 4 are confused; this could indicate a possible mislabelling of these two samples for that assessor. The scaling factors for each assessor give information on how concentrated or spread out the scoring for that assessor is, with a large scaling factor corresponding to scoring over a small range and conversely a small scaling factor showing a large range of scoring. The final column of Table 1 shows these scale factors, all of which are reasonably similar except in the case of assessor D where it is considerably larger. This indicates that D scored over a much narrower range of the scale thus requiring the configuration to be stretched to obtain closer agreement with the other assessors.

The configurations after translation, rotation/reflection and possibly scaling are conventionally referred to principal axes which, in effect, define new transformed attributes or factors. These, like principal components, account for progressively decreasing proportions of total variance. Figures 3 and 4 are plotted using these principal axes.

The final consensus configuration is the mean of the individual transformed configurations shown in Fig. 4, and replaces the panel mean of the untransformed configurations in further analyses. The percentage of variation accounted for by each of the principal axes can be obtained both for the individual and the consensus final configurations, which gives an indication of how good an approximation a lower dimensional solution is. For this example however both original and final configurations are in two dimensions.

The totals of the Procrustes statistics at the foot of each column in Table 1 can be used to construct a Procrustes Analysis of Variance (PANOVA) table and approximate F-tests carried out to test the statistical significance of each stage (Langron and Collins, 1985). In this particular example (Table 2) only the scaling stage is not significant; this is mainly due to the large contribution in the residual from assessor E who appears to have assessed the samples somewhat differently from the other assessors.

TABLE 2
PROCRUSTES ANALYSIS OF VARIANCE (PANOVA) TABLE

Source	df	Sums of squares	Mean squares	F ratio
Residual after scaling	16	7·012	0·438	
Scaling	4	3·731	0·933	2·13
Residual after rotation/reflection	20	10·743		
Rotation/reflection	4	23·876	5·969	13·63
Residual after translation	24	34·619		
Translation	8	31·575	3·947	9·01
Total of original configuration squared distances	32	66·194		

As well as being partitioned between assessors the residual sum of squares can also be split between the samples. A small value for a particular sample will indicate good agreement by assessors for that sample and, conversely, a high value will indicate poor agreement. In this example the residuals for samples 1, 2, 3 and 4 are 0·577, 0·529, 3·267 and 2·639 respectively, the larger values for samples 3 and 4 being due to the differing assessment by E.

This simulated example has dealt with only two attributes for simplicity, but the same concepts can be applied when many more attributes have been scored. The first few axes of the consensus configuration normally contain most of the information and can be thought of as the 'best' lower-dimensional representation of the sample space in a Procrustes sense. The consensus configuration can then be used in subsequent investigations such as relating the sensory information to experimental variables or analytical data. Langron (1983; *et al.*, 1984) has shown the consensus gives more meaningful results than the untransformed mean configuration when relating sensory data on apples to storage conditions.

2.3. Interpretation of the Consensus Configuration

The transformed attributes obtained after a Procrustes analysis can be interpreted in terms of the original attributes for each of the assessors. One method is to obtain the rotation matrix for each assessor which transforms his original centred configuration to the consensus. Another approach is to look at the correlations between original attributes for each assessor and the transformed attributes of the consensus. Such analyses can show if particular attributes are important in discriminating between the samples and can indicate the existence of disagreements among the assessors in the identification of attributes.

For the simulated example of bitterness and astringency shown in Section 2.2, Table 3 gives the rows of the transposed rotation matrices described above. This shows that for assessors A, C and D the first transformed attribute is almost totally described as bitterness whereas for taster B it is astringency. Conversely the second transformed attribute is described as astringency by assessors A, C and D and as bitterness by assessor B. This is clearly a case where one assessor has confused these two attributes. For assessor E the pattern is not similar to the other assessors; this is indeed the assessor which did not conform to the others after the Procrustes analysis.

TABLE 3
FINAL TRANSFORMED ATTRIBUTES

Assessor	1st transformed attribute		2nd transformed attribute	
	Bitterness	Astringency	Bitterness	Astringency
A	0·995	−0·098	0·098	0·995
B	0·005	1·000	1·000	−0·005
C	1·000	−0·015	0·015	1·000
D	0·998	−0·059	0·059	0·998
E	0·761	0·649	−0·649	0·761

2.4. Investigation of Outliers

As described in Section 2.2 the application of Procrustes analysis adjusts for the first three types of assessor variation listed in Section 2.1. It does not attempt to deal with assessors who perceive different stimuli in a sample, rather than merely giving the same stimuli different labels. It also assumes that an assessor is self-consistent in use of terms and scales throughout all sessions of a profiling experiment.

By considering each transformed configuration as an $NV \times 1$ vector, an alternative to the $M \times M$ matrix of a pairwise Procrustes analysis can be obtained from the variance/covariance matrix of the M vectors (Langron, 1981). Coordinates can then be produced for each assessor using this derived dissimilarity matrix as an input into a classical scaling procedure sometimes known as principal coordinate analysis (see for example Chatfield and Collins (1980) Chapter 10). The resulting coordinates for the assessors after any stage of the transformation can be examined, for example, by plotting the first two dimensions, and obvious outliers or different groupings of assessors discovered. Figure 5 shows this assessor plot for the example described earlier, both for the original configurations (lower case letters) and after a full Procrustes analysis (upper case letters), clearly indicating assessor E to be an outlier.

Replicate sessions for profiling can determine whether an outlying assessor is differing from the main panel by perceiving different stimuli or

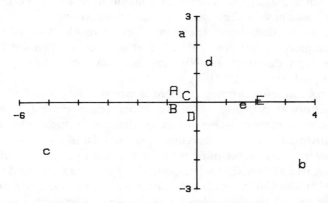

FIG. 5. Assessor plot for simulated data set: Principal Axis 2 versus Principal Axis 1. Lower case letters (a, b, c, d, e) denote assessors relative distances before transformation, with upper case letters (A, B, C, D, E) denoting their relative distances after all stages of a generalised Procrustes analysis.

just by inconsistent scoring. If different stimuli are perceived the use of assessor plots can indicate possible subsets of the assessors which can then be analysed separately. For the example given, eliminating assessor E from the analysis reduces the final residual mean square from 0·438 (16 df) to 0·0954 (12 df), thus considerably improving the overall agreement.

3. FREE-CHOICE PROFILING

3.1. An Alternative Approach to Profiling

Sensory profiling, as it is generally practised, is rather time-consuming. For each set of products to be assessed a language has to be developed and the panelists need to agree on the meaning of each of the terms used. The vocabulary development stage in particular can take a long time, and complete agreement on terms between panelists is virtually impossible to achieve.

One use of generalised Procrustes analysis of profile data is to eliminate variation due to confusion of terms between assessors. An extension suggested by this fact is that completely differently labelled terms can equally well be matched in the same way. It has also been shown that matching configurations of different column dimension (i.e. different numbers of terms/attributes) using generalised Procrustes analysis gives an unambiguous consensus configuration up to the minimum of the dimensions in the initial configurations (Langron and Collins, unpublished results). From these two facts a much more flexible approach to profiling has been devised. This is called Free-choice Profiling and has been described in Williams and Langron (1983, 1984) and Williams and Arnold (1984).

The procedure for carrying out free-choice profiling is initially similar to conventional profiling, with the panel being presented with the products or a representative subset of them, to sample and describe. Each individual is asked to develop a personal list of terms for assessing the samples. These terms must mean something to that individual who must then be able to use them consistently, but there is no need to try to convey that meaning to anyone else. Each assessor can use as many or as few terms as desired although all assessors should be encouraged to use at least as many terms as dimensions required in the final configuration. These individual sets of profile terms can be put onto score sheets for each assessor who, as with conventional profiling, proceeds to score all the products on the individual list of terms using a properly designed experimental plan. The individual configurations thus obtained can then be matched by generalised Procrustes analysis. The stage of rotation/reflection in this approach will obviously be highly significant as no attempt is made prior to this to associate the terms used by one individual assessor with those of any other. The relationships between the samples for each assessor are not altered by the analysis, although they may have been rotated and the whole sample space for an individual stretched or shrunk isotropically to improve agreement between assessors.

The new transformed attributes can be interpreted, as described in Section 2.3, in terms of each individual assessor's profile vocabulary and different terms for different assessors related. In a free-choice profiling approach to the simulated example described in Section 2.2, assessor B may have called the two terms, for example, acetic and sharpness, and in the rotation/reflection stage these would be matched as before to the terms of astringency and bitterness respectively, as used by assessors A, C and D.

3.2. An Example of a Procrustes Analysis of Free-choice Profile Data

Williams and Langron (1984) describe an experiment conducted on commercial ports using the free-choice profiling method of assessment. Ten assessors (here labelled A–J) took part in the experiment and profiled eight different commercial ports (here labelled 1–8) for appearance, aroma and flavour using individually selected profile terms. Figure 6 shows the samples plotted for the first two transformed attributes after a generalised Procrustes analysis of the appearance data, and Table 4 gives the terms of importance used by each of the assessors to describe these new attributes. The first of these attributes clearly separates samples 1 and 3 from the other samples and appears to be generally described as a contrast between red/ruby terms and brown/tawny terms. The second transformed attribute separates samples 1 and 7 from the rest and is described mainly in terms of total colour/intensity/depth.

The first two dimensions of the final assessor plot for this example are shown in Fig. 7. It appears that assessors C, E, G, H, I and J are behaving as a reasonably consistent subgroup with assessors A, D, F and particularly B behaving somewhat differently from other assessors. Table 5 gives the amount of variation accounted for by the first three dimensions and, whereas generally two dimensions appear adequate to describe

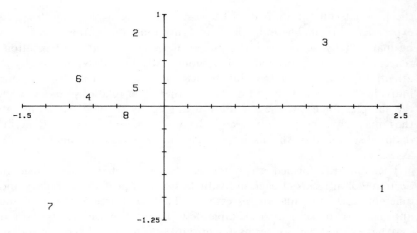

FIG. 6. Sample consensus plot for appearance of ports (1, 2, 3, 4, 5, 6, 7, 8) assessed by free-choice profiling: Principal Axis 2 versus Principal Axis 1.

TABLE 4

FINAL TRANSFORMED AXES RESULTING FROM A GENERALISED PROCRUSTES ANALYSIS (EACH ASSESSOR'S CHOSEN TERMS ARE GIVEN IN ORDER OF THE IMPORTANCE OF THEIR CONTRIBUTION TO EACH OF THE TRANSFORMED ATTRIBUTES)

Assessor	1st transformed axis	2nd transformed axis
A	− Tawny + Ruby + Purple	+ Ruby − Purple + Clarity
B	+ Depth	− Brightness
C	+ Purple − Brown + Red	+ Red + Brown
D	+ Redness	+ Intensity + Yellowness
E	+ Mauve − Brown − Soft + Plum	− Soft
F	− Tawny + Ruby	+ Depth
G	+ Red + Blue	+ Intensity + Brown
H	− Tawny + Ruby + Intensity	+ Intensity + Tawny
I	+ Red − Brown	+ Colour + Brown
J	+ Red − Brown + Intensity	+ Intensity

the variation, assessor **B** in particular and, to a certain extent, assessor **A** appear to require three dimensions. Assessor **D** has the variation explained by the first two dimensions much more equally distributed between both dimensions than the main subgroup. The reasons for assessor **F** being an outlier on this plot are not immediately apparent from this table and would thus need further investigation.

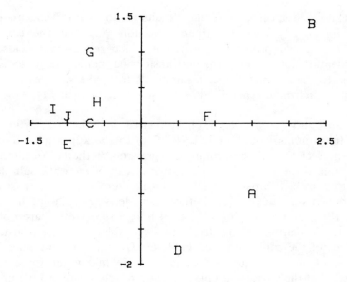

FIG. 7. Plot of assessors (A, B, C, D, E, F, G, H, I, J) showing their relative distances after a generalised Procrustes analysis of their free-choice profiling data of port appearance.

TABLE 5

PERCENTAGE OF VARIATION EXPLAINED BY FIRST THREE FINAL DIMENSIONS

Assessor	Variation explained by final dimensions (%)		
	1st	2nd	3rd
A	64·9	24·6	8·5
B	32·9	24·7	41·5
C	63·6	33·9	1·9
D	45·5	49·1	3·2
E	75·1	14·0	5·5
F	80·1	17·7	1·4
G	80·5	14·7	3·0
H	68·5	27·0	4·2
I	84·1	14·8	0·3
J	69·6	26·6	3·7
Consensus	73·6	22·8	3·0

3.3. Relating Free-choice Profiling Results to Analytical Measurements

It has previously been mentioned (Section 2.2) that the consensus configuration can produce information which relates more closely to experimental factors than the untransformed panel mean. It is also possible to relate analytical measurements from the samples to such a configuration from a generalised Procrustes analysis of any type of profile data.

Williams and Langron (1983) have related analytical colour measurements (tristimulus values—CIELAB 1976) to the appearance data discussed in Section 3.2 using multiple regression methods. An alternative description of the relationships is shown in Fig. 8. Here the sample plot from Fig. 6 has superimposed upon it vectors for the tristimulus measurements L, a and b, together with derived variables hue angle ($\tan^{-1} (b/a)$) and saturation (sq rt($a^2 + b^2$)). These vectors are obtained from the correlations of the tristimulus variables with the transformed attributes of the consensus (see Table 6). The fact that the magnitudes (lengths) of these vectors are close to their maximum value of one indicates that the sensory sample space is strongly related to the underlying physical dimensions represented by the tristimulus measurements. The directions of the vectors relate well to the appearance terms used to describe the consensus axes. The main analytical component in a positive sense along the first axis is a which, within the colour range of ports,

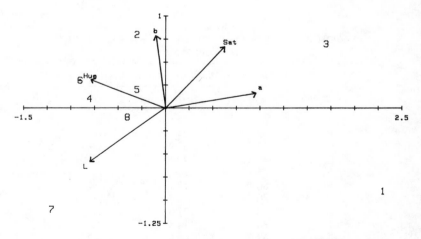

FIG. 8. Plot of vectors for tristimulus measurements on sample consensus plot previously shown in Fig. 6.

TABLE 6
CORRELATIONS OF TRISTIMULUS MEASUREMENTS WITH THE CONSENSUS

Tristimulus variables	Consensus Axes 1st	2nd	Vector magnitude
L	−0·786	−0·554	0·962
a	0·952	0·185	0·970
b	−0·106	0·892	0·898
Hue angle	−0·898	0·329	0·956
Saturation	0·620	0·688	0·926

denotes increasing redness. The analytical components in a negative sense are 'hue angle', a measure of brownness, and L, a measure of lightness. For the second axis the main analytical components are both in a positive sense. These are b, which denotes increasingly the progression from blueness to yellowness, and 'saturation', a measure of colour intensity. This example indicates that although assessors used different terms to describe the ports they were clearly assessing the same underlying physical dimensions in the samples and a generalised Procrustes analysis has abstracted this information from free-choice profiling data.

3.4. Comparing Free-choice Profiling with Other Sensory Assessment Procedures

The final consensus configuration obtained from a generalised Procrustes analysis of free-choice profile data has been shown, in an experiment dealing with coffee aroma, to give similar information about the relationships between samples as other sensory assessment techniques (Williams and Arnold, 1985). Figure 9 shows the final two-dimensional configurations obtained from:

(a) Principal Component Analysis of conventional profile data.
(b) INDSCAL Analysis of similarity data.
(c) Generalised Procrustes Analysis of free-choice profile data.

Although the actual rotation of these configurations is different the inter-relationships between the samples are very similar. This can be seen in Fig. 9(d) where the three two-dimensional solutions given in (a)–(c) are matched by Procrustes rotation/reflection and scaling. In addition, Williams and Arnold (1985) show that the scatter of individual assessor configurations about the consensus is considerably less for (b) and (c) than for (a). This is due to the adjustment made for assessor variation,

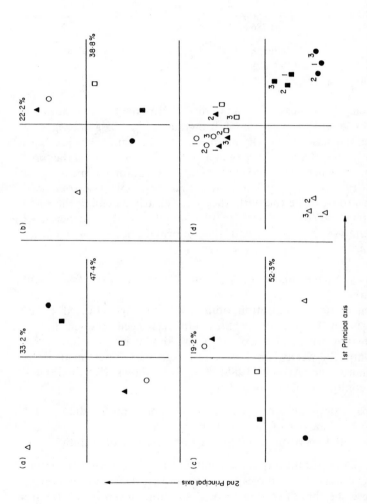

FIG. 9. Sample consensus plots for coffee aroma assessments after (a) Principal Component Analysis of conventional profile data; (b) INDSCAL analysis (two-dimensional solution) of similarity data; (c) Generalised Procrustes Analysis (GPA) of free-choice profile data; (d) Final configurations from (a), (b), (c) after matching by GPA; (1), (2), (3) denote analyses (a), (b), (c) respectively. Principal Axis 2 versus Principal Axis 1. The six samples are denoted by ●, ▲, ○, ■, △ throughout. (Reproduced with permission from Williams and Arnold, 1985.)

albeit in different ways, by both INDSCAL and Generalised Procrustes Analysis.

Free-choice profiling has been shown to give results compatible to those obtained by more conventional procedures, and has many practical advantages (Williams and Arnold, 1985). It is only by the development of generalised Procrustes analysis for use in sensory analysis, however, that such improvements have become possible.

4. THE MATHEMATICS UNDERLYING GENERALISED PROCRUSTES ANALYSIS

4.1. Derivation of the Equations

Let $\mathbf{X}_i$ denote the $N \times V$ matrix (configuration) for assessor i ($i = 1, 2, \ldots,$ M). Translation to a new origin is given by adding the same $1 \times V$ row-vector $\mathbf{t}_i$ to every row of $\mathbf{X}_i$; rotation/reflection is equivalent to post-multiplying $\mathbf{X}_i$ by an orthogonal matrix $\mathbf{H}_i$; scaling is expressed by a multiplicative constant ρ_i. If $\mathbf{T}_i$ denotes the $N \times V$ matrix with all rows equal to $\mathbf{t}_i$, then the transformation given by generalised Procrustes analysis can be expressed as

$$\mathbf{X}_i \rightarrow \rho_i (\mathbf{X}_i + \mathbf{T}_i) \mathbf{H}_i$$

It can be shown that all configurations should be translated to the same centroid, which is conveniently chosen to be the origin. If $\mathbf{X}_i$ now denotes the centre-at-origin matrix for assessor i, the transformed matrix is $\rho_i \mathbf{X}_i \mathbf{H}_i$ and the consensus matrix is calculated as $\mathbf{C} = (1/M) \Sigma_{i=1}^{M} \rho_i \mathbf{X}_i \mathbf{H}_i$. The squared distance of the ith configuration from the consensus is calculated as the sum of squares, over samples, of the distances between the points as represented by the consensus and by the ith assessor. The sum of these squared distances over assessors may be calculated as

$$S = \sum_{i=1}^{M} \text{trace} \left((\rho_i \mathbf{X}_i \mathbf{H}_i - \mathbf{C})' (\rho_i \mathbf{X}_i \mathbf{H}_i - \mathbf{C}) \right)$$

$\mathbf{H}_i$ and ρ_i are then determined to minimise S, the minimum value of S being known as the Procrustes statistic or the residual sum of squares after transformation. Gower (1975) shows that $\mathbf{H}_i$ is given by $\mathbf{H}_i = \mathbf{U}_i' \mathbf{V}_i$ arising from the singular value decomposition of $\rho_i \mathbf{X}_i' \mathbf{C}$ as $\rho_i \mathbf{X}_i' \mathbf{C} = \mathbf{U}_i' \mathbf{\Gamma}_i \mathbf{V}_i$ with $\mathbf{U}_i$ and $\mathbf{V}_i$ orthogonal and $\mathbf{\Gamma}_i$ diagonal matrices. $\mathbf{C}$ is not known initially so that $\mathbf{H}_i$ cannot be calculated directly and the solution has to be obtained by an iterative procedure which will now be described.

4.2. An Algorithm for Computing a Generalised Procrustes Analysis

The following algorithm, implemented in the generalised Procrustes macro available in GENSTAT, is based on the iterative procedure given by Gower (1975).

(1) Centre each $\mathbf{X}$ and scale by a constant ψ so that

$$\psi \sum_{i=1}^{M} \text{trace}(\mathbf{X}_i' \mathbf{X}_i) = M$$

(2) Using these centred and scaled configurations, rotate $\mathbf{X}_2$ to $\mathbf{X}_1$ and compute $\mathbf{C}$ as the mean of the two current configurations (i.e. of $\mathbf{X}_1$ and rotated $\mathbf{X}_2$). $\mathbf{X}_3$ is then rotated to $\mathbf{C}$ and $\mathbf{C}$ recomputed as the mean of the three current configurations. This procedure is continued until all the assessors are included. The current $\mathbf{X}_i$ are taken as initial values for the iterative procedure to follow. The final value of $\mathbf{C}$ is taken as the initial consensus configuration.

(3) Evaluate initial residual sum of squares as $S_r = M(1\text{-trace}(\mathbf{C}'\mathbf{C}))$ and set $\rho_i = 1$ $(i = 1, 2, \ldots, M)$.

(4) For $i = 1, 2, \ldots, M$ rotate the current matrix (initially $\rho_i \mathbf{X}_i$) to fit $\mathbf{C}$ giving

$$\mathbf{X}_i^* = \rho_i \mathbf{X}_i \mathbf{H}_i$$

Compute $\mathbf{C}^*$ as mean of $\mathbf{X}_i^*$ $(i = 1, 2, \ldots, M)$
and $S_r^* = S_r - M \, \text{trace}(\mathbf{C}^{*'}\mathbf{C}^* - \mathbf{C}'\mathbf{C})$.
Set $S_r^{**} = S_r^*$

(5) If scaling is not required go to step 7.
(6) For $i = 1, 2, \ldots, M$, evaluate

$$\rho_i^*/\rho_i = \text{sq rt}((\text{trace}(\mathbf{X}_i^* - \mathbf{C}^*)/(\text{trace}(\mathbf{X}_i^{*'}\mathbf{X}^*)\text{trace}(\mathbf{C}^{*'}\mathbf{C}^*)))$$

Scale $X_i^{**} = (\rho_i^*/\rho_i)\mathbf{X}^*$ as the new current matrix
Set $\rho_i = \rho_i^*$

Compute new mean $\mathbf{C}^{**}$ and new residual sum of squares

$$S_r^{**} = S_r^* - M \, \text{trace}(\mathbf{C}^{**'}\mathbf{C}^{**} - \mathbf{C}^{*'}\mathbf{C}^*)$$

(7) If $S_r - S_r^{**} >$ tolerance, set $S_r = S_r^{**}$ and go to step 4, else go to step 8.

(8) Find principal axes of **C** (i.e. compute the orthogonal latent-vector matrix **H** satisfying $(\mathbf{C'C})\mathbf{H} = \mathbf{H\Lambda}$ where $\mathbf{\Lambda}$ is the diagonal matrix of latent roots), and refer all sets of coordinates to these principal axes.

In practice the tolerance in step 7 is set to 0·0001 and the algorithm will usually converge. An additional constraint applying throughout is that

$$\sum_{i=1}^{M} \rho_i^2 \, \mathrm{trace}(\mathbf{X}_i'\mathbf{X}_i) = \sum_{i=1}^{M} \mathrm{trace}\,(\mathbf{X}_i'\mathbf{X}_i) = \sum_{i=1}^{M} \mathrm{trace}(\mathbf{X}_i^{**'}\mathbf{X}_i^{**})$$

which states that the total sum of squares about the origin is unchanged by the transformation. Consequently to return to the original units before the scaling in step 1 the configurations obtained in step 8 must be divided by sq rt(ψ) and the sums of squares by ψ, where

$$\psi = M \bigg/ \sum_{i=1}^{M} \mathrm{trace}(\mathbf{X}_i'\mathbf{X}_i).$$

This algorithm can be modified in various ways to take account of the methods given by Kristof and Wingersky (1971) and TenBerge (1977). A full discussion of these alternative rotation and scaling procedures is given in Langron (1981), along with suggestions for modified algorithms.

5. CONCLUSIONS

Generalised Procrustes analysis has proved to be a valuable statistical tool in sensory profiling. It enables the sensory analyst to investigate and adjust for several types of variation in the way assessors describe samples. In conjunction with the free-choice approach to profiling it also overcomes many of the inherent problems associated with conventional profiling techniques, in particular those related to training assessors to describe products in the same way.

In any form of sensory analysis assessors are individuals and will, to a certain extent, inevitably respond differently to stimuli. It is important not to ignore these differences, pretend they do not exist and merely average over them, but to recognise their presence and adequately adjust for them.

REFERENCES

Banfield, C. F. and Harries, J. M. (1975). A technique for comparing judges' performance in sensory tests. *J. Food Technol.*, **10**, 1–10.

Caul, J. F. (1957). The profile method of flavor analysis. *Adv. Food Res.*, **7**, 1–40.

Chatfield, C. and Collins, A. J. (1980). *Introduction to Multivariate Analysis*, Chapman and Hall, London, pp. 189–211.

Gower, J. C. (1971). Statistical methods of comparing different multivariate analyses of the same data. In: *Mathematics in the Archaeological and Historical Sciences*, F. R. Hodson *et al.* (Eds), University Press, Edinburgh, pp. 138–49.

Gower, J. C. (1975). Generalized Procrustes analysis. *Psychometrika*, **40**, 33–51.

Gower, J. C. (1976). Procrustes rotational fitting problems. *Mathematical Scientist*, **1**, 12–15 (Suppl.).

Harries, J. M. and Macfie, H. J. H. (1976). The use of a rotational fitting technique in the interpretation of sensory scores for different characteristics. *J. Food Technol.*, **11**, 449–56.

Hurley, J. R. and Cattell, R. B. (1962). The Procrustes program: Producing direct rotation to test a hypothesized factor structure. *Behav. Sci.*, **7**, 258–62.

Kristof, W. and Wingersky, B. (1971). Generalization of the orthogonal Procrustes rotation procedure to more than two matrices. *Proceedings, 79th Annual Convention, American Psychological Association*, pp. 89–90.

Krzanowski, W. J. (1971). A comparison of some distance measures applicable to multinomial data, using a rotational fit technique. *Biometrics*, **27**, 1062–8.

Langron, S. P. (1981). The statistical treatment of sensory analysis data. Ph.D. thesis, University of Bath.

Langron, S. P. (1983). The application of Procrustes statistics to sensory profiling. In: *Sensory Quality in Foods & Beverages: Definition, Measurement & Control*, A. A. Williams and R. K. Atkin (Eds), Ellis Horwood Ltd, Chichester, pp. 89–95.

Langron, S. P. and Collins, A. J. (1985). Perturbation theory for generalised Procrustes analysis. *J. R. Statist. Soc. B*, **47**, 277–84.

Langron, S. P. and Collins, A. J. (unpublished). Procrustes Rotation and Singularity.

Langron, S. P., Williams, A. A. and Collins, A. J. (1984). A comparison of the consensus configuration from a generalised Procrustes analysis with the untransformed panel mean in sensory profile analysis. *Lebensm. -Wiss. u. - Technol.*, **17**, 296–8.

Schonemann, P. H. (1966). A generalized solution of the orthogonal Procrustes problem. *Psychometrika*, **31**, 1–10.

Schonemann, P. H. and Carroll, R. M. (1970). Fitting one matrix to another under choice of a central dilation and a rigid motion. *Psychometrika*, **35**, 245–55.

Sibson, R. (1978). Studies in the robustness of multidimensional scaling: Procrustes Statistics. *J. R. Statist. Soc. B*, **40**, 234–8.

Sibson, R. (1979). Studies in the robustness of multidimensional scaling: Perturbational analysis of classical scaling. *J. R. Statist. Soc. B*, **41**, 217–29.

TenBerge, J. M. F. (1977). Orthogonal Procrustes rotation for two or more matrices. *Psychometrika*, **42**, 267–76.

Williams, A. A. and Arnold, G. M. (1984). A new approach to the sensory analysis of foods and beverages. In: *Progress in Flavour Research 1984, Proceedings of the 4th Weurman Flavour Research Symposium*, J. Adda (Ed.), Elsevier, Amsterdam, pp. 35–50.

Williams, A. A. and Arnold, G. M. (1985). A comparison of the aromas of six coffees characterised by conventional profiling, free-choice profiling and similarity scaling methods. *J. Sci. Food Agric.*, **36**, 204–14.

Williams, A. A. and Langron, S. P. (1983). A new approach to sensory profile analysis. In: *Flavour of Distilled Beverages: Origin & Development*, J. R. Piggott (Ed.), Ellis Horwood Ltd, Chichester, pp. 219–24.

Williams, A. A. and Langron, S. P. (1984). The use of free-choice profiling for the evaluation of commercial ports. *J. Sci. Food Agric.*, **35**, 558–68.

Chapter 8

MULTIDIMENSIONAL SCALING AND ITS INTERPRETATION

Susan S. Schiffman and Timothy G. Beeker

Department of Psychiatry and Psychology, Duke University, Durham, North Carolina, USA

1. INTRODUCTION

Multidimensional scaling (MDS) is a mathematical method that permits us to portray the similarities among stimuli such as odors by a picture or map. MDS techniques can construct a geometric representation of olfactory data, for example, such that odors judged similar to one another are located close to one another in space; odor sensations judged dissimilar are positioned far away from each other. The fundamental feature of MDS is simply that the spatial representation of data reflects perceived similarities. The use of similarity data by MDS procedures eliminates experimenter contamination because *a priori* knowledge of the attributes of the stimuli to be scaled is not required. Rather MDS provides a map that reveals the relevant dimensions.

The purpose of this chapter is to describe briefly the basic concepts of multidimensional scaling. In addition mathematical techniques that can be used to interpret the geometric representations derived by MDS will be described.

2. BASIC CONCEPTS OF MDS

Multidimensional scaling procedures take as input a set of similarities or distances (for example, those found in a table at the bottom of a map) and recreate the map. Data suitable for input for an MDS procedure are illustrated in Table 1 (from Kruskal and Wish, 1978). These are the airline distances between pairs of 10 US cities measured in miles. When

TABLE 1

AIRLINE DISTANCES BETWEEN PAIRS OF 10 US CITIES IN MILES
(modified from Kruskal and Wish, 1978)

	Atl	Chic	Denw	Hous	LA	Miami	NY	SF	Seatle	DC
Atlanta	—									
Chicago	587	—								
Denver	1 212	920	—							
Houston	701	940	879	—						
Los Angeles	1 936	1 745	831	1 374	—					
Miami	604	1 188	1 726	968	2 339	—				
New York	748	713	1 631	1 420	2 451	1 092	—			
San Francisco	2 139	1 858	949	1 645	347	2 594	2 571	—		
Seattle	2 182	1 737	1 021	1 891	959	2 734	2 408	678	—	
Washington DC	543	597	1 494	1 220	2 300	923	205	2 442	2 329	—

these data are analyzed by MDS procedures, the geometric configuration of points represents a map of the United States.

The two-dimensional map achieved by the multidimensional scaling procedure KYST (Kruskal, 1964a,b; Kruskal and Wish, 1978) for the data in Table 1 is given in Fig. 1. This map is derived from perfect data, that is, 0% noise. In practice, however, we seldom have perfect data since experimental measures contain error. For this reason 10%, 30% and 50% noise respectively were added to the data in Table 1 and the resulting spaces derived by KYST are given in Figs. 2, 3 and 4. The method and program by which the noise was added to the data is given in the Appendix. First, it can be seen that KYST can rotate, translate and reverse axes. This illustrates an important point about MDS. It simply recovers the underlying structure among the stimuli that is hidden in the data. Meaningful interpretation of the data such as North–South or East–West directions may have to be determined by the experimenter. The next section on interpretation of the stimulus configuration will illustrate how this is done. Second, with increasing noise in the data, the arrangement of the points becomes less meaningful. While 10% noise added to a single matrix gives an acceptable geometric configuration, 50% noise does not.

There are various computer programs that have been written to recover the structure from sets of similarity data. Six of the main procedures are given in Table 2. These procedures are discussed extensively by Schiffman *et al.* (1981) and are beyond the scope of this paper. All of the methods, however, recover structure from data sets that consist of the amount of perceived difference between each pair in a set of stimuli. The data sets are often called 'dissimilarities' or 'proximities'. Each of the six programs given in Table 2 computes positions in space (or coordinates for each stimulus) such that the distances between stimuli will correspond as closely as possible to the experimental proximities or transformations of them. The success of the analysis is reflected by how well the distances, d, match the proximities, δ, or their transformations.

The positions of the stimuli in space are specified by their coordinates on each dimension. In the two-dimensional case, the coordinates to be found for stimulus 1 are x_{11} and x_{12}; for stimulus 2, x_{12} and x_{22}, and so on. From the Pythagorean theorem, the distance between stimulus 1 and 2 is:

$$d_{12} = [x_{11} - x_{21})^2 + (x_{12} - x_{22})^2]^{1/2}$$

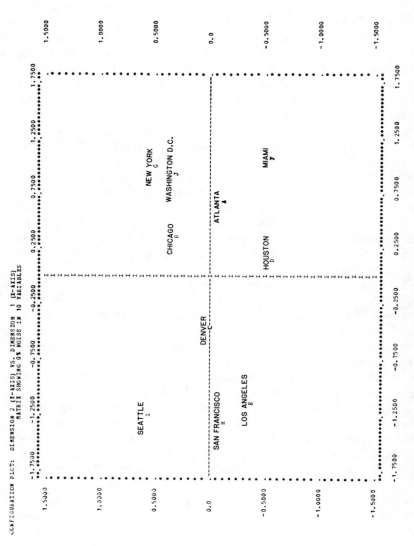

FIG. 1. Two-dimensional arrangement derived by KYST for the data in Table 1.

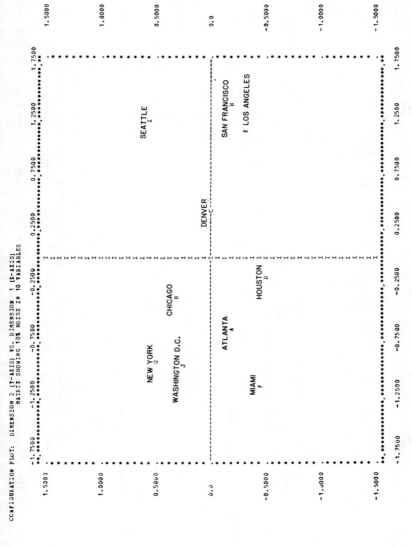

FIG. 2. Two-dimensional arrangement derived by KYST when 10% noise was added to the data in Table 1.

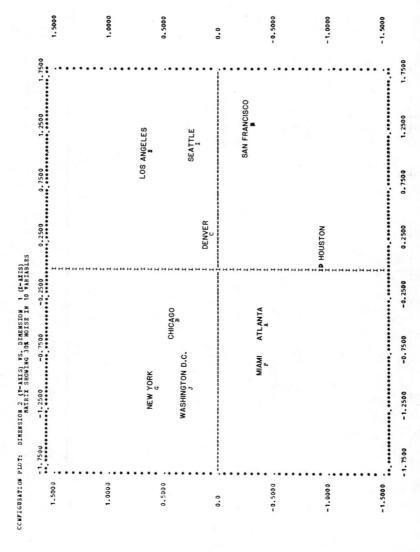

FIG. 3. Two-dimensional arrangement derived by KYST when 30% noise was added to the data in Table 1.

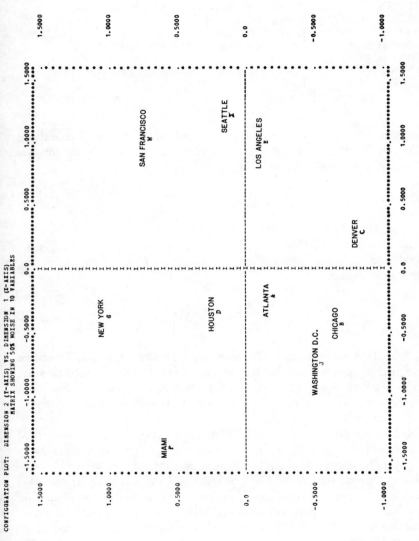

FIG. 4. Two-dimensional arrangement derived by KYST when 50% noise was added to the data in Table 1.

TABLE 2
SIX OF THE MAJOR MDS PROGRAMS IN COMMON USE

MINISSA	Guttman (1968); Lingoes (1973); Roskam (1968)
POLYCON	Young (1972, 1973)
KYST	Kruskal (1964a,b); Kruskal *et al.* (1973)
INDSCAL and SINDSCAL	Carroll and Chang (1970); Pruzansky (1975)
ALSCAL	Takane *et al.* (1977); Young and Lewyckyj (1979)
MULTISCALE	Ramsay (1977, 1978a,b)

This equation can be generalized so that each distance, calculated according to the Euclidean distance formula for two dimensions, is expressed in summation notation as:

$$d_{ij} = \left[\sum_{a=1}^{2} (x_{ia} - x_{ja})^2 \right]^{1/2}$$

where d_{ij} is the Euclidean distance between points i and j, and x_{ia} is the coordinate on some unspecified dimension a. For r dimensions the algebraic formula is:

$$d_{ij} = \left[\sum_{a=1}^{r} (x_{ia} - x_{ja})^2 \right]^{1/2}$$

Each MDS program has different computational strategies. These are described at length by Schiffman *et al.* (1981). It suffices here to state simply that all MDS programs derive geometric representations from measures of similarity permitting systematic classification and compression of large amounts of data.

Multidimensional scaling (MDS) in conjunction with mathematical techniques for interpretation of the spaces has been employed extensively by psychophysicists, food technologists, and market researchers to uncover the perceptual dimensions of taste and odor stimuli. It has also been used to provide novel leads for molecular structures with specific odor and taste qualities. Increasingly MDS is used as a tool for molecular modeling to permit rational design of flavor molecules and eliminate the blind synthesis of compounds in the laboratory (see Schiffman, 1983).

3. INTERPRETATION OF MULTIDIMENSIONAL SPACES

The power of the MDS approach depends in part on the effectiveness of the mathematical techniques used to interpret multidimensional spaces. Unfortunately, interpretation of spaces has received less attention than development of the MDS programs themselves. This section will deal with methods for interpreting MDS spaces and will include a brief discussion of vector and ideal point models, and a more detailed description of canonical correlation, maximum redundancy analysis, and partial least squares. Vector and ideal point models relate a single attribute to a multidimensional space. The other techniques relate a series of variables to a space.

In order to interpret a multidimensional space, it is necessary to have basic information about the individual stimuli in addition to their coordinates derived from an MDS analysis. The specific application used in this chapter to illustrate the property fitting will be an example from odor psychophysics.

3.1. Experiment Used to Illustrate Interpretation Techniques

Twelve nonsmoking university students judged the similarity in odor quality among all 171 pairs of nineteen reagent grade chemicals. The odorants were delivered from the sniffing port of an olfactometer and mixed with an airstream to provide moderate sensations of approximately equal intensity (see Schiffman et al., 1977).

Judgments of similarity were made along an undifferentiated five inch line:

exact _____ completely
same   different

The ratings were transcribed on a scale from 0 to 99 with 0 representing 'exact same' and 99, 'completely different'. The transcribed data were analyzed by the SAS version of ALSCAL using the replicated interval option. The two-dimensional space is shown in Fig. 5.

Twenty-three physicochemical parameters were related to the spatial arrangement in Fig. 5 to search for those variables that correlate most highly with odor quality. The physicochemical parameters are given in Table 3 and include Raman frequencies, functional groups, molecular weight, and Laffort parameters (see Schiffman et al., 1977). Raman spectra from 176–1000 reciprocal wave numbers were examined to

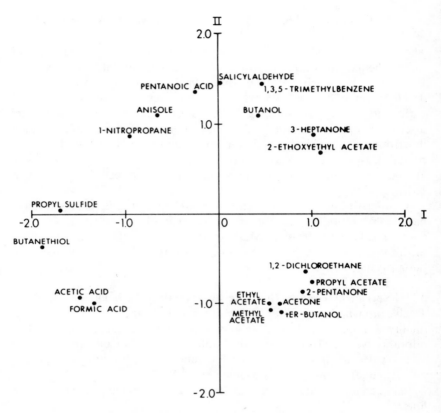

FIG. 5. Two-dimensional space derived by ALSCAL for a range of odorants. Compounds located near one another have similar odor quality. (From Schiffman *et al.*, 1977.)

determine the relationship of low energy molecular vibrations to olfactory quality. The Laffort parameters are alpha (an apolar factor proportional to molecular volume), rho (a proton receptor factor), epsilon (an electron factor), and pi (a proton donor factor).

3.2. Relating a Single Variable to a Stimulus Space

Two methods, a vector model and an ideal point model, will be described here that can be used to relate an individual physicochemical descriptor, such as molecular weight, to the spatial arrangement in Fig. 5.

TABLE 3
THE TWENTY-THREE PHYSICOCHEMICAL PARAMETERS RELATED TO THE SPATIAL ARRANGEMENT IN Fig. 5

1. 176–250 cm^{-1} ⎫	13. Ester (ES)
2. 251–325 cm^{-1} ⎪	14. Acid (AC)
3. 326–400 cm^{-1} ⎪	15. Aromatic ring (AR)
4. 401–475 cm^{-1} ⎪	16. Ketone (KE)
5. 476–550 cm^{-1} ⎬ Raman	17. Hydrogen bonding (HB)
6. 551–625 cm^{-1} ⎪ frequencies	18. Boiling point (BP)
7. 626–700 cm^{-1} ⎪	19. Vapor pressure (VP)
8. 701–775 cm^{-1} ⎪	20. Alpha ⎫
9. 776–850 cm^{-1} ⎪	21. Rho ⎬ Laffort
10. 851–925 cm^{-1} ⎭	22. Epsilon ⎬ parameters
11. 926–1 000 cm^{-1}	23. Pi ⎭
12. Molecular weight (MW)	

3.2.1. Vector Model

The vector model makes the assumption that there is a direction through the space that corresponds to increasing amounts of a chemical descriptor. The direction of the vector is found by multiple regression techniques (see Darlington, 1968; Schiffman *et al.*, 1981). A single physicochemical parameter is regressed over the coordinates of the configuration. The goal is to find weighted combinations of the configuration coordinates that best explain the variable.

The basic equation for ordinary multiple regression is:

$$p_i \cong \tilde{p}_i = b_0 + b_1(x_{i1}) + \cdots + b_r(x_{ir})$$

In summation notation, this is

$$p_i \cong \tilde{p}_i = b_0 + \sum_{a=1}^{r} b_a(x_{ia})$$

where: p_i is the specific value stimulus i on the attribute;
$\tilde{p}_i$ is the best estimate of p_i;
x_{ia} is the coordinate of stimulus i on dimension a;
r is the number of dimensions;
b_a is the regression weight on dimension a;
b_0 is the intercept.

There are n equations for the n stimuli.

Figure 6 illustrates how an attribute vector can be drawn through a space. The projections for each stimulus on the vector correspond to the degree of the attribute (here molecular weight) possessed by the stimulus.

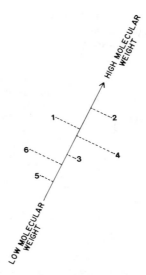

FIG. 6. Representative arrangement of six odorants by MDS with a vector regressed through the space representing molecular weight. The projections of each stimulus on the vector correspond to the molecular weight.

3.2.2. Ideal Point Model

Another technique based on multiple regression analysis is the ideal point model. The ideal point model is useful when a point in the multidimensional space can be found that is most like a physicochemical parameter. It can be conceptualized as a hypothetical stimulus, if it existed, that would contain the maximum amount of the physicochemical attribute (e.g. molecular weight). The maximum for the attribute is found at the ideal point and falls off in all directions as the square of the distance from the ideal point (see Fig. 7). The ideal point is located by a special kind of regression technique proposed by Carroll (1972) that correlates the values of the physicochemical parameter for each stimulus with the stimulus coordinates and a dummy variable constructed from the sum of squares of the coordinates for each point:

$$\hat{y}_i = b_0 + \sum_{a=1}^{r} b_a(x_{ia}) + b_{r+1}\left(\sum_{a=1}^{r} x_{ia}^2 \right)$$

There are many statistical packages available for doing multiple regression techniques. Practical examples are found in Schiffman et al. (1981).

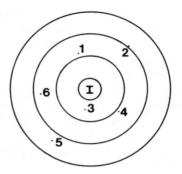

FIG. 7. Representative arrangement of six odorants by MDS with an ideal point imbedded in the space. The ideal point I can be conceptualized as a hypothetical stimulus, if it existed, that would contain the maximum amount of the physicochemical attribute, here molecular weight.

When multiple regression techniques were applied to each of the 23 variables in Table 3, no one attribute was found to relate well to the space in Fig. 5. For this reason, canonical correlation, maximum redundancy, and PLS were utilized to relate a set of quantitative physicochemical descriptors to the arrangement of odor stimuli.

Canonical correlation analysis. Canonical correlation analysis (see Muller, 1982; Schiffman *et al.*, 1981) is a means of finding linear relationships between two sets of variables, e.g. coordinates of a multidimensional space and physicochemical parameters. Canonical correlation analysis finds linear relationships between two sets of variables as expressed by the following equations:

$$\tilde{y}_{ik} = a_{0k} + a_{1k}(y_{i1}) + \cdots + a_{pk}(y_{ip})$$

and

$$\tilde{x}_{ik} = b_{0k} + b_{1k}(x_{i1}) + \cdots + b_{qk}(x_{iq})$$

where y_{i1}, y_{i2}, are the stimulus values on dimensions 1, 2, ... of the multidimensional space, and where x_{i1}, x_{i2}, ... are ratings of stimulus i on the physicochemical parameters. The values a_{0k} and b_{0k} are intercepts and a_{1k}, b_{1k}, etc., are canonical coefficients.

The first pair of *canonical variates* is extracted simultaneously from the two sets of variables in a manner that maximizes the correlation between $\tilde{y}_{i1}$ and $\tilde{x}_{i1}$ which is the first *canonical correlation*. Subsequent pairs of canonical variates are chosen to maximize the correlation between $\tilde{y}_{ik}$ and $\tilde{x}_{ik}$ subject to the restriction that they are uncorrelated with all previous canonical variates. Thus, for each canonical variate there is a complete set of canonical coefficients and intercepts. The intercepts are arbitrary and are generally chosen to give canonical variates a mean of zero. The number of canonical variates cannot exceed the number of variables in the smaller set, in this case, two.

Canonical coefficients are an index of the relationship between a physicochemical parameter and the canonical variate. However, a better index of the relative contribution of the physicochemical parameters to each canonical variate is given by the *canonical structure matrix* that contains the correlation between a particular physicochemical parameter and a particular canonical variate.

Canonical correlation analysis was applied to the psychophysical odor data. The SAS procedure CANCORR was used to relate eight of the physicochemical parameters given in Table 3, molecular weight through vapor pressure, to the coordinates of the two-dimensional space in Fig. 5. The SAS program used is given in Fig. 8. SAS refers to the Statistical Analysis System (SAS Institute, Inc., SAS Circle, P.O. Box 8000, Cary, N. C. 27511–8000, USA).

Lines 1–2 create a data set called DIMS that consists of the coordinates of the two-dimensional space. Lines 24–29 create a data set called STIM which specifies the values of the series of physicochemical parameters including molecular weight through vapor pressure for the 19 stimuli. Lines 70–71 join corresponding observations in the new SAS data set called COMBO.

In lines 72–79, a canonical correlation procedure is applied to the combined data COMBO. The prefix for naming canonical variates from the VAR statement is DIMM; the prefix from the WITH statement is PHYS. The output is placed in a SAS data set called SCORE, printed, and the results are shown in Fig. 9(a–f).

It can be seen in Fig. 9(a) that the first but not the second canonical correlation is statistically significant for this data set. To get a pictorial impression of how effective these eight parameters are in predicting the arrangement in Fig. 5, it is possible to apply PROC SCORE. This procedure multiplies two SAS data sets, one containing the data (COMBO) and one containing the canonical coefficients. This can be done in two ways using either standardized (lines 80–97) or unstandardized (lines 101–116) data. The output of SCORE using standardized and unstandardized coefficients is given in Fig. 10(a) and (b). The canonical coordinates computed from the standardized coefficients have mean zero while those computed from the raw coefficients have a

```
1              DATA DIMS;
2              INPUT CHEMICAL $1-8 DIM1 9-15 DIM2 16-22;
3              CARDS;

NOTE: DATA SET WORK.DIMS HAS 19 OBSERVATIONS AND 3 VARIABLES. 680 OBS/TRK.
NOTE: THE DATA STATEMENT USED 0.06 SECONDS AND 324K.

23             ;
24             DATA STIM;
25             INPUT RAM1 1-5 RAM2 6-10 RAM3 11-15 RAM4 16-20 RAM5 21-25
26             RAM6 26-30 RAM7 31-35 RAM8 36-40 RAM9 41-45 RAM10 46-50
27             RAM11 51-55 MW 56-60
28             #2 ES 1-5 AC 6-10 AF 11-15 KF 16-20 HB 21-25 BP 26-30
29             VP 31-35 LAF1 36-40 LAF2 41-45 LAF3 46-50 LAF4 51-55;
30             CARDS;

NOTE: DATA SET WORK.STIM HAS 19 OBSERVATIONS AND 23 VARIABLES. 101 OBS/TRK.
NOTE: THE DATA STATEMENT USED 0.10 SECONDS AND 324K.

69             ;
70             DATA COMBO;
71             MERGE DIMS STIM;

NOTE: DATA SET WORK.COMBO HAS 19 OBSERVATIONS AND 26 VARIABLES. 89 OBS/TRK.
NOTE: THE DATA STATEMENT USED 0.09 SECONDS AND 356K.

72             PROC CANCORR DATA=COMBO RED NCAN=2 OUTSTAT=SCORE
73                          VPREFIX=DIMM VNAME='DIMENSIONS'
74                          WPREFIX=PHYS WNAME='PHYSICOCHEMICAL PARAMETERS';
75             VAR DIM1 DIM2;
76             WITH MW--VP;
77             TITLE2 CANONICAL CORRELATION OF PHYSICOCHEMICAL PARAMETERS MW--VP;

NOTE: DATA SET WORK.SCORE HAS 26 OBSERVATIONS AND 12 VARIABLES. 190 OBS/TRK.
NOTE: THE PROCEDURE CANCORR USED 0.27 SECONDS AND 444K AND PRINTED PAGES 1 TO 5.

78             PROC PRINT DATA=SCORE;
79             TITLE3 OUTPUT OF CANCORR;

NOTE: THE PROCEDURE PRINT USED 0.17 SECONDS AND 384K AND PRINTED PAGE 6.

80             PROC SCORE DATA=COMBO SCORE=SCORE OUT=SCOROUT;
81             VAR DIM1 DIM2 MW--VP;
82             MACRO PLOTAXIS
83             VPOS=70;
84             %

NOTE: DATA SET WORK.SCOROUT HAS 19 OBSERVATIONS AND 30 VARIABLES. 78 OBS/TRK.
NOTE: THE PROCEDURE SCORE USED 0.15 SECONDS AND 352K.

85             PROC PRINT DATA=SCOROUT;
86             TITLE2 OUTPUT OF SCORE USING STANDARDIZED DATA;

87             PROC PLOT DATA=SCOROUT;
88             PLOT PHYS2*PHYS1=CHEMICAL
89                  /PLOTAXIS;
93             TITLE2 PLOT OF FIRST TWO CANONICAL CORRELATES FOR MW--VP;
94             TITLE3 USING STANDARDIZED DATA;

NOTE: THE PROCEDURE PLOT USED 0.21 SECONDS AND 380K AND PRINTED PAGE 8.

95             PROC PLOT DATA=SCOROUT;
96             PLOT DIMM2*DIMM1=CHEMICAL
97                  /PLOTAXIS;

NOTE: THE PROCEDURE PLOT USED 0.21 SECONDS AND 380K AND PRINTED PAGE 9.

101            PROC SCORE DATA=COMBO SCORE=SCORE TYPE=RAWSCORE NOSTD OUT=RAWOUT;
102            VAR DIM1 DIM2 MW--VP;

NOTE: DATA SET WORK.RAWOUT HAS 19 OBSERVATIONS AND 30 VARIABLES. 78 OBS/TRK.
NOTE: THE PROCEDURE SCORE USED 0.15 SECONDS AND 352K.

103            PROC PRINT DATA=RAWOUT;
104            TITLE2 CANONICAL CORRELATES OF PHYSICOCHEMICAL PARAMETERS MW--VP;
105            TITLE3 OUTPUT OF SCORE USING UNSTANDARDIZED DATA;

NOTE: THE PROCEDURE PRINT USED 0.24 SECONDS AND 408K AND PRINTED PAGE 10.

106            PROC PLOT DATA=RAWOUT;
107            PLOT PHYS2*PHYS1=CHEMICAL
108                 /PLOTAXIS;
112            TITLE2 PLOT OF FIRST TWO CANONICAL CORRELATES FOR MW--VP;
113            TITLE3 USING UNSTANDARDIZED DATA;

NOTE: THE PROCEDURE PLOT USED 0.21 SECONDS AND 380K AND PRINTED PAGE 11.

114            PROC PLOT DATA=RAWOUT;
115            PLOT DIMM2*DIMM1=CHEMICAL
116                 /PLOTAXIS;
```

FIG. 8. SAS code to do a canonical correlation analysis.

SAS

CANONICAL CORRELATION OF PHYSICOCHEMICAL PARAMETERS MW--VP

CANONICAL CORRELATION ANALYSIS

19 OBSERVATIONS
2 DV
8 PHYSICOCHEMICAL PARAMETERS

CANONICAL CORRELATIONS AND TESTS OF H0: THE CANONICAL CORRELATION IN THE CURRENT ROW AND ALL THAT FOLLOW ARE ZERO

	CANONICAL CORRELATION	ADJUSTED CAN CORR	APPROX STD ERROR	VARIANCE RATIO	CANONICAL R-SQUARED	LIKELIHOOD RATIO	F STATISTIC	NUM DF	DEN DF	PROB>F
1	0.973206389	0.956238477	0.012461419	17.9146	0.947130675	0.020613086	6.7108	16	18	0.0001
2	0.781097026	0.653556805	0.091897350	1.5648	0.610112563	0.389887437	2.2335	7	10	0.1202

MULTIVARIATE TEST STATISTICS AND F APPROXIMATIONS

STATISTIC	VALUE	F	NUM DF	DEN DF	PROB>F
WILKS' LAMBDA	0.002009985	24.02457	16	18	6.15552E-09
PILLAI'S TRACE	24.66657		16	20	.0000400421
HOTELLING-LAWLEY TRACE	24.64516	12.32258	16	20	.0000400421
ROY'S GREATEST ROOT	17.91456	22.3932	8	10	.0000201069

NOTE: F STATISTIC FOR ROY'S GREATEST ROOT IS AN UPPER BOUND
      F STATISTIC FOR WILKS' LAMBDA IS EXACT

RAW CANONICAL COEFFICIENTS FOR THE DIMENSIONS

	DIM1	DIM2
DIM1	-.4588610728	0.8584874635
DIM2	0.8521299910	0.4705495585

RAW CANONICAL COEFFICIENTS FOR THE PHYSICOCHEMICAL PARAMETERS

	PHYS1	PHYS2
MW	-0.042867495	0.029210330
ES	-0.6679891115	1.345977367
AC	-0.7392286401	-.135250038
AB	-1.7010602618	0.976730943
KH	-1.0892026600	1.534753942
HB	0.0484863943	1.003171175
BP	0.001847933	-0.001206788
VP		

FIG. 9a.

FIG. 9(a–f). The output of the SAS program in Fig. 8.

SAS
CANONICAL CORRELATION OF PHYSICOCHEMICAL PARAMETERS MW--VP
CANONICAL CORRELATION ANALYSIS

STANDARDIZED CANONICAL COEFFICIENTS FOR THE DIMENSIONS

	DIMM1	DIMM2
DIM1	-0.4714	0.8820
DIM2	0.8755	0.4834

STANDARDIZED CANONICAL COEFFICIENTS FOR THE PHYSICOCHEMICAL PARAMETERS

	PHYS1	PHYS2
MW	-1.0244	0.6980
ES	-0.2972	0.5638
AC	-0.4268	-0.4239
AR	-0.2628	0.2651
KE	-0.4574	0.7169
HB	-0.5199	0.7349
BP	1.8307	-0.1294
VP	0.1441	-0.0941

FIG. 9b.

SAS
CANONICAL CORRELATION OF PHYSICOCHEMICAL PARAMETERS MW--VP
CANONICAL STRUCTURE

CORRELATIONS BETWEEN THE DIMENSIONS AND THEIR CANONICAL VARIABLES

	DIMM1	DIMM2
DIM1	-0.4834	0.8754
DIM2	0.8819	0.4714

CORRELATIONS BETWEEN THE PHYSICOCHEMICAL PARAMETERS AND THEIR CANONICAL VARIABLES

	PHYS1	PHYS2
MW	0.4813	0.6550
ES	-0.4577	0.2906
AC	0.1430	-0.5557
AR	0.5256	0.3384
KE	-0.3169	0.3288
HB	0.1946	0.5905
BP	0.8638	0.3616
VP	-0.4140	-0.0514

CORRELATIONS BETWEEN THE DIMENSIONS AND THE CANONICAL VARIABLES OF THE PHYSICOCHEMICAL PARAMETERS

	PHYS1	PHYS2
DIM1	-0.4704	0.6838
DIM2	0.8583	0.3682

CORRELATIONS BETWEEN THE PHYSICOCHEMICAL PARAMETERS AND THE CANONICAL VARIABLES OF THE DIMENSIONS

	DIMM1	DIMM2
MW	0.4684	0.5116
ES	-0.4449	0.2270
AC	0.1392	-0.4341
AR	0.5115	0.2643
KE	-0.3084	0.2568
HB	0.1894	-0.1488
BP	0.8407	0.2825
VP	-0.4029	-0.0401

FIG. 9c.

SAS
CANONICAL CORRELATION OF PHYSICOCHEMICAL PARAMETERS HW--VP

CANONICAL REDUNDANCY ANALYSIS

RAW VARIANCE OF THE DIMENSIONS
EXPLAINED BY

	THEIR OWN CANONICAL VARIABLES			THE OPPOSITE CANONICAL VARIABLES	
	PROPORTION	CUMULATIVE PROPORTION	CANONICAL R-SQUARED	PROPORTION	CUMULATIVE PROPORTION
1	0.5057	0.5057	0.9471	0.4790	0.4790
2	0.4943	1.0000	0.6101	0.3016	0.7806

RAW VARIANCE OF THE PHYSICOCHEMICAL PARAMETERS
EXPLAINED BY

	THEIR OWN CANONICAL VARIABLES			THE OPPOSITE CANONICAL VARIABLES	
	PROPORTION	CUMULATIVE PROPORTION	CANONICAL R-SQUARED	PROPORTION	CUMULATIVE PROPORTION
1	0.2906	0.2906	0.9471	0.2752	0.2752
2	0.0576	0.3481	0.6101	0.0351	0.3103

STANDARDIZED VARIANCE OF THE DIMENSIONS
EXPLAINED BY

	THEIR OWN CANONICAL VARIABLES			THE OPPOSITE CANONICAL VARIABLES	
	PROPORTION	CUMULATIVE PROPORTION	CANONICAL R-SQUARED	PROPORTION	CUMULATIVE PROPORTION
1	0.5057	0.5057	0.9471	0.4790	0.4790
2	0.4943	1.0000	0.6101	0.3016	0.7806

STANDARDIZED VARIANCE OF THE PHYSICOCHEMICAL PARAMETERS
EXPLAINED BY

	THEIR OWN CANONICAL VARIABLES			THE OPPOSITE CANONICAL VARIABLES	
	PROPORTION	CUMULATIVE PROPORTION	CANONICAL R-SQUARED	PROPORTION	CUMULATIVE PROPORTION
1	0.2242	0.2242	0.9471	0.2123	0.2123
2	0.1518	0.3760	0.6101	0.0926	0.3049

FIG. 9d.

nonzero mean because the CANCORR procedure doesn't bother to compute an intercept term.

The arrangement of the stimuli in the reconstructed space using either raw or standardized coefficients will be identical. The scores for the unstandardized data are plotted in Fig. 11. It can be seen that the space based on these physicochemical parameters is a moderately good reconstruction of the arrangement in Fig. 5. Plotting unstandardized scores makes it slightly easier to plot the location of a new stimulus.

Canonical correlation analysis has some drawbacks for recreating a multidimensional space. The most potentially serious is that it can weight the dimensions of the original space so that it is stretched elliptically. Figure 12 shows the arrangement of the stimuli after application of PROC CANCORR. It is rotated but not badly distorted. In

CANONICAL CORRELATION OF PHYSICOCHEMICAL PARAMETERS MW--VP

SAS

CANONICAL REDUNDANCY ANALYSIS

SQUARED MULTIPLE CORRELATIONS BETWEEN THE DIMENSIONS AND THE FIRST 'M' CANONICAL VARIABLES OF THE PHYSICOCHEMICAL PARAMETERS

M	1	2
DIM1	0.7217	0.6889
DIM2	0.7363	0.8722

SQUARED MULTIPLE CORRELATIONS BETWEEN THE PHYSICOCHEMICAL PARAMETERS AND THE FIRST 'M' CANONICAL VARIABLES OF THE DIMENSIONS

M	1	2
MW	0.2194	0.4811
ES	0.1979	0.2495
AC	0.2094	0.3278
AR	0.2614	0.3311
KE	0.0359	0.0480
HB	0.7067	0.7365
BP	0.1624	0.1640

FIG. 9e.

CANONICAL CORRELATION OF PHYSICOCHEMICAL PARAMETERS MW--VP

SAS

OUTPUT OF CANCORR

FIG. 9f.

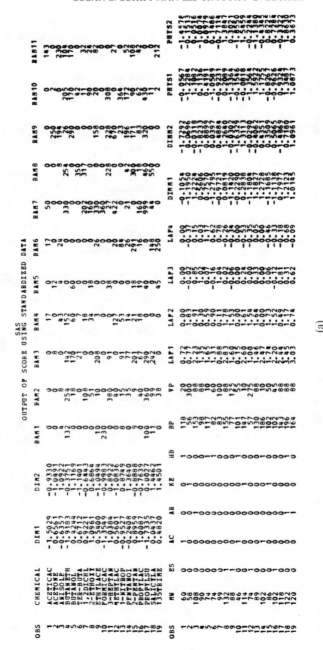

FIG. 10. The output of SCORE using (a) standardized and (b) unstandardized coordinates.

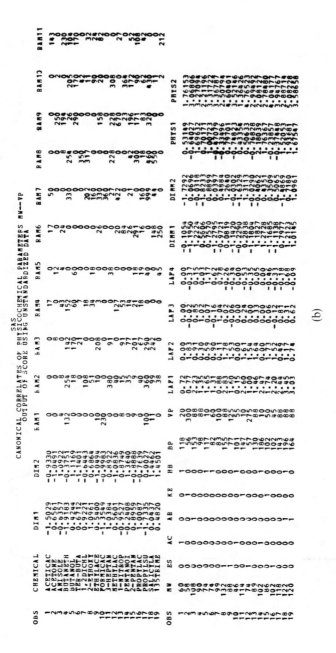

Fig. 10—*contd.*

(b)

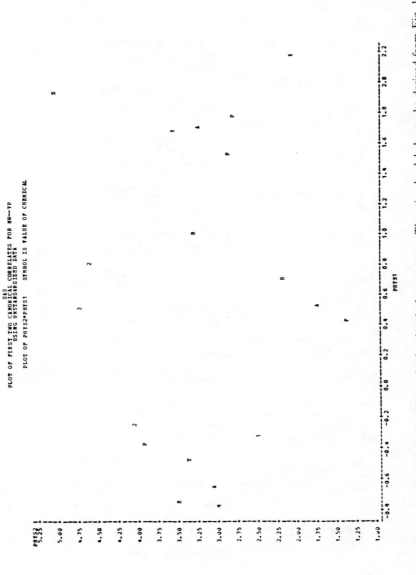

Fig. 11. Reconstructed space based on physicochemical parameters. The stimulus labels can be derived from Fig. 10.

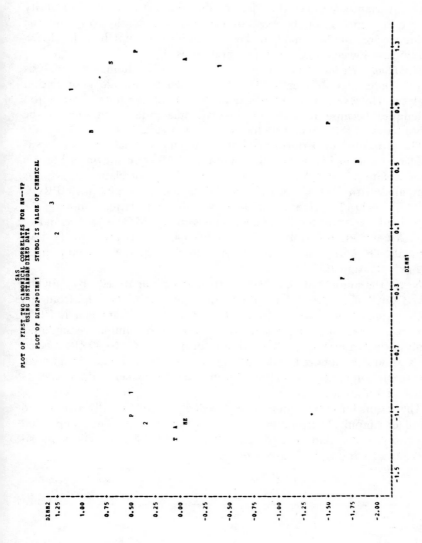

FIG. 12. Arrangement of the stimuli after application of PROC CANCORR. The labels are identical to Fig. 11.

practice, we have found only minimal stretching of spaces but it is certainly a possible consequence of the model.

The reason for the lack of distortion is that MDS solutions tend to have covariance matrices that are roughly proportional to the identity matrix, the correlation between dimensions is generally low, and the variances are roughly equal. If these conditions did not hold for MDS solutions, a lower dimensionality could be used.

Maximum Redundancy Analysis. Maximum redundancy analysis (Wollenberg, 1977; Muller, 1981) is very similar to canonical correlation analysis. However, it eliminates a drawback of canonical correlation techniques because it does not involve differential weighting of the coordinates of the original multidimensional space.

The procedure to perform maximum redundancy analysis with SAS is similar to that in Fig. 8 with the additional SAS code shown in Fig. 13. After creating the SAS data set COMBO, a correlation matrix is computed with PROC CORR and subsequently printed with PROC PRINT; a DATA step is used to set the correlations among the dependent variables (here the coordinates in the MDS space) equal to zero. A complete description of the code's meaning is given in the SAS manuals. The correlation matrix before and after the DATA step is given in Fig. 14(a) and (b).

Next the modified correlation matrix is analyzed by PROC CANCORR. The prefix for naming the linear combinations from the VAR statement is XXX; the prefix from the WITH statement is PHY. The equivalent of a canonical correlation in maximum redundancy analysis is redundancy. All output from PROC CANCORR labeled XXX should be ignored. Also, all significance tests should be ignored. The linear combinations computed from the physicochemical parameters are the redundancy variates.

The results for maximum redundancy analysis are virtually identical to those for canonical correlation analysis for this example. The comparison of canonical correlations and redundancy for 4 different sets of physicochemical parameters is given below:

	Canonical correlation		Redundancy correlation	
	I	II	I	II
RAM1–RAM11	0·89	0·66	0·89	0·66
MW–VP	0·97	0·78	0·97	0·77
LAF1–LAF4	0·84	0·66	0·84	0·66
RAM1–LAF4	1·00	1·00	1·00	0·99

```
 1              DATA DIMS;
 2              INPUT CHEMICAL $1-8 DIM1 9-15 DIM2 16-22;
 3              CARDS;

NOTE: DATA SET WORK.DIMS HAS 19 OBSERVATIONS AND 3 VARIABLES. 680 OBS/TRK.
NOTE: THE DATA STATEMENT USED 0.06 SECONDS AND 324K.

23             ;
24             DATA STIM;
25             INPUT RAM1 1-5 RAM2 6-10 RAM3 11-15 RAM4 16-20 RAM5 21-25
26             RAM6 26-30 RAM7 31-35 RAM8 36-40 RAM9 41-45 RAM10 46-50
27             RAM11 51-55 MW 56-60
28             #2 ES 1-5 AC 6-10 AR 11-15 KE 16-20 HB 21-25 BP 26-30
29             VP 31-35 LAF1 36-40 LAF2 41-45 LAF3 46-50 LAF4 51-55;
30             CARDS;

NOTE: DATA SET WORK.STIM HAS 19 OBSERVATIONS AND 23 VARIABLES. 101 OBS/TRK.
NOTE: THE DATA STATEMENT USED 0.10 SECONDS AND 324K.

69             ;
70             DATA COMBO;
71             MERGE DIMS STIM;

NOTE: DATA SET WORK.COMBO HAS 19 OBSERVATIONS AND 26 VARIABLES. 89 OBS/TRK.
NOTE: THE DATA STATEMENT USED 0.09 SECONDS AND 356K.

72             PROC CORR DATA=COMBO OUTP=COR;
73             VAR DIM1 DIM2 MW--VP;

NOTE: DATA SET WORK.COR HAS 13 OBSERVATIONS AND 12 VARIABLES. 190 OBS/TRK.
NOTE: THE PROCEDURE CORR USED 0.20 SECONDS AND 388K AND PRINTED PAGES 1 TO 2.

74             PROC PRINT DATA=COR;
75             TITLE2 OUTPUT OF CORR--MATRIX BEFORE MANIPULATION;

NOTE: THE PROCEDURE PRINT USED 0.15 SECONDS AND 384K AND PRINTED PAGE 3.

76             DATA COR(TYPE=CORR); SET;
77             LENGTH VARNAME $8; DROP VARNAME MATCH;
78             ARRAY PREF DIM1--DIM2;
79             IF _TYPE_='CORR' THEN DO OVER PREF;
80                 CALL VNAME(PREF,VARNAME);
81                 IF VARNAME=_NAME_ THEN GOTO ZERO;
82                 END;
83             RETURN;
84             ZERO:
85             MATCH=_I_;
86             DO OVER PREF;
87                 PREF=0;
88                 END;
89             _I_=MATCH;
90             PREF=1;
91             RETURN;

NOTE: THE VARIABLE VARNAME IS UNINITIALIZED.
NOTE: DATA SET WORK.COR HAS 13 OBSERVATIONS AND 12 VARIABLES. 190 OBS/TRK.
NOTE: THE DATA STATEMENT USED 0.10 SECONDS AND 324K.

92             PROC PRINT DATA=COR;
93             TITLE2 OUTPUT OF CORR--AFTER MATRIX MANIPULATION;

NOTE: THE PROCEDURE PRINT USED 0.15 SECONDS AND 384K AND PRINTED PAGE 4.

94             PROC CANCORR REDUNDANCY NCAN=2 OUTSTAT=SCORE
95                 VPREFIX=RED VNAME='DIMENSIONS'
96                 WPREFIX=PHY WNAME='PHYSICOCHEMICAL PARAMETERS';
97             VAR DIM1 DIM2;
98             WITH MW--VP;
99             TITLE2 MAXIMUM REDUNDANCY ANALYSIS OF PHYSICOCHEMICAL PARAMETERS;

NOTE: DATA SET WORK.SCORE HAS 26 OBSERVATIONS AND 12 VARIABLES. 190 OBS/TRK.
NOTE: THE PROCEDURE CANCORR USED 0.24 SECONDS AND 444K AND PRINTED PAGES 5 TO 9.

100            PROC PRINT DATA=SCORE;
101            TITLE2 OUTPUT OF PROC CANCORR;

NOTE: THE PROCEDURE PRINT USED 0.16 SECONDS AND 384K AND PRINTED PAGE 10.

102            PROC SCORE DATA=COMBO SCORE=SCORE OUT=RED;
103            VAR DIM1 DIM2 MW--VP;

NOTE: DATA SET WORK.RED HAS 19 OBSERVATIONS AND 30 VARIABLES. 78 OBS/TRK.
NOTE: THE PROCEDURE SCORE USED 0.14 SECONDS AND 352K.

104            PROC PRINT DATA=RED;
105            TITLE2 OUTPUT OF PROC SCORE;
106            MACRO LIST
107                PROC SORT DATA=RED;
108                BY LISTVAR;
109            PROC PRINT;
110                ID CHEMICAL;
111                VAR LISTVAR;
112            %
```

FIG. 13. SAS code for maximum redundancy analysis.

```
NOTE: THE PROCEDURE PRINT USED 0.22 SECONDS AND 416K AND PRINTED PAGE 11.

NOTE: DATA SET WORK.RED HAS 19 OBSERVATIONS AND 30 VARIABLES. 78 OBS/TRK.
NOTE: THE PROCEDURE SORT USED 0.23 SECONDS AND 760K.
113          MACRO LISTVAR RED1% LIST TITLE2 SORTED BY FIRST REDUNDANCY VARIABLE;
NOTE: THE PROCEDURE PRINT USED 0.17 SECONDS AND 372K AND PRINTED PAGE 12.

NOTE: DATA SET WORK.RED HAS 19 OBSERVATIONS AND 30 VARIABLES. 78 OBS/TRK.
NOTE: THE PROCEDURE SORT USED 0.23 SECONDS AND 760K.
123          MACRO LISTVAR RED2% LIST TITLE2 SORTED BY SECOND REDUNDANCY VARIABLE;
133          MACRO PLOTAXIS
134              HAXIS=-2.5 TO 2.5 BY .5 VAXIS=-2.5 TO 2.5 BY .5 VPOS=70;
135          %
NOTE: THE PROCEDURE PRINT USED 0.16 SECONDS AND 368K AND PRINTED PAGE 13.

136          PROC PLOT DATA=RED;
137              PLOT RED2*RED1=CHEMICAL
138              /PLOTAXIS;
142              TITLE2 PLOT OF THE FIRST TWO REDUNDANCY VARIABLES;
NOTE: THE PROCEDURE PLOT USED 0.18 SECONDS AND 382K AND PRINTED PAGE 14.

143          DATA PAT; SET SCORE;
144              KEEP _NAME_ DIM1 DIM2;
145              IF _TYPE_='STRUCTUR';
NOTE: DATA SET WORK.PAT HAS 4 OBSERVATIONS AND 3 VARIABLES. 680 OBS/TRK.
NOTE: THE DATA STATEMENT USED 0.08 SECONDS AND 328K.
146          PROC TRANSPOSE OUT=PAT;
NOTE: DATA SET WORK.PAT HAS 2 OBSERVATIONS AND 5 VARIABLES. 433 OBS/TRK.
NOTE: THE PROCEDURE TRANSPOSE USED 0.10 SECONDS AND 366K.
147          DATA ZERO;
148              NAME_ = '+
149              RED1=0;
150              RED2=0;
NOTE: DATA SET WORK.ZERO HAS 1 OBSERVATIONS AND 3 VARIABLES. 680 OBS/TRK.
NOTE: THE DATA STATEMENT USED 0.06 SECONDS AND 328K.
151          DATA BIPLOT; SET PAT ZERO RED(IN=INPRIN);
152              IF INPRIN THEN _NAME_='.';
NOTE: DATA SET WORK.BIPLOT HAS 22 OBSERVATIONS AND 31 VARIABLES. 75 OBS/TRK.
NOTE: THE DATA STATEMENT USED 0.11 SECONDS AND 336K.
153          PROC PLOT;
154              PLOT RED2*RED1=_NAME_
155              /PLOTAXIS;
159              TITLE3 SHOWING BOTH CHEMICALS AND REDUNDANCY PATTERN;
NOTE: THE PROCEDURE PLOT USED 0.18 SECONDS AND 382K AND PRINTED PAGE 15.

160          DATA VEC; SET SCORE;
161              KEEP _NAME_ MW--VP;
162              IF _TYPE_='STRUCTUR';
NOTE: DATA SET WORK.VEC HAS 4 OBSERVATIONS AND 9 VARIABLES. 250 OBS/TRK.
NOTE: THE DATA STATEMENT USED 0.08 SECONDS AND 328K.
163          PROC TRANSPOSE OUT=VEC;
NOTE: DATA SET WORK.VEC HAS 8 OBSERVATIONS AND 5 VARIABLES. 433 OBS/TRK.
NOTE: THE PROCEDURE TRANSPOSE USED 0.11 SECONDS AND 366K.
164          DATA BIPLOT; SET VEC ZERO RED(IN=INPRIN);
165              IF INPRIN THEN _NAME_='.';
NOTE: DATA SET WORK.BIPLOT HAS 28 OBSERVATIONS AND 31 VARIABLES. 75 OBS/TRK.
NOTE: THE DATA STATEMENT USED 0.12 SECONDS AND 336K.
166          PROC PLOT;
167              PLOT RED2*RED1=_NAME_
168              /PLOTAXIS;
172              TITLE3 SHOWING BOTH CHEMICALS AND PHYSICOCHEMICAL PARAMETERS;
NOTE: THE PROCEDURE PLOT USED 0.18 SECONDS AND 386K AND PRINTED PAGE 16.

NOTE: DATA SET WORK.RED HAS 19 OBSERVATIONS AND 30 VARIABLES. 78 OBS/TRK.
NOTE: THE PROCEDURE SORT USED 0.20 SECONDS AND 760K.
173          MACRO LISTVAR PHY1% LIST TITLE2 SORTED BY FIRST REDUNDANCY VARIABLE;
NOTE: THE PROCEDURE PRINT USED 0.15 SECONDS AND 376K AND PRINTED PAGE 17.
```

FIG. 13.—contd.

```
NOTE: DATA SET WORK.RED HAS 19 OBSERVATIONS AND 30 VARIABLES. 78 OBS/TRK.
NOTE: THE PROCEDURE SORT USED 0.20 SECONDS AND 760K.

183        MACRO LISTVAR PHY2% LIST TITLE2 SORTED BY SECOND REDUNDANCY VARIABLE;

NOTE: THE PROCEDURE PRINT USED 0.15 SECONDS AND 376K AND PRINTED PAGE 18.

193        PROC PLOT DATA=RED;
194            PLOT PHY2*PHY1=CHEMICAL
195        /PLOTAXIS;
199        TITLE2 PLOT OF THE FIRST TWO REDUNDANCY VARIABLES;

NOTE: THE PROCEDURE PLOT USED 0.19 SECONDS AND 390K AND PRINTED PAGE 19.

200        DATA PAT; SET SCORE;
201            KEEP _NAME_ DIM1 DIM2;
202            IF _TYPE_='STRUCTUR';

NOTE: DATA SET WORK.PAT HAS 4 OBSERVATIONS AND 3 VARIABLES. 680 OBS/TRK.
NOTE: THE DATA STATEMENT USED 0.08 SECONDS AND 336K.

203        PROC TRANSPOSE OUT=PAT;

NOTE: DATA SET WORK.PAT HAS 2 OBSERVATIONS AND 5 VARIABLES. 433 OBS/TRK.
NOTE: THE PROCEDURE TRANSPOSE USED 0.10 SECONDS AND 374K.

204        DATA ZERO;
205            NAME_='+
206            PHY1=0;
207            PHY2=0;

NOTE: DATA SET WORK.ZERO HAS 1 OBSERVATIONS AND 3 VARIABLES. 680 OBS/TRK.
NOTE: THE DATA STATEMENT USED 0.06 SECONDS AND 336K.

208        DATA BIPLOT; SET PAT ZERO RED(IN=INPRIN);
209            IF INPRIN THEN _NAME_='.';

NOTE: DATA SET WORK.BIPLOT HAS 22 OBSERVATIONS AND 31 VARIABLES. 75 OBS/TRK.
NOTE: THE DATA STATEMENT USED 0.11 SECONDS AND 344K.

210        PROC PLOT;
211            PLOT PHY2*PHY1=_NAME_
212        /PLOTAXIS;
216        TITLE3 SHOWING BOTH CHEMICALS AND REDUNDANCY PATTERN;

NOTE: THE PROCEDURE PLOT USED 0.20 SECONDS AND 390K AND PRINTED PAGE 20.

217        DATA VEC; SET SCORE;
218            KEEP _NAME_ MW--VP;
219            IF _TYPE_='STRUCTUR';

NOTE: DATA SET WORK.VEC HAS 4 OBSERVATIONS AND 9 VARIABLES. 250 OBS/TRK.
NOTE: THE DATA STATEMENT USED 0.08 SECONDS AND 336K.

220        PROC TRANSPOSE OUT=VEC;

NOTE: DATA SET WORK.VEC HAS 8 OBSERVATIONS AND 5 VARIABLES. 433 OBS/TRK.
NOTE: THE PROCEDURE TRANSPOSE USED 0.11 SECONDS AND 374K.

221        DATA BIPLOT; SET VEC ZERO RED(IN=INPRIN);
222            IF INPRIN THEN _NAME_='.';

NOTE: DATA SET WORK.BIPLOT HAS 28 OBSERVATIONS AND 31 VARIABLES. 75 OBS/TRK.
NOTE: THE DATA STATEMENT USED 0.11 SECONDS AND 344K.

223        PROC PLOT;
224            PLOT PHY2*PHY1=_NAME_
225        /PLOTAXIS;
229        TITLE3 SHOWING BOTH CHEMICALS AND PHYSICOCHEMICAL PARAMETERS;
```

FIG. 13.—contd.

Although PROC CANCORR when utilized to perform either canonical correlation or maximum redundancy analysis permits the input of more physicochemical parameters than stimuli, as in the last case above (RAM1–LAF4) where there were 23 physicochemical parameters for 19 stimuli, the analysis only provides canonical or redundancy coefficients for the first 19 physicochemical parameters. A new procedure called PLS (partial least squares) that is discussed in the next section can be used to find coefficients for all 23 physicochemical parameters if this is desired

SAS
OUTPUT OF CORR--MATRIX BEFORE MANIPULATION

OBS	_TYPE_	_NAME_	DIM1	DIM2	MW	ES	AC	AR	KE	HB	BP	VP
1	MEAN		-0.0000	0.0000	92.4211	0.2105	0.1579	0.1579	0.1579	0.3158	119.316	88.2105
2	STD		1.0274	1.0274	23.8963	0.4189	0.3746	0.3746	0.3746	0.4776	40.800	77.9840
3	N		19.0000	19.0000	19.0000	19.0000	19.0000	19.0000	19.0000	19.0000	19.000	19.0000
4	CORR	DIM1	1.0000	-0.0137	0.2214	0.4138	-0.4472	-0.0159	0.3739	-0.2218	-0.159	0.1597
5	CORR	DIM2	-0.0137	1.0000	0.6543	-0.2854	-0.0819	0.5757	-0.1509	0.0969	0.875	-0.3743
6	CORR	MW	0.2214	0.6543	1.0000	0.1461	-0.4298	0.4514	-0.1195	-0.3725	0.692	-0.2306
7	CORR	ES	0.4138	-0.2854	0.1461	1.0000	-0.2236	-0.2236	-0.2236	-0.3508	-0.280	0.3064
8	CORR	AC	-0.4472	-0.0819	-0.4298	-0.2236	1.0000	-0.1875	-0.1875	0.6374	0.171	-0.3416
9	CORR	AR	-0.0159	0.5757	0.4514	-0.2236	-0.1875	1.0000	-0.1875	0.0163	0.564	-0.0012
10	CORR	KE	0.3739	-0.1509	-0.1195	-0.2236	-0.1875	-0.1875	1.0000	-0.2942	-0.192	0.1814
11	CORR	HB	-0.2218	0.0969	-0.3725	-0.3508	0.6374	0.0163	-0.2942	1.0000	0.240	-0.4270
12	CORR	BP	-0.1591	0.8746	0.6917	-0.2804	0.1710	0.5636	-0.1924	0.2398	1.000	-0.5433
13	CORR	VP	0.1597	-0.3743	-0.2306	0.3064	-0.3416	-0.0012	0.1814	-0.4270	-0.543	1.0000

(a)

SAS
OUTPUT OF CORR--AFTER MATRIX MANIPULATION

OBS	_TYPE_	_NAME_	DIM1	DIM2	MW	ES	AC	AR	KE	HB	BP	VP
1	MEAN		-0.0000	0.0000	92.4211	0.2105	0.1579	0.1579	0.1579	0.3158	119.316	88.2105
2	STD		1.0274	1.0274	23.8963	0.4189	0.3746	0.3746	0.3746	0.4776	40.800	77.9840
3	N		19.0000	19.0000	19.0000	19.0000	19.0000	19.0000	19.0000	19.0000	19.000	19.0000
4	CORR	DIM1	1.0000	0.0000	0.2214	0.4138	-0.4472	-0.0159	0.3739	-0.2218	-0.159	0.1597
5	CORR	DIM2	0.0000	1.0000	0.6543	-0.2854	-0.0819	0.5757	-0.1509	0.0969	0.875	-0.3743
6	CORR	MW	0.2214	0.6543	1.0000	0.1461	-0.4298	0.4514	-0.1195	-0.3725	0.692	-0.2306
7	CORR	ES	0.4138	-0.2854	0.1461	1.0000	-0.2236	-0.2236	-0.2236	-0.3508	-0.280	0.3064
8	CORR	AC	-0.4472	-0.0819	-0.4298	-0.2236	1.0000	-0.1875	-0.1875	0.6374	0.171	-0.3416
9	CORR	AR	-0.0159	0.5757	0.4514	-0.2236	-0.1875	1.0000	-0.1875	0.0163	0.564	-0.0012
10	CORR	KE	0.3739	-0.1509	-0.1195	-0.2236	-0.1875	-0.1875	1.0000	-0.2942	-0.192	0.1814
11	CORR	HB	-0.2218	0.0969	-0.3725	-0.3508	0.6374	0.0163	-0.2942	1.0000	0.240	-0.4270
12	CORR	BP	-0.1591	0.8746	0.6917	-0.2804	0.1710	0.5636	-0.1924	0.2398	1.000	-0.5433
13	CORR	VP	0.1597	-0.3743	-0.2306	0.3064	-0.3416	-0.0012	0.1814	-0.4270	-0.543	1.0000

(b)

FIG. 14. Correlation matrix (a) before and (b) after the DATA step in the maximum redundancy analysis.

even if the number of physicochemical parameters exceeds the number of stimuli.

Partial Least Squares. Partial least squares (PLS) is a relatively new technique that can be used when the number of physicochemical parameters exceeds the number of stimuli (see Lindberg *et al.*, 1983). In the example presented here, the relation between 23 physicochemical parameters and 19 stimuli was examined. PLS is an iterative principal components method that employs a cross validation approach with 1/3 of the data deleted per cycle. Basically the goal is to continue to improve the model, selecting the better model over the less effective one. PLS is best described in matrix notation (see Fig. 15(a) and (b) where $\mathbf{X}$ represents the calibration matrix (training set, here physicochemical parameters) and $\mathbf{Y}$ represents the test matrix (in this case, the coordinates of the odor space). Since principal components techniques are known to be scaling dependent, the means are first subtracted from the data; then the data are scaled so each variable has unit variance.

The $\mathbf{C}$ matrix in Fig. 15(a) is an $m \times p$ coefficient matrix to be determined where m is the number of dimensions of the stimulus space (here 2) and p is the number of physicochemical parameters (here 23). $\mathbf{C}$

$$\mathbf{Y} = \mathbf{X}\mathbf{C}' + \mathbf{E}_p$$

FIG. 15(a). Algorithms for PLS in matrix notation. $\mathbf{X}$ represents the physicochemical data for n stimuli; $\mathbf{Y}$, the coordinates in the multidimensional space; $\mathbf{C}$, the matrix of calibration coefficients determined by the statistical analysis.

$$\mathbf{X} = \mathbf{T}\mathbf{B} + \mathbf{F}$$

FIG. 15(b). The $\mathbf{X}$ matrix is decomposed into two matrices, $\mathbf{T}$ and $\mathbf{B}$, plus the $\mathbf{F}$ or error matrix.

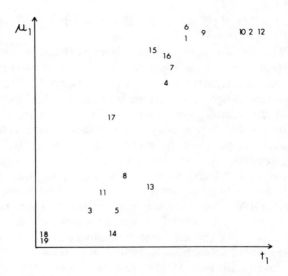

FIG. 16(a). Plot of the first latent y variable (μ_1) versus the first latent x variable (t_1). The numbers correspond to the stimuli given in Fig. 10(a).

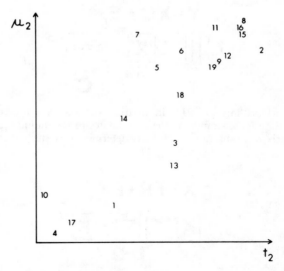

FIG. 16(b). Plot of the second latent y variable (μ_2) versus the second latent x variable (t_2).

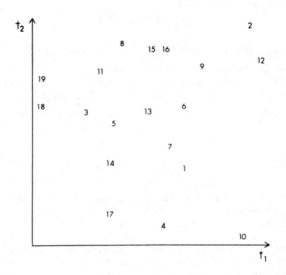

FIG. 17. Plot of the latent x variables, t_1 versus t_2, that represents the best reconstruction by PLS of the two-dimensional space in Fig. 5. The numbers correspond to the stimuli listed in Figure 10a.

is estimated by ordinary least squares. The residuals not explained by the model are designated $\mathbf{E}_p$. The $\mathbf{X}$ matrix is decomposed as shown in Fig. 15(b) into the product of two small matrices, $\mathbf{T}$ and $\mathbf{B}$ whose dimensions are $n \times a$ and $a \times p$ respectively and where n is the number of stimuli and $a \ll n$ and $a \ll p$. Here, $\mathbf{F}$ is the error matrix. The solution for PLS resembles principal components regression (PCR) except that the computation of $\mathbf{T}$ is such that it both models $\mathbf{X}$ and correlates with $\mathbf{Y}$. (In PCR, the projection $\mathbf{T}$ only models $\mathbf{X}$.) The PLS solution is accomplished with a weight matrix $\mathbf{W}$ as well as a set of latent variables $\mathbf{U}$ with the corresponding loading matrix $\mathbf{B}$.

Figure 16(a) shows a plot of the first latent y variable (μ_1) against the first latent x variable (t_1); Fig. 16(b) shows a plot of μ_2 versus t_2. The plot of the latent x variables, t_1 versus t_2, is given in Fig. 17. This is the best reconstruction of the multidimensional odor space (in Fig. 5) based on application of PLS to the data. All twenty-three physicochemical parameters were utilized to achieve the plot in Fig. 17. The arrangements in Figs 5 and 12 are similar (correlation $=0.70$) although the PLS algorithm rotated the space.

4. SUMMARY

Multidimensional scaling techniques can arrange stimuli in a map on the basis of their perceived similarity. Vector and ideal point models can be used to relate individual stimulus properties to the map. Canonical correlation, maximum redundancy, and PLS (partial least squares techniques) can relate a set of stimulus properties to a space.

REFERENCES

Carroll, J. D. (1972). Individual differences and multidimensional scaling. In: *Multidimensional Scaling. Theory and Application in the Behavioral Sciences*, R. N. Shepard, A. K. Romney, and S. B. Nerlove (Eds), Seminar Press, New York.

Carroll, J. D. and Chang, J. J. (1970). Analysis of individual differences in multidimensional scaling via an n-way generalization of 'Eckhart-Young' decomposition. *Psychometrika*, **35**, 283–319.

Darlington, R. B. (1968). Multiple regression in psychological research and practice. *Psychological Bulletin*, **69**, 161–82.

Guttman, L. A. (1968). A general nonmetric technique for finding the smallest coordinate space for a configuration of points. *Psychometrika*, **33**, 469–506.

Kruskal, J. B. (1964a). Multidimensional scaling by optimizing goodness of fit to a nonmetric hypothesis. *Psychometrika*, **29**, 1–27.

Kruskal, J. B. (1964b). Nonmetric multidimensional scaling: A numerical method. *Psychometrika*, **29**, 115–29.

Kruskal, J. B. and Wish, M. (1978). Multidimensional scaling. A Sage University Paper. Series/Number 07–011. Sage Publications, Beverly Hills.

Kruskal, J. B., Young, F. W. and Seery, J. B. (1973). *How to Use KYST, a Very Flexible Program to Do Multidimensional Scaling and Unfolding*, Bell Laboratories, Murray Hill, N.J.

Lindberg, W., Persson, J-A. and Wold, S. (1983). Partial least-squares method for spectrofluorometric analysis of mixtures of humic acid and ligninsulfonate. *Anal. Chem.*, **55**, 643–8.

Lingoes, J. C. (1973). *The Guttman-Lingoes Nonmetric Program Series*, Mathesis Press, Ann Arbor, Michigan.

Muller, K. E. (1981). Relationships between redundancy analysis, canonical correlation, and multivariate regression. *Psychometrika*, **46**, 139–42.

Muller, K. E. (1982). Understanding canonical correlation through the general linear model and principal components. *American Statistician*, **36**, 342–54.

Pruzansky, S. (1975). *How to Use SINDSCAL. A Computer Program for Individual Differences in Multidimensional Scaling*, Bell Laboratories, Murray Hill, N.J.

Ramsay, J. O. (1977). Maximum likelihood estimation in multidimensional scaling. *Psychometrika*, **42**, 241–66.

Ramsay, J. O. (1978a). Confidence regions for multidimensional scaling analysis. *Psychometrika*, **43**, 241–66.

Ramsay, J. O. (1978b). *MULTISCALE: Four Programs for Multidimensional Scaling by the Method of Maximum Likelihood* National Educational Resources, Inc., Chicago.

Roskam, E. E. C. I. (1968). *Metric Analysis of Ordinal Data in Psychology*, Voorshoten, Amsterdam.

Schiffman, S. S. (1983). Future design of flavor molecules by computer. *Chemistry and Industry*, **3**, 39–42.

Schiffman, S. S., Reynolds, M. L. and Young, F. W. (1981). *Introduction to Multidimensional Scaling. Theory, Methods and Applications*, Academic Press, New York.

Schiffman, S., Robinson, D. E. and Erickson, R. P. (1977). Multidimensional scaling of odorants: Examination of psychological and physicochemical dimensions. *Chemical Senses*, **2**, 375–90.

Takane, Y., Young, F. W. and de Leeuw, J. (1977). Nonmetric individual differences in multidimensional scaling: An alternating least squares method with optimum scaling features. *Psychometrika*, **42**, 7–67.

Wollenberg, A. L. van den (1977). Redundancy analysis. An alternative for canonical correlation analysis. *Psychometrika*, **42**, 207–19.

Young, F. W. (1972). A model for polynomial conjoint analysis algorithms. In: *Multidimensional Scaling*, R. W. Shepard, A. K. Romney, and S. B. Nerlove (Eds), Seminar Press, New York.

Young, F. W. (1973). *Conjoint Scaling*. University of North Carolina, Chapel Hill, N. C. (April, No. 118). (Revised March 1977.)

Young, F. W. and Lewyckyj, R. (1979) *ALSCAL–4. User's Guide*. University of North Carolina, Chapel Hill, N. C.

APPENDIX

The distances between the ten cities used in these analyses are given in Table 1. Those matrices representing the original intercity distances with 10, 20, 30 and 50% noise added were created by the program listed below. This program, written in Basic on an IBM XT, operates as follows:

1. Lines 1–220 create a one-dimensional array, $M(X)$, from the data matrix, here the intercity distances. $M(X)$ was constructed as a single column matrix for simplicity; after subsequent manipulation it is later rearranged into the lower half matrix form. An exact copy of $M(X)$, here called $S(X)$, is created for use later in the program.

2. Lines 110–210 file raw data into $M(X)$ and obtain the sum of all the *positions*, here called S, of its elements. For example, if there are 4 elements in $M(X)$ then $S = 1 + 2 + 3 + 4 = 10$. This sum is required in the next step, the randomization process.

3. Lines 290–380 are the heart of the program. The purpose is to create another matrix, $N(P)$, having the same elements as $M(X)$ but in a completely randomized order. This new matrix represents $M(X)$ with '100%' noise and becomes the source for all later additions of noise to the original data. Note that $N(P)$ is still mathematically related to $M(X)$ since it has the same mean.

$N(P)$ is initially comprised of dummy numbers, in this case, -999. This part of the program is a loop in which elements of $M(X)$ are randomly selected and placed in an orderly manner into $N(P)$. On the first time through the loop a random number, Q, is generated. This number is any of the whole numbers within the range of the *number of elements* in $M(X)$. If there are 20 elements in $M(X)$ then Q could be any whole number between and including 1 and 20. Next, the *value* of that element, $M(Q)$, is placed in the first position (top of the column) in $N(P)$. Then $M(Q)$ is replaced by another dummy number, this time, -888, indicating that the previous value of this element has been transferred to $N(P)$. Upon subsequent runs through the loop, if an $M(Q) = -888$ is found, then a new Q is generated until an $M(Q)$ is located that has not previously been selected. Line 320 was necessary in order to avoid values where $Q = 0$ because there are no real data located in $M(0)$.

A problem arises when there is only one more available Q to select, i.e. there is only one more element in $M(X)$ to be placed in $N(P)$. Due to the way random numbers are generated in an IBM XT and the type of logical loop involved here, the selection of the last Q would require an indefinite amount of time. This is because the probability of its selection is small compared to the chance that any of the many other values of Q would first be selected. Therefore, a counter variable is created that represents, upon completion of this loop, the sum of all the positional values, (Qs), used so far in $M(X)$ minus the remaining unselected value. The final value of this variable, $S1$, is then subtracted from the value of variable S, calculated in Step 2, to obtain the identity of the remaining value of Q. Once done, its value, $M(Q)$, is then positioned in the last remaining spot in $N(P)$.

4. The matrix with a fractional percentage of noise is obtained by adding to $S(X)$, created in Step 1, a fractional value of the corresponding element in $N(P)$. For example, if the first value in $S(X)$ were 5 and the first value in $N(P)$ were 10, then a resulting value containing 30% noise would be $5 + 0.3(10) = 8$. Therefore, a matrix representing 30% noise would be created by the addition of 30% of the value of the first element in $N(P)$ added to the value of the first element in $S(X)$. This process

continues for the remaining values in $S(\mathbf{X})$ and $N(\mathbf{P})$. The result is a new matrix, here called $F(\mathbf{W})$, that is equal to $S(\mathbf{X})$ but with a fractional amount of noise added.

5. Subsequent lines of this program contain procedures for printing to the screen or printer or saving on disk the resultant matrix in lower half form.

In order to obtain a random number for the IBM XT a random number seed must first be given by the operator or made permanent in the program. Permanent seeds have the drawback of always creating the same randomization of $M(\mathbf{X})$, i.e. $N(\mathbf{P})$, the 100% noise matrix, will always be arranged in the same way. This is not useful if your intention is to create several different matrices each having the same percentage noise value. To circumvent this problem, line 30 in the program creates different seeds whose values are chosen from the seconds reading of the XT's internal clock. This provides a seed that changes enough to allow for a different arrangement of $M(\mathbf{X})$ to occur each time the randomization process is used.

```
10 WIDTH 80:SCREEN 0,0,0:COLOR 7,0,0
20 CLS
30 RANDOMIZE VAL(RIGHT$(TIME$,2))
40 S=0
50 INPUT "PLEASE ENTER THE NUMBER OF VARIABLES IN THE MATRIX ";K
60 R=K-1
70 FOR R=R TO 1 STEP -1
80 Y=Y+R
90 NEXT R
100 DIM M(Y),N(Y),F(Y),S(Y)
110 INPUT "GIVE NAME OF DATA SET TO USE"; Z$
120 OPEN Z$ FOR INPUT AS #1
130 PRINT "ORIGINAL DISTANCE DATA"
140 FOR X=1 TO Y
150 INPUT #1,M(X)
160 S=S+X
170 NEXT X
180 CLOSE #1
190 FOR X=1 TO Y
200 S(X)=M(X)
210 NEXT X
220 GOTO 250
230 REM INFILE RAW DATA INTO MATRIX M(X) AND OBTAIN THE SUM OF ALL X'S
240 CLS:WIDTH 80
250 FOR P=1 TO Y
260 N(P)=-999
270 NEXT P
280 S1=0
290 FOR T=1 TO Y
300 IF T=Y THEN Q=S-S1:GOTO 350
310 Q=INT(RND*(Y+1))
320 IF Q=0 THEN GOTO 310
330 IF M(Q)=-888 THEN GOTO 310
```

```
340 S1=S1+Q
350 N(T)=M(Q)
360 M(Q)=-888
370 NEXT T
380 CLOSE #1
390 REM THIS SECTION CREATES MATRIX N(T), HAVING THE SAME NUMBER OF ELEMENTS
400 '    AS M(X), BUT CONTAINING DUMMY VALUES.  THESE ARE REPLACED IN RANDOM
410 '     FASHION USING ELEMENTS OF M(X)
420 INPUT "WHAT PERCENTAGE OF NOISE WOULD YOU LIKE? ";B
430 A=B/100
440 FOR W=1 TO Y
450 F(W)=S(W) +(A*(N(W)-S(W)))
460 NEXT W
470 REM CREATES A MATRIX WHOSE VALUES HAVE HAD A FRACTION OF THE NOISE FROM
480 '    THE RANDOMIZED MATRIX ADDED TO THE ORIGINAL DATA MATRIX
490 PRINT "WOULD YOU LIKE TO:" TAB(19);"1) PRINT MATRIX TO SCREEN?"
500 PRINT TAB(19);"2) LIST MATRIX AT THE PRINTER?"
510 PRINT TAB(19);"3) SAVE MATRIX?"
520 PRINT TAB(19);"4) END PROGRAM?"
530 PRINT TAB(19);"5) CREATE ANOTHER MATRIX?"
540 INPUT "ENTER YOUR SELECTION:";E
550 IF E=1 GOTO 630
560 IF E=2 GOTO 780
570 IF E=3 GOTO 920
580 IF E=4 THEN GOTO 1130
590 IF E=5 THEN ERASE M,N,F,S:X=0:Y=0:P=0:GOTO 10
600 IF 1>E>6 THEN BEEP
610 GOTO 540
620 '******PRINTS MATRIX TO SCREEN*****************************
630 CLS
640 PRINT "DATA RANDOMIZED AT "B"%"
650 DIM Q(K,K)
660 C=0
670 FOR J=1 TO K
680 FOR I=1 TO J-1
690 C=C+1
700 Q(I,J)=F(C)
710 PRINT USING "####.## ";Q(I,J),
720 NEXT I
730 PRINT
740 NEXT J
750 ERASE Q
760 GOTO 490
770 '******LISTS MATRIX AT PRINTER*****************************
780 LPRINT "DATA RANDOMIZED AT "B"%"
790 DIM Q(K,K)
800 C=0
810 FOR J=1 TO K
820 FOR I=1 TO J-1
830 C=C+1
840 Q(I,J)=F(C)
850 LPRINT USING "####.## "; Q(I,J),
860 NEXT I
870 LPRINT
880 NEXT J
890 ERASE Q
900 GOTO 490
910 '******SAVES FILES***************************************
920 CLS
930 INPUT "NAME OF FILE TO CREATE"; B$
940 DIM Q(K,K)
950 PRINT "DO YOU WANT " B$ " SAVED ON THIS DIRECTORY OR THE ONE"
960 INPUT "THAT CONTAINS THE MODEM"; R$
970 IF R$="Y" THEN GOTO 1000
980 IF R$="N" THEN GOTO 990
990 OPEN "C:SMARTMOD\"+B$ FOR OUTPUT AS #2:GOTO 1010
```

```
1000 OPEN B$ FOR OUTPUT AS #2
1010 C=0
1020 FOR J=1 TO K
1030 FOR I=1 TO J-1
1040 C=C+1
1050 Q(I,J)=F(C)
1060 PRINT #2,USING "####.## ";Q(I,J),
1070 NEXT I
1080 PRINT #2,
1090 NEXT J
1100 ERASE Q
1110 CLOSE #2
1120 GOTO 490
1130 CLS: PRINT "END OF PROGRAM"
```

Chapter 9

PARTIAL LEAST SQUARES REGRESSION

M. MARTENS and H. MARTENS

Norwegian Food Research Institute, Ås, Norway

1. INTRODUCTION

1.1. Problems in Food Science and Technology

Food research and food production involve problems of biochemical, chemical, physical, technological, agronomical as well as sociological and psychological nature. Quality may be defined as the totality of features and characteristics of a product that bear on its ability to satisfy a given need (EOQC, 1976). In food research we want to understand the basic chemical and physical characteristics that cause our perception of quality. In the food industry we want to develop and maintain products of high quality from the producer to the consumer, also taking economical and political aspects into consideration, i.e. total quality control (Martens, M., 1984). For both problems achieving the final aim requires that we are able to relate 'products to persons'—relate hard fact instrumental measurements to more soft human data. In addition, high-speed instruments for quality control require conversion of non-selective data to selective information.

However, although there are thousands of variabilities in this two-block or multi-block space, biological systems are not infinitely complex: there exist systematic interrelationships reflecting the same basic phenomena (Fig. 1).

The *first* purpose of this chapter is to show that it is possible to extract the main information from various types of quality measurements by focusing the data onto a few, underlying latent variables.

1.2. Data Analytic Methods in Food Research

Two facts concerning food research measurements are clear:

COMPLICATED BUT SYSTEMATIC :

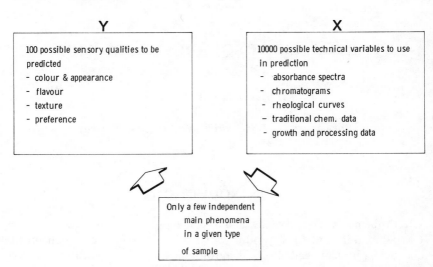

FIG. 1. A multitude of sensory as well as chemical, physical and optical measurements can reflect the same basic phenomena in a given type of biological material. Thus, e.g. 10 000 technical variables (**X**) might be used to predict 100 sensory variables (**Y**).

— We need *many* data to cover the complexity.
— We need data analytic tools so we, on one hand don't drown in data, and on the other hand, don't oversimplify by looking only at those data that we feel comfortable with, ignoring the rest, or lose information by averaging systematically opposing trends.

Data analysis involves fitting some sort of mathematical 'model' or 'formula' to the data by estimating certain 'model parameters', followed by an evaluation of the obtained parameters and the residual lack-of-fit:

$$\text{Data} = \text{'model'} \text{ (with parameters)} + \text{residual} \tag{1}$$

Any data analysis, be it simple or sophisticated, consists of:

(1) *A choice of data model*—a mathematical 'formula' expected to be suitable for the purpose of the experiment and the expected structure of the relationships and uncertainties in the data.

(2) A procedure for *fitting this model to the data*—for estimating the model's parameters. The procedure should correspond to the

design of the experiment and should be based on reasonable assumptions about the uncertainties involved.

(3) *Validation* of the results obtained: Is the chosen model suitable for these data? Have we overfitted the data? Are there abnormalities (outliers) in the data? Are the results reasonable? The validation should not be performed on the data used for the fitting of the model to the data, unless special precautions are taken (e.g. cross-validation or leverage correction).

(4) *Presentation* of the data analytic results (parameters and residuals), for one's self during the data analysis and for others after the conclusions have been drawn.

Multivariate data analysis has increasingly been applied in food research during the last decade (Martens, M. and Harries, 1983). More popularly (Powers, 1984; Gacula and Singh, 1984; Martens, H. *et al.*, 1983c) as well as theoretically (Cooley and Lohnes, 1971) based descriptions of various methods have been given.

Multivariate data analytic techniques for finding the main information or structure in *one* data table (e.g. principal component analysis, factor analysis, cluster analysis) are described in other chapters of this book. However, the problems discussed in Section 1.1 also concern relationships between *two* or *more* data tables.

Thus, the *second* purpose of this chapter is to give a short overview of possible methods for quantitatively relating two or more blocks of data (Section 2), especially focusing on Partial Least Squares (PLS) regression (Sections 3, 4) and its properties on real data compared to other methods (Section 5).

1.3. What Does the Data Analysis Require from the Food Scientist?

Computerized multivariate data modelling can be of great help in food research and development. But there are many pitfalls in multivariate data analysis, at least in the way many standard statistical programs are used:

* An analytical chemist may be so fond of his favourite theory of what takes place in his samples that he forces a certain mathematical model onto his data and does not want to look at alternatives or error warnings. Examples: Linearized kinetic models of reactions, 'Beer's Law' models in spectrometry of mixtures.
  He should first have used a 'soft' modelling technique like the PLS regression in order to let the data talk for themselves. He might then

have detected an obvious flaw in his theory! Or he may see that he
only has one single observation of a certain experimental condition,
and therefore must improve his experimental design before reliable
conclusions can be drawn from the data.

* A statistician may receive excellent and informative data from the
food scientist: A thousand different variables have been measured by a
sophisticated orchestra of instruments like spectrophotometers and
chromatographs. The food scientist wants to know how they correlate
to sensory quality measured on the same samples. The statistician has
to disregard all but a few of these thousand instrument variables,
because his regression method cannot use more variables than objects.
A lot of good data are wasted.

Instead, the statistician or the food scientist himself should have used
a method like the PLS regression, finding the main harmonies from
the instrument orchestra, and using them for modelling the sensory
quality. In that way the food scientist can learn about the different
phenomena that affect his samples, seeing which variables give similar
information, which give unique information and which give no information at all.

Traditionally, data analysis was more or less synonymous with statistical hypothesis testing. Except for the simplest types of t-tests and F-tests,
hypothesis testing requires special expertise to ensure that the underlying
assumptions of the test are fulfilled. But in food research today the main
data analytic problem is not to *test* well defined hypotheses, but rather to
find the information in a mass of data.

Gower (1983) discusses the division of responsibilities between the
food scientist and the professional data analyst in more detail. All
scientists should be familiar not only with the characteristics of their data
but also with the models fitted and assumptions made.

Irrespective of data analytic technique, an evaluation of validity and
practical relevance of the results is always required from the food
scientist. Thus, the *third* purpose of this chapter is to discuss validation
and interpretation procedures, especially concerning PLS regression
(Section 6).

1.4. Short History of PLS

Partial Least Squares regression is a relatively new approach to multivariate data analysis. The basic concept was originally developed by the
statistician Herman Wold and is described in Wold, H. (1982). The

particular version of PLS regression to be focused on in this chapter is the Orthogonalized mode A two-block predictive PLS regression on latent variables (Wold, S. *et al.*, 1983a).

This 'PLS regression' has proven itself very useful both for calibration (Martens, H. and Jensen, 1983; Martens, H. *et al.*, 1983a,b; Wold, S. *et al.*, 1983a) and for general data interpretation (Wold, S. *et al.*, 1983b, 1984). It is a robust and intuitively appealing algorithm, rather than a theoretically derived method based on minimizing a certain statistical criterion. For this reason it has gained considerably more popularity among, for example, chemometricians than among statisticians, although even the latter group has given it some attention lately (Næs and Martens, H., 1985; Aastveit and Martens, H., 1986). Its mathematical relationship to matrix inversion is treated in Wold, S. *et al.* (1985).

Food research scientists should pay extra attention to the possibilities of relating different types of chemical, physical and biological as well as sensory and sociological information to each other. Thus, the *fourth* purpose of this chapter is to give a list of areas expressing PLS's potential for interdisciplinary applications (Section 7). Finally, a list of available PLS programs is given (Section 8).

2. OVERVIEW OF MULTIVARIATE TWO-BLOCK DATA ANALYTIC METHODS

2.1. Definitions and Distinctions

In the following, bold-face upper-case letters (e.g. **X**) refer to matrices (=tables=blocks of variables). Bold-face lower-case letters (e.g. **x**) refer to vectors (a column or row of data elements), and ordinary lower-case letters (e.g. x) refer to scalars (individual data elements=individual numbers). Upper-case ordinary letters are used to describe upper limits for running indices (e.g. $k = 1, 2, \ldots, K$).

The present chapter mainly concerns how to find quantitative relationships between two blocks of variables, **X** and **Y**.

Variable (=manifest variable) means input data from a certain analytic method, e.g. pH, absorbance at a certain wavelength, or sensory score for a certain flavour attribute. In this chapter a variable is represented by a *column* of numbers: by index $k = 1, 2, \ldots, K$ if it is represented in matrix **X**, and by index $j = 1, 2, \ldots, J$ if it is represented in matrix **Y**. Sometimes, K and J are replaced by p and q as the total number of variables in the **X**-block and **Y**-block, respectively.

Latent variable (=factor) means a 'variable' that is estimated during the data analysis in order to represent a general variability more or less common to a set of input variables directly or indirectly intercorrelated. It is represented by index $a = 1, 2, \ldots, A$.

Sample (=object) is used in its chemical sense of a single object, not in its statistical sense of a 'sampled subset of a population'. In this chapter a sample is represented by a *row* of numbers. It is represented by index $i = 1. 2, \ldots, I$. Sometimes, symbol I is replaced by n as the total number of samples.

Matrix means two-way table (samples × variables).

Vector means a row or column of data elements.

Model is mainly used to represent the formula or type of formula chosen to be fitted to the experimental data. The model consists of a certain combination of mathematical rules (e.g. conventional linear regression: $y = b_0 + x b_1 + e$) between variables (here: y and x) and a set of model parameters to be estimated from the data (here: b_0, b_1). The estimation of the parameters also implies an estimation of the residual or lack-of-fit (here: e). Distributional assumptions about parameters and residuals are implicit parts of the model.

Parameters are the unknown 'numbers' in the model, to be estimated from fitting the model to the data. Note that parameters are not the same as constants; the term *constant* should in data analysis be reserved for true physical constants (e.g. Planck's constant).

Estimation is a procedure for finding the best possible values of the unknown parameters in a mathematical model. It is here used to mean the choice of method for computing the parameter values, plus the actual fitting of the mathematical model to a certain set of data. In this chapter the method of computing is always based on the principle of least squares residuals, but different least squares methods can be used for estimating the same parameter. Estimated values of parameters are represented by the 'hat' symbol, e.g. $\hat{b}$, $\hat{y}$, $\hat{e}$.

Least Squares (LS) methods of fitting a mathematical model to a certain set of data involve minimizing the sum of the squared residuals, i.e. the squared differences between data and the corresponding predictions from the model. The fitting yields estimates for the parameters in the model. LS methods require a weighting of the relative reliability of the different residuals (different samples and/or variables) to be summed in multivariate LS methods.

Regression means fitting a mathematical model to a certain set of data by projecting some variables onto other variables, usually by Least Squares.

Calibration concerns how to find the mathematical formula that optimally converts, for example, instrument data X to results $\hat{Y}$. Once this formula has been determined (statistically 'estimated') the levels of the Y-variables can be predicted in new, unknown samples of the same kind, from their X-variables.

Prediction means to use the chosen model and the estimated model parameters to predict certain variables from other variables available. Example: after linear regression, predict y from the input data for variables x by: $\hat{y} = \hat{b}_0 + x\hat{b}_1$.

Predictive methods are here used for regression methods that imply a prediction of certain variables Y from other available variables X, as opposed to '*correlative*' methods, in which no predictive direction is implied.

Classification also called 'supervised learning' or 'pattern recognition' (PARC), concerns the analysis of differences between classes of objects. Only classification followed by a quantitative prediction is relevant for this chapter (PARC level 3 and 4; Wold, S. *et al.*, 1984).

Validation is a procedure to ensure that the model and its estimated parameters really have predictive ability for future, unknown samples of the same general kind. Validation is an important step in data analysis and guards against overfitting, i.e. modelling just nonsense. The validation may be based on results from a new test set of samples not used in the actual model fitting. But the methods of *cross-validation* and *leverage correction* make it possible to use data from the same samples both for model fitting and validation (see Section 3.6).

2.1.1. Metric Data and Linear Additive Models

This chapter mainly concerns *metric* data analytic methods (assuming quantitative data at the 'ratio' (e.g. $4°K$ is twice as hot as $2°K$) or 'interval' (e.g. $42 °F$ is $10 °F$ higher than $32 °F$) measurement levels), as opposed to *non-metric* methods (accepting qualitative input data at 'ordinal' (cold $<$ cool $<$ hot) or 'nominal' (milk $\neq$ beer $\neq$ water) measurement levels); see Young (1981). But non-metric input data can be useful even as part of metric data sets, as some of the presented examples will show (Sections 4.3, 4.5, 5.2, 5.3 and 5.4).

Within psychometry different non-metric two-block multivariate data analytic techniques have been developed which may be of great interest for food scientists, e.g. a non-linear canonical correlation analysis (Burg and Leeuw, 1983) and non-metric regression analyses (Young, 1985). Non-metric multidimensional scaling methods are discussed in Chapter 6 in this book and in MacFie and Thomson (1984).

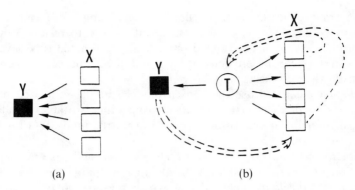

(a)   (b)

FIG. 2. Conceptual difference between (a) MLR and (b) PLS (here PLS1). In MLR, all the **X**-variables (here: 4) simultaneously model **Y** (here: only one **y**) (solid arrows). In PLS1, **Y** is used as a guide in the extraction of latent variables **T** from **X** (dotted arrows). These latent variables **T** (here: only one **t**) are in turn used for modelling both **X** and **Y** (solid arrows).

Further, this chapter mainly concerns *linear additive* mathematical models, as opposed to *non-linear* models. But by centring the data, linear additive models can approximate many types of non-linearities in data (Martens, H. *et al.*, 1983a; Geladi *et al.*, 1985).

2.1.2. Multicollinearity: Regression on Manifest or on Latent Variables?
The multivariate two-block data analytic methods differ in one fundamental aspect of great practical importance (see Fig. 2): One family of methods, like Multiple Linear Regression (MLR) is based on regressions of **y** directly onto the individual **X**-variables (the 'manifest' variables). In the other family of methods based, for example, on the Partial Least Squares (PLS), the regression of **y** is done on so-called 'latent' variables, **T**, representing the main variation found to be common to many **X**-variables. Thus, multicollinearity among the **X**-variables gives a stability advantage instead of creating an instability problem. The two families are similar when the number of samples is very high. But when the number of samples is low, the more traditional methods can give graver estimation errors (see Section 5.1).

2.2. Regressing X on Y or Y on X, or both on Latent Variables?
One way of classifying the different methods for two-block modelling concerns the way irrelevant phenomena in the data are treated. By 'irrelevant phenomena' we here mean systematic types of variations in

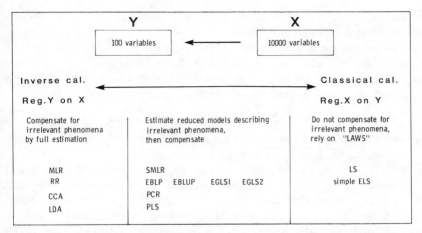

FIG. 3. Multivariate methods for relating two blocks of variables (e.g. **X** and **Y** from Fig. 1) to each other. Inverse versus classical methods distinguish between different treatments of irrelevant phenomena. Abbreviations: see text.

one data table that have no relationship to the variations in the other table.

Figure 3 positions a number of the two-block methods in this respect. In the univariate calibration literature a long debate has taken place on whether to regress **x** on **y** (classical calibration) or **y** on **x** (inverse calibration) in order to get the best predictions of **y** from future **x**-data. The conclusion from this univariate/bivariate field was that when the correlation between **x** and **y** was high, it did not matter very much. But if the correlation was low, then one should regress **y** on **x** if the calibration samples were representative for the distribution of future unknown samples, while one should regress **x** on **y** if they were not and one therefore might have to extrapolate outside the range of calibration. Noise in the **x**- and **y**-data complicates this conclusion.

This 'classical versus inverse' distinction has been extended to multivariate linear regression methods (Næs and Martens, H., 1984). Figure 3 uses this terminology to distinguish between different treatments of irrelevant phenomena.

2.2.1. Regressing **X** on **Y**-variables
Assume, for instance, that the available input variables $\mathbf{X}=(\mathbf{x}_1, \mathbf{x}_2, \mathbf{x}_3, \mathbf{x}_4, \ldots)$ from an instrument are affected by the con-

centration of the constituent to be determined, y_1, and by some well characterized interfering constituents, $y_2, y_3, \ldots$.

In *classical* modelling one relies on assumed physical 'laws' for how the X-data are generated from the Y-data. These methods have the ambition of explicitly modelling every *important phenomenon* $y_1, y_2, y_3,$ ... that affects the X-data in the samples:

$$X = f(y_1, y_2, y_3, \ldots) + E \tag{2}$$

where $f(\ )$ defines the mathematical model and E is the residual, ideally representing random measurement noise in X.

Thereby the well known interferences $y_2, y_3, \ldots$ can be described and compensated for, allowing determination of $\hat{y}_1$. If the correct physical model has been chosen, then this type of modelling gives the best results from a given set of data. But alas, in food science, such complete modelling is virtually never possible in anything but very pure model systems! The danger is therefore that irrelevant and/or unexpected phenomena $z_1, z_2, \ldots$ in X are ignored and never even checked for, with potential alias errors as result:

$$X = f(y_1, y_2, y_3, \ldots, z_1, z_2, \ldots) + E \tag{3}$$

The unmodelled phenomena $z_1, z_2, \ldots$ manifest themselves as apparent variations in the modelled phenomena $\hat{y}_1, \hat{y}_2, \hat{y}_3, \ldots$ leading to mistaken conclusions.

Least Squares (LS) curve fitting and the simplest types of Estimated Least Squares (ELS) regressions based on, for example, 'Beer's Law' and similar mixture models fall into this category of potential oversimplifications. Data models that cannot take into account unidentified covariance structures in the data are not recommended for anything but simple model experiments.

2.2.2. Regressing Y on X-variables

On the other hand, in *inverse* modelling, the aim is to use the covariance structure within the data blocks to *compensate* for irrelevant variations in the samples analyzed, but without any attempts at modelling these irrelevant phenomena explicitly:

$$Y = g(x_1, x_2, x_3, \ldots) + F \tag{4}$$

where $g(\ )$ is the model and F the residual, ideally representing random measurement noise in Y. For example, MLR for one y-variable, this can be written

$$\mathbf{y} = b_0 + \mathbf{Xb} + \mathbf{f} \tag{5}$$

where b_0 and $\mathbf{b}$ are the regression coefficients (see Section 5.1.). If several Y-variables are to be modelled in terms of X, the MLR is called Multivariate Linear Regression.

The advantage of this approach over the classical one is that the user does not have to describe explicitly every phenomenon that affects the data; it is sufficient to ensure that all the important types of variations, including irrelevant phenomena, do vary in the data set used in the modelling. A disadvantage of this full inverse approach is the lack of explicit modelling of the various phenomena in the data; the resulting model shows how to avoid interferences, but not what the interferences are. A second, and in many practical situations graver disadvantage, is the problem of multicollinearity. With MLR, strongly intercorrelated X-variables create grave uncertainties in the modelling and interpretation, and corresponding decrease in prediction ability. Strong intercorrelations are often encountered when using instrument variables such as different wavelengths from a spectrophotometer, and will in addition always occur if the number of samples is low. In fact, MLR cannot be used at all if the number of samples is lower than the number of X-variables. Intercorrelations force the user to select a subset of X-variables and ignore the rest. This makes it impossible for the user to get a complete overview of the relationships in the data, and information is wasted.

This problem is caused by an unnatural and unnecessary mathematical assumption in these methods, namely that every regressor variable has unique information—it tells a story that is not being told by the others. Variables which only differ in their noise will be amplified grotesquely and force their noise nonsense into the final regression solution; this leads to numerical instability and statistical estimation uncertainties, as well as strong tendency for overfitting.

Attempts have been made at overcoming these estimation problems, for example, in MLR by artificially modifying the obtained covariance; this is called Ridge Regression (RR). If only the most dominant 'harmonies' (eigenvalues) in X are relevant for Y, then RR will work, but if intermediate and minor eigenvalues are important for Y, then RR will not be satisfactory, as has been shown for Near Infrared Reflectance (NIR) determination of protein in wheat (Fearn, 1983; Farebrother, 1984; Næs *et al.*, 1986).

Several other traditional multivariate methods like Canonical Correlation Analysis (CCA, see Section 5.2) and Linear Discriminant

Analysis (LDA, see Section 5.5) are based on the same assumption that each input variable has unique information. Hence these methods have the same limitations as MLR. They cannot be used directly unless the number of samples is much higher than the number of variables, and unless the variables are not otherwise too intercorrelated.

2.2.3. Intermediate Regression Methods

In between these two extremes we find a number of two-block regression methods designed to avoid the problems of the two extremes. Stepwise Multiple Linear Regression (SMLR) is a family of procedures to make MLR work by selecting only the 'best' X-variables. This may decrease the interpretability and represents a waste of information, unless one explicitly wants to find such a representative subset of X-variables to describe Y.

The remaining methods in this intermediate group have the ability that they both *describe* and *compensate for* irrelevant phenomena. Thus, for example, for predicting y_1 from X, (e.g. via Eqn. (3)) both the identified interferents y_2, y_3, ... and the unidentified phenomena z_1, z_2, ... are modelled from the data.

The Estimated Best Linear Predictor (EBLP), the Estimated Best Linear Unbiased Predictor (EBLUP), and the two Estimated Generalized Least Squares predictors (EGLS1 and EGLS2) are similar. But they allow different distributional assumptions on whether or not the training set is representative for future samples, with respect to identified and unidentified phenomena in X. They rely on rather demanding matrix algebra, but have been shown to work well both from a theoretical (Brown, 1982; Næs, 1985a,b; Martens, H. and Næs, 1986; Sundberg, 1985) and practical (Skrede *et al.*, 1983) point of view.

An algebraically simple and versatile approach to multivariate regression methods is that based on 'soft modelling on latent variables' represented by Principal Component Regression (PCR) and PLS regression.

The latent variable methods can give a physical understanding like classical mixing models, while at the same time providing the statistical ability of the inverse regression methods of compensating for unidentified phenomena in the calibration data X.

This approach combines readings from all the relevant chemical or instrumental variables $X = (x_1, x_2, x_3, x_4, ...)$ onto a few factors or latent variables that can be regarded as the main 'harmonies' between the X-variables. The intensities of these main harmonies in different samples are represented by a small factor score table $T = (t_1, t_2, ..., t_A)$ which models both **X** and **Y**:

$$X = f(T) + E$$

and (6)

$$Y = g(T) + F$$

where $f(\ )$ and $g(\ )$ define the factors mathematically. One may calibrate for a single **y**-variable or for a set of variables $\mathbf{Y} = (\mathbf{y}_1, \mathbf{y}_2, \mathbf{y}_3, \ldots)$. Keeping to, for example, Eqn. (3), both the identified **X**-phenomena $(\mathbf{y}_1, \mathbf{y}_2, \mathbf{y}_3, \ldots)$ and the unidentified **X**-phenomena $(\mathbf{z}_1, \mathbf{z}_2, \ldots)$ are modelled by the latent variables in **T**.

In practice an additive model is easiest to use. Here $f(\ )$ and $g(\ )$ are defined by estimates of so-called 'loading spectra' for each factor: Table $\mathbf{P} = (\mathbf{p}_1, \mathbf{p}_2, \ldots)$ defines the main harmonies in **X** and table $\mathbf{Q} = (\mathbf{q}_1, \mathbf{q}_2, \ldots)$ defines how their intensities **T** relate to the variables in **Y**:

$$X = TP + E$$

and (7)

$$Y = TQ + F$$

Figure 4(a) shows this graphically for explicit modelling of only one **y**-variable. Figure 4(b) shows it for simultaneous calibration for J different **Y**-variables. Some sort of validation is used to select A, the number of factors optimal for the model.

Thus, soft multivariate calibration results in coefficients $\bar{\mathbf{x}}$, $\bar{\mathbf{y}}$, $\hat{\mathbf{P}}$ and $\hat{\mathbf{Q}}$. These can be used in the prediction of **Y** from **X** in future samples. This first maps the variation onto $\hat{\mathbf{T}}$ and $\hat{\mathbf{E}}$ and then predicts the **Y**-variables. Alternatively, this full spectral prediction can be simplified mathematically into a purely predictive model:

$$\hat{Y} = X\hat{B}$$ (8)

where $\hat{\mathbf{B}}$ represents 'calibration coefficients' that directly predict **Y** from **X** without any estimation of scores **T** or residuals **E**. These $\hat{\mathbf{B}}$-coefficients are method-dependent functions of the calibration parameters $\bar{\mathbf{x}}$, $\bar{\mathbf{y}}$, $\hat{\mathbf{P}}$ and $\hat{\mathbf{Q}}$. In the limiting case they are identical to the MLR coefficients.

These two different modes for predicting **Y** from **X** give identical results; one yields better outlier detections, while the other is computationally faster.

The coefficients $\hat{\mathbf{B}}$ may also be regarded as a *rotation* of the factor axes $\hat{\mathbf{P}}$ to maximum prediction relevance: The A individual loading vectors $\hat{\mathbf{p}}_1, \hat{\mathbf{p}}_2, \ldots, \hat{\mathbf{p}}_A$ do not necessarily represent the individual 'spectra' or response-vectors of the various physical phenomena affecting the **X**-data; they may well represent combinations of the physical phenomena due to

a)

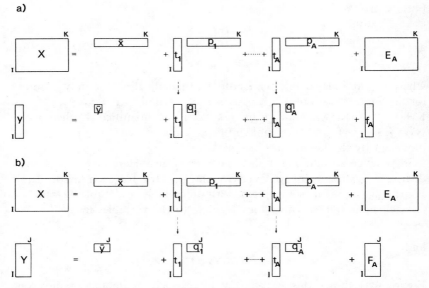

b)

FIG. 4. (a) The data model of latent-variables regression methods for one individual y-variable (e.g. PCR, PLS1). (b) The corresponding data model for several Y-variables (PLS2).

intercorrelations between the phenomena in terms of amounts of 'spectra'. Columns $\hat{b}_1, \hat{b}_2, \ldots, \hat{b}_J$ represent the directions in the X-space that correspond to the highest increase in $y_1, y_2, \ldots, y_J$, respectively.

PCR and PLS here represent a larger family of latent-variable methods. There are several different methods of two-block regressions based on latent variables (Martens, H. and Næs, 1986): PCR, PLS regression, Fourier regression, Hruschka regression, latent root regression, etc. They differ mainly in the way the latent variables T are estimated as described above. PCR is the statistically most established method, and PLS regression may be considered as an extension of PCR.

3. PARTIAL LEAST SQUARES MODELLING: THEORY AND ALGORITHMS

3.1. What is Special about PLS?

Assessing the within and between block structures in, for example, two-block multivariate relationships can be quite complicated, because it requires statistical description of a number of aspects concerning intercorrelations and mathematical rank, unique variances, etc. This is in statistics called the 'identification problem'. General programs like Jöreskog's LISREL (see Jöreskog and Wold, H., 1982) can be applied to such systems analysis, but they are difficult to use and sometimes have convergence problems. The PLS concept of H. Wold (1982) solves this identification problem in a simplified and user-friendly way.

The PLS regression is a systems analysis approach that optimizes several 'partial' (separate) sub-models, each by minimizing lack-of-fit residuals by the principle of least squares. Based on certain orthogonality properties, this allows a wide variety of modifications of the individual steps in the algorithm.

3.2. The PLS Family of Methods

Because of its flexibility, the PLS approach to systems analysis allows a number of different PLS algorithms to be developed to suit different analytical situations. Figure 5 shows some of the members of the PLS family already born.

The PLS family is here grouped first according to whether the methods are predictive or correlative.

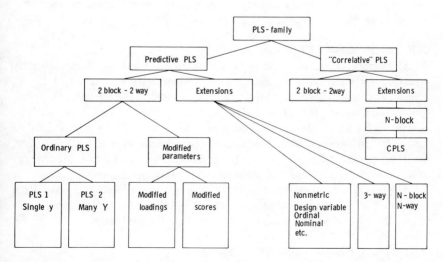

FIG. 5. The 'family' of Mode A PLS algorithm for 'soft modelling on latent variables.'

Among the predictive PLS methods we shall concentrate on analyses of two-block $(\mathbf{X}, \mathbf{Y})$ two-way data tables (samples × variables).

Among the two-block two-way methods we shall concentrate on the 'ordinary' PLS methods PLS1 and PLS2. PLS1 regression predicts a single $\mathbf{y}$-variable from a block of $\mathbf{X}$-variables, and thus resembles MLR. PLS2 regression predicts a whole block of $\mathbf{Y}$-variables from a block of $\mathbf{X}$-variables, and is thus akin to a predictive version of Canonical Correlation. These methods will be described in more detail below.

A range of Modified PLS versions have been published. Some of these concern modification of the factor scores with respect to additional information about the samples (Esbensen and Wold, S., 1983), others concern modifications of loading spectra by, for example, smoothing of continuous spectral data (see Martens, H. *et al.*, 1983b; Martens, H. and Næs, 1986). Preliminary tests have shown good results for Stepwise PLS, a loading modification designed to eliminate irrelevant $\mathbf{X}$-variables with no information (Martens, H. and Næs, 1986).

In general the same types of modifications and extensions can be envisioned in both the predictive and the correlative groups. We shall in this chapter show the use of design variables and briefly mention the desirability of extensions like non-metric and three-way methods.

Concerning the correlative PLS methods we shall in the present paper only look at one, namely the new three-way or multiblock extension that we have termed Consensus PLS (CPLS).

3.3. The Predictive PLS1 Algorithm

PLS1 regression relates a single $\mathbf{y}$-variable to a block of $\mathbf{X}$-variables by focusing the $\mathbf{X}$-variables $\mathbf{x}_1, \mathbf{x}_2, \mathbf{x}_3, \mathbf{x}_4, \ldots, \mathbf{x}_K$ onto a few factors $\hat{\mathbf{t}}_1, \hat{\mathbf{t}}_2, \ldots \hat{\mathbf{t}}_A$ $(A \ll K)$ and using these estimated factors as regressors for the variable $\mathbf{y}$. The general data model from Fig. 4(a) is described in more detail in this section.

The PLS1 algorithm is non-iterative and therefore very fast. It can be expressed in two apparently equivalent forms that give the same results for the orthogonal loadings and for prediction of $\mathbf{y}$. The two algorithms (the *orthogonalized* and the *oblique*) were developed simultaneously in 1981 when it was discovered that the original two-block predictive PLS algorithm did not compensate for its non-orthogonal factor scores and therefore did not work on high-precision instrumental data.

3.3.1. The Orthogonalized PLS1 Algorithm

S. Wold (University of Umeå, Sweden) developed the orthogonalized algorithm that has been implemented in most PLS programs such as the

SIMCA and the UNSCRAMBLER (see Section 8), and which is most easily modified. In this algorithm an extra set of loadings is estimated for the X-variables to ensure that the factor scores $\hat{t}_1, \hat{t}_2, \ldots, \hat{t}_A$ are orthogonal to each other.

In order to understand the algorithm, consider a teaching process: In the data analysis, a set of variables $x_1, x_2, x_3, x_4, \ldots, x_K$ are 'taught' how to reproduce y in a 'teaching' set of data. To ensure predictive ability, the training data should be accurate, representative and should not be overfitted!

This is parallel to a classroom situation:

The students $x_1, x_2, x_3, x_4, \ldots, x_K$ are taught how to reproduce the knowledge of the teacher y by training on certain didactic material that should be accurate and representative and that should not be misunderstood.

Assume that the class is to learn the main aspects of their country's history, in order to foresee the future development of their country. The teacher selects a history book, believed to be accurate and representative, and reads it aloud to the class. The teacher faithfully reads every sentence $i = 1, 2, 3, 4, \ldots, I$, including certain sentences with misprints.

The different students have different backgrounds and other previous knowledge on which they have to rely in order to understand what the teacher reads.

The analogue of MLR would be for the teacher to read the book once, and then rely on every student to tell something unique about the history. The first students will tell most of the important points. So, the last students are forced to try to make sense out of the misprint; their understanding of the main points is wasted.

In contrast, PLS1 regression attempts to give the best possible account of the history's main aspects, and tries to ignore the misprints: all the students are allowed to cooperate; what one student forgets others may remember, and what one student misunderstands others may correct.

The orthogonalized PLS1 algorithm goes like this:

ORTHOGONAL FACTORS ESTIMATED ONE AT A TIME (Fig. 4(a))

First, the individual x-variables are scaled by a weight to ensure that their variances correspond to their relative signal/noise levels. Then the average for $\mathbf{y}$ and every variable $\mathbf{x}_k$ $(k=1, 2, \ldots, K)$ in the I samples are calculated and subtracted, giving residual matrices: $\hat{\mathbf{E}} = \mathbf{X} - \mathbf{1}\bar{\mathbf{x}}$ and $\hat{\mathbf{f}} = \mathbf{y} - \mathbf{1}\bar{\mathbf{y}}$. This centring of the data set is done in order to develop the subsequent multidimensional bilinear model around the estimated centre of the population of samples. This minimizes the effect of non-linearities, differences in offset, etc., and gives the best prediction ability if the training set of samples is representative for the future samples.

In the classroom picture each student is given a weight corresponding to how well he or she is expected to learn. The centring may correspond to ensuring that the teacher and the class concentrate on the history book and nothing else.

Then the parameters of the first factor $a=1$ are estimated (see below). The effect is subtracted to create new residuals $\hat{\mathbf{E}} = \hat{\mathbf{E}}_1$ and $\hat{\mathbf{f}} = \hat{\mathbf{f}}_1$, from which the second factor $a=2$ is estimated and subtracted. From residuals $\hat{\mathbf{E}} = \hat{\mathbf{E}}_2$ and $\hat{\mathbf{f}} = \hat{\mathbf{f}}_2$ the third factor $a=3$ is estimated, subtracted, etc. This process continues until no more valid factors can be obtained from the data.

In the classroom picture, the students pick up one aspect of the history each time the teacher reads. The teacher checks out what the students have understood and only repeats those parts of the history that have not yet been correctly reproduced. After a few such rounds, $a=1, 2, 3, \ldots, A$, all the significant points in the history may have been brought across.

The number of factors A cannot exceed $\min(K, I)$ for mathematical reasons; at that stage the $\mathbf{X}$-matrix has been emptied for both information and noise, and consists of only zeroes. When $I > K$ so that MLR can be applied to the same data, then the limiting solution of $A = K$ is identical to the MLR solution when expressed in terms of $\hat{\mathbf{b}}$. As the example in Section 5.1 will show, in many practical cases this is carrying the modelling too far; the data become overfitted: minor noise phenomena and other nonsense have been drawn into the model and given apparent importance.

Overfitting the data is analogous to the over-zealous teacher going too far: After having ensured that the class has learnt all the important aspects of the history that they are mature enough to understand, he goes on trying to teach the class every little detail in the book. And the students will politely try to make some sense out of this nonsense.

Although not having understood, they will mumble something trivial that the teacher acknowledges as a sign that they still can learn more. In the end the teacher will even teach them the misprints in the book, and those students who never mastered spelling, will finally have their day.

A more careful teacher might have used 'history repeats itself', as validation criterion: new kings replace old kings. An incidental misprint should not be modelled; if for no other reason because it comes alone.

THE PARAMETERS OF EACH FACTOR ESTIMATED BY PARTIAL MODELS (Fig. 6(a))

Using y as a guide in the estimation of the next loading-weight of X:
The residual left in X and y after subtracting the effect of the previous factors are called $\hat{E}$ and $\hat{f}$. The remaining variation in $\hat{f}$ is first used to ensure y-relevance of the new X-factor, t: The $\hat{f}$ is used as preliminary estimate for the new factor itself. Every variable in $\hat{E}$ is projected onto this preliminary $\hat{t}$, yielding preliminary estimates of the loading weight vector: $\hat{w} = \hat{t}' \hat{E}/\hat{t}' \hat{t}$.

In the classroom picture, the teacher now repeats one more time those parts of the history that the students have not yet grasped. The students this time grasp a little more (as described by their loading weights). If the students are similar, they will all grasp the same points at the same time; if they are very different, they will grasp different things.

It is necessary to stabilize bilinear score × loading models against affine transformations of the type $2 \times 6 = 3 \times 4$. In PLS regression the conventional way of doing this has been to normalize this preliminary $\hat{w}$ by a factor that ensures that the final $\hat{w}$ has a square sum of one ($\hat{w}\hat{w}' = 1 \cdot 0$).

Estimating how different objects relate to this factor in X:
The X-residual matrix $\hat{E}$ is now projected onto the normalized loading weight vector $\hat{w}$, to produce a score vector for the objects $i = 1, 2, \ldots, I$: $\hat{t} = \hat{E}\hat{w}'$.

In the classroom picture, all the students take a vote on what aspect of the story they should agree to account for now (as described by the factor score for each sentence). Ideally, the best students should carry stronger weight than the others. But even the best student can err, and

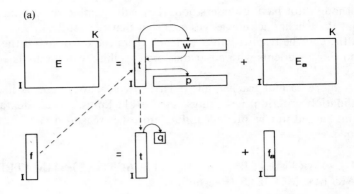

(b) Let $\hat{\mathbf{w}}_{21}$ and $\hat{\mathbf{W}}_{22}$ be the ordinary sample covariance estimators for $\mathrm{cov}(y, \mathbf{x})$ and $\mathrm{cov}(\mathbf{x})$. The first PLS vector $\hat{\mathbf{p}}_1$ is found by normalizing $\hat{\mathbf{w}}_{21}$ to unit length, i.e.

$$\hat{\mathbf{p}}_1 = \hat{\mathbf{w}}_{21}/\|\hat{\mathbf{w}}_{21}\|$$

and by induction

$$\hat{\mathbf{p}}_{a+1} \propto \sum_{m,n \leqslant a} \hat{q}_{an} \hat{\mathbf{p}}_n \hat{\mathbf{W}}_{22} \hat{\mathbf{p}}'_m \hat{\mathbf{p}}_m - \sum_{n \leqslant a} \hat{q}_{an} \hat{\mathbf{p}}_n \hat{\mathbf{W}}_{22} \quad \text{for } a \geqslant 1$$

$$\hat{\mathbf{q}}_a = (\hat{q}_{a1}, \ldots, \hat{q}_{aa})' = (\hat{\mathbf{P}}_a \hat{\mathbf{W}}_{22} \hat{\mathbf{P}}'_a)^{-1} \hat{\mathbf{P}}_a \hat{\mathbf{w}}'_{21}$$

If $I < K$, we have matrix inversion problems (i.e. rank problems) when determining the $\hat{q}_a$ for $a > I$. We then define $\hat{q}_{an} = 0$ and $\hat{p}_a = 0$ if $a > I$.

(c) Principal Component Regression (PCR):

$$\hat{y} = \mathbf{x}\left[y'\mathbf{X}\left(\hat{\mathbf{p}}_1 \frac{1}{\lambda_1} \hat{\mathbf{p}}'_1 + \cdots + \hat{\mathbf{p}}_A \frac{1}{\lambda_A} \hat{\mathbf{p}}'_A \right) \right]$$

PLS1 (Without Orthogonalized Scores):

$$\hat{y} = \mathbf{x}\left[y'\mathbf{X}\left(\hat{\mathbf{l}}_1 \frac{1}{\phi_1} \hat{\mathbf{l}}'_1 + \cdots + \hat{\mathbf{l}}_A \frac{1}{\phi_A} \hat{\mathbf{l}}'_A \right) \right]$$

FIG. 6. The predictive PLS regression. (a) The conceptual PLS1 algorithm with orthogonal factor scores. (b) The PLS1 model. (c) PCR and PLS1 predictors have similar structure. (d) The conceptual PLS2 algorithm with orthogonal factor scores. (b) and (c) are discussed in Section 3.3.2. (d) is discussed in Section 3.4.

(d)

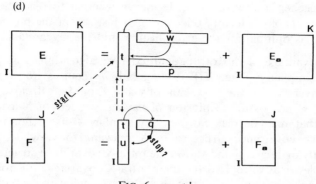

FIG. 6.—*contd.*

in the consensus he can still be over-ruled by a majority of other students.

Estimating how different X-variables relate to this factor:
In the orthogonalized PLS algorithm, $\hat{\mathbf{E}}$ is projected onto $\hat{\mathbf{t}}$, to ensure that subsequent factors' scores are orthogonal to this one. This gives a second loading vector: $\hat{\mathbf{p}} = \hat{\mathbf{t}}' \, \hat{\mathbf{E}}/\hat{\mathbf{t}}' \, \hat{\mathbf{t}}$. Then the effect of this factor is subtracted from **X**, creating new residuals $\hat{\mathbf{E}}$: $\hat{\mathbf{E}}_a = \hat{\mathbf{E}}_{a-1} - \hat{\mathbf{t}}_a \hat{\mathbf{p}}_a$.

In the classroom, all the students now accept the result of their vote, and make sure that everyone has understood this aspect of the story as well as they can (as described by the factor loading for each student). Disagreements among the students are for the time being postponed and kept as residuals in the back of their minds.

Estimating how the y-variable relates to this factor:
Since the consecutive $\hat{\mathbf{t}}$-variables are orthogonal, it is sufficient to use univariate regression in fitting **y** (via $\hat{\mathbf{f}}$) to the scores from **X**. This gives the loading for **y**: $\hat{q} = \hat{\mathbf{t}} \hat{\mathbf{f}}/\hat{\mathbf{t}}' \, \hat{\mathbf{t}}$. Then the effect of this factor $\hat{\mathbf{t}}$ is subtracted even from y, creating new residuals $\hat{\mathbf{f}}$: $\hat{\mathbf{f}}_a = \hat{\mathbf{f}}_{a-1} - \hat{\mathbf{t}}_a \hat{q}_a$.
Now the algorithm is ready for validation: deciding on whether to estimate one more factor or not (see Section 3.6).

In the classroom, the teacher listens to what the class has agreed about this time (as described by the factor loading for the teacher). He will later omit what was understood, correct what was misunderstood, and repeat what went unnoticed when reading it next time.

The teacher is now ready to decide on whether to read the remaining aspects of the history once more, or just accept the present performance as optimal for the given history and the given class.

The advantage of this orthogonalized PLS algorithm is its flexibility and its simplicity: Since $\hat{T}'\hat{T}$ is diagonal, it requires no complicated matrix inversions in the regression of y and X on $\hat{T}$. A disadvantage for the user is the possible confusion of having two sets of X-loadings, $\hat{W}$ and $\hat{P}$, that may or may not be very similar. $\hat{W}$ is orthonormal and shows the covariance structure in X relevant to y, while $\hat{P}$ is not necessarily orthogonal and shows the intra-X covariance structure of the X-variables relative to $\hat{T}$. If the main intra-X covariance phenomena are also the ones relevant for y, then $\hat{W}$ and $\hat{P}$ are similar to each other (and to the eigenvectors of $X'X$; in such cases PLS1 and PCR give the same results).

3.3.2. The Oblique PLS1 Algorithm

H. Martens (NINF, Norway) developed the other algorithm for PLS1, which simply corrects for the problem of intercorrelated factor scores instead of eliminating it. The method was used in the calibration of fluorescence spectra for botanical components in wheat flour (Jensen *et al.*, 1982; Jensen and Martens, H., 1983).

It is slightly more complicated to program since it involves a matrix inversion of non-diagonal $\hat{T}'\hat{T}$ for the multiple linear regression of y on the non-orthogonal factor scores $\hat{T}$. But on the other hand, it has fewer steps and is easier to study from a theoretical point of view. It yields only one set of loading vectors, $\hat{P}$, which is identical to $\hat{W}$ in the orthogonalized PLS1.

Næs and Martens, H. (1985) give a description of the PLS1 regression from a statistical point of view. Their study is based on the oblique PLS algorithm, and their description of the PLS1 model is given in Fig. 6(b). In Fig. 6(c) they show that the PLS1 predictor can be expressed in a way quite similar to the more well known PCR: ignoring for simplicity the averages, the formula that predicts y from the x-vector of a new sample is a product of this new x-vector and a function of the cross product of the calibration data y and X, times a sum of a weighted contribution from different eigenvectors. In PCR these are the eigenvectors of $X'X$ itself, p_a, $a = 1, \ldots, A$. The weights are the inverse of the corresponding eigenvalues λ_a. (PCR with $A = K$ corresponds to MLR, which shows why MLR gives problems when X

is multicollinear; this implies some eigenvalues λ_a close to zero, and division by near zeroes inflates $\hat{\mathbf{b}}$ and is detrimental to the prediction ability.)

In PLS1 it is the eigenvectors and eigenvalues of a *function* of **X** that enter into the predictor, but otherwise the two methods are similar. In Fig. 6(c) the vectors $\hat{\mathbf{l}}_1, \ldots, \hat{\mathbf{l}}_a$ are the eigenvectors of $\mathbf{X}'\mathbf{X}$ projected onto the PLS space **P**, and $\phi_1, \ldots, \phi_A$ are the corresponding eigenvalues. In practice the authors could verify theoretical considerations that showed the PCR and PLS1 to be relatively similar. But PLS1 in general gave simpler models (fewer factors, A) and equal or better predictions than PCR, apparently since the use of $\hat{\mathbf{f}}$ in the estimation of $\hat{\mathbf{p}}$ ensures that **X**-variations relevant to **y** are estimated before **X**-variations irrelevant to **y**.

3.4. The Predictive PLS2 Algorithm

The PLS2 algorithm gives a predictive modelling of a whole block consisting of J different **Y**-variables from a block of **X**-variables, as illustrated generally in Fig. 4(b). It is most easily implemented as an extension of the orthogonalized PLS1 algorithm. Figure 6(d) shows that the algorithm, in contrast to PLS1, is iterative for each factor. Convergence is apparently no problem in the algorithm.

For a given factor number a, the preliminary loadings **w** are estimated as in orthogonalized PLS1 by regressing $\hat{\mathbf{E}}$ on some column of starting values from $\hat{\mathbf{F}}$.

As before, score vector **t** for a certain factor is estimated for the **X**-variables by regressing $\hat{\mathbf{E}}$ on normalized $\hat{\mathbf{w}}$. The **Y**-variables are then modelled by regressing their residuals $\hat{\mathbf{F}}$ on the estimated scores. Since we have more than one **Y**-variable and hence get a whole $\hat{\mathbf{q}}$-vector instead of the single $\hat{q}$ element for each factor in PLS1, it is possible to obtain a preliminary estimate of the factor scores $\hat{\mathbf{u}}$ from the **Y**-variables: by regressing the old **Y**-residuals $\hat{\mathbf{F}}$ on the **Y**-loadings $\hat{\mathbf{q}}$ we get **Y**-scores $\hat{\mathbf{u}} = \hat{\mathbf{F}}\hat{\mathbf{q}}'/\hat{\mathbf{q}}\hat{\mathbf{q}}'$.

In order for the final **X**-scores $\hat{\mathbf{t}}$ to model the largest remaining phenomenon in the **Y**-variables, the PLS2 algorithm for each factor iterates back and forth between modelling $\hat{\mathbf{E}}$ from $\hat{\mathbf{u}}$ (the main variation in $\hat{\mathbf{F}}$) by $\hat{\mathbf{w}} = \hat{\mathbf{u}}'\hat{\mathbf{E}}/\hat{\mathbf{u}}'\hat{\mathbf{u}}$ and modelling $\hat{\mathbf{F}}$ from $\hat{\mathbf{t}}'$ (the main variation in $\hat{\mathbf{E}}$) by $\hat{\mathbf{q}} = \hat{\mathbf{t}}'\hat{\mathbf{F}}/\hat{\mathbf{t}}'\hat{\mathbf{t}}$. In the final solution, $\hat{\mathbf{t}}$ defines the factor while $\hat{\mathbf{u}}$ only represents a temporary estimation tool in this predictive version of PLS regression.

In the classroom picture we have J different teachers $\mathbf{y}_1, \mathbf{y}_2, \ldots, \mathbf{y}_J$

teaching the history in slightly different ways to the students x_1, $x_2, \ldots, x_K$. The students first try to grasp those aspects that many of the teachers seem to agree upon. This probably gives the most important aspects of the history. Once that has been understood, the students go for the peculiarities of the individual teachers. The class will eventually end up trying to mimic their mistakes if no one tells the class what is significant and what is not.

3.5. Consensus PLS

The consensus PLS (CPLS) aims at relating several data-matrices to each other. For instance, in sensory descriptive analysis: What is the 'result' from a panel of several sensory judges? If half of the judges misunderstand the instructions and systematically give score 9 when the others give score 1 and vice versa, a simple averaging over all the judges may result in zero information. Confusion of terms likewise reduces information if simple averaging is used.

Another problem also has to be dealt with if several sensory attributes have been evaluated: Even the average or consensus of the sensory panel is an $I \times K$ table that often is too large to be interpreted directly. Further multivariate data compression is needed in order to focus the attention on the main reliable information in the consensus table, summarizing redundancy and leaving out random noise.

With CPLS we want to describe the samples and the judges as parsimoniously as possible by interrelating the main systematic differences between the judges, instead of just averaging over them. The CPLS algorithm allows that by combining a translation/rotation/scaling of Procrustes Rotation type (see Chapter 7 in this book) with a PCA-like rank reducing data compression in one single algorithm.

The correlative three-way CPLS algorithm was recently developed by Wold, S. *et al.* (1986). For simplicity it will only be illustrated graphically here. Figure 7(a) shows the basic data model exemplified for analysis of sensory panel data: I samples or objects have been assessed by J judges, each judge evaluating each sample with respect to K sensory terms. Thus the input data is the $I \times J \times K$ three-way matrix $\mathbf{X} = (x_{ijk})$.

The mean of every judge's evaluation on every term, $\bar{\mathbf{X}} = (\bar{x}_{jk})$, is first subtracted. A succession of orthogonal consensus factors $\hat{\mathbf{t}}_1$, $\hat{\mathbf{t}}_2$, ..., $\hat{\mathbf{t}}_A$ are then extracted in order to account for as much as possible of the systematic variance in $\mathbf{X}$. These score vectors are the columns of $\hat{\mathbf{T}}$ in the figure.

Each factor score vector $\hat{\mathbf{t}} = (\hat{t}_{ia})$ is a weighted aggregate of the

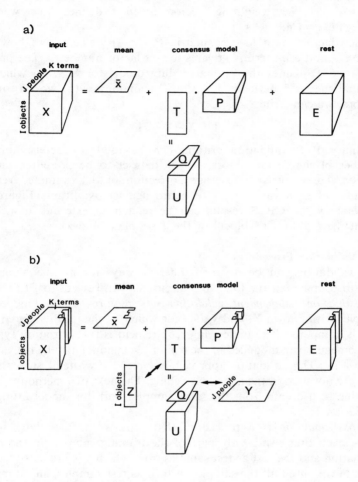

FIG. 7. The conceptual CPLS data model. (a) The parameters $\bar{\mathbf{X}}$, $\mathbf{T}$, $\mathbf{P}$ and $\mathbf{E}$ are extensions of those in Fig. 4. (b) CPLS has been modified compared to (a) to illustrate that the CPLS can handle input data when the J different people have not evaluated the same terms or even the same number of terms, K_j. Further extensions of the CPLS algorithm to incorporate additional information for interpretation, e.g. certain independent information $\mathbf{Y}$ about the J people, and certain independent information $\mathbf{Z}$ about the I objects.

individual judges' score of the object with respect to this factor number a: $\hat{\mathbf{U}} = (\hat{u}_{ija})$. The weighting vector $\hat{\mathbf{q}} = (\hat{q}_{ja})$ defines this weighted aggregate: $\hat{\mathbf{t}} = \hat{\mathbf{U}}\hat{\mathbf{q}}$.

Each factor has a loading matrix $\hat{\mathbf{P}} = (\hat{p}_{jka})$ which shows how each person, j, and each term, k, relates to this factor number a. The product of $\hat{\mathbf{T}}$ and $\hat{\mathbf{P}}$ defines the estimated data model for $\mathbf{X}$, from which the residual matrix $\hat{\mathbf{E}}$ is defined. Using the analogy with two-way matrix algebra, we can write:

$$\hat{\mathbf{E}} = \mathbf{X} - \bar{\mathbf{X}} - \hat{\mathbf{T}}\hat{\mathbf{P}} \qquad (9)$$

Ordinary PLS validation criteria can be used for determining the number of significant factors. In the dataset to be presented later in Section 4.6, we used a leverage correction of the estimated residual variance of each variable x_{jk} to guard against overfitting. Figure 7(b) shows how the CPLS results can be related to external information about the I objects ($\mathbf{Z}$-block) or the J people ($\mathbf{Y}$-block).

3.6. Validation Procedures

The validation can be done in different ways for all the algorithms described above, in the following discussed with respect to PLS1.

Testing on independent validation sets requires extra, independent samples with known $\mathbf{X}$- and y-data for which s^2, the mean squared error of $\hat{\mathbf{f}}$, is computed. The underlying requirement is that variation types or phenomena being modelled in the training set should also be relevant for the test set. This validation approach is somewhat wasteful, since the test data are not used in the actual modelling. The next two methods make it possible to use data from the same samples both for model fitting and validation.

Cross-validation is a procedure that repeats the modelling several times, each time using only part of the training samples in the model estimation and the rest as test samples from which y is predicted from $\mathbf{X}$. After having used all the samples in turn as test samples, an estimate of the prediction error, s^2, is obtained as their mean squared error of $\hat{\mathbf{f}}$. Thus, its underlying requirement is that every phenomenon being modelled must be present in several samples. This method works well but is computationally somewhat time consuming.

Leverage correction is a new approach for directly converting the residuals $\hat{\mathbf{f}} = \mathbf{y} - \hat{\mathbf{y}}$ of the training set used for model estimation to estimates of the corresponding prediction error. The method is described for MLR in, for example, Cook and Weisberg (1982) and adapted for PLS regression by Martens, H. and Næs (1986).

Its underlying requirement is that even phenomena being modelled should be detectable in at least two samples in the training set in order to be accepted as valid. The leverage correction of a sample's residual $\hat{f}$ is $\hat{f}_i/(1 - h_i)$ where the leverage h_i is approximated by:

$$h_i = \sum_{\alpha=1}^{a} t_{i\alpha}^2/(t'_\alpha \, t_\alpha) \qquad (10)$$

The leverage-corrected prediction variance for $\hat{y}$ used here is:

$$s^2 = \sum_{i=1}^{I} (\hat{f}_i /(1 - h_i))^2/(I - A - 1) \qquad (11)$$

(The degrees-of-freedom correction $(I - A - 1)$ is included in order to compensate for the influence exerted by $\hat{y}_{ij}$ on the estimation of $\mathbf{W}$.)

To our knowledge the present paper is the first time leverage correction has been used in practice for PLS regression; and in our experience it gives results identical to or very similar to the cross-validation, although with considerably less computation time.

Irrespective validation method, new factors $a = 1, 2, \ldots, A$ may be accepted as long as s^2 continues to decrease (unless common sense indicates that systematic data errors are being modelled) as described in more detail in Section 6.2.

At the dimensionality A, corresponding to the minimal prediction error s^2, the PLS model consisting of $\hat{\mathbf{W}}$, $\hat{\mathbf{P}}$ and $\hat{\mathbf{q}}$ can be expressed in terms of the y-rotation, $\hat{\mathbf{b}}$:

$$\hat{\mathbf{b}} = \hat{\mathbf{W}}' \, (\hat{\mathbf{P}}\hat{\mathbf{W}}')^{-1}\hat{\mathbf{q}} \qquad (12)$$

These estimates $(\hat{\mathbf{W}}, \hat{\mathbf{P}}, \hat{\mathbf{q}}, \hat{\mathbf{b}})$ obtained from the validated A-dimensional solution procedure should be used to present the optimal PLS model (see Section 6).

4. APPLICATIONS OF PLS REGRESSION

4.1. Overview of the Examples

4.1.1. Concerning the Measurements
Some of the principles discussed above are to be illustrated by recent work at the Norwegian Food Research Institute (NINF). The examples aim at relating two or more blocks of variables with at least one of the blocks containing data from sensory analysis; see Piggott (1984) for basic

literature in sensory analysis. The input data represent various types of quality measurements.

Descriptive sensory analysis using a panel of 12 trained judges under controlled conditions at the NINF's sensory laboratory. Each sensory attribute was evaluated along a 1–9 point intensity scale (1 = low; 9 = high intensity); the sensory data being input directly through a microcomputer system (Martens, M., 1985).

Consumer testing using about 100 untrained consumers at a central location giving preference scores along a 1–9 point hedonic scale (1 = dislike extremely; 9 = like extremely).

Instrumental methods which here means either traditional chemical and physical measurements or data from modern rapid spectrophotometers.

Product registrations including information about the origin of the product, or processing parameters, e.g. agronomical yield, growth location or temperature data.

4.1.2. Concerning the Data Analysis

Some details concerning the data analytic treatment were common for all the examples. The following list may serve as a model for information necessary to give from PLS-analysis.

Input data consisted of mean values across replicates where nothing else is mentioned.

Missing values: In some data sets a few reasonably well distributed missing values in the input data were handled by the software by ignoring these data elements in the PLS algorithm steps where they occurred.

Weighting of variables: In most of the predictive PLS analyses each variable was standardized to unit variance prior to the multivariate analyses in order to ensure each variable an equal chance of influencing the modelling. In the CPLS analysis the input data were analyzed directly.

Weighting of objects: All the objects were given the same weight since we assume the same analytical precision for each of them.

Design variables, often called dummy variables, here refer to variables with values 1 or 0, identifying different objects with respect to, for example, season, site and process parameter.

Validation criteria: Cross-validation and leverage-corrected residuals were used as well as interpretability of the solutions (defined in Sections 3.6 and 6).

4.1.3. Presentation of PLS Model Results

Factor loadings: $\hat{\mathbf{p}}_k$ (for the **X**-variables $k = 1, 2, \ldots, K$) and $\hat{\mathbf{q}}_j$ (for the **Y**-variables $j = 1, 2, \ldots, J$) give the direction of each factor through the object space spanned by the **X**- and **Y**-variables. A non-zero loading means that the variable's variation is correlated to and hence more or less described by this factor. Positive and negative loadings refer to positive or negative relationships to the factor (see Fig. 8).

Factor scores: $\hat{\mathbf{t}}_i$ gives the position of each object, i, on the obtained factor axis, i.e. the distance from the average or centre of the training set of the projection point of the object on the factor axis. A non-zero factor score means that the object's deviation from the average to some degree is described by this factor. Positive and negative scores refer to positive or negative relationships to the factor (see Fig. 8).

Rest variances express conceptually what variation is left unmodelled for the different **Y** (or **X**) variables by the PLS-analysis after a certain number of factors. More statistically it is here the mean square of the

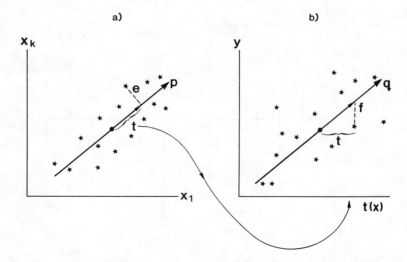

FIG. 8. The geometrical meaning of the PLS parameters. (a) Objects are represented by points in the K-dimensional **X**-space shown for two of these **X**-variables. The loading vector $\hat{\mathbf{p}}$ of a factor gives its direction in this **X**-space, its scores $\hat{\mathbf{t}}$ give the position of the objects, projected down on the factor relative to the origin (the average of objects). The residual vector, $\hat{\mathbf{e}}_i$, gives the lack-of-fit of each object to the factor axis. (b) Each score vector, $\hat{\mathbf{t}}$, is in turn used as regressor for the **Y**-variables, giving $\hat{\mathbf{q}}$ and $\hat{\mathbf{f}}$.

deviation **f** (or **e**) (see Fig. 8) of each variable. Its square root is also called standard error of prediction or prediction error (see Section 3.6). In most of the examples leverage-corrected residuals are given as the rest variance as a percentage of the total prediction variance.

Percent explained variance is (100-percent rest variance).

Rotation of the PLS-solution other than **b̂** is not done due to the clear interpretability of plots of **p̂** and **q̂**.

4.2. PLS1 with One y-variable and Many X-variables

Example: Predict consumer preference of peas (*Pisum sativum* L.) from descriptive sensory analysis.

Model: In the PLS1 in Fig. 4(a), model $J = 1$ preference variable **y** from $K = 11$ sensory variables (**X**-block) over $I = 16$ objects.

Experimental: The preference variable was obtained by averaging the

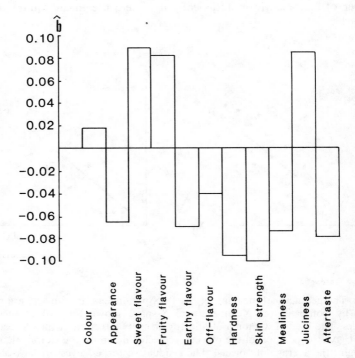

FIG. 9. Estimated regression coefficients **b̂** for predicting consumer preference from **X** = 11 sensory descriptive attributes calculated for PLS1 using one factor.

data from 96 consumers for each of the 16 pea samples. This was done here to give an example of predictive modelling by PLS1. But for the purpose of understanding consumers' response, the preference data were also treated individually (see Section 4.5) as well as grouped according to demographic variables (reported elsewhere). The 11 sensory attributes described in Fig. 9 were evaluated in three replicates. Details about sensory profiling of the same pea batches are given in Martens, M. (1986b).

The 16 pea samples were blanched, frozen and analyzed within one month from harvesting in 1984. They were selected to represent relevant variation with respect to maturity levels and varieties.

Results and discussion: About 73% of the total leverage-corrected variance in preference could be explained by the sensory descriptive variables (X-block) after three PLS1 factors. The first and main factor related high preference to the sweet, fruity, juicy, not earthy and no aftertaste attributes. To focus on which variable was best at predicting y, the estimated regression coefficients, $\hat{b}$, obtained from the PLS1 modelling were calculated as seen in Fig. 9. Strongly non-zero $\hat{b}_k$ for an x-variable means high predictive relevance. From this it seems clear that both flavour and texture variables and to a less extent colour, are important for pea preference.

The practical consequences of these results may be illustrated by an example (Fig. 10): some results from the descriptive sensory analysis for three of the pea samples and evaluation of the same samples by the consumer plotted together, made it possible to see how these tests were related. The sample profiled to be sweet and fruity and less hard than the others, was liked the most (hedonic score = 6·7). The instrumentally measured tenderometer value (TV), not used in the PLS1 modelling, but conventionally used to express maturity of peas, was obtained for interpretation, and showed that this preferred pea (TV = 102) was relatively immature.

Conclusions: The PLS1 regression indicated that sensory descriptive analysis of frozen green peas to some degree can predict an average consumer response; about 73% of the variation in the consumers' preference could be explained by a sensory profile panel by the bilinear modelling. The many PLS parameters $\hat{\mathbf{W}}$, $\hat{\mathbf{P}}$ and $\hat{\mathbf{q}}$ could be summarized by a single $\hat{b}$-vector.

4.3. PLS2 with Many Y-variables and Many X-variables

Example: Explore relationships between analytic sensory and chemical

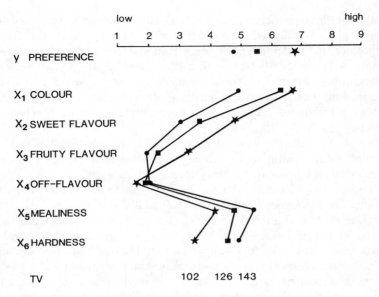

FIG. 10. Example of laboratory sensory analysis used to predict consumer preference. Three pea samples are profiled (1–9 point scale) with respect to some of the X-attributes from Fig. 9, and related to consumer preference (y). The 'star'-line represents a sensory description of a well liked pea. A maturity index (TV) is given for the same samples.

measurements of swedes (*Brassica napus* var. *napobrassica* L.) from different seasons and growth-sites.

Model: In the PLS2 in Fig. 4(b), model $J = 10$ sensory variables (Y-block) from seven chemical variables + six design variables, in total $K = 13$ (X-block) over $I = 46$ objects.

Experimental: The 10 sensory attributes (total colour, crispness, chewing resistance, juiciness, total texture, fruity-, sweet-, bitter-, and sulphurous flavour, total flavour) were evaluated for each sample in three replicates. The seven chemical measurements (soluble solids, dry matter, total titratable acids, pH, sucrose, glucose and fructose) were performed in two replicates and calculated as a percentage of fresh weight. Details about the sensory and chemical analyses are given elsewhere (Fjeldsenden *et al.*, 1981; Martens, M. *et al.*, 1983a).

The 46 raw swede samples were chosen to span the relevant range of variation with respect to swedes bound for the Norwegian market. Three different growth seasons (1978, 1979 and 1980) and three different sites (east-, west-, north-Norway) constituted the six design variables; for simplicity no interaction variables were included in the example.

Results and discussion: Leverage-corrected residuals showed optimal prediction ability for four PLS regression factors, explaining about 46% of the total variance in **Y** (Fig. 11). The prediction error variance is plotted as a function of increasing numbers of PLS factors. The prediction error reached a certain minimum (i.e. lowest rest variance) in **Y**, before increasing again with increasing model complexity. This general phenomenon is discussed in Section 6 (Fig. 27(a)). The corresponding **X**-residuals showed a continual decrease, ending at zero residual after 13 PLS factors, i.e. the MLR solution. This MLR solution has no predictive ability for **Y**. Figure 11 gives a good illustration of the PLS philosophy that a maximum of variation in **X** is drawn out to describe **Y** with a minimum risk of modelling just noise in **X** and **Y**.

PLS factors 1 versus 2 and 1 versus 3 are respectively shown for the loadings in Fig. 12(a,b) and for the scores in Fig. 13(a,b). Factor 1 constituted a relationship between, on one hand, the flavour variables, especially sweet ($-$) but also bitter ($+$), and, on the other hand, the

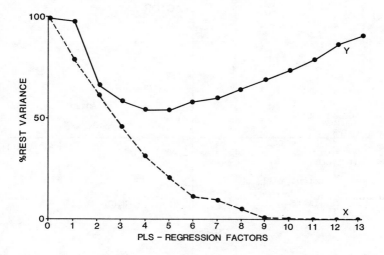

FIG. 11. Percentage rest variance after each of 13 factors for the **Y**-block (10 sensory variables) and the **X**-block (13 chemical and design variables) from a PLS2 analysis of the 46 swede samples. Leverage-corrected variances for both **X** and **Y** are given. The curved behaviour of the prediction error in **Y**, is discussed in Fig. 27.

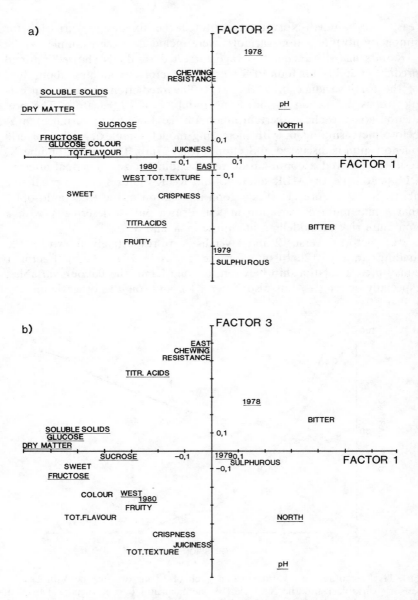

FIG. 12. PLS2 loadings for the 10 sensory variables (**Y**-block), seven chemical and six design variables (**X**-block) analysed on the 46 swede samples treated as in Fig. 11. (a) Factors 1 and 2. (b) Factors 1 and 3. The **X**-variables are underlined.

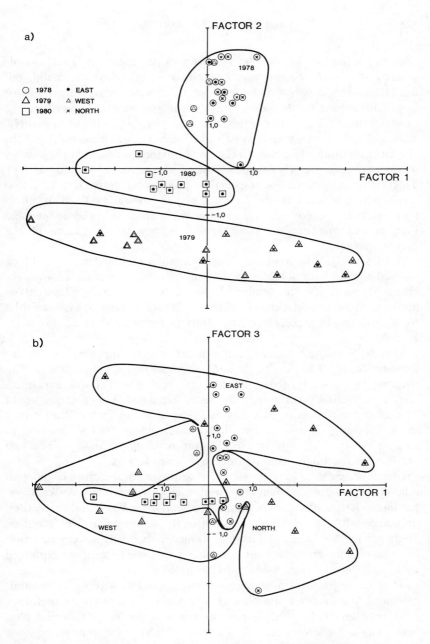

FIG. 13. PLS2 scores for the 46 swede samples analyzed as in Figs. 11 and 12. (a) Factors 1 and 2; (b) Factors 1 and 3.

chemical variables fructose $(-)$, glucose $(-)$, dry matter $(-)$ and soluble solids $(-)$. This variation was apparently independent of season, but weakly showing a variation between sites (i.e. west versus north). Factor 2 was dominated by the yearly variation in the material, describing the swedes from 1979 as more sulphurous and bitter than those from 1978. This may reflect a sensory flavour variation not easily measurable by the chemical methods. The third factor was obviously describing a sensory texture variation weakly related to the titratable acids $(+)$ and pH $(-)$. This reflected a variation especially in chewing resistance $(+)$ and juiciness $(-)$ between swedes from the east of Norway $(+)$ and the north $(-)$. The fourth factor was small and of minor interest in this connection. Further interpretation of these results is beyond the scope of the present paper.

A PLS-analysis without the design variables included in the X-block showed that only about 20% of the sensory variation covaried with the chemical variables, confirming factor 1 in the total PLS-analysis above as the main relationship. Similar effects by using design variables were observed in a corresponding study of carrots (Martens, M. *et al.*, 1985).

This PLS-analysis illustrates a general way of approaching the interpretation of PLS2 results: Although a small *average* variation in Y in the first factor (only about 4% as seen from Fig. 11) was explained, certain individual y-variables were better explained. For instance, about 23% of the variation in sweetness was explained in factor 1; after four factors about 43% was explained. However, using a PLS1 analysis to study $y =$ sweetness more specifically improved its percentage explained variance to about 68% after its three significant factors.

Conclusions: PLS2 may be useful for getting a total picture of different relationships between many Y- and many X-variables. A weak relationship between sensory and chemical variables was found for swedes; only about 20% of the total variation in the sensory variables could be predicted by the chemical variables alone. A relatively strong variation between seasons and sites caused an increase of the percentage explained variance in the sensory Y-block to about 46%.

After getting a total overview, within-season and within-site variabilities need to be further investigated. The design variables were useful for interpretation of the loading plot, in a way replacing the scoring plot. Modelling a single y-variable by individual PLS1 regression on the same X-variables gave improved prediction ability.

4.4. PLS2 with Many Y-variables and Different Numbers of X-variables and Objects

Example: Explore how combinations of chemical and physical measurements improve prediction of sensory quality of cauliflowers (*Brassica oleracea* var. *botrytis* L.). Study the effect of having few objects in the training set.

Model: In the PLS2 in Fig. 4(b), model $J = 12$ sensory variables (**Y**-block) from between $K = 1$ and $K = 8$, i.e. 1–8 chemical and physical variables (**X**-block), over $I = 27$ or $I = 6$ objects.

Experimental: The 12 sensory attributes (total colour, total appearance, crispness, chewing resistance, juiciness, total texture, sweet-, fruity-, bitter-, sulphurous flavour, flavour strength and total flavour) were evaluated for each sample in three replicates. The seven chemical measurements (dry matter, pH, total titratable acids, vitamin C (ascorbic acid), fructose, glucose and sucrose) were performed in two replicates and calculated as percentage of fresh weight. The physical variable, weight (g) of each sample, was taken as a mean of 15 individual cauliflower heads. Details about the sensory and chemical analyses are given elsewhere (Fjeldsenden *et al.*, 1981; Martens, M. *et al.*, 1983a,b).

The different samples were chosen in order to include variation due to season, sites and variety.

Results and discussion: Fig. 14 shows percentage explained variance in the **Y**-block for six PLS2-analyses, calculated by cross-validation, using various **X**-variables alone and in combinations. Only about 4% of the variation in the sensory variables could be explained by the **x** = weight alone. A slight increase was observed for (**X** = weight and dry matter), while the sugar analyses (**X** = sucrose, fructose and glucose) alone seemed to describe the same *amount* of variation. But these two groups of **X**-variables did not describe the same *type* of variation. This was seen by combining (**X** = weight, dry matter and the three sugars). While the weight and dry matter reflected sweetness, crispness and juiciness, the sugars were apparently related to the sweet–bitter balance. The 'acids' variables (**X** = total titratable acids, pH and vitamin C) were relatively strongly related to the sensory variables, first of all fruity flavour, but also crispness and juiciness were explained. However, the combination of all the chemical and physical variables were found to predict the total variation in **Y** optimally; about 75% variance explained after three factors.

The latter PLS2 analysis predicting the 12 sensory variables from all

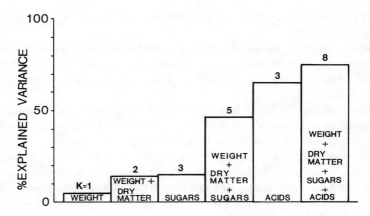

FIG. 14. Percentage explained variances of 12 sensory **Y**-attributes of cauliflower (27 samples) described by chemical and physical variables alone and in different combinations ($K = 1$–8). Averaged results after 1–3 PLS factors found to be significant are shown.

the eight chemical/physical variables, was repeated on a lower number of samples: six selected samples were chosen to span the main variations. This PLS2 analysis gave PLS loading plots very similar to those obtained by analyzing all 27 samples (not shown here).

Conclusions: PLS2 regression allowed us to model **Y** by a low-number of 'harmonies' $\hat{\mathbf{T}}$ from an 'orchestra' of instruments **X**. Multicollinearities between the **X**-variables were no problem. Sensory quality of cauliflowers was found to be best described by a combination of dry matter, sugars and acids variables. PLS worked well even on small sample sets with fewer samples than variables.

4.5. PLS2 with only Design Variables in the X-block

Example: Explore relationships between demographic variables of consumers and their preference of different types of peas (*Pisum sativum* L.).

Model: In the PLS2 in Fig. 4(b), model the preference for $J = 16$ pea batches (**Y**-block) from $K = 11$ demographic design variables (**X**-block) over $I = 96$ objects (i.e. 'samples'=consumers). For simplicity, design variables for interactions were not used. An opposite model with only design variables in the **Y**-block will be discussed in Section 5.5.

Experimental: The ability to predict the average consumer preference by a laboratory sensory panel was studied in Section 4.2. The individual response from the 96 consumers were now further investigated: in addition to the hedonic evaluations of the 16 pea batches, a questionnaire gave information about sex (2), age (4), frequency of use (3) and place of belonging (2) for each person; the numbers in parenthesis refer to the categories of each demographic variable (in total 11). These 11 **X**-variables were used for modelling the disagreements between the people on the different pea batches.

Results and discussion: On average about 20% of the between-people variation in the preference of the peas was accounted for by differences in sex, age, etc., among the consumers (two PLS-factors). Place, sex, age and frequency of use were described to 87%, 60%, 38% and 20% respectively by these two factors. Figure 15 shows that the **X**-variables age, place and sex were contributing the most to PLS factor 1; i.e. there was a tendency that young people (age 15–25), men and people from place 2 seemed to prefer peas of low maturity (low TV). Elderly people (age above 60), females and people from place 1 apparently accepted peas of higher maturity. In factor 2 a weak relationship was revealed between preference of certain peas by consumers that 'often use' peas compared

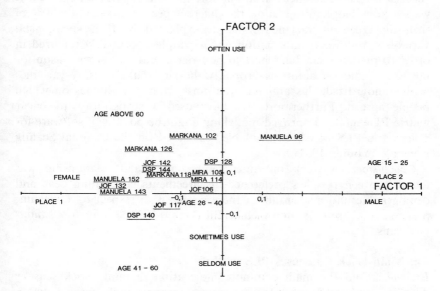

FIG. 15. PLS2 loadings for factors 1 and 2 for 16 preference variables on different pea samples (**Y**-block) and 11 demographic variables (**X**-block) registered for 96 consumers. The **Y**-variables are underlined and marked according to pea variety and maturity level (tenderometer value, TV).

to consumers that 'seldom use' peas, and people in the 'age 41–60' group. The fact that elderly people also seemed to contribute to preference of low maturity peas, confirm other statistical analyses indicating that consumers of that group were split according to frequency of use. This might have been revealed if interaction variables, e.g. age × usage frequency, had been included in the study. Further, Fig. 15 shows that consumers' preference for a certain pea variety was not evident from the present linear modelling, and that consumers of age 26–40 and people only sometimes using peas, showed preference pattern in between those of the other age and usage groups. Further PLS discussions with respect to the experimental design and potential consequences are left out here.

In summary, the results in Section 4.2 showed that a large proportion (73%) of the *between-batches* preference variations was systematic enough to be predicted linearly from laboratory sensory data; in that example the average of the consumer results were used as y, and the PLS1 showed that sensory quality appeared to be important for the consumers. In the present extension of the same example we studied the *between-people* preference variations for the different pea batches. Now we see how people disagree on the different pea qualities. Only 20% of their disagreement variance could be explained by their sociological variables. Additional information about people is probably required in order to predict their differences in preference. But one other reason for the low prediction ability is probably the fact that the 16 Y-variables were standardized; this amplifies the noise from pea batches on which people agreed. Furthermore, we have used a straightforward linear metric PLS model; improved modelling might be possible if software for non-metric PLS had been available, e.g. based on the Optimal Scaling principle (Young, 1981).

Conclusions: A weak but interpretable and valid relationship was found between people's preference disagreements concerning peas and demographic information about these people with respect to, for example, age and sex. A non-metric PLS may be relevant for similar problems.

4.6. Multi-block Consensus PLS (CPLS)

Example: Find the main common information in multi-block sensory data in order to correct for systematic response differences between judges on different sensory attributes.

Model: In the CPLS model (Wold, S. *et al.*, 1986) in Fig. 7(a) let $J = 7$ judges, $K = 6$ sensory texture variables and $I = 5$ alginate solutions. How can 7 X-blocks $(x_j, j = 1, 2, \ldots, 7)$ efficiently be combined into a common concentrated consensus table with respect to I objects?

Experimental: The 6 sensory variables (1 = viscosity, 2 = hardness, 3 = cohesiveness, 4 = body, 5 = resistance to deformation, 6 = smoothness) were evaluated for 5 alginate solutions of different concentrations (4·0, 2·0, 1·3, 0·65 and 0·25% weight/volume). Data from 7 judges were used (6 judges A–F plus a seventh 'judge' G, G representing the average of 12 judges).

This experimental part was taken from a larger study on relationships between fundamental rheological data and sensory perceived mouthfeel, Bohlin *et al.* (1985), where further details about the experiment as well as results with focus on sensory–instrumental relationships by PLS2 are described.

Results and discussion: In the CPLS analysis (Fig. 7(a)) the average was first estimated and subtracted in order to compensate for systematic differences in the general level of results. Then the CPLS algorithm estimated a series of orthogonal consensus scores $\hat{t}_1, \hat{t}_2, \ldots$, each with their associated people × terms rotation and scaling matrix, loading $\hat{P}$, their samples × people individual score matrix $\hat{U}$, and their individual consensus influence weights $\hat{q}$. After each factor the residual variances were computed, with respect to the K terms, the J people and the I samples.

The leverage-corrected total residual variance revealed only one CPLS factor to be significant, explaining 73% of the variation in X. But for illustration, the next two factors are also discussed. Figure 16(a) shows that terms 1, 4, 5 and 6 were well explained in factor 1; there was drastic reduction in rest variances from 0 to 1 factor. Terms 2 and 3 had low initial variance; they were not important with respect to describing the texture variation in the material. Especially term 6, but also terms 4 and 5 were modelled by factor 2. Looking at the judges' contribution to each factor (Fig. 16(b)), all of them reflected the type of variation described in factor 1, but to different degrees. Factor 2 revealed some confusion among the judges, in particular, judges A and E, and to a smaller extent C and D, differed from the average (i.e. 'judge G').

These differences between the judges (A–G) may be understood from the CPLS loading plot for the first two factors (Fig. 17). Along $\hat{P}_1$ all of the judges seemed to agree (circled results). They even seemed to span the 1–9 point scales rather similarly. It may be noticed that this main variation is also reflected in the average value (G). Term 1 contributed strongly and positively in a consistent way (judges A–G grouped to-

a)

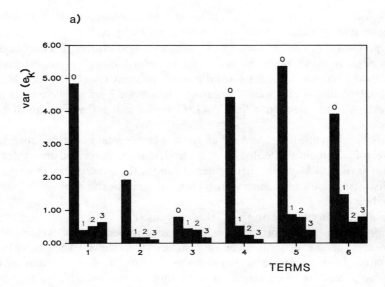

b)

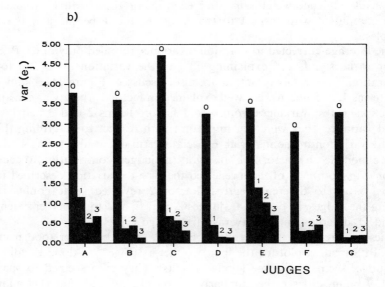

FIG. 16. Rest variances in $\hat{E}$ after 0, 1, 2 and 3 CPLS factors: (a) for six different sensory terms (1–6); (b) for seven different judges (A–G).

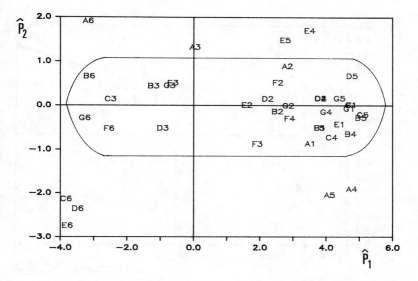

FIG. 17. CPLS loadings $\hat{\mathbf{P}}$ for factors 1 and 2. The letters (A–G) refer to different judges and the numbers (1–6) to different sensory terms.

gether), term 6 contributed strongly and negatively, while terms 2 and 3 didn't vary much with this consensus factor. In factor 2 judges A and E used the terms 4, 5 and 6 in an opposite way; for example, when A scored higher than the others on term 6, then E scored lower and vice versa. Term 6 (smoothness) in general was perceived differently by the judges. Factor 2, being minor and non-significant, should not be paid attention to when interpreting the results about the alginate solutions.

The results obtained were easy to interpret by plotting the CPLS factor 1 scores versus the alginate concentrations. (This corresponds to relating $\hat{t}_1$ to $\mathbf{Z}$ in Fig. 7(b).) Figure 18 shows the consensus $\hat{t}_1$ to be a nice, smooth and non-linear function of alginate addition: with increased alginate concentration the solutions became first of all more viscous (term 1) and less smooth (term 6), but also a tendency toward stronger body (term 4) and higher resistance to deformation (term 5) was evident.

To study the validity of this first CPLS solution further, a general evaluation of the judges along a good–bad scale (10 = very good; 0 = no good) was done by sensory staff not involved in the data analysis. These results, corresponding to the $\mathbf{Y}$-block in Fig. 7(b), are plotted versus the

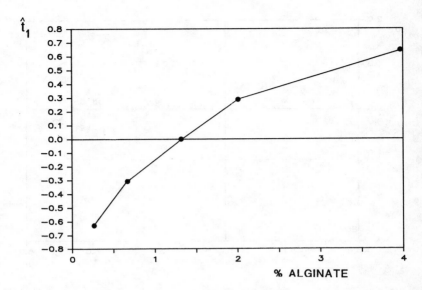

FIG. 18. CPLS scores $\hat{t}_1$ for factor 1 plotted against alginate concentration in the five different samples.

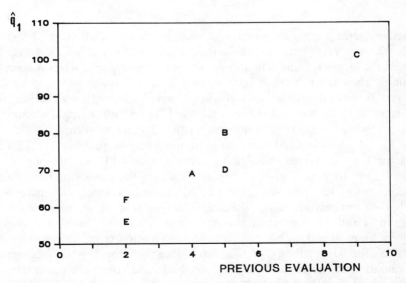

FIG. 19. Weights $\hat{q}_1$ for the CPLS factor score 1 plotted against an independent previous evaluation of judges A–F.

weights for the CPLS factor score 1, $\hat{q}_1$ (Fig. 19). This shows that the best judge in the panel also contributed the most to the consensus solution $\hat{t}_1$.

Since this was a small data set with a relatively simple structure, CPLS needs to be tested on other data sets as well before its real usefulness is clear. Also, the CPLS should be compared to Procrustes analysis (see Chapter 7 in this book).

Conclusions: CPLS was found to extract and concentrate the essential information from a multi-block system, thereby 'cleaning' up noisy data before relating them to, for example, instrumental data. CPLS seems to be a promising method to study the performance of judges in a sensory panel. It may also have relevance in comparison of different analytical techniques, e.g. multivariate ring tests.

5. APPLICATIONS OF PLS VERSUS OTHER METHODS

5.1. PLS versus Multiple Linear Regression (MLR)

Principles: For modelling quantitative relationships between a y-variable and a block of X-variables, the conventional statistical method is MLR. The distinction between MLR and PLS is described in Section 2.1. Because of a mathematical peculiarity MLR cannot use highly intercorrelated X-variables, therefore a number of different methods have been developed for eliminating apparently redundant X-variables (Stepwise Multiple Linear Regression, SMLR).

These SMLR methods are routinely used in standard statistical software packages (often without proper validation routines). It is often difficult to choose which and how many X-variables to use, and even more difficult to interpret the result, since we then do not know the importance of the X-variables eliminated. PLS regression offers an easier and better alternative, as the next example will show.

Example: We want to predict the degree of sweet taste (y) in cauliflower from a set of seven different chemical variables $x_1, \ldots, x_7$. The sweetness was measured by a trained panel of 12 judges in three replicates and averaged, while the seven chemical variables were measured by various conventional methods, averaging two replicates.

Data were available for 12 well selected cauliflower samples. A conventional upward-selection SMLR program was first used. Different criteria in the program indicated different dimensionalities of the optimal solution, but a four-dimensional regression appeared to be the most sensible (*F*-test was significant). The four **X**-variables selected were total titratable acids (x_1), vitamin C (x_2), glucose (x_3) and sucrose (x_4).

But was this four-dimensional calibration model really optimal for predicting the sweetness in future cauliflowers of the same type calibrated for? Figure 20 shows the leverage-corrected prediction error as a function of the dimensionality of the PLS model based on the four **X**-variables selected by the SMLR program. The 'noise line' at variance 0·03 indicates the expected uncertainty of the sweetness data themselves, based on between-replicate variances.

The SMLR program indicated an estimated error variance of 0·03. This four-regressor MLR solution, i.e. the present SMLR, is mathematically identical to the full four-factor PLS solution ($\hat{E} = 0$). The validation showed that even this SMLR gave overfitting of the data. The SMLR prediction error seen from Fig. 20 (same as prediction error after four PLS-factors) turned out to be 0·08, almost three times higher than what the original SMLR program had indicated! The PLS program, in contrast, showed that a two-factor solution had better predictive ability, variance = 0·05, corresponding to ±0·22 on the 1–9 point sweetness scale.

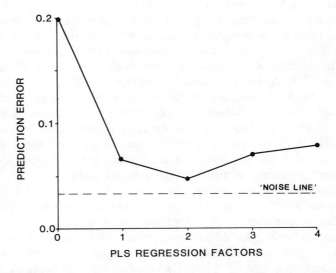

FIG. 20. Prediction error for sensory sweetness (**y**) of cauliflower, given as mean-square error as a function of the number of PLS regression factors. 'Noise line' represents the measurement noise (standard error of the mean for the three sensory replicates).

The prediction error is a function of $(y - \hat{y})$ (see Section 6.2). The dotted 'noise line' at variance 0·03 gives the expected uncertainty of the input sweetness assessments y. Below this line the prediction error cannot ever be expected to come, even if the number of samples in the training set had been very high. Actually, the prediction error must be higher than this y-noise alone, because it also contains more or less errors from $\hat{y}$, e.g. due to non-linearities and to errors in the estimations of the model parameters, as well as prediction errors due to noise in X. Thus it was not surprising to find that the apparent SMLR variance 0·03 (similar to the 'noise line'), was too optimistic due to overfitting. In the above PLS1 regression the four X-variables were used unscaled.

Figure 21 shows the estimated coefficients $\hat{b}$ from the two-factor PLS solution, compared to the original SMLR coefficient estimates. The two estimates have the same general pattern, opposing the sucrose against the other three variables. But the SMLR-based coefficients are much larger than the PLS based ones, indicating that the SMLR, even after the

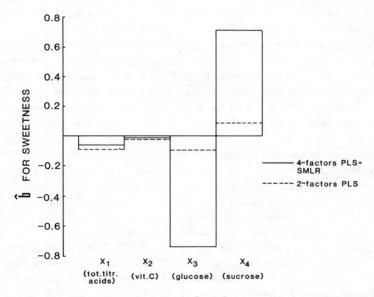

FIG. 21. Estimated regression coefficients $\hat{b}$ for predicting sensory sweetness from the four chemical X-variables, given for the four-factors PLS solution, which is equal to the SMLR solution (solid lines), and the optimal two-factors PLS solution (dotted lines).

stepwise elimination procedure, overemphasizes minor variations in the data and thereby overamplifies noise and irrelevant phenomena.

Conclusions: In this example we first used conventional SMLR to select the 'best' subset of **X**-variables. Then we applied PLS1 regression on these to evaluate this solution. The results indicated that the SMLR had been overfitted. The example shows that PLS1 regression may be easier to use than SMLR. It also illustrates the importance of validating the results with respect to prediction error. This is seldom done in regression software.

5.2. PLS versus Canonical Correlation Analysis (CCA)

Principles: CCA is a statistically oriented two-block method analogous to PLS2; it constructs linear combinations of the variables from the **X**-block that correlate maximally with the **Y**-block and vice versa. The computation requires that the number of objects is higher than the number of variables in **X** and **Y**. In essence both PLS2 and CCA estimate a small number of factors or dimensions in order to express the systematic variations common to the two data matrices, the **X**-block and the **Y**-block in Fig. 22. The loadings of the variables in each factor are correlations (CCA) or modified correlations (PLS).

The major difference between the two techniques concerns the way these factors are estimated from the raw data, as popularly illustrated in Fig. 22. If there are many variables in **X** or **Y** compared to the number of objects, then CCA first requires the use of a rank reduction step (PCA, factor analysis, etc.) prior to the CCA analysis. In PLS regression these two steps are done simultaneously in one algorithm. This ensures statistical parsimony.

Hence, from a statistical point of view the two techniques are expected to respond differently to multicollinearities and to the relative number of variables compared to objects. One other difference, indicated by the horizontal arrows in Fig. 22, is that CCA is a purely correlative method, while PLS2 regression gives a predictive direction from **X** to **Y**. The PLS algorithm can be modified to a correlative one if desired.

Example (from Martens, M. and Burg, 1985): The following data set was studied by PLS2 regression and CCA: 34 pea samples were analyzed by 12 sensory variables (**Y**-block) and 14 chemical and physical variables (**X**-block). Thus, $I = 34$, $J = 12$ and $K = 14$ variables.

PLS2 regression revealed four significant factors with which about 74% of the total variation in the **Y**-block was explained by the **X**-block (Fig. 23(a)).

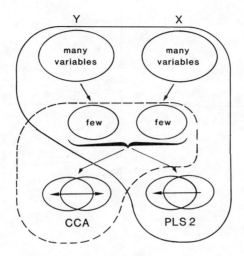

Fɪɢ. 22. Conceptual difference between CCA and PLS2 regression. If the number of variables is larger than the number of objects, then CCA needs a prior variables reduction step (e.g. PCA, factor analysis) before relating the two blocks of variables, while PLS2 is doing this simultaneously. The PLS regression has a predictive direction while CCA is correlative.

A non-metric CCA used directly on the data, failed due to rank problems; the number of objects was not high enough. A non-metric PCA (PRINCALS) was therefore first used on each of the blocks separately to reduce the number of variables. This gave two intermediate score matrices, each describing a few principal factors from **X** and **Y**, respectively. These were subsequently related to each other by a metric CCA, which revealed two significant canonical dimensions. With this two-factor solution about 67% of the total variation in the **Y**-block was explained by the **X**-block (Fig. 23b).

Summarized from Fig. 23(a, b) the PLS and the PRINCALS-CCA solution gave mainly the same results and were, as such, both suited for studying relations between two blocks of data. However, this example as well as other references stress the necessity of keeping the number of variables low in CCA, as in MLR. This is a limitation of serious consequences since modern analytical instruments very easily and relatively cheaply give data on a large number of variables on each object. But getting many objects, especially for analysing food samples or biological material in general, may be difficult and expensive. This

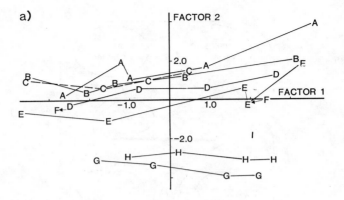

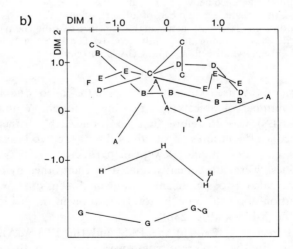

FIG. 23. Results from 12 sensory variables (**Y**-block) and 14 chemical/physical variables (**X**-block) measured on 34 pea batches, marked according to varietal name in the figures: (a) PLS scores for factor 1 and 2; (b) CCA mean canonical scores for dimensions 1 and 2. Factor or dimension 1 describes maturation of peas (solid lines connecting the same pea varieties) from right to left, while factor or dimension 2 describes differences between varieties. (Reprints from Martens and Burg, 1985, with kind permission from Elsevier, Amsterdam).

problem was exemplified by Canaway *et al.* (1984) in an attempt to use CCA to establish relationships between individual vocabularies from sensory profiling. They apparently had to carry out the canonical correlation analysis on the replicates in order to get enough 'samples', and thereby obtained results that were difficult to interpret. For a similar problem connected to sensory profiling, Martens, M. and Russwurm (1980) used factor analysis to reduce the number of variables below the numbers of samples prior to relating the sensory to chemical data by CCA. Piggott and Jardine (1979) used CCA successfully to relate sensory descriptive terms of whisky to chemical constituents, and CCA gave interpretable results in a study of odour perception of food-relevant chemical components (Schiffman, 1981). In an attempt to relate dynamical criteria from a baking process to baking quality variables, Möttönen (1975) concludes that CCA was not powerful for studying quality.

5.3. PLS versus Multidimensional Scaling (MDS)

Principles: MDS is designed for the analysis of square tables where the number of rows equals the number of columns, for instance symmetrical similarity or dissimilarity tables. Chapter 8 in this book describes MDS; we shall here show that even PLS2 can be used for square tables.

Example: 132 persons from the food industry were asked to evaluate similarities between 20 flavour attributes on a 1–9 point scale, resulting in 132 symmetric 20×20 similarity matrices (Fig. 24).

A non-metric MDS (Young and Lewyckyj, 1979) was performed on the one-mode, two-way matrix representing the 20×20 averages over all 132 persons; treating these similarities as ordinal data.

The metric PLS2 modelling was performed by regarding the 20×20 average of the first 66 persons as **X** and the 20×20 average of the last 66 persons as **Y**. These **X** and **Y** similarity data (scale 1–9) were transformed to dissimilarities (scale 8–0). In order to reduce the effect of giving 'non-related' and 'opposite' the same high scores, the square roots of the dissimilarities were used in the PLS-analysis. Since the **X** and **Y** matrices are symmetric, they were double centred prior to the PLS-analysis, i.e.

$$e_{ik} = x_{ik} - \bar{x}_i - \bar{x}_k + \bar{\bar{x}}, \text{ where } \bar{\bar{x}} \text{ is the average of vector } \bar{x}.$$

Six PLS factors appeared to be significant, judging from the similarity between $\hat{\mathbf{p}}$ and $\hat{\mathbf{q}}$. The scores of the 20 attributes along the first two factors are shown in Fig. 25(a). Figure 25(b) correspondingly shows the first two factors or 'dimensions' from a six-factor MDS solution. In both plots factor 1 separates the fruity, aromatic quality properties from

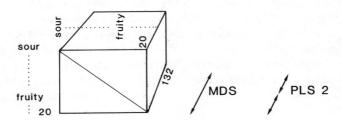

FIG. 24. Conceptual difference between MDS as a one-block method, and two-block PLS2. Experimental design of a study of similarities between 20 different flavour attributes evaluated by 132 persons using a 1–9 point scale.

rancid, metallic, etc., while factor 2 separates sour, acid from boiled, oily flavour attributes.

After six factors the non-metric MDS modelled 92% and the metric PLS modelled only 73% of the total variation in the perception data. (A corresponding six-factor PLS solution for the same data without having taken square root, explained only 56%.)

A combination of MDS and PLS as a link between, for example, a cognitive perception matrix *and* some external demographic variables or chemical and physical variables, opens up many possibilities. Works on such PLS combinations are in progress. Hoffman and Young (1983) successfully used a non-metric MLR to interpret MDS-results from a study of different persons' perception of various beverages.

The ALSCAL program can also analyze three-way two-mode square matrices, using the 'INDSCAL' MDS model. The three-way CPLS algorithm can probably be used in a similar way, replacing 'I objects' in Fig. 7(a) by 'K terms'. The scores $\hat{T}$ would then show the consensus between the J people, concerning the relationships between the K terms.

Conclusions: The MDS explained much more variance than the PLS regression, probably because the former allowed for non-metric characteristics in the input data. But the plots of their main parameters were

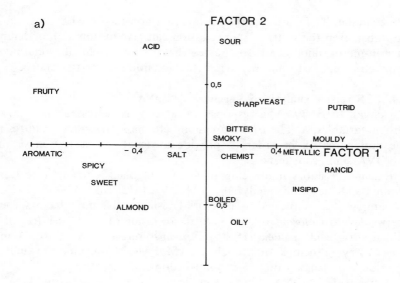

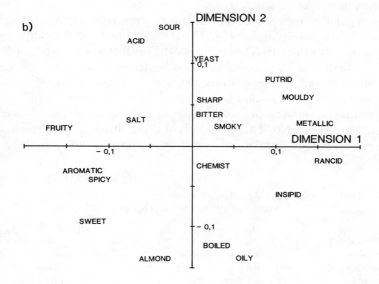

FIG. 25. Results from the study described in Fig. 24: (a) PLS scores for factors 1 and 2; (b) MDS coordinates for dimensions 1 and 2.

quite similar. This indicates that although a non-metric PLS program is desirable, even the metric PLS regression can give meaningful modelling of non-metric data. It also indicates that PLS is useful for relating a symmetric matrix to another symmetric (or non-symmetric) matrix.

5.4. PLS versus Analysis of Variance (ANOVA)

Principles: In ANOVA, a response variable, y, is regressed on a set of design variables, X. The PLS regression here maps the salient features in the design matrix in order to provide a visual representation of the ANOVA significant tests.

Example: Factors influencing preference of black currant juice were studied and the results analyzed by ANOVA (Martens, M. *et al.*, 1983c). 32 samples were subjected to a factorial design of five main factors, each in two levels: *Colorant* (regular-added green colorant), *acidity* (regular-added citric acid), *volume* (15–25 ml), *temperature* ($+5\,°C–+20\,°C$) and *time* of serving (before–after lunch, i.e. AM–PM). 24 consumers evaluated their degree of liking on a 1–9 point hedonic scale.

A five-way ANOVA showed significant differences between three of the main factors (Table 1). For the PLS2 regression each of the five factors in two levels was described by two design variables in an X-block (e.g. regular colour: $x_1 = 1$, $x_2 = 0$; added green colorant: $x_1 = 0$, $x_2 = 1$). Thus, $I = 32$, $K = 10$ and $J = 24$. The results from Table 1 could then be directly seen in the PLS2 loading plot (Fig. 26(a)). The two first PLS2 factors (25% and 7% explained cross-validated variance in Y respectively) mapped the variation in colorant (PLS factor 1) and acidity (PLS factor 2), the two most significant experimental factors from the ANOVA. The individual consumer's preference may also be studied from this loading plot, e.g. person No. 14 particularly disliked black currant juice with green colour but liked it somewhat sour. Persons No. 8 and 24 had

TABLE 1

MAIN EFFECTS FROM A 5-WAY ANOVA FOR BLACK CURRANT JUICE; 32 SAMPLES (2^5 FACTORIAL DESIGN) EVALUATED BY 24 PERSONS

Factor	*Order of mean value*	*Level of significance*
Colorant	Reg. C. > Green	$p < 0.001$
Acidity	Reg. A. > Citric	$p < 0.05$
Volume	25 ml > 15 ml	$p < 0.05$
Temperature	$5\,°C \simeq 20\,°C$	not sign.
Time	AM $\simeq$ PM	not sign.

a)

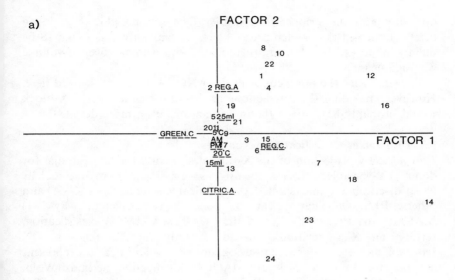

b)

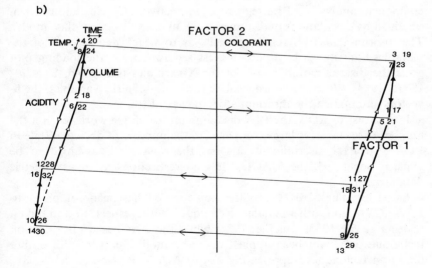

FIG. 26. Results from a study of relationship between five different design variables (**X**-block) and 24 persons' hedonic scores (**Y**-block) on 32 samples of black currant juice: (a) PLS loadings for the design variables (underlined) and the persons (1–24) for factors 1 and 2; (b) PLS scores for the samples (1–32) for factors 1 and 2.

opposite preferences concerning acidity. The scoring plot (Fig. 26(b)) nicely confirmed that preference of black currant juice was found to be mainly influenced by colorant, then acidity, but also an effect of volume was significant.

For simplicity the interactions in the ANOVA are not discussed here. However, including the interactions as design variables in the X-block would probably have made the interpretations even more detailed.

5.5. PLS versus Classification Techniques

Principles: By projection of the X-variables down on a set of design (or dummy) Y-variables, PLS may be used as a classification method such as linear discriminant analysis (LDA), canonical variate analysis (CVA) and others. PLS classification can be done in two different ways. (1) MACUP, the PLS equivalent of the PCA-based SIMCA classification, relying on X–Y relations instead of only intra-X relations. (2) Discriminant PLS regression, using design variables Y to represent classification. In the SIMCA and MACUP classification methods (Wold, S. *et al.*, 1983b, 1984), each class is separately modelled by a principal component analysis or PLS regression, respectively. Classification is then obtained by calculations of distances from an object to every class model. The discriminant PLS regression tells us to which degree each of the variables contributes to a certain class separation, i.e. the loading plot gives the discrimination power of the X-variables (see Wold, S. *et al.*, 1983b, 1984). When expressed relative to the noise in the variables, the $\hat{b}$-vectors summarize the discriminatory power of the variables.

In contrast to LDA, the PLS discriminant technique works even if the number of variables is large compared to the number of objects. While in LDA and PLS discriminant analysis the classes are assumed to be linearly separated, the MACUP has no restrictions as to asymmetric data structure.

Examples: The SIMCA classification method has been compared to LDA, CVA and other similar techniques with respect to food data (Forina *et al.*, 1983; MacFie, 1983) while the PLS-based classification techniques have not been applied much by food scientists. PLS outlier detection techniques, representing simple MACUP classifications, have been developed for calibration (Wold, S. *et al.*, 1983b; Martens, H. and Næs, 1986) and applied to food-relevant spectra: Martens, H. and Jensen (1983) distinguished between wheat and barley by NIR reflectance spectra; Martens, H. *et al.* (1986) revealed heme protein abnormalities in uv/vis transmission spectra. Discriminant PLS analysis (Wold, S. *et al.*,

1983b) was applied by Martens, M. (1986a) in a study of sensory and chemical quality criteria for stored versus not-stored frozen peas by treating 11 sensory and 9 chemical variables as the X-block and using design variables (1 and 0 for stored and not-stored, respectively) as the Y-block.

6. VALIDATION WITH RESPECT TO PRACTICAL INTERPRETATION

6.1. Optimal Model?

For a given set of data and a given application purpose it is important to check that a suitable mathematical model has been used. The 'soft' bilinear additive PLS model consisting of a series of orthogonal factors is very general. If several Y-variables are to be modelled, then a simultaneous PLS2 gives an overview, while a separate PLS1 solution for each individual y-variable often gives better prediction ability (see Section 4.3).

However, some sort of data pretreatment may be necessary to give an optimal fit of the data to the model; plots of parameters and residuals from preliminary PLS-fits to raw data will often indicate what type of pretreatment is needed. PLS regression may require some sort of weighting of the variables within a block to balance their signal/noise ratios. If the actual error level of a variable x_k or y_j is very different from the error level assumed in its weighting, this will decrease the prediction ability of the PLS results. But such error can automatically be detected by checking the estimated residual variances of the individual variables after the PLS-fit. Similarly, outliers among the samples $i = 1, 2, \ldots, I$ can automatically be detected after the PLS-fit, in part based on their residual variance in X or Y, in part based on their leverage h_i (see Section 3.6). Abnormal individual data elements x_{ik} or y_{ij} can likewise be detected. Once an outlier has been detected in the data, the user must decide whether to knock it out from the data set and repeat the PLS modelling, to obtain new data from this object or just to accept it as an extreme, but not erroneous data point.

Other types of pretreatment like CPLS or Procrustes rotation techniques appear to be useful for cleaning up sensory data before putting them into a two-block study (see Section 4.6). If there are purely multiplicative effects in the model, these ought to be removed in advance (Martens, H. et al., 1983a; Geladi et al., 1985) or made additive by logarithmic pretreatments. Other linearizations of the input data can also sometimes improve the fit (see Section 5.3), although this is not so important for higher-precision data, for example, from diffuse fluorescence (Jensen *et al.*, 1982) or Near Infrared Reflectance (Martens, H. and Næs, 1986).

In general, it is important to note that data pretreatment should not be used to make nonsense data fit a model.

6.2. Optimal Modelling Complexity?

Data modelling of **Y** (or a single **y**) from **X** can be done at different levels of ambitions, ranging from general causal modelling via predictive modelling to *ad hoc* fitting (Aakesson *et al.*, 1974). In this chapter we emphasize predictive modelling and try to avoid *ad hoc* modelling but leave the causal explanation to the subsequent interpretation of the results. Optimal predictive modelling means achieving a minimum prediction error.

The prediction error $(\mathbf{y}-\hat{\mathbf{y}})$ contains several errors; model errors due to incomplete or invalid modelling, and estimation errors due to insufficient training set data and propagation of noise from the **X**-data, plus, of course, errors in the 'true' test-data **y** (see Fig. 27(a)).

As illustrated in two of the examples in this chapter (Figs. 11 and 20), the prediction error usually reaches a minimum after a certain number of PLS factors, i.e. a certain complexity of the calibration model. This curved behaviour of the prediction error is a general phenomenon, and is explained conceptually in Fig. 27(a): as more 'harmonies' $\hat{\mathbf{t}}_1, \hat{\mathbf{t}}_2, \ldots$ (PLS factors) from the **X**-data are extracted and used as regressors for **Y**, the model errors and hence the prediction error goes down. But at the same time the effect of measurement noise and other irrelevant phenomena in the **X** and **Y** data cause an increased statistical uncertainty in the predictions. The total prediction error therefore reaches a minimum when the advantage of modelling yet another phenomenon equals the disadvantage of becoming yet more sensitive to noise, etc.

The PLS modelling requires a satisfactory design of the training set, both for valid interpretation of the obtained parameters and for optimal prediction. Figure 27(b) illustrates conceptually how, for a given data-analytic problem, different qualities of the training set data give different prediction errors.

The prediction ability of the PLS1 and PLS2 methods shown in this chapter is optimal for new samples similar to the average, $(\bar{\mathbf{x}}, \bar{\mathbf{y}})$, and it may decrease strongly for samples outside the ranges of the training set. Thus, the prediction testing requires a sensible selection of test samples in

a)

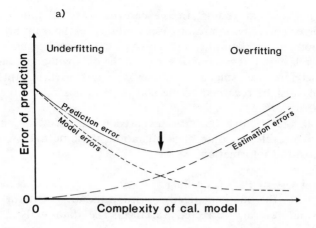

b)

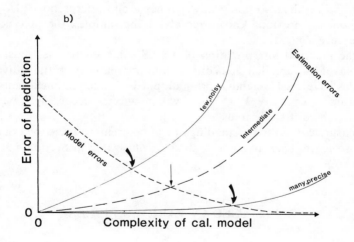

FIG. 27. (a) Conceptual illustration showing the total prediction error to be the sum of two main contributions: The model errors to be removed and the statistical uncertainty errors that can lead to overfitting. The arrow marks the optimal complexity, yielding minimal prediction error. (b) Effect of the quality and quantity of the input data: For calibration samples of a given type the optimal complexity of the solution (arrows) and the corresponding prediction error depends on the quality and quantity of data. Having few or noisy data gives worse prediction than having many or precise data.

order to give relevant results. In the case of cross-validation and of leverage-corrected prediction testing (see Section 3.6) the training set and the validation set are the same, and this puts extra requirements on the sampling: irrelevant, but systematic errors in the data will appear as valid factors. Therefore, the smaller examples in the present chapter (e.g. Section 4.6) must be regarded as method illustrations rather than conclusive experiments.

In general, the scientist must be prepared to accept zero significant factors as a possible outcome of a validation; in some data sets there simply is no valid information.

6.3. Practical Use of PLS Modelling

In addition to the mathematically based validation criteria (cross-validation and leverage-corrected variance), the data-analytic results must also be evaluated by other criteria: if outliers have been detected, should they be eliminated and the data reanalyzed? Are the statistically 'significant' results also practically significant and interpretable? Do they correspond to previous knowledge about the samples, the precision of the measurements, etc.?

In the practical interpretation of a PLS solution the user must take care to avoid scaling delusions due to data pretreatment. If the individual variables have been weighted (pre-multiplied by different coefficients), all the parameters $\bar{x}$, $\bar{y}$, $\hat{W}$, $\hat{P}$, $\hat{Q}$ and $\hat{B}$ will be affected accordingly, but can be de-weighted if so desired.

To ensure correct understanding, it can be useful to trace the obtained factor structure back to the raw data, as illustrated in Section 4.2 (Fig. 10).

7. PLS USED IN VARIOUS FIELDS

The PLS method, as described in this chapter, has recently been applied to other chemical and instrumental data with food research relevance, for instance:

* In physical chemistry: Predicting protein molecular conformation from circular-dichroism spectra; predicting food gel properties from fundamental rheological measurements; predicting mineral composition of rock samples from X-ray diffraction spectra; predicting particle size in powders from reflectance spectra.

* For 'classical' chemical data: Predicting concentrations of dyes from conventional UV/visual-range transmission spectra; predicting chemical composition of foods from NIR spectroscopy; predicting composition of protein mixtures from amino acid chromatograms (ion exchange and HPLC).

* In biologically oriented chemistry: Predicting chemical composition of living animals from X-ray computer tomography images; predicting botanical components in wheat flour mill streams from autofluorescence spectra; predicting growth of cereal varieties from climatic and agronomical information; predicting biochemical compositions from NIR spectroscopy in biotechnological fermentation.

PLS applications from the chemometric field outside food research are increasing rapidly (see Kowalski, 1984). Also, PLS has been found useful on ecological, economical, geological and medical data as well as data from the oil industry.

8. PLS PROGRAMS AVAILABLE

Since PLS is a fairly new multivariate data-analytic technique, it is not yet found in standard statistical packages. The PLS1 and PLS2 algorithms described here are implemented in the following two programs:

* The SIMCA-3B (and 3F) package developed by S. Wold, Umeå, Sweden (Wold, S., 1985). It is written in Microsoft Basic and runs on MS-DOS, PC-DOS and CP/M micros. The program is available from SEPANOVA AB, Östrandsvägen 14, S-12243 ENSKEDE, Sweden (Europe) and PRINCIPAL DATA COMPONENTS, 2505 Shepard Blvd, Colombia, MO 65201, USA. Fortran versions for minis and mainframes are available from SGAB, Box 801, S-951 28 Luleå, Sweden (PDP-11, VAX, CD Cyber, IBM, Prime, ...) and from O. Kvalheim, Chemical Institute, University of Bergen, N-5000 Bergen, Norway (VAX, NORD).

* The UNSCRAMBLER program package for multivariate calibration, used in most of the present examples, is being developed by H. Martens. It is written in Fortran 77 and runs on IBM–PC and VAX computers. The program package is available from Computer-Aided Modelling (CAMO A/S), P.O. Box 2893, N-7001 Trondheim, Norway.

While SIMCA-3B mostly aims at solving classification problems, the UNSCRAMBLER directs more towards calibration type of problems. Both programs have the characteristics listed in Fig. 28.

PLS is a desired method because it:
— handles many **X**-variables and **Y**-variables
— takes small sample sets
— takes missing values
— is realistic with respect to
        random noise in **X** and in **Y**
        multicollinearity in **X** and in **Y**
— gives warnings of outliers
— gives estimated parameters: easy to interpret
— gives predictive validation
— gives automatic determination of
        optimal model complexity

FIG. 28. Relating two blocks of variables: list of desired characteristics of a data analytic method from a user's point of view.

9. SUMMARY AND CONCLUSIONS

The predictive PLS1 and PLS2 regression methods and the new Consensus PLS analysis have been demonstrated on various food research data, especially for studies of sensory–chemical relationships. References to other applications are given. Advantages of PLS to more traditional statistical methods are exemplified. Validation with respect to practical interpretation is discussed.

Systems analysis based on the principle of Partial Least Squares regression offers new methods for studying relationships between two or more tables of variables measured on a set of objects. The methods avoid multicollinearity problems by modelling latent variables that account for the systematic and most **Y**-relevant 'harmonies' in the **X**-data.

Thus, with PLS modelling a general tool for relating different types of data tables to each other, is available. This enables the food scientist with one single program to analyze problems ranging from understanding consumer perception of food quality to calibration of advanced multivariate instruments.

ACKNOWLEDGEMENTS

The PLS method could not have been tested out in real life without constructive scientific consultations and skilful technical assistance. Thus, many thanks to M. Rødbotten, S. Hurv, L. Blümlein and E. Risvik (i.e.

the sensory group at NINF); H. Russwurm Jr. and M. K. Hårstad (from the chemical group); H. J. Rosenfeld (ensuring agronomical interpretation); P. Lea, C. Irgens and I. Pedersen (from the data group) and L. Bakke and U. Dyrnes (for typing and technical drawings respectively). S. Wold (Umeå University, Sweden) is thanked for continuous support and inspiration.

REFERENCES

Aakesson, C., Persson, T. and von Sydow, E. (1974). Predicting sensory and preference values of aroma and flavour by use of gas chromatographic data. *Proc. IV Int. Congress Food Sci. and Technol.*, Vol. II, pp. 183–9.

Aastveit, A. and Martens, H. (1986). ANOVA interactions interpreted by PLS regression: Straw length in barley genotypes related to climate, *Biometrics*, in press.

Bohlin, L., Egelandsdal, B. and Martens, M. (1985). Relationship between fundamental rheological data and mouthfeel for a model hydro-colloid system. In: *Proc. 3rd Int. Conf. and Industrial Exhibition 'Gums and Stabilisers for the Food Industry'*, Wrexham, UK, July 8–11.

Brown, P. J. (1982). Multivariate calibration, *J. R. Stat. Soc. B*, **44**, 287–308.

Burg, van der E. and Leeuw, de J. (1983). Non-linear canonical correlation. *Brit. J. Math. Stat. Psychol.*, **36**, 54–80.

Canaway, P. R., Piggott, J. R., Sharp, R. and Carey, R. G. (1984). Comparison of sensory and analytical data for cereal distillates. *Proc. Flavour Research of Alcoholic Beverages*, L. Nykänen and P. Lehtonen (Eds), Foundation for Biotechnical and Industrial Fermentation Research, Vol. 3, pp. 301–11.

Cook, R. D. and Weisberg, S. (1982). *Residuals and Influence in Regression*, Chapman and Hall, London.

Cooley, W. W. and Lohnes, P. R. (1971) *Multivariate Data Analysis*, John Wiley, New York.

EOQC: European Organization for Quality Control (1976). *Glossary of terms used in quality control*, 4th ed.

Esbensen, K. and Wold, S. (1983). SIMCA, MACUP, SELPLS, GDAM, SPACE and UNFOLD: The ways towards regionalized principal components analysis and subconstrained *N*-way decomposition—with geological illustrations. In: *Proc. Nordic Symp. Appl. Stat.*, O. H. Christie (Ed.), Stokkand Forlag Publishers, Stavanger, Norway, pp. 11–36.

Farebrother, R. W. (1984). A note on Fearn's 'Misuse of ridge regression'. *Appl. Stat.*, **33**, 74–5.

Fearn, T. (1983). Misuse of ridge regression in the calibration of a near infrared reflectance instrument. *Appl. Stat.*, **32**, 73–9.

Fjeldsenden, B., Martens, M. and Russwurm, H. Jr. (1981). Sensory quality criteria of carrots, swedes and cauliflower. *Lebensm.-Wiss. u. Technol.*, **14**, 237–41.

Forina, M., Armanino, C., Lanteri, S. and Tiscornia, E. (1983). Classification of olive oils from their fatty acid composition. In: *Food Research and Data Analysis*, H. Martens and H. Russwurm Jr. (Eds), Applied Science Publishers, London, pp. 189–214.

Gacula, M. and Singh, J. (1984). *Statistical Methods in Food and Consumer Research*, Academic Press, Orlando, 505 pp.

Geladi, P., MacDougall, D. and Martens, H. (1985). Linearization and scatter-correction for near-infrared reflectance spectra of meat. *Appl. Spectrosc.*, May–June, 491–9.

Gower, J. C. (1983). Data analysis: Multivariate or univariate and other difficulties. In: *Food Research and Data Analysis*, H. Martens and H. Russwurm Jr. (Eds), Applied Science Publishers, London, pp. 39–67.

Hoffman, D. L. and Young, F. W. (1983). Quantitative analysis of qualitative data: applications in food research. In: *Food Research and Data Analysis*, H. Martens and H. Russwurm Jr. (Eds), Applied Science Publishers, London, pp. 69–93.

Jensen, S. Å. and Martens, H. (1983). Multivariate calibration of fluorescence data for quantitative analysis of cereal composition. In: *Food Research and Data Analysis*, H. Martens and H. Russwurm Jr. (Eds), Applied Science Publishers, London, pp. 253–70.

Jensen, S. Å., Munck, L. and Martens, H. (1982). The botanical constituents of wheat and wheat milling fractions. I. Quantification by autofluorescence. *Cereal Chem.*, **59**(6), 477–84.

Jöreskog, K. G. and Wold, H. (1982). *Systems under Indirect Observation*, Vols. I and II, North-Holland, Amsterdam.

Kowalski, B. R. (1984). *Chemometrics: Mathematics and Statistics in Chemistry*, D. Reidel, Dordrecht, The Netherlands.

MacFie, H. J. H. (1983). Some useful multivariate techniques relevant to classifying and identifying microbes. In: *Food Research and Data Analysis*, H. Martens and H. Russwurm Jr. (Eds), Applied Science Publishers, London, pp. 215–37.

MacFie, H. J. H. and Thomson, D. M. H. (1984). Multidimensional scaling methods. In: *Sensory Analysis of Foods*, J. R. Piggott (Ed.), Elsevier Applied Science Publishers, London, pp. 351–75.

Martens, H. and Jensen, S. Å. (1983). Partial Least Squares regression: A new two-stage NIR calibration method. In: *Progress in Cereal Chemistry and Technology 5a*, J. Holas and J. Kratochvil (Eds), Elsevier Amsterdam, pp. 607–47.

Martens, H. and Næs, T. (1984). Multivariate calibration I. Concepts and distinctions. *Trends in Analytical Chemistry*, **3**, 204–10.

Martens, H. and Næs, T. (1986). Multivariate calibration by data compression. In: *Near Infrared Reflection Spectroscopy*, P. Williams (Ed.), American Association of Cereal Chemists, St. Paul, Minnesota, in press.

Martens, H., Jensen, S. Å. and Geladi, P. (1983a). Multivariate linearity transformation for near infrared reflectance spectrometry. In: *Proc. Nordic Symp. Appl. Stat.*, O. H. Christie (Ed.), Stokkand Forlag Publishers, Stavanger, Norway, pp. 205–33.

Martens, H., Vangen, O. and Sandberg, E. (1983b). Multivariate calibration of an

X-ray computer tomograph by smoothed PLS regression. In: *Proc. Nordic Symp. Appl. Stat.*, O. H. Christie (Ed.), Stokkand Forlag Publishers, Stavanger, Norway, pp. 235–68.

Martens, H., Wold, S. and Martens, M. (1983c). A layman's guide to multivariate data analysis. In: *Food Research and Data Analysis*, H. Martens and H. Russwurm Jr. (Eds), Applied Science Publishers, London, pp. 473–92.

Martens, H., Karstang, T., Martens, M., Nilsson, M. B., Hovland, J., Vangen, O., Sandberg, E., Næs, T. and Birth, G. (1986). From dirty data to clean information: multivariate calibration in the analysis of intact samples. *Proc. VIIth Int. Conf. on Computers in Chemical Research and Education*, Garmish-Partenkirchen, June 1985, John Wiley, New York, in press.

Martens, M. (1984). Quality and quality evaluation. *Acta Hort.*, **163**, 15–30.

Martens, M. (1985). Data collection by a microcomputer system in a sensory laboratory, and analysis of sensory data. Lecture notes from *Computers in Sensory Research*, Society of Food Science and Technology, Helsinki, Finland, 10th April.

Martens, M. (1986a). Sensory and chemical quality criteria of stored versus not-stored frozen peas studied by multivariate data analysis. In: *The Shelf Life of Foods and Beverages*, G. Charalamboos (Ed.), Elsevier, Amsterdam, pp. 775–90.

Martens, M. (1986b). Sensory and chemical/physical quality criteria of frozen peas studied by multivariate data analysis. *J. Food Sci.*, **51**(3), 599–603.

Martens, M. and Russwurm, H. Jr. (1980). Evaluation of sensory and chemical quality criteria of dry sausage. In: *Proc. 24th Conf. EOQC*, Warsaw, pp. 88–93.

Martens, M. and Harries, J. (1983). A bibliography of multivariate statistical methods in food science and technology. In: *Food Research and Data Analysis*, H. Martens and H. Russwurm Jr. (Eds), Applied Science Publishers, London, pp. 493–518.

Martens, M. and Burg van der, E. (1985). Relating sensory and instrumental data from vegetables using different multivariate techniques. In: *Progress in Flavour Research*, J. Adda (Ed.), Elsevier, Amsterdam, pp. 131–48.

Martens, M., Fjeldsenden, B., Russwurm, H. Jr. and Martens, H. (1983a). Relationships between sensory and chemical quality criteria for carrots studied by multivariate data analysis. In: *Sensory Quality in Foods and Beverages*, A. A. Williams and R. K. Atkin (Eds), Ellis Horwood Ltd, Chichester, pp. 233–46.

Martens, M., Martens. H. and Wold, S. (1983b). Preference of cauliflower related to sensory descriptive variables by partial least squares (PLS) regression. *J. Sci. Food Agric.*, **34**, 715–24.

Martens, M., Risvik, E. and Schutz, H. G. (1983c). Factors influencing preference: A study on black currant juice. In: *Research in Food Science and Nutrition*, Vol. 2, J. V. McLoughlin and B. M. McKenna (Eds), Boole Press, Dublin, pp. 193–4.

Martens, M., Rosenfeld, H. J. and Russwurm, H. Jr. (1985). Predicting sensory quality of carrots from chemical, physical and agronomical variables: a multivariate study. *Acta Agric. Scand.*, **35**(4), 407–20.

Möttönen, K. (1975). *On the Baking Process Dynamics of Wheat.* Part IV,

Technical Research Centre of Finland, Materials and Processing Technology, 11, 40 pp.

Næs, T. (1985a). Comparison of approaches to multivariate linear calibration. *Biometr. J.*, 27, 265–75.

Næs, T. (1985b). Multivariate calibration when the error covariance matrix is structured. *Technometrics*, Aug.

Næs, T. and Martens, H. (1984). Multivariate calibration II. Chemometric methods. *Trends Analyt. Chem.*, 3, 266–71.

Næs, T. and Martens, H. (1985). Comparison of prediction methods for multicollinear data. *Commun. Statist.-Simula. Computa.*, 14(3), 545–76.

Næs, T., Irgens, C. and Martens, H. (1986). Calibration of NIR reflectance instruments. *Appl. Stat.*, in press.

Piggott, J. R. (Ed.) (1984). *Sensory Analysis of Foods*, Elsevier Applied Science Publishers, London.

Piggott, J. R. and Jardine, S. P. (1979). Descriptive sensory analysis of whisky flavour. *J. Inst. Brew.*, 85, 82–5.

Powers, J. J. (1984). Descriptive methods of analysis. In: *Sensory Analysis of Foods*, J. R. Piggott (Ed.), Elsevier Applied Science Publishers, London, pp. 179–242.

Schiffman, S. S. (1981). Perception of odors of simple pyrazines by young and elderly subjects: a multidimensional analysis. *Pharmacol. Biochem. Behav.*, 14, 787–98.

Skrede, G., Næs, T. and Martens, M. (1983). Visual color deterioration in blackcurrant syrup predicted by different instrumental variables. *J. Food Sci.*, 48, 1745–9.

Sundberg, R. (1985). When is the inversed regression estimator MSE superior to the standard regression estimator in multivariate controlled calibration situations? *Statistics and Probabilities Letters*, 3, 75–9.

Wold, H. (1982). Soft modelling: The basic design and some extensions. In: *Systems under Indirect Observation*, Part II, K. G. Jöreskog and H. Wold (Eds), North-Holland, Amsterdam, pp. 1–54.

Wold, S. (1985). *SIMCA 3B & 3F: Soft Independent Modelling of Class Analogy. Brief program description*, Umeå University, Umeå, Sweden.

Wold, S., Martens, H. and Wold, H. (1983a). The multivariate calibration problem in chemistry solved by the PLS method. In: *Lecture Notes in Mathematics*, no. 973, B. Kågström and A. Ruhe (Eds), Matrix Pencils, Springer-Verlag, Berlin, pp. 286–93.

Wold, S., Albano, C., Dunn III, W. J., Esbensen, K., Hellberg, S., Johansson, E. and Sjöström, M. (1983b). Pattern recognition: Finding and using regularities in multivariate data. In: *Food Research and Data Analysis*, H. Martens and H. Russwurm Jr. (Eds), Applied Science Publishers, London, pp. 147–88.

Wold, S., Albano, C., Dunn III, W. J., Edlund, U., Esbensen, K., Geladi, P., Hellberg, S., Johansson, E., Lindberg, W. and Sjöström, M. (1984). Multivariate data analysis in chemistry. In: *Chemometrics: Mathematics and Statistics in Chemistry*, B. R. Kowalski (Ed.), D. Reidel, Dordrecht, The Netherlands, pp. 17–95.

Wold, S., Wold, H., Dunn III, W. J. and Ruhe, A. (1985). The collinearity problem in linear and non-linear regression. The partial least squares (PLS) approach to generalized inverses, in press.

Wold, S., Martens, H. and Martens, M. (1986). Finding the main common information in multi-table sensory data by Consensus Partial Least Squares (CPLS) modelling. In preparation.

Young, F. W. (1981). Quantitative analysis of qualitative data. *Psychometrika*, **46**, 357–88.

Young, F. W. (1985). Alternating Least Squares. Building individuals into the model. Lecture at Int. meeting on Relating sensory data to physical and chemical measurements, Society of Chemical Industry & Royal Statistical Society, London, 29th April.

Young, F. W. and Lewyckyj, R. (1979). *ALSCAL-4 User's Guide*, 2nd edn, Data Analysis and Theory Association, Carrboro, N. C.

Chapter 10

APPLIED CLUSTER ANALYSIS

T. Jacobsen

Bryggeriindustriens Forskningslaboratorium, Oslo, Norway

and

R. W. Gunderson

Department of Mathematics, Utah State University, Logan, Utah, USA

1. INTRODUCTION

This last chapter in the book should, in our opinion, be where the practical reader starts. Everyone who has tried to gain information from a large data matrix has felt the need for a simplification. A simplification may involve the search for clusters or substructures. Such an investigation will, at least, give one result: better knowledge of the data. It can then be evaluated whether the information from cluster analysis is sufficient, or whether other methods should be used.

1.1. Applied Cluster Analysis in Food Science
Every student of chemistry meets a classical example of applied cluster analysis: the periodic table of elements. Mendeleev used the available information about the nature of each element to 'see' that the elements actually formed groups, and that the similarity within each group was higher than the similarity between groups. This was, however, done without what we today would mean by cluster analysis: the use of computational methods, aimed at forming subgroups or clusters of similar objects. In fact, all clustering methods would be impractical for use on all but the smallest data set if a computer was not available.

The food scientist of today will meet many problems where 'similarity'

361

is one of the key-words. Unlike Mendeleev, he or she can benefit from the availability of computers and computer programs. In food science literature, we find examples of applied cluster analysis from various fields: identification of contaminating microorganisms, training and selection of judges for a sensoric panel, chemical analyses in the quality control department, research or development of new products. Table 1 gives a survey of different food science applications of cluster analysis. Interesting projects have been carried out both through clustering of *objects* (e.g. beer samples, sensoric judges), as well as through clustering of measurements upon the objects (*attributes*, *features*, e.g. sensoric descriptors or chemical analyses).

1.2. A Preview of the Following Sections

We start with the class of *hierarchical* clustering methods, which is by far the most popular class of clustering techniques appearing in the food science literature. They are characterized by the property that the clusters evolve in the form of a *nested* structure, where it is never possible for two sample data vectors to appear in two distinct clusters, after they have once appeared together in a single cluster. Although we shall see that there is almost an infinite possibility for variations within the class of hierarchical clustering methods, they are all similar in the sense that they share a general procedure of execution. The output is almost always in the form of a *dendrogram*, or a *tree*, which conveniently displays the hierarchy of classes defined by the clusters.

We have concentrated upon methods belonging to the class of *agglomerative* clustering methods, as opposed to *divisive* methods. This means that the trees we construct will evolve from the top down as their procedure steps through its various levels.

At the end of this chapter, the reader will find a program, written in BASIC. The program is specifically intended for use on any of the many microcomputers commonly available today, and covers the three first hierarchical methods we describe.

One might suspect that the appeal of hierarchical methods may be more a function of their ready availability and conceptual simplicity than any technical superiority over other methods. Certainly these methods are appropriate and have distinct advantages for some applications. Taxonomists, for example, expect their classifications to have a hierarchical structure and have good reason to prefer them in their investigations. However, while availability and mathematical simplicity may be appealing, and while the long list of taxonomical clustering successes is impressive, these are not necessarily the sole criteria by which a clustering method should be selected.

Obviously, one reason to look beyond hierarchical methods is to find a method which does not *impose* a hierarchical structure. Many authors distinguish between a hierarchical structure and a *partitional* structure. In the latter case, the objective is not to uncover an overall nested, tree-like structure, but instead to group the data into a (usually small) prespecified number of mutually exclusive and exhaustive subsets of similarity groups. Data sets may fail to possess any hierarchical structure, but still partition nicely into a prescribed number of classes. To arbitrarily impose a hierarchical structure on such data sets would be wholly inappropriate and misleading.

Non-hierarchical methods represent, therefore, an important part on the menu of clustering methods. They also represent the newest additions to the method collections. We will present one such method here.

Finally, for the reader who gets eager to try different methods on their own data, and who is not satisfied with the BASIC program, references to program packages are given.

1.3. Textbooks of Cluster Analysis

We have not been able to cover all the aspects of cluster analysis in this chapter. Those of the readers who want to study the different methods in more detail, are recommended to choose some of the available textbooks. The book by Romesburg (1984) starts at a fundamental level, and gives illustrations of calculations and applications. The book contains references to several other textbooks from various fields. Two books can be added to the list: a recent one by Massart and Kaufman (1983), where cluster analysis in analytical chemistry is described, and the introduction to fuzzy cluster analysis by Bezdek (1981).

Furthermore, several textbooks on pattern recognition contain chapters about cluster analysis. The books by Duda and Hart (1973) and Fukunaga (1972) can be mentioned, in addition to the ones quoted by Romesburg.

2. STEP-BY-STEP THROUGH AN EXAMPLE OF HIERARCHICAL CLUSTERING

The first method of cluster analysis we wish to present is not necessarily the best, but it is widely known and used. The method may be referred to

TABLE 1

FOOD SCIENCE RELATED EXAMPLES OF APPLIED CLUSTER ANALYSIS

	Similarity/dissimilarity measure and clustering method	Ref.
In microbiology		
68 tests are performed upon 460 strains of *Bacillus*. This collection was divided into ten groups, four of these could not be identified with recognized species. Estimates are given as to how many tests are necessary to divide two species	A qualitative dissimilarity matrix is used. Clustering method: Nearest neighbor	Bonde (1975)
The fatty acid composition of strains from *Enterobacteriaceae* and *Vibrionaceae* is clustered. Good separation of species, genera and families is obtained	The data are logarithmically transformed and normalized to one of the esters. Both a correlation matrix and Euclidean distance are used. Clustering method: Average distance	Bøe and Gjerde (1979)
Clustering of DNA and RNA from some unusual bacteria leads to the identification of a new group of organisms in addition to the eucaryotes and the procaryotes		Woese (1981)
Sensoric analysis or sensoric/objective comparisons		
Cluster analysis used among other multivariate methods with data from a profile sensory evaluation of chocolate	Several distance measures are used. Clustering method: Average distance	Vuataz et al (1974)
PCA, stepwise discriminant analysis, and cluster analysis are used with flavor terms for describing tea	The CLUSTAN program (Section 6) is used. PCA-models (see Chapter 6) are computed for each cluster.	Palmer (1974)
The panel is clustered in two groups: one with preference for canned beans, the other one with preference for frozen beans. For each group, the sensory or objective attributes are clustered		Godwin et al. (1978)

Objective measurements and sensoric measurements for blueberry samples are clustered in order to discern the most useful in characterizing the products	Powers *et al.* (1978)
A panel for sensoric analysis is selected by means of clustering the results from threshold sensitivity determinations	Golovnja *et al.* (1981)
The influence of oxygen in beer upon the relationship between objective and sensoric analysis is studied by means of several multivariate methods	Schmidt *et al.* (1981)
From GC profiles of soy sauces, 10 peaks are selected either from discriminant analysis or from multiple regression analysis. Cluster analysis with these peaks show that extraneous samples are distinguished from a normal sample set	Aishima (1983)	Euclidean distance. A BMDP2M program (see Section 6) is used
'Quality profiles' by means of chemical analysis	
Wines from one region are grouped together due to their similarity in trace element patterns	Siegmund and Bächmann (1977)
Clustering of meat aroma concentrates by means of objective analyses demonstrates the possibility for an instrumental determination of sensoric quality	Rothe *et al.* (1981)
Instrumental analyses of blue cheese are used to form clusters with different rancidity	Rothe *et al.* (1982)
Several features associated with good flavor and acceptable cooking characteristics of yams are used to select the clusters which are interesting for industrial application	Rhodes and Martin (1972)

The middle column (methods):

Correlation coefficient used as similarity measure — Schmidt *et al.* (1981)

Euclidean distance. A BMDP2M program (see Section 6) is used — Aishima (1983)

Euclidean distance between objects. Clustering method: Average distance — Siegmund and Bächmann (1977)

Correlation, Sokal's distance coefficient. Clustering method: Average distance. The results are compared with results from PCA. — Rhodes and Martin (1972)

(continued).

TABLE 1—*contd.*

	Similarity/dissimilarity measure and clustering method	Ref.
Quality profiles—contd.		
Chemical profiles are formed for three breweries. The chemical descriptions are in accordance with descriptions given by a sensoric panel. The flavor formation is due to yeast strain rather than brewery	Euclidean distance. Clustering method: non-hierarchical, fuzzy	Jacobsen and Gunderson (1983a)
Breweries are clustered according to the trace element concentration in (a) their worts, or (b) yeast samples. The first data set gives a more complicated optimal solution than the second one	Euclidean distance. Clustering method: non-hierarchical, fuzzy. The method involves an automatical PCA-model for each cluster	Jacobsen and Gunderson (1983b)
Cluster analysis is used among other multivariate methods to identify hop variety from hop oil analyses	Correlation? The methods from ARTHUR are used (Section 6)	Stenroos and Siebert (1984)

Significant peaks in GC profiles of orange juice are chosen as the peaks which, when a clustering algorithm is applied, will group chromatograms of the same type together and separate the different types of juices.

Euclidean distance and the nearest neighbor algorithm

Carpenter *et al.* (1983)

Taxonomy in botanics

'Tidying up' in maize name and races by means of cluster analysis

Euclidean distance. Clustering method: Average distance

Goodman and Bird (1977)

Clustering of blueberry strains

A non-metric similarity coefficient Clustering method: Average distance

van der Kloet (1978)

Other applications

Market research. The relationship between consumer characteristics and buying behavior

Euclidean distance. Clustering method: Average distance

Parker Lessing and Tollefson (1971)

Menu planning. Menus are prepared by selections from clusters of similar foods

Moskowitz and Klarman (1977)

by any of several names. The most commonly used are the *nearest neighbor* method and the *single linkage* method. It is the method used by Bonde, 1975, Tab. 8.1.

Step 1. The Input Data Matrix

Table 2 shows 12 gas chromatographic analyses of beer from two Norwegian breweries. The example is a shortened version of the one presented by Jacobsen and Gunderson (1983a). The rows of the matrix correspond to twelve samples, and the columns correspond to measurements of twelve common *attributes*, or *features*, taken on each of the twelve beer samples. Each *sample data vector* has twelve components corresponding to the twelve features. That means, for a human being who can only see in three dimensions, nine components 'too much'. But that's one of the advantages of computerized data analyses: one attempts to have the computer serve as our 'eyes' for looking at data displayed in a higher dimensional geometric space than we are able to visualize.

In this chapter we shall consistently identify the *rows* of the data matrix as the sample data vectors and the *columns* as the attributes. That is purely an arbitrary decision, usually decided as a function of format. For obvious reasons, the reader should be careful to identify the labels on the rows and columns used by different authors, and pay particular attention to the preference of individual computer programmers.

Step 2. Scaling the Data

In a cluster analysis, we reach points where it becomes necessary to make some fairly arbitrary, but important decisions. The question of whether to scale the data and, if so, how to scale it, is one of those points. This is not a difficulty which is unique to clustering. The very same question must be addressed if one is involved in, for example, a principal component analysis.

Given that the attributes are measured in a mixture of units (e.g. pounds, liters, feet, slugs, and whatever), an argument could be made for at least *standardizing* (normalizing) the data to some dimensionless form. Centering the attributes to mean zero and scaling to unit variance achieves this goal, and tends to prevent certain attributes from dominating subsequent computations because of their relatively large numerical values. In Table 3, we have performed this type of scaling upon the data from Table 2. Duda and Hart (1973) point out, however, that this almost routine standardization of most data analysts may be precisely the wrong strategy for a cluster analysis, since the differing spreads in

TABLE 2
EXAMPLE INPUT DATA SET

			2-Methyl propanol	Amyl alcohols	1-Propanol	2-Phenyl ethanol	Acetal-dehyde	Ethyl acetate	Isoamyl acetate	2-Phenyl ethyl acetate	Octanoic acid	Decanoic acid	Ethyl hexanoate	Ethyl octanoate
			Attributes											
			1	2	3	4	5	6	7	8	9	10	11	12
Sample data	Brewery B	1	6·60	44·00	7·40	6·00	13·50	17·30	1·30	0·23	3·10	0·10	0·17	0·14
		2	6·40	44·00	8·00	6·50	15·50	19·70	1·20	0·23	2·70	0·20	0·16	0·13
		3	7·10	46·00	8·20	5·50	11·50	20·40	1·20	0·25	2·70	0·20	0·16	0·12
		4	6·60	43·00	7·80	5·20	8·20	16·00	1·40	0·24	2·90	0·50	0·18	0·17
		5	6·60	43·00	7·30	5·90	9·10	18·80	1·20	0·26	3·00	0·20	0·14	0·16
		6	6·50	42·00	8·00	5·40	9·70	16·50	1·10	0·28	2·70	0·20	0·22	0·17
vectors	Brewery C	7	10·00	46·00	8·40	10·00	20·20	12·40	1·30	0·25	7·00	0·60	0·30	0·17
		8	9·90	46·00	9·20	20·00	15·40	14·30	1·00	0·37	5·40	0·50	0·14	0·16
		9	8·50	47·00	8·20	10·50	19·30	14·50	1·00	0·27	5·50	0·50	0·20	0·14
		10	10·20	53·00	8·00	12·30	8·50	13·00	1·20	0·27	5·80	0·80	0·23	0·17
		11	15·30	55·00	9·30	11·50	13·20	13·50	1·00	0·24	5·20	0·70	0·20	0·15
		12	15·50	56·00	9·00	10·90	14·00	13·70	1·00	0·31	6·50	0·80	0·41	0·20

TABLE 3
THE INPUT DATA MATRIX OF TABLE 2 AFTER SCALING TO MEAN VALUE=0·0 AND UNIT VARIANCE

	Attributes											
	1	2	3	4	5	6	7	8	9	10	11	12
1	−0·76	−0·64	−1·29	−0·72	0·08	0·54	1·03	−0·92	−0·77	−1·35	−0·51	−0·76
2	−0·82	−0·64	−0·36	−0·61	0·58	1·42	0·30	−0·92	−1·01	−0·95	−0·63	−1·22
3	−0·61	−0·22	−0·05	−0·83	−0·42	1·68	0·30	−0·42	−1·01	−0·95	−0·63	−1·68
4	−0·76	−0·84	−0·67	−0·90	−1·24	0·06	1·75	−0·67	−0·89	0·23	−0·38	0·61
5	−0·76	−0·84	−1·44	−0·74	−1·02	1·09	0·30	−0·17	−0·83	−0·95	−0·89	0·15
6	−0·79	−1·05	−0·36	−0·86	−0·87	0·24	−0·42	0·33	−1·01	−0·95	0·14	0·61
7	0·27	−0·22	0·26	0·20	1·76	−1·27	1·03	−0·42	1·58	0·62	1·17	0·61
8	0·24	−0·22	1·49	2·49	0·56	−0·57	−1·15	2·59	0·62	0·23	−0·89	0·15
9	−0·18	−0·02	−0·05	0·31	1·53	−0·49	−1·15	0·08	0·68	0·23	−0·12	−0·76
10	0·33	1·22	−0·36	0·72	−1·17	−1·05	0·30	0·08	0·86	1·41	0·27	0·61
11	1·88	1·63	1·65	0·54	0·01	−0·86	−1·15	−0·67	0·50	1·02	−0·12	−0·30
12	1·94	1·84	1·18	0·40	0·21	−0·79	−1·15	1·09	1·28	1·41	2·59	1·98

Sample data vectors

attribute values may well exist because of the presence of subclasses within the data.

Perhaps the best solution to this problem is for the cluster analyst to be *aware* of the consequences of scaling, or not scaling, the raw input data. Before drawing any earthshaking and revolutionary conclusions from the results of the analysis, the question should always be asked to what extent those results are dependent upon the form of the data. We hold the view that cluster analysis is, before anything else, an *exploratory* data analysis technique. Different ways of scaling the raw input data correspond to different ways of 'looking' at the data, and may occasionally suggest an hypothesis which fails to hold up under closer investigation. So what?

Step 3. Compute a Similarity Matrix

At the first level of a *nearest neighbor* (single linkage) clustering, we are at the bottom of the hierarchy, where there are as many clusters as there are sample data vectors. At the second level, two clusters from the previous level are merged into a single cluster; and so on at the next level, until finally there is only one cluster (which contains all of the sample data vectors).

Every merger is made after an evaluation of the similarity between clusters. We need, therefore, to define two terms: first, a measure of similarity, and second, a rule for how to measure similarity when there is more than one sample in a cluster.

Another look at Table 1 will show that the most popular method of measuring the similarity between sample data vectors is the use of the so-called Euclidean distance. In familiar two-dimensional geometry, the Euclidean distance between two points $P = (a, b)$ and $Q = (c, d)$ is just the straight line distance shown in Fig. 1, and the value of the distance can be quickly computed by an application of the Pythagorean theorem of plane geometry. In our example, the data are in a twelve-dimensional feature space, but the formula for computing the distance differs only by adding to the term under the radical the squares of the differences of the ten additional attributes. The Euclidean distance between two sample data vectors measures the similarity between the vectors, in the sense that the smaller the value of the coefficient, the more similar we assume the vectors.

We have computed this distance between each pair of the twelve sample data vectors in Table 3. The result is given in Table 4. This matrix is called a *similarity*, or a *resemblance*, matrix. The number found

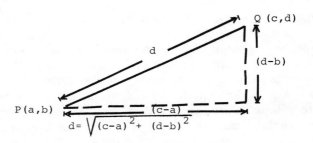

FIG. 1. Computing the Euclidean distance.

at the intersection of the ith row and the jth column is called a *similarity coefficient* and is a measure of the 'similarity' between the ith and jth sample data vectors, respectively. The similarity matrix is symmetric, since distance measure is reflexive. It would have been sufficient to have just shown those coefficients below (or above) the main diagonal. However, we will find it convenient a little later to have the full matrix available.

Before going on to the next step in the procedure, we will only mention some of the infinitely many other possibilities for mathematically defining the concept of 'similarity' between clusters of sample data vectors. Since the entire idea is to group together 'similar' sample data vectors into clusters, any change in the definition of similarity could be expected to result in a change in the cluster configuration. It can be hoped that enough is known beforehand about the data and questions to be answered with it, that there may be a natural choice for the similarity definition. If not, the remark we made about scaling, earlier in this section, may be also the best advice to be given here. That is, the investigator should be *aware* of the likely consequences of changing similarity definitions. Given that there is no prior knowledge about the data to guide such decisions, the choice of similarity must be regarded as arbitrary. Conclusions based upon the use of a particular choice should be examined carefully for significance, and shown not to be merely an artifact of the decision.

As we have said, by far the most common choice for obtaining a similarity matrix is to choose the coefficient obtained by computing pairwise distance with the Euclidean norm. We will only mention a few other possibilities such as the correlation, cosine, Bray–Curtis, and Canberra coefficients, or coefficients particularly designed for qualitative

TABLE 4

EXAMPLE SIMILARITY MATRIX. COLUMNS AND ROWS CORRESPOND TO SAMPLE DATA VECTORS AS NUMBERED IN Table 2

	C(1)	C(2)	C(3)	C(4)	C(5)	C(6)	C(7)	C(8)	C(9)	C(10)	C(11)	C(12)
C(1)	0·000	1·697	2·271	2·723	1·951	2·868	4·993	6·568	4·121	5·096	6·060	7·766
C(2)	1·697	0·000	1·376	3·517	2·537	3·122	5·252	6·222	3·756	5·472	5·724	7·730
C(3)	2·271	1·376	0·000	3·602	2·563	3·164	5·795	6·226	4·212	5·370	5·614	7·696
C(4)	2·723	3·517	3·602	0·000	2·439	2·775	4·850	6·555	4·921	4·115	5·899	7·122
C(5)	1·951	2·537	2·563	2·439	0·000	2·011	5·643	6·235	4·506	4·835	6·158	7·540
C(6)	2·868	3·122	3·164	2·775	2·011	0·000	5·041	5·483	3·997	4·508	5·557	6·465
C(7)	4·993	5·252	5·795	4·850	5·643	5·041	0·000	5·294	3·243	3·755	4·464	4·711
C(8)	6·568	6·222	6·226	6·555	6·235	5·483	5·294	0·000	4·002	4·824	4·732	5·595
C(9)	4·121	3·756	4·212	4·921	4·506	3·997	3·243	4·002	0·000	3·902	3·713	5·379
C(10)	5·096	5·472	5·370	4·115	4·835	4·508	3·755	4·824	3·902	0·000	3·464	4·240
C(11)	6·060	5·724	5·614	5·899	6·158	5·557	4·464	4·732	3·713	3·464	0·000	4·091
C(12)	7·766	7·730	7·696	7·122	7·540	6·465	4·711	5·595	5·379	4·240	4·091	0·000

measurements. These and a number of others are given a clear and uncomplicated discussion in the book by Romesburg (1984).

We should make one final remark about the choice of a similarity coefficient and its relationship to the scaling problem. That is, most scalings of the raw data of interest can be accomplished just as well by employing some other norm than the Euclidean norm to compute distance. For example, the Mahalanobis norm (Duda and Hart, 1973) accomplishes the usual standardization to zero mean and unit variance. Thus, to choose any norm other than the Euclidean for computing the similarity coefficient may only result in further distortions of the raw data.

Step 4. The Clustering Procedure

In Fig. 2(a), measurements are plotted which form two groups or clusters. In the hierarchical clustering, we start with every sample as a cluster, and work towards the top, where there is only one cluster. The two 'natural' groups will be detected on the way from the bottom to the top.

With only one sample in a cluster, there is only one way to measure the distance between two clusters. When a merger has taken place, however, there will be several alternatives for the distance between two clusters. Three alternatives are shown in Fig. 2(b), d_1, d_2 or d_3. As the name of the method we are presenting indicates, the nearest neighbor method uses the alternative d_1, i.e. the distance between a member of one cluster and *the nearest neighbor* in the other cluster. To perform the first level of the clustering of the beer samples, we compute (or read off from the similarity matrix) all of the distances between pairs of sample data vectors, one in each cluster (sometimes called *spanning pairs*). The nearest neighbor distance between the two clusters is merely the smallest of all the values.

The basic rule of the nearest neighbor, or single linkage, clustering method is as follows: *At each level, merge those two clusters whose nearest neighbor distance is the smallest.* Ties, when the distances between two or more pairs happen to be equal and smallest, are broken arbitrarily. A common choice is to merge the first of the pairs.

At level 1, each sample data vector defines a cluster consisting of a single member. At level 2, the two clusters will be merged whose nearest neighbor distance is smallest. Since each of the clusters at level 1 is a singleton cluster, it is only necessary to refer to Table 4 and look for the smallest coefficient. That occurs at the intersection of row 2 and column

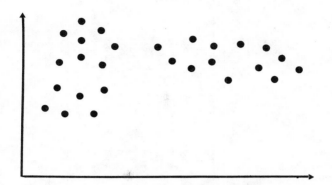

FIG. 2(a). A two-dimensional data set. Cluster analysis can be used to detect the two 'natural' clusters.

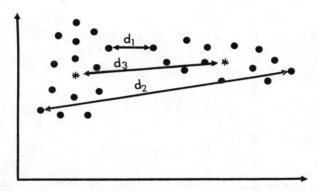

FIG. 2(b). The distance between clusters with more than one object can be measured in several ways, e.g. d_1 (nearest neighbor), d_2 (furthest neighbor), or d_3 (average neighbor).

3, so we merge cluster C(2) and C(3) to get a new cluster C(2, 3); C(2, 3), for example, denotes the cluster consisting of samples 2 and 3.

In order to merge clusters at level 3 it is necessary that we know all of the nearest neighbor distances between the clusters C(1), C(4), C(5), C(6), C(7), C(8), C(9), C(10), C(11), C(12), C(2, 3). This is not as bad as it looks, since the only distances not already computed at the previous level are the ones associated with the new cluster C(2, 3), i.e. the distances $d_1[C(k), C(2, 3)]$ for $k = 1, 4, 5, 6, 7, 8, 9, 10, 11, 12$. In terms of the *distance matrix*, Table 5, it is only necessary to compute the last row of distances since all

TABLE 5
NEAREST NEIGHBOR DISTANCES BETWEEN CLUSTERS—LEVEL 3

	C(1)	C(4)	C(5)	C(6)	C(7)	C(8)	C(9)	C(10)	C(11)	C(12)	C(2,3)
C(1)	0·000	2·723	1·951	2·868	4·993	6·568	4·121	5·096	6·060	7·766	1·697
C(4)	2·723	0·000	2·439	2·775	4·850	6·555	4·921	4·115	5·899	7·122	3·517
C(5)	1·951	2·439	0·000	2·011	5·643	6·235	4·506	4·835	6·158	7·540	2·537
C(6)	2·868	2·775	2·011	0·000	5·041	5·483	3·997	4·508	5·557	6·465	3·122
C(7)	4·993	4·850	5·643	5·041	0·000	5·294	3·243	3·755	4·464	4·711	5·252
C(8)	6·568	6·555	6·235	5·483	5·294	0·000	4·002	4·824	4·732	5·595	6·222
C(9)	4·121	4·921	4·506	3·997	3·243	4·002	0·000	3·902	3·713	5·379	3·756
C(10)	5·096	4·115	4·835	4·508	3·755	4·824	3·902	0·000	3·464	4·240	5·370
C(11)	6·060	5·899	6·158	5·557	4·464	4·732	3·713	3·464	0·000	4·091	5·614
C(12)	7·766	7·122	7·540	6·465	4·711	5·595	5·379	4·240	4·091	0·000	7·696
C(2,3)	1·697	3·517	2·537	3·122	5·252	6·222	3·756	5·370	5·614	7·696	0·000

the rest can be copied from Table 4, after crossing out rows 2 and 3 and columns 2 and 3. The last row is just the smallest of the distances $d_1(k, 2)$ and $d_1(k, 3)$ for each $k = 1, 4, 5, 6, 7, 8, 9, 10, 11, 12$, i.e. look for the smallest of the two distances occurring at the intersection of column k and rows 2 and 3 in Table 4.

Inspection of Table 5 (it is only necessary to examine the entries below the main diagonal) shows that the nearest neighbor distances occur at the intersection of the row corresponding to cluster $C(2, 3)$ and the column corresponding to cluster $C(1)$; so, we merge these clusters to get a new one $C(1, 2, 3)$. The search for the smallest distance is continued until all clusters are merged into one final cluster, containing all of the original vectors.

We implied earlier that the method we have just described may also be called the *single linkage* method. According to Duda and Hart (1973), the single linkage designation is usually applied if the procedure is allowed to terminate when the distance between nearest clusters exceeds some arbitrary threshold. The name is derived from a graph-theoretical interpretation of the procedure, which we shall not undertake in this chapter. The graph-theoretical interpretation of the method is presented in the books by Massart, *et al.*, (1978), Massart and Kaufman (1983), and in the ASI proceedings edited by Kowalski (1984). The reader interested in pursuing the subject further can also start with Chapter 6 of Duda and Hart's excellent book.

Step 5. Constructing the Dendrogram (Tree)

There is a convenient way to depict graphically the result of the clustering procedure we have just completed. Along the left side of the tree-like Fig. 3 are equally spaced points numbered in correspondence with the original twelve sample data vectors. Notice that the numbers have been arranged to provide a clear representation of the hierarchical clustering as it evolves through the various levels. Along the bottom is a scale, which provides a value for the nearest neighbor distance at which two clusters from a preceding level are merged. These values represent the nearest neighbor distances found in Tables 4 and 5, and similar tables corresponding to the higher levels of clustering, converted to a 0–1 scale.

At the top, we have placed arrows (not usually shown) to indicate the corresponding clustering levels. Thus, the dendrogram, or tree, provides a quick way of evaluating the nesting relationship of the hierarchical

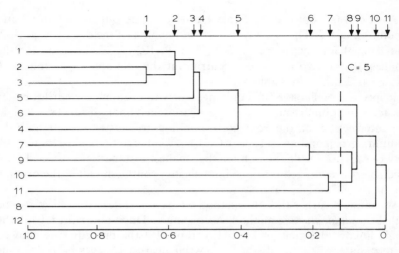

FIG. 3. Nearest neighbor clustering of the data in Table 3.

structure, the level at which various cluster configurations are formed, and the nearest neighbor distance at which clusters were merged.

Step 6. Interpreting the Results

The most straightforward use of the tree is to identify the cluster membership, in terms of the original n sample data vectors, at a given level k. At level k, the original vectors have been merged into $c = n - (k - 1)$ clusters. If we would like to see the cluster constituency for the case of decomposing the original data into c clusters, we need only 'cut' the tree with a vertical line anywhere between the arrow pointing at level $k = n - (c - 1)$ and the next level higher, $k + 1$.

In Fig. 3, we have cut the tree so as to determine the cluster makeup for $c = 5$ clusters. Thus the dashed line is shown cutting between level $k = 11 - (5 - 1) = 7$ and level $k + 1 = 8$. This cut places all the beer samples from brewery B (Table 2) in one cluster. Samples nos. 7 and 9 and nos. 10 and 11, all from brewery C, cluster together. All four of them will be in one cluster at the next level. The samples 8 and 12 are treated as outliers.

More often than not, the number of clusters is not known or specified beforehand, and one of the major questions to be answered in the analysis is to *find* the cluster configurations, i.e. values for c, which seem to provide natural, as opposed to forced, representations of the class substructure. Drawing the tree to the similarity scale of Euclidean nearest neighbor distances, at the bottom of the figure, provides one way of selecting these preferred values for c. For example, in going from level 8 to level 9, one observes only a very small increase in dissimilarity, but a relatively large increase occurs in going from level 5 to level 6. Using the criteria that a relatively large spacing between clustering levels suggests a natural grouping, one suspects that the cluster with beer samples 1–6 may be 'natural', whereas the group 7–9–10–11 is more or less formed by an artifact. It will be interesting to see what happens when we apply methods other than the nearest neighbor method.

3. OTHER HIERARCHICAL METHODS

The major criticism of the nearest neighbor method, as compared to other hierarchical methods, is its sensitivity to the *chaining effect*. This occurs when there is a convenient nearest-neighbor bridge from one apparent cluster to another, as shown in Fig. 4. As a consequence, small variations in the data can occasionally result in major changes in the dendrogram. These disadvantages might be overlooked, if it were necessary to look for pathological data sets to illustrate their occurrence. Unfortunately, this is not the case. Noise and outliers in the data can easily create just such behavior.

In order to avoid these problems, we consider some alternatives to the nearest neighbor criteria for merging two clusters. Not wanting to take half-measures, we next introduce the *furthest neighbor*, or *complete linkage* method.

3.1. The Furthest Neighbor Method
In the case of the nearest neighbor method, the distance between two

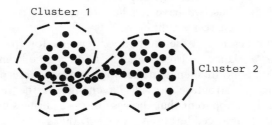

FIG. 4. Two apparent clusters joined by a 'bridge'. Dashed line shows result of clustering using single linkage.

clusters, at any level, was obtained by finding the *minimum* distance between all pairs of sample data vectors, one in each cluster. For the furthest neighbor method, the distance between any two clusters is defined to be the *maximum* distance between all pairs of sample data vectors, one in each cluster, i.e., d_2 in Fig. 2.

With that major exception, the two methods are identical. In particular, the criteria for merging two clusters is only slightly changed to read: *Merge those two clusters with minimum furthest neighbor distance between them.* Therefore, we can start the discussion of the furthest neighbor method at step 4 of the basic hierarchical clustering procedure outlined in the previous section.

As before, each sample data vector will define a unique cluster at level 1. At level 2, two clusters will be merged whose furthest neighbor distance d_2 is *smallest*. Ties may, once again, be broken by some arbitrary rule. Since each of the clusters going into level 2 is a singleton cluster, we still may use Table 4 to find that distance (as the smallest similarity coefficient). The same two clusters, C(2) and C(3), will be merged to get the new cluster C(2, 3).

It is not until level 3 before a change is encountered. The last row of the distance matrix corresponding to Table 5, must now be computed using the furthest neighbor distances $d_2[C(k), C(2,3)]$, for $k = 1, 4, 5, 6, 7, 8, 9, 10, 11, 12$. It is still possible to use Table 4; however, now we must look for the *largest* of the two distances (similarity coefficients) occurring at the intersection of row k and columns 2 and 3. The result is shown as Table 6.

Since we are trying to determine the *minimum* of the furthest neighbor distances between clusters in Table 6, we look for the *smallest* entry in that table, and find it at the intersection of the row corresponding to cluster C(1) and the column corresponding to C(5). Following the furthest neighbor rule, we merge the corresponding clusters to form a new one, C(1, 5). Thus, we have reached a departure from the results obtained using the nearest neighbor rule.

There is no difference in the method, or reasons, for constructing the tree. However, a glance at Figs 3 and 5 shows a significant change in structure. There is no difference in the way the tree is interpreted either, but the change in structure provides a change in the results of the interpretation. It is apparent that the case of $c = 2$ clusters now provides the most natural, unforced, grouping. Further, this grouping places each of the beer samples in its 'proper' brewery.

It is tempting to conclude at this point that the furthest neighbor

TABLE 6
FURTHEST NEIGHBOR DISTANCE BETWEEN CLUSTERS–LEVEL 3

	C(1)	C(4)	C(5)	C(6)	C(7)	C(8)	C(9)	C(10)	C(11)	C(12)	C(2,3)
C(1)	0·000	2·723	1·951	2·868	4·993	6·568	4·121	5·096	6·060	7·766	2·271
C(4)	2·723	0·000	2·439	2·775	4·850	6·555	4·921	4·115	5·899	7·122	3·602
C(5)	1·951	2·439	0·000	2·011	5·643	6·235	4·506	4·835	6·158	7·540	2·563
C(6)	2·868	2·775	2·011	0·000	5·041	5·483	3·997	4·508	5·557	6·465	3·164
C(7)	4·993	4·850	5·643	5·041	0·000	5·294	3·243	3·755	4·464	4·711	5·795
C(8)	6·568	6·555	6·235	5·483	5·294	0·000	4·002	4·824	4·732	5·595	6·226
C(9)	4·121	4·921	4·506	3·997	3·243	4·002	0·000	3·902	3·713	5·379	4·212
C(10)	5·096	4·115	4·835	4·508	3·755	4·824	3·902	0·000	3·464	4·240	5·472
C(11)	6·060	5·899	6·158	5·557	4·464	4·732	3·713	3·464	0·000	4·091	5·724
C(12)	7·766	7·122	7·540	6·465	4·711	5·595	5·379	4·240	4·091	0·000	7·730
C(2, 3)	2·271	3·602	2·563	3·164	5·795	6·226	4·212	5·472	5·724	7·730	0·000

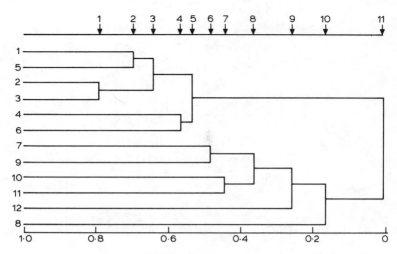

FIG. 5. Furthest neighbor clustering of the data in Table 3.

method, because of its apparent success with our example, should therefore be designated the method of choice. In particular, it begins to appear that we may have been victimized by the 'chaining effect' when we tried to apply the nearest neighbor method.

But we could just as well have constructed a sample data set to give us the reverse result. That is, the chaining effect may sometimes work to our advantage, instead of our disadvantage. As might be inferred from our example, the furthest neighbor tends to work very well, when the basic cluster structure is 'round'. But, it doesn't do so well when the basic structure is 'chain-like', or 'linear', as illustrated by Fig. 6. Precisely because of its sensitivity to the chaining effect, that is when the nearest neighbor method will give the better result. The problem is, of course, that the analyst is unlikely to have enough prior knowledge about the data to be able to predict the shapes likely to be encountered. Thus, we

FIG. 6. Two apparent 'linear' clusters.

appear to be forced into making an arbitrary decision between two extremes. Rather than do so, many analysts prefer to steer a middle course.

3.2. The Average Distance Method

A compromise to the nearest and furthest neighbor methods is provided by still another variation on the basic hierarchical clustering rule. This time, we use d_3 in Fig. 1. This distance goes from the center of one cluster to the center of the other. It is computed by summing up all of the distances between spanning pairs, and then dividing that sum by the total number of sample data vectors in both clusters. For example, from Table 4, we get

$$d_3[C(1, 5), C(2, 3)] = (1/4)*(1\cdot697 + 2\cdot271 + 2\cdot537 + 2\cdot563) = 2\cdot267$$

The mechanics of carrying out the merging of clusters at the various levels differs only in the computation of distances between clusters, so it is probably not worth our while to duplicate the discussion from the previous sections. Again, the result of clustering the data of our example using the average distance method should be a tree, or dendrogram, like the one shown in Fig. 7.

Comparing the three dendrograms of Figs. 3, 5 and 7, it appears that

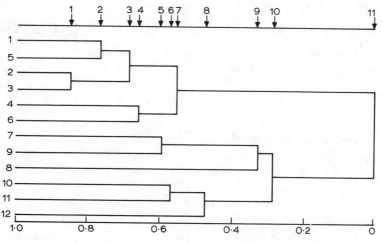

FIG. 7. Average distance clustering of the data in Table 3.

the tree derived with the average distance method does seem to accomplish the objective of providing a result midway between the extremes of the other two methods. That result is quite satisfactory, both with regard to identifying $c = 2$ as being the most 'natural' clustering of the data, and with regard to sample data vector membership in the two clusters.

Table 1 reveals that the average distance method (often called UnWeighted Pair Group Average, UWPGA) is the most popular clustering method in food science. Searches in other fields of application will reveal similar results (see Romesburg, 1984), and that Ward's method, which we shall discuss in the next section, holds the second place.

3.3. Ward's Method
Aside from the popularity of this method, we have an ulterior motive for presenting it. Ward's method, it turns out, provides us with a link to the most popular *non-hierarchical* family of clustering techniques, the objective function methods.

Before stating the cluster merging rule for Ward's method, we introduce some notation. It will be convenient in this, and the next section, to refer to a sample data vector using the notation

$$\mathbf{x}_n = (x_{1n}, x_{2n}, \ldots, x_{dn})$$

i.e. we shall write $\mathbf{x}_n$ as a *row vector* whose *components*, x_{jn}, are the d attributes of the data vector. For example, the first sample data vector $\mathbf{x}_1$ in Table 2 can be written as

$$\mathbf{x}_1 = (6\cdot60, 44\cdot00, 7\cdot40, 6\cdot00, 13\cdot50, 17\cdot30, 1\cdot30, 0\cdot23, 3\cdot10, 0\cdot10, 0\cdot17, 0\cdot14)$$

With this change, the (Euclidean) distance between two n-dimensional vectors $\mathbf{x}_i$ and $\mathbf{x}_j$ can be written as

$$d_e(\mathbf{x}_i, \mathbf{x}_j) = \sum_{m=1}^{d} [(x_{mi} - x_{mj})^2]^{1/2}$$

It is now easier to state the basic condition which is to be used for deciding which clusters to merge when using Ward's method. That condition involves the sum-of-squared-error functional

$$J[C(n_1, n_2, \ldots, n_k), \bar{\mathbf{m}}] = \sum_{j=1}^{k} d_e^2(\mathbf{x}_j, \bar{\mathbf{m}})$$

where $\bar{\mathbf{m}}$ is a vector of the same dimension as the sample data vector $\mathbf{x}_j$, but is not required to belong to the data set. Since $d_e(\mathbf{x}_j, \bar{\mathbf{m}})$ measures the distance from x_j to $\bar{m}$, it is not unreasonable to identify that distance as being the 'error' of approximating $\bar{m}$ by x_j; hence the sum-of-squared-error designation. It is not at all difficult to show (or guess) that J will be smallest if $\bar{m}$ is chosen to be the mean of the sample data vectors making up the cluster $C(n_1, n_2, \ldots, n_k)$, i.e.

$$\bar{m} = \sum_{j=1}^{k} x_j / k$$

We now can state the criteria for merging two clusters at step 4 in the discussion of the other hierarchical methods using Ward's method. To do so, it is first necessary to carry out the following computation involving J: for *every* pair of clusters going into a given level, compute J for that pair merged into one cluster *and* compute J for *each* of the surviving unmerged clusters. Sum up the *total* sum-of-squared-error for that configuration. Ward's method says to *merge those two clusters for which the total sum-of-squared-error is smallest.*

If Ward's method is applied to the scaled data of our example, Table 3, the dendrogram obtained should appear as shown in Fig. 8. Notice that this dendrogram seems to clearly show $c = 2$ as being the best choice for the number of clusters. From our prior knowledge of the data, we know that to be the case in fact, and it is tempting to conclude that Ward's

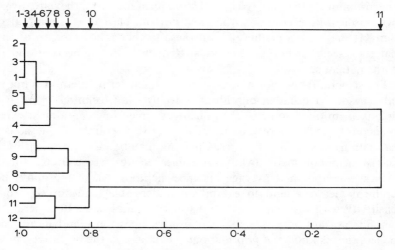

FIG. 8. Clustering of the data in Table 3, according to Ward's method.

method did the best job of detecting the structure known to exist in the data. Unfortunately, Ward's method has a built-in non-linear 'stretch factor' which causes the dendrogram to be biased in favor of the higher clustering levels (i.e. in favor of fewest clusters). That comes about because the error is being *squared* when computed.

There are some definite advantages to Ward's method, even if it does tend to favor clustering to fewest clusters. The main one is that, unlike the preceding methods, Ward's, to a certain degree, is an optimal method. At each level, Ward's method decided to merge those two clusters which minimized an objective functional. Thus, the method is at least a step-wise optimal method. It is far less sensitive to chaining than the single-linkage method, but can be modified to look for other than 'round' clusters. The latter objective can be realized by simply changing the norm used to compute distances from Euclidean to a more elliptical norm. For these and other reasons, Ward's method is quite popular as a hierarchical clustering approach.

4. NON-HIERARCHICAL CLUSTERING METHODS

In the next section we shall discuss one of the many so-called *objective function* methods. While it is possible to apply these algorithms recursively so as to impose a hierarchical structure, the real reason for their existence is to satisfy the need for a non-hierarchical method of obtaining a partitioning of the data. Next to hierarchical methods, they are, by our own unscientific accounting, the most popular class of clustering algorithms. It may say something about these methods, however, to observe that they seem to be used the most frequently in engineering and the mathematical sciences.

The structural need for a non-hierarchical clustering method is not the only reason to broaden our library of clustering techniques. We have already mentioned some of the difficulties which one can almost expect to encounter when applying any of the above, hierarchical, methods to real data from the food sciences. Chaining may be most prevalent in the nearest neighbor method, but sometimes creates havoc even with the furthest neighbor and average distance methods. All of the above hierarchical methods tend to exhibit an undesirable tendency to exhibit sensitivity with respect to variations in the initial data. In general, the methods are not very *robust*. Their use becomes more and more risky, the less that is known, *a priori*, about the data, and the objectives, of the investigation.

We remind the reader, once again, that the objective of this chapter is not to provide a comprehensive survey of the many different clustering methods currently available, hierarchical or non-hierarchical. We have selected the non-hierarchical method of this section because (1) we are quite familiar with it, having used it frequently in many applications for diverse sets of real data; and (2) it is a very powerful method, robust and versatile. For the reader interested in more traditional, and possibly better known, objective function methods we suggest starting with Chapter 6 in Duda and Hart's book (1973), or Hartigan's book (1975). One method not mentioned in those books, because of its later development, should be mentioned here. That is the MASLOC non-hierarchical clustering method presented by Massart *et al.* (1983). They present the interesting concept of a *robustness hierarchy* which, in a certain sense, provides a bridge between the hierarchical and non-hierarchical methods.

4.1. The Fuzzy C-Varieties (FCV) Clustering Algorithms

The title of the clustering method we shall be discussing in this section may, at first glance, appear to be somewhat frivolous. The word 'fuzzy', however, refers to the concept of a fuzzy set, introduced by L. Zadeh (1965) as a possible way to rigorously handle various aspects of *imprecision* in mathematical modelling. Since its introduction, there has been a steadily rising interest in attempting to apply these ideas in a variety of disciplines: for example, automata, control theory, linguistics, decision theory and optimization. A pioneering application to cluster analysis was provided by Ruspini (1969). However, it was not until Dunn and Bezdek published their Fuzzy ISODATA algorithm (Bezdek, 1973), that the applicability and importance of these concepts to the clustering problem became fully appreciated. Since then there have been many contributions to the subject and the number of theoretical and practical contributions has risen so rapidly as to make it impossible to mention only but a representative few here.

There is really nothing 'fuzzy' about the mathematical content of the FCV algorithms. It refers more to a point of view than to the use of new or non-traditional mathematical techniques. The real contribution of Ruspini, Dunn and Bezdek was to recognize that Zadeh's concept of *partial set membership* was particularly appropriate to the clustering problem. They dropped the traditional requirement that *every sample data vector be eventually assigned to one, and only one, of the cluster classes*, and replaced it with the pair of requirements:

(i) that a sample data vector could simultaneously 'belong' to more than one of the data classes, with its *degree of membership* in a particular cluster represented by a number in the interval [0, 1].

(ii) that the total 'membership' of a given sample data vector over all the clusters must sum to unity.

The FCV algorithms use the notation

$$u_{ik} = u_i(\mathbf{x}_k)$$

to represent the degree of membership of the sample data vector **x** in the cluster i. The two conditions can then be given a convenient mathematical statement

(i) $0 \leqslant u_{ik} \leqslant 1$ (for every i and k)

(ii) $\sum_{i=1}^{c} u_{ik} = 1$ (for every k)

where c is the number of clusters.

The idea of shared membership and what it might mean to the clustering problem is suggested by the membership values given in Table 7. Those values are the final cluster membership assignments obtained by applying the program FCVPC (a microcomputer program described in Section 6) to the data shown in Fig. 9. Notice that most of the samples possess a strong degree of membership in one cluster or the other. Sample data vector number 27, on the other hand, possesses an almost equal degree of membership in both clusters, which is what one would expect from visual inspection of Fig. 9.

The program FCVPC, and its companion FCVAX (see also Section 6), are implementations of the c-varieties algorithms presented by Bezdek *et al.* (1981). They generalized the Fuzzy ISODATA algorithms of Dunn and Bezdek so that it was possible to seek out not only round clusters, but any cluster shape which could be described as a linear surface (mathematically, a linear variety). For example, if the data were three-dimensional, i.e. each with three measured attributes, it would be possible to seek out round, linear (chain-like), or planar cluster shapes. It was necessary, however, for the user to specify ahead of time how many clusters were wanted, and to specify the shape wanted. It was also tacitly assumed that all of the detected clusters would be of the same basic shape. These restrictions may be removed, as demonstrated by Gunderson (1983). Even with those restrictions, however, the FCV

TABLE 7
FUZZY CLUSTER ANALYSIS OF THE DATA IN
Fig. 9 (MEMBERSHIP MATRIX)

Sample	Cluster 1	Cluster 2
1	0·04	0·96
2	0·06	0·94
3	0·02	0·98
4	0·03	0·97
5	0·04	0·96
6	0·03	0·97
7	0·01	0·99
8	0·01	0·99
9	0·04	0·96
10	0·05	0·95
11	0·07	0·93
12	0·04	0·96
13	0·12	0·88
14	0·82	0·18
15	0·94	0·06
16	0·96	0·04
17	0·96	0·04
18	0·98	0·02
19	1·00	0·00
20	0·98	0·02
21	0·96	0·04
22	0·97	0·03
23	0·97	0·03
24	0·97	0·03
25	0·95	0·05
26	0·96	0·04
27	0·48	0·52

algorithms provide a very powerful and versatile method for detecting the cluster substructure of the original data, and it is upon this original form of the algorithms that the programs FCVPC and FCVAX have been written.

Technically, the FCV algorithms arrive at a partitioning of the data into clusters by an iterative solution of a system of simultaneous non-linear equations. These equations are obtained as necessary conditions for minimizing a generalized sum-of-squared-error objective function, somewhat related to the one we used in Ward's method. Once having obtained those equations, it is not difficult to see why the algorithms

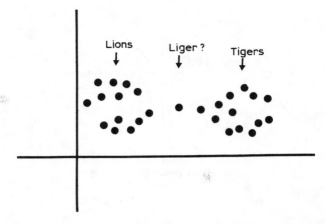

FIG. 9. In a two-dimensional system, the measurements indicate two groups of samples (lions and tigers) and a mutant (liger?).

work without having to get bogged down in mathematical manipulations. For the reader who is interested in those details, we recommend the original publication (Bezdek *et al.*, 1981), or the book by Bezdek (1981). We shall take a more heuristic approach here.

Let us assume that we have decided to impose a round structure on the data of Fig. 9. This case of the FCV algorithms is often called a clustering to *fuzzy c-means*. At the first iteration, the user furnishes an initial guess as to the location of the *cluster centers*. These may be obtained, if the user is so inclined, by a preliminary application of Ward's method, with the center being the mean of the individual clusters obtained by cutting the tree to obtain a partition. For the data shown in Fig. 9, it has been assumed that a partitioning of the n samples to two clusters is desired ($c = 2$). Initial guesses for the centers of those two clusters are shown by the open circles in Fig. 10. Notice that the centers are not required to belong to the original data set. The next step is to compute the distance of each of the sample data vectors to each of the assumed centers. Having done that, the degree of membership of each of the samples in each of the cluster classes is assigned by the equation

$$u_{ik} = \frac{1}{\displaystyle\sum_{i=1}^{c} \left(\frac{D_{ik}}{D_{ij}}\right)^2} \qquad (D_{ij} \neq 0)$$

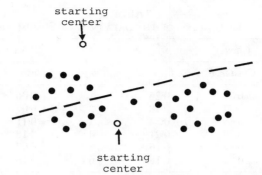

starting
center

starting
center

FIG. 10. The lions and tigers of Fig. 9 are clustered in two groups. The starting
centers for the first iterative step are marked.

where D_{ik} denotes the distances between the vector $\mathbf{x}_k$ and the center of
the ith cluster. The dashed line in Fig. 10 divides the sample data vectors
into groups, depending upon in which group the vector has its maximum
membership. As one would expect, the next step is to compute two new
centers v_1 and v_2, which the algorithm does using the equations

$$v_i = \sum_{k=1}^{n} u_{ik}^2 (\mathbf{x}_k) \Big/ \sum_{k=1}^{n} u_{ik}^2$$

These new centers are then used to compute the membership assignments for the next iteration, which are in turn used to compute new
centers. The iterations continue until reaching a stopping condition, such
as stopping when the maximum shift in the position of the centers in two
consecutive iterations fails to exceed a prespecified threshold level.

Notice that the membership value u_{ik} could be interpreted as a special
weighting factor which models the relative importance of each data
vector to each class. Notice also, that the computed cluster centers could
be interpreted as being the 'fuzzy' means of each class, or simply a special
weighted mean for each class. Thus, the fuzzy approach leads to a useful
and practical variation of the traditional concept of weighted
membership.

The convergence of the iterative procedure was investigated in Bezdek
et al., (1981), but the best answer was probably given by Windham
(1985), who showed that the procedure will always reach a stopping
point, regardless of how small a threshold is set.

The beer example was also clustered with the FCVPC program. Table
8 gives the final membership values obtained with FCVPC on the scaled

TABLE 8

FCVPC-CLUSTER ANALYSIS OF THE DATA IN Table 3–MEMBERSHIP VALUES

	Cluster 1			Cluster 2	
Sample	Cluster 1	Cluster 2	Sample	Cluster 1	Cluster 2
7	0·74	0·26	1	0·06	0·94
8	0·72	0·28	2	0·09	0·91
9	0·66	0·34	3	0·11	0·89
10	0·79	0·21	4	0·18	0·82
11	0·84	0·16	5	0·07	0·93
12	0·82	0·18	6	0·16	0·84

data (Table 3) for the case of $c = 2$ clusters. The table presents the sample data vectors in two clusters, with a vector being assigned to a particular cluster depending upon its maximum cluster membership.

It is a simple matter to obtain a traditional 'hard' cluster partitioning (every vector in one cluster only) from the partial membership values of a 'fuzzy' clustering. To limit the interpretation of the output of the algorithms to only that objective would, however, waste some very valuable information. For example, notice that sample number 9 appears to have a significant extent of sharing between both classes. That observation should prompt us to go back to Table 3 and take a closer look at that sample data vector. So doing, we find that the first attribute of vector 9, 2-methyl propanol, is quite a bit smaller than the first attribute of the remaining sample data vectors 'in' that class. We also observe from the membership values that cluster number 2 seems to have a noticeably tighter, more compact structure (less membership sharing), than does cluster number 1. Thus, we are able to infer not only *between-cluster* differences, but also gain information on variations *within-cluster*.

The output of FCVPC also includes additional information: Table 9 shows the locations of the final centers, and the principal components of each cluster. If we interpret the centers as providing prototypical *models* of each of the classes, we are able to extract some important additional information concerning the apparent discriminatory importance of the measured attributes: that is, the relative importance of the chemical variables in discriminating between the two breweries. A negative center value in Table 9 means that the average value for that particular variable in the cluster is lower than the *total* average for the variable in question.

TABLE 9

FCVPC-CLUSTER ANALYSIS OF THE DATA IN Table 3. CENTER VALUES AND PRINCIPAL COMPONENTS

	Cluster 1			Cluster 2		
	Center	1-Princ. comp.	2-Princ. comp.	Center	1-Princ. comp.	2-Princ. comp.
2-Methyl propanol	0·834	0·413	0·441	−0·668	0·160	0·039
Amyl alcohols	0·800	−0·203	−0·115	−0·623	−0·185	−0·250
1-Propanol	0·721	0·199	0·337	−0·630	0·080	0·149
2-Phenyl ethanol	0·713	−0·266	0·048	−0·653	−0·116	−0·254
Acetaldehyde	0·349	0·217	−0·019	−0·355	0·107	0·159
Ethyl acetate	−0·824	−0·178	0·314	0·753	−0·367	−0·547
Isoamyl acetate	−0·524	0·043	0·377	0·453	0·064	0·140
2-Phenyl ethyl acetate	0·398	−0·067	−0·088	−0·401	−0·171	0·040
Octanoic acid	0·880	0·435	0·088	−0·785	0·419	0·196
Decanoic Acid	0·859	−0·335	0·245	−0·751	−0·498	0·376
Ethyl hexanoate	0·544	0·311	0·219	−0·452	−0·350	−0·109
Ethyl octanoate	0·448	0·441	−0·558	−0·389	−0·441	0·558

The differences in frequencies of minus signs between cluster 1 and cluster 2 demonstrate large differences in the chemical makeup for the two breweries. The principal components aid us in pin-pointing the variation within each brewery. Knowledge in analytical chemistry, microbial physiology or brewing technology can further elucidate this variation.

4.2. Strategy for Finding Other Than Round Clusters

The only real change in algorithm operation when asked to seek out structures other than round clusters is in how the distances are computed, prior to computing the degree of membership of the sample data vectors. It is only necessary to start each iteration knowing the degree of membership assignments from the previous iteration. A weighted covariance matrix is computed corresponding to each of the clusters. Each of these matrices are computed over all of the sample data vectors, exactly as if one were computing a covariance matrix for obtaining the principal components of the total original data, but with the contributions from each sample data vectors weighted by its degree of membership in the cluster for which the computation is being carried out. The eigenvalues and eigenvectors are then computed, which furnish a disjoint weighted principal component model for each of the c clusters. If, for example, it is desired to seek out linear cluster shapes, the distance of a given sample data vector to a specified cluster is defined to be *the orthogonal distance of the vector to the line running through the center of the cluster, in the direction of its first principal component.* If planar clusters are desired, the distances are measured to the *plane* containing the center of the cluster, and formed by the first two principal components..., and so forth. Colinear or coplanar, etc., clusters may be found by slightly modifying the distance equations to penalize sample data vectors if they are far removed from the center of the cluster in question.

Some examples obtained by using the FCV algorithms to cluster to shapes other than round clusters are shown in Figs. 11(a) and 11(b). The results of Figs. 11(c) and 11(d) were obtained using an experimental shape adaptive form of the FCV algorithms, (Gunderson, 1983). As can be seen, it is capable of *simultaneously* seeking out clusters of different linear shapes. Thus, use of this form of the FCV algorithms should be much less likely to result in the investigator inadvertently imposing a misleading or inappropriate structure on the input data. It also results in a clustering algorithm which is, at least to a certain extent, invariant to scalings of the data.

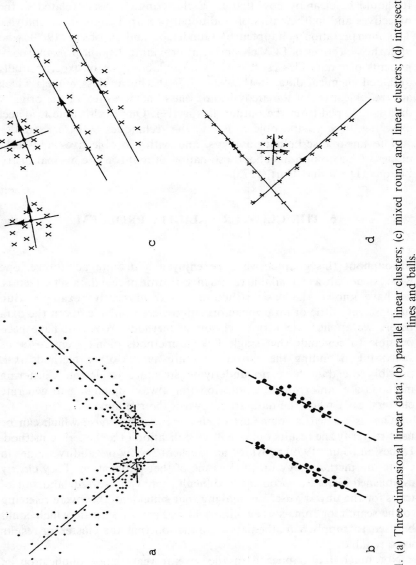

FIG. 11. (a) Three-dimensional linear data; (b) parallel linear clusters; (c) mixed round and linear clusters; (d) intersecting lines and balls.

4.3. FCV Versus Other Types of Multivariate Data Analyses

It should be clear by now that FCV clustering is closely related to the objectives and mathematics of traditional principal component analysis. This interpretation is adopted by Gunderson and Jacobsen (1983), who view the objectives of FCV clustering as providing disjoint principal components of c data classes defined by an unlabeled set of experimentally obtained chemical data. In this view, it is the linear class models which are the objectives of the analysis, and class 'membership' of the original data is dropped from the output all together. One is also able to detect close ties between the objectives and the techniques of Fisher's multivariate linear discriminate analysis, and with the objectives and techniques of maximum likelihood estimation of multivariate normal distributions (Duda and Hart, 1973).

5. THE CLUSTER VALIDITY PROBLEM

Throughout this chapter we have enjoyed a definite advantage, one which is not always available to the investigator of real data sets. That is, we have known the basic structure of our illustrative example. But, suppose very little or no prior information were available about the data before we applied the various clustering methods. Would it have been possible to conclude that single linkage methods didn't seem to be as successful in finding the cluster structure as the other methods? Or, possibly the data have no underlying structure to detect. Clustering methods are, unfortunately, notorious for always managing to generate clusters, even when the data are known to be random.

What is needed is some sort of *cluster validity criteria* which can be used to verify the results obtained by application of a clustering method. Dubes and Jain (1979) provided an excellent review of validity studies in clustering methodology up to the time of that publication. They clearly established that 'the problem is difficult, mainly unsolved, and full of traps for the unwary user'. In making that statement, they were referring to the search for some sort of analytical measure or statistic which could be used to supply a mathematical validation that the clustering results were reliable.

Not much has happened in the several years since publication of Dubes and Jain's survey to ease their rather pessimistic conclusion. In that survey they ended with the following recommendation: *that the user of clustering algorithms interested in establishing cluster validity would be well advised to apply several clustering approaches and check for common clusters instead of searching for a technical measure of validity for an individual clustering.* We consider that excellent advice today. That being the case, we prefer to present here only one approach to cluster validity, relevant only to investigations involving hierarchical cluster structure, and valid only for trying to answer the question of how well a hierarchical clustering provides a conceptualization of a given similarity matrix. There has been some success in this important area, however, and the problem is one which can be expected to continue to attract research interest and activity. In addition to the references provided in Dubes and Jain's publication, we refer the reader to the book by Bezdek (1981) and his chapter on some of the possibilities offered by the fuzzy objective function approach.

In this chapter, we shall describe a more traditional approach to the cluster validity problem. The measure has had a large number of applications, especially in numerical taxonomy, and may be the most widely accepted measure of this type. It applies specifically to investigations involving hierarchical data structure, and attempts to evaluate the degree to which the entire hierarchy matches, or correlates, with the information contained in the similarity matrix from which the hierarchy was derived.

5.1. The Cophenetic Correlation Coefficient

Sneath and Sokal (1973) suggest the use of the *cophenetic correlation coefficient* (CPCC) as a standard for comparing the tree from a hierarchical structure with a similarity matrix. The measure works best where the similarity coefficients are obtained in interval-scaled, as opposed to ordinal, values. The method depends on defining the *cophenetic matrix* **D**, whose element at the intersection of the ith row and kth column is the similarity level at which sample data vectors $\mathbf{n}_i$ and $\mathbf{n}_k$ are put into the same cluster. Put another way, to find the value it is only necessary to trace the path connecting the pair, $\mathbf{n}_i$ and $\mathbf{n}_k$, to its highest point and read off its scaled value. Since the tree and the cophenetic matrix are really one and the same thing, it is possible to compare the tree with the original similarity matrix by comparing the elements of the two matrices. Tables 10(a) and 10(b) provide a side-by-side comparison of these two matrices for average distance clustering methods, where only the values below the main diagonal have been listed, since the matrices are symmetric. The CPCC is then computed as the ordinary Pearson product–

TABLE 10(a)
COPHENETIC MATRIX FOR AVERAGE DISTANCE CLUSTERING (Fig. 7)

	1	2	3	4	5	6	7	8	9	10	11
2	2·208										
3	2·208	1·280									
4	2·848	2·848	2·848								
5	1·888	2·208	2·208	2·848							
6	2·208	2·848	2·848	2·688	2·848						
7	6·145	6·145	6·145	6·145	6·145	6·145					
8	6·145	6·145	6·145	6·145	6·145	6·145	5·185				
9	6·145	6·145	6·145	6·145	6·145	6·145	3·201	5·185			
10	6·145	6·145	6·145	6·145	6·145	6·145	3·904	5·185	3·904		
11	6·145	6·145	6·145	6·145	6·145	6·145	3·904	5·185	3·904	3·393	
12	6·145	6·145	6·145	6·145	6·145	6·145	4·577	5·185	4·577	4·577	4·577

TABLE 10(b)

DISTANCE MATRIX FOR THE DATA SET (cf. Table 4)

	1	2	3	4	5	6	7	8	9	10	11
2	1·697										
3	2·271	1·376									
4	2·723	3·517	3·602								
5	1·951	2·537	2·563	2·439							
6	2·868	3·122	3·164	2·775	2·011						
7	4·993	5·252	5·795	4·850	5·643	5·041					
8	6·568	6·222	6·226	6·555	6·235	5·483	5·294				
9	4·121	3·756	4·212	4·921	4·506	3·997	3·243	4·002			
10	5·096	5·472	5·370	4·115	4·835	4·508	3·755	4·824	3·902		
11	6·060	5·724	5·614	5·899	6·158	5·557	4·464	4·732	3·713	3·464	
12	7·766	7·730	7·676	7·122	7·540	6·465	4·711	5·595	5·379	4·240	4·091

moment correlation coefficient between the entries. i.e.

$$r_{x,y} = \frac{\Sigma xy - (1/n)(\Sigma x)(\Sigma y)}{\{[\Sigma x^2 - (1/n)(\Sigma x)^2][\Sigma y^2 - (1/n)(\Sigma y)^2]\}^{1/2}}$$

The larger the CPCC, the better the match between similarity matrix and dendrogram. Dubes and Jain consider the CPCC as a measure of *global fit* of the structure to the data. Romesburg (1984), views the measure as an indicator of how much the clustering method 'distorts' the input data to produce the output dendrogram. He suggests that practitioners in most fields would accept a value in the neighborhood of 0·8 or more, as indicating satisfactory performance. The CPCC values computed for the nearest neighbor, furthest neighbor and average distance hierarchical clustering methods applied to the data of our example gave the numbers 0·810, 0·819 and 0·833. The method is not appropriate to Ward's method since the similarity levels of the dendrogram are not to the same scale as the similarity matrix.

6. CLUSTERING PROGRAMS AVAILABLE

Several textbooks contain FORTRAN source codes for the most popular clustering methods, e.g. Anderberg (1973), Mather (1976), and Hartigan (1975). A paper by Dubes and Jain (1975) compares several published methods, and can be used to estimate the necessary computer resources of one method relative to another.

The easiest way to get familiar with cluster analysis is to try some of the methods in the commercially available packages. These packages are mainly for mainframes or minicomputers, but micro-versions seem to be coming. We will give a closer description of some of the available cluster analysis packages below. Similar lists can also be found in the books by Romesburg (1984) and Massart and Kaufman (1983).

ARTHUR
ARTHUR is a collection of programs specialized for chemical pattern recognition. The package is available from Infometrix Inc., P.O. Box 25808, Seattle, WA 98125, USA. ARTHUR contains seven different resemblance measures. Among the clustering methods, the user can choose between a hierarchical approach (nearest neighbor and furthest neighbor) or a graph theoretical approach (minimal spanning tree). ARTHUR runs on several minicomputers/mainframes.

BMDP
Biomedical Computer Programs P-Series is a set of programs for data display, univariate, and multivariate statistics. BMDP has four programs for cluster analysis. One of these is non-hierarchical (k-means), the other three aim at hierarchical analysis of (a) attributes, (b) objects, (c) simultaneous clustering of attributes and objects. The last three refer to different menus for resemblance coefficients. More information on the BMDP programs can be obtained from: BMDP Program Librarian, Health Services Computing Facility, AV-11, CHS, University of California, Los Angeles, California 90024, USA.

CLUE
CLUE is a program for hierarchical divisive clustering, and will be available from Elsevier Scientific Software, P.O. Box 330, 1000 AH Amsterdam, The Netherlands.

CLUSTAN
This statistical package contains both hierarchical and non-hierarchical cluster analysis. Principal component analysis and discriminant function analysis are also included.

The package contains thirteen resemblance coefficients for quantitative data, and twenty seven for qualitative data. Eight methods from hierarchical clustering are included, in addition to the k-means and several other non-hierarchical methods. The package is designed as an adjunct to SPSS (Statistical Package for the Social Sciences).

CLUSTAN is available from the CLUSTAN project, 16 Kingsburgh Road, Murrayfield, Edinburgh EH 126 DZ, UK.

CLUSTAR/CLUSTID
The two programs allow the user to choose from ten quantitative and fourteen qualitative resemblance coefficients. The clustering methods consist of the nearest neighbor, the furthest neighbor, the average linkage, and Ward's method. CLUSTID is designed to be run after CLUSTAR, and will identify unknown objects into classifications that have been created using CLUSTAR. The programs run on medium sized computers (e.g. VAX 11/780), and can then handle data matrices with 400×400 elements.

The programs are available from Lifetime Learning Publications, Ten Davis Drive, Belmont, California 94002, USA.

FCVPC/FCVVAX

These packages contain the PASCAL code for the fuzzy c-means clustering algorithm described in this chapter. FCVPC runs on an IBM PC (256 Kb). An 8087 co-processor is recommended. Data sets with maximum 50 attributes measured on maximum 500 objects can be clustered into maximum 20 clusters (not all maximums may be simultaneously achievable).

FCVVAX is the VAX-version of the program. Further information on the packages can be obtained from Prof. R. W. Gunderson, Department of Mathematics, Utah State University, Logan, UT 84322, USA.

MASLOC

MASLOC is a FORTRAN program for non-hierarchical clustering (Massart *et al.*, 1983). The program is developed at Brussels University, and is a non-hierarchical method based on the k-means method. Depending upon the size of the problem, the user can choose between three solution techniques. With a central memory of 256 Kb, most problems can be solved for data sets up to 500 objects and 100 variables.

In the second part of the program, it is determined which of the clusters found in the first part are particularly significant (called robust).

NTSYS

The Numerical Taxonomy System of Multivariate Programs are designed primarily for research in numerical taxonomy. The programs follow the presentation of Sneath and Sokal's (1973) book. Both hierarchical (eight methods) and non-hierarchical (a variant of k-means) methods are present. The user can choose between nine quantitative and sixteen qualitative resemblance coefficients.

The programs are written in FORTRAN for IBM computers, and can be purchased from Dr F. James Rohlf, Department of Ecology and Evolution, The State University of New York, Stony Brook, New York 11794, USA.

SAS

SAS (Statistical Analysis System) is a collection of programs for data display, univariate analysis, and multivariate analysis. The programs have been used principally with large IBM computers, but a version for microcomputers is in preparation. Three of the programs are for cluster analysis: (1) CLUSTER, (2) FASTCLUS, and (3) VARCLUS. CLUSTER performs hierarchical cluster analysis of objects, and is restricted to quantitative data. Three clustering methods are provided (Average linkage, Centroid, Ward), and there is only one resemblance coefficient for each method. FASTCLUS is a variant of the *k*-means method. VARCLUS can be used for either hierarchical or non-hierarchical analysis of attributes. The data must be quantitative, and the resemblance coefficient to be used is either the correlation coefficient or a covariance measure.

Further information on SAS can be obtained from SAS Institute Inc., Box 8000, Cary, North Carolina 27511, USA.

7. A CLUSTERING PROGRAM

The BASIC code below allows the user to run the nearest neighbor, the furthest neighbor, or the average linkage clustering upon a data set with maximum 15 features measured upon maximum 50 samples. The program runs under the MS-DOS version 2.0 BASICA interpreter.

```
10 DEFINT I,J,K,M,N,O,P,S
20 DIM  X(50,15), DIS(50,50), BMAP$(100), SKIP%(50), TAIL%(50), STACK%(50)
30 DIM  PNUM%(100), PLOC%(100), PNEXT%(100), PDIS!(100)
40 CLS
50 PRINT "Linkage Clustering Program"
60 INPUT "Enter the input file name: "; FIN$
70 INPUT "Enter the output file name: "; FOUT$
80 OPEN FIN$ FOR INPUT AS #1
90 OPEN FOUT$ FOR OUTPUT AS #2
100 INPUT #1, ND
110 I = 1
120 IF EOF(1)  GOTO 180
130    INPUT #1, PNUM%(I)
140    FOR J = 1 TO ND: INPUT #1, X(I,J): NEXT J
150    PDIS!(I) = 0!:  PLOC%(I) = 0:  PNEXT%(I) = 0
160    TAIL%(I) = I:  SKIP%(I) = 0:  I = I + 1
170 GOTO 120
180 NS = I - 1
190 PRINT "Select linkage method:"
200 PRINT "1: Nearest Neighbor (Single-Linkage),"
210 PRINT "2: Farthest Neighbor (Complete-Linkage),"
220 PRINT "3: Average Neighbor."
230 INPUT "Enter the code for linkage method: "; METHOD
240 REM   Compute distance matrix
250 PRINT " Computing the distance matrix..."
260 FOR I = 1 TO (NS - 1)
270 FOR J = I + 1 TO NS
280    DIST = 0!
290    FOR K = 1 TO ND
300       TT = X(I,K) - X(J,K)
310       DIST = DIST + TT * TT
320    NEXT K
330    DIS(I,J) = SQR(DIST)
340 NEXT J
350 NEXT I
```

```
360 OW = 80    'Output form width
370 STP = 15
380 NC = NS:  PT = NS + 1
390 PRINT " Start Clustering ..."
400 PRINT " Count-down: ";
410 FOR I = NC TO 2 STEP -1
420   PRINT " ";I;
430   DISMIN = 1E+37
440   FOR J = 2 TO NS
450     IF SKIP(J) = 1 GOTO 490
460       FOR K = 1 TO J - 1
470         IF DISMIN > DIS(K,J) THEN DISMIN = DIS(K,J): M = K: N = J
480       NEXT K
490   NEXT J
500   REM Modify the DIS matrix
510   ON METHOD GOTO 520, 670, 820
520   'Single-Linkage
530     FOR J = M + 1 TO N-1
540       IF DIS(M,J) > DIS(J,N) THEN DIS(M,J) = DIS(J,N)
550       DIS(J,N) = 1E+37
560     NEXT J
570     DIS(M,N) = 1E+37
580     FOR J = N+1 TO NS
590       IF DIS(M,J) > DIS(N,J) THEN DIS(M,J) = DIS(N,J)
600       DIS(N,J) = 1E+37
610     NEXT J
620     FOR J = 1 TO M-1
630       IF DIS(J,M) > DIS(J,N) THEN DIS(J,M) = DIS(J,N)
640       DIS(J,N) = 1E+37
650     NEXT J
660     GOTO 970
670   'Complete-Linkage
680     FOR J = M+1 TO N-1
690       IF DIS(M,J) < DIS(J,N) THEN DIS(M,J) = DIS(J,N)
700       DIS(J,N) = 1E+37
710     NEXT J
720     DIS(M,N) = 1E+37
730     FOR J = N+1 TO NS
740       IF DIS(M,J) < DIS(N,J) THEN DIS(M,J) = DIS(N,J)
750       DIS(N,J) = 1E+37
760     NEXT J
770     FOR J = 1 TO M-1
780       IF DIS(J,M) < DIS(J,N) THEN DIS(J,M) = DIS(J,N)
790       DIS(J,N) = 1E+37
800     NEXT J
810     GOTO 970
820   'Average-Linkage
830     FOR J = M+1 TO N-1
840       IF (DIS(M,J) <> 1E+37) AND (DIS(N,J) <> 1E+37) THEN
            DIS(M,J) = (DIS(M,J) + DIS(J,N)) / 2!
          ELSE  DIS(M,J) = 1E+37
850       DIS(J,N) = 1E+37
860     NEXT J
870     DIS(M,N) = 1E+37
880     FOR J = N+1 TO NS
890       IF (DIS(M,J) <> 1E+37) AND (DIS(N,J) <> 1E+37) THEN
            DIS(M,J) = (DIS(M,J) + DIS(N,J)) / 2!
900       DIS(N,J) = 1E+37
910     NEXT J
920     FOR J = 1 TO M-1
930       IF (DIS(J,M) <> 1E+37) AND (DIS(J,N) <> 1E+37) THEN
            DIS(J,M) = (DIS(J,M) + DIS(J,N)) / 2!
940       DIS(J,N) = 1E+37
950     NEXT J
960   REM  Modify the link list
970   PNUM%(PT) = -1: PDIS!(PT) = DISMIN: PLOC%(PT) = 0: PNEXT%(PT) = 0
```

```
980     PNEXT%(TAIL%(N)) = PT: PNEXT%(TAIL%(M)) = N
990     TAIL%(N) = 0: TAIL%(M) = PT: SKIP%(N) = 1
1000    PT = PT + 1
1010 NEXT I
1020 LIM% = 2 * NS - 1: TOP% = 0
1030 REM  Build the tree, normalize the differences to the MAX difference
1040 PRINT " ":  PRINT " Building tree..."
1050 FOR I = 2 TO LIM% STEP 2:  BMAP$(I) = "     ":  NEXT I
1060 DISMAX = PDIS!(TAIL%(1))
1070 I = 1:  NN = PT - 1:  PT = 1
1080 FOR K = 1 TO NN
1090    IF PNUM%(PT) < 0 THEN GOTO 1160
1100       PLOC%(PT) = 2 * I - 1
1110       I = I + 1
1120          BMAP$(PLOC%(PT)) = "  " + STR$(PNUM%(PT))
1130          BMAP$(PLOC%(PT)) = "  " + STR$(PNUM%(PT))
1140       GOTO 1340
1150    REM  PNUM%(PT) < 0
1160       PT2 = STACK%(TOP%): TOP% = TOP% - 1    'Pop off from stack
1170       PT1 = STACK%(TOP%): TOP% = TOP% - 1
1180       N1 = PLOC%(PT1): N2 = PLOC%(PT2)
1190       PLOC%(PT) = (N1 + N2) \ 2
1200       PDIS!(PT) = PDIS!(PT) / DISMAX
1210       LOCT% = (PDIS!(PT) * (OW - 4)) + 4
1220       LOCS1% = LEN(BMAP$(N1)) + 1:  LOCS2% = LEN(BMAP$(N2)) + 1
1230       FOR J = LOCS1% TO LOCT% - 1
1240          BMAP$(N1) = BMAP$(N1) + "-"
1250       NEXT J
1260       FOR J = LOCS2% TO LOCT% - 1
1270          BMAP$(N2) = BMAP$(N2) + "-"
1280       NEXT J
1290       FOR J = N1 TO N2
1300          LOCS1% = LEN(BMAP$(J)) + 1
1310          FOR M = LOCS1% TO LOCT%-1: BMAP$(J) = BMAP$(J) + " ": NEXT M
1320          BMAP$(J) = BMAP$(J) + "|"
1330       NEXT J
1340    PT1 = PT
1350    PT = PNEXT%(PT)
1360    TOP% = TOP% + 1: STACK%(TOP%) = PT1    'Push into stack
1370 NEXT K
1380 REM  Write parameters and other information into output file
1390 PRINT #2, CHR$(12)  ' Top of New Page
1400 IF METHOD = 1 THEN  PRINT #2, " Single-Linkage Cluster Analysis."
1410 IF METHOD = 2 THEN  PRINT #2, " Complete-Linkage Cluster Analysis."
1420 IF METHOD = 3 THEN  PRINT #2, " Average-Linkage Cluster Analysis."
1430 PRINT #2, " "
1440 PRINT #2, " Input data file: "; FIN$
1450 PRINT #2, " "
1460 PRINT #2, " Number of data samples, NS: "; NS
1470 PRINT #2, " Number of features, ND: "; ND
1480 PRINT #2, " Normalization factor: ", DISMAX
1490 PRINT #2, " "
1500 PRINT #2, " "
1510 PRINT #2, " The resulting dendrogram:"
1520 PRINT #2, " "
1530 REM  Print the Scale
1540 PRINT #2, "    ";
1550 T1 = 1!
1560 FOR I = 4 TO OW STEP STP
1570    IF I = OW-1 THEN PRINT #2,USING"#.";T1; ELSE PRINT #2,USING"#.#";T1;
1580    IF (I + STP) < OW THEN
             FOR J = 1 TO STP-3:  PRINT #2, " ";:  NEXT J
1590    T1 = T1 - .2
1600 NEXT I
1610 PRINT #2, " "
1620 PRINT #2, "    +";
```

```
1630 K = (OW \ 5) - 1
1640 FOR I = 1 TO K:  PRINT #2, "----+";:  NEXT I
1650 PRINT #2, " "
1660 FOR I = 1 TO LIM%: PRINT #2, BMAP$(I): NEXT I  'Print the bit-map
1670 REM Print the scale
1680 PRINT #2, "    +";
1690 FOR I = 1 TO K:  PRINT #2, "----+";:  NEXT I
1700 PRINT #2, " "
1710 PRINT #2, "   ";
1720 T1 = 1!
1730 FOR I = 4  TO OW STEP STP
1740   IF I = (OW-1) THEN PRINT #2,USING"#.";T1; ELSE PRINT #2,USING"#.#";T1
1750   IF (I + STP) < OW THEN
        FOR J = 1 TO STP-3: PRINT #2, " ";:  NEXT J
1760   T1 = T1 - .2
1770 NEXT I
1780 CLOSE #1, #2
1790 SOUND 262, 9: SOUND 330, 9: SOUND 392, 18
1800 PRINT     " All done, the results in file: ";FOUT$
1810 END
```

REFERENCES

Aishima, T. (1983) In: *Instrumental Analysis of Foods, Recent Progress*, Vol. 1. G. Charalambous and G. Inglett (Eds). Academic Press, New York, pp. 37–56.

Anderberg, M. R. (1973). *Cluster Analysis for Applications*, Academic Press, New York.

Bezdek, J. C. (1973). Fuzzy mathematics in pattern classification. Ph.D. thesis, Cornell University, Ithaca, N.Y.

Bezdek, J. (1981). *Pattern Recognition with Fuzzy Objective Function Algorithms*, Plenum Press, New York.

Bezdek, J., Gunderson, R., Coray, C. and Watson, J. (1981). Detection and characterization of cluster substructure. *SIAM J. Appl. Math.*, **40**(2), 339–57.

Bonde, G. J. (1975). The genus *Bacillus*. An experiment with cluster analysis. *Danish Medical Bulletin*, **22**, 41–61.

Böe, B. and Gjerde, J. (1980). Fatty acid patterns in the classification of some representatives of the families *Enterobacteriaceae* and *Vibrionacea. Journal of General Microbiology.* **116**, 41–9.

Carpenter, R. S., Burgard, D. R., Patton, D. R. and Zwerdling, S. S. (1983). In: *Instrumental Analysis of Foods, Recent Progress*, Vol. 2, G. Charalambous and G. Inglett (Eds). Academic Press, New York. pp. 173–86.

Dubes, R. and Jain, A. K. (1975) Clustering techniques: the user's dilemma. *Pattern Recognition*, **8**, 247–60.

Dubes, R. and Jain, A. K. (1979). Validity Studies in Clustering. *Pattern Recognition*, **11**, 235–54.

Duda, R. D. and Hart, P. E. (1973) *Pattern Classification and Scene Analysis*, John Wiley, New York.

Fukunaga, K. (1972). *Introduction to Statistical Pattern Recognition*, Academic Press, New York.

Godwin, D. R., Bärgmann, R. E. and Powers, J. J. (1978). Use of cluster analysis to evaluate sensory-objective relations of processed green peas. *Journal of Food Science*, **43**, 1229–34.

Golovnja, R. V., Jakovleva, V. N., Cesnokova, A. E., Matveea, L. V. and Borisov, J. A. (1981). A method of selecting a panel for taste assessment of new food products. *Die Nahrung*, **25**, 53–8.

Goodman, M. M. and Bird, R. McK. (1977). The races of maize IV: tentative grouping of 219 Latin American races. *Economic Botany*, **31**, 204–21.

Gunderson, R. W. (1983). An adaptive FCV clustering algorithm. *Int. J. Man-Machine Studies*, **19**, 97–104.

Gunderson, R. W. and Jacobsen, T. (1983). Unsupervised learning of disjoint principal component models. *Nordic Symposium on Applied Statistics*. Stokkand Forlag Publishers, Stavanger, 37–63.

Hartigan, J. A. (1975). *Clustering Algorithms*, John Wiley, New York.

Jacobsen, T. and Gunderson, R. W. (1983a). Cluster analysis of beer flavor components. II. Case study of yeast strain and brewery dependency. *J. American Society of Brewing Chemists*, **41**, 78–80.

Jacobsen, T. and Gunderson, R. W. (1983b). Trace element distribution in yeast and wort samples: an application of the FCV clustering algorithms. *Int. J. Man-Machine Studies*, **19**, 105–16.

Kloet, S. P. van der (1978). The taxonomic status of *Vaccinium pallidium*, the Hillside Blueberries including *Vaccinium vacillans*. *Canadian Journal of Botany*, **56**, 1559–74.

Kowalski, B. R. (Ed) (1984). *Chemometrics. Mathematics and Statistics in Chemistry*, NATO ASI Series Vol. 138, D. Reidel Publishing Company, Dordrecht.

Massart, D. L., Dijkstra, A. and Kaufmann, L. (1978). *Evaluation and Optimization of Laboratory Methods and Analytical Procedures*, Elsevier Scientific Publishing Company, Amsterdam.

Massart, D. L. and Kaufmann, L. (1983) *The Interpretation of Analytical Chemical Data by the Use of Cluster Analysis*, John Wiley, London.

Massart, D. L., Plastria, F. and Kaufmann, L. (1983). Non-hierarchical clustering with MASLOC, Vrüje Universiteit Brussel, Brussels, Belgium.

Mather, P. M. (1976). *Computational Methods of Multivariate Analysis in Physical Geography*, John Wiley, London.

Moskowitz, H. R. and Klarman, L. (1977). Food compatibilities and menu planning. *J. Inst. Can. Sci. Technol. Aliment.*, **10**, 256–74.

Palmer, D. H. (1974). Multivariate analysis of flavour terms used by experts and non-experts for describing tea. *J. Sci. Fd Agric.*, **25**, 153–64.

Parker Lessing, V. and Tollefson, J. O. (1971). Market segmentation through numerical taxonomy. *Journal of Marketing Research*, **8**, 480–7.

Powers, J. J., Smit, C. J. B. and Godwin, D. R. (1978). Relations among sensory and objective attributes of canned rabbiteye (*Vaccinium ashei* Reade) Blueberries. II. Cluster and discriminant analysis examination. *Lebensm.-Wiss. u. Technol.*, **11**, 275–8.

Rhodes, A. M. and Martin, F. W. (1972). Multivariate studies of variations in yams (*Dioscorea alata* L.). *J. Am. Soc. Hort. Sci.*, **97**, 685–8.

Romesburg, H. C. (1984). *Cluster Analysis for Researchers*, Lifetime Learning Publications, Belmont, California.

Rothe, M., Engst, W. and Erhardt, V. (1982). Studies on blue cheese flavour. *Die Nahrung*, **26**, 591–602.

Rothe, M., Specht, M. and Erhardt, V. (1981). Kennwerte zur Beurteilung der Aromaqualität von Lebensmitteln, 1. Mitt. Bedeutung und Lösungswege. *Die Nahrung*, **25**, 495–506.

Ruspini, E. (1969). A new approach to clustering. *Inf. and Conf.*, **15**, 22–32.

Schimdt, F., Rosendal, I. and Sejersen, L. (1981). Correlation between flavour profiles, chemical parameters, and gas chromatograms of beer, demonstrated by the influence of variation of air in head space. In: *EBC Flavour Symposium, European Brewery Convention*, Monograph-VII. Copenhagen, 103–15.

Siegmund, H. and Bächman, K. (1977). Die Lagezuordnung von Weinen durch Bestimmung des Spurenelementmusters. *Z. Lebesm. Unters. -Forschung*, **164**, 1–7.

Sneath, P. H. A. and Sokal, R. R. (1973). *Numerical Taxonomy. The Principles and Practice of Numerical Classification*, W. H. Freeman, San Francisco.

Stenroos, L. E. and Siebert, K. J. (1984). Application of pattern-recognition techniques to the essential oil of hops. *J. American Society of Brewing Chemists*, **42**, 54–61.

Vuataz, L., Sotek, J. and Rahim, H. M. (1974). Profile analysis and classification, *Proc. IV Int. Congress Food Sci. and Technol.*, Vol. I, pp. 68–78.

Windham, M. P. (1985). Optimization in Classification. Department of Mathematics Research Report No. 1985/27, Utah State University, Logan, UT., USA.

Woese, C. R. (1981). Archaebacteria. *Scientific American*, **244**, 94–106.

Zadeh, L. A. (1965). Fuzzy sets. *Inf. and Conf.*, **8**, 338–53.

INDEX